# BOUNDARIES OF STATE, BOUNDARIES OF RIGHTS

This collection of essays draws together innovative scholars to examine the relationship between two legal and political phenomena: the shrinking of the state as a monopoly of power in favour of the expansion of power over individuals in private hands, and the change in the nature of rights. The authors expertly discuss the implications of the changing boundaries of state power, the legal responses to this development, its application to human rights and re-conceptualizations of public life as obligations are handed over to private hands. This innovative book deals with an important set of problems and offers a fresh perspective of different legal themes in an integrated fashion.

TSVI KAHANA is Associate Professor at Queen's University, Toronto.

ANAT SCOLNICOV is Professor of Law at the University of Winchester.

# BOUNDARIES OF STATE, BOUNDARIES OF RIGHTS

Human Rights, Private Actors, and
Positive Obligations

Edited by
TSVI KAHANA
ANAT SCOLNICOV

CAMBRIDGE
UNIVERSITY PRESS

# CAMBRIDGE
UNIVERSITY PRESS

University Printing House, Cambridge CB2 8BS, United Kingdom

One Liberty Plaza, 20th Floor, New York, NY 10006, USA

477 Williamstown Road, Port Melbourne, VIC 3207, Australia

314-321, 3rd Floor, Plot 3, Splendor Forum, Jasola District Centre, New Delhi-110025, India

79 Anson Road, #06-04/06, Singapore 079906

Cambridge University Press is part of the University of Cambridge.

It furthers the University's mission by disseminating knowledge in the pursuit of education, learning and research at the highest international levels of excellence.

www.cambridge.org
Information on this title: www.cambridge.org/9781107665743

© Cambridge University Press 2016

This publication is in copyright. Subject to statutory exception and to the provisions of relevant collective licensing agreements, no reproduction of any part may take place without the written permission of Cambridge University Press.

First published 2016
First paperback edition 2017

*A catalogue record for this publication is available from the British Library*

Library of Congress Cataloging in Publication data
Names: Kahana, Tsvi, 1967– editor. | Scolnicov, Anat, editor.
Title: Boundaries of state, boundaries of rights : human rights, private actors, and positive obligations / edited by Tsvi Kahana and Anat Scolnicov.
Description: Cambridge, United Kingdom : Cambridge University Press, 2016. | Includes papers presented at a conference held in Cambridge, England in 2011.–ECIP Introduction. | Includes bibliographical references and index.
Identifiers: LCCN 2015050948 | ISBN 9781107066502 (Hardback)
Subjects: LCSH: Human rights–Congresses. | Liability for human rights violations–Congresses. | Privatization–Law and legislation–Congresses. | State action (Civil rights)–Congresses.
Classification: LCC K3239.8 .B68 2016 | DDC 341.4/8–dc23 LC record available at
http://lccn.loc.gov/2015050948

ISBN 978-1-107-06650-2 Hardback
ISBN 978-1-107-66574-3 Paperback

Cambridge University Press has no responsibility for the persistence or accuracy of URLs for external or third-party internet websites referred to in this publication, and does not guarantee that any content on such websites is, or will remain, accurate or appropriate.

Dedicated to the memory of my father Samuel Scolnicov.
*AS*

# CONTENTS

*List of contributors* ix

Introduction 1
TSVI KAHANA AND ANAT SCOLNICOV

1 Our rights, but whose duties? Re-conceptualizing rights in the era of globalization 6
JEAN THOMAS

2 On suffering and societal constitutionalism: at the border of international investment arbitration and human rights 25
DAVID SCHNEIDERMAN

3 Beware: boundary crossings 43
JOSÉ E. ALVAREZ

4 Dialogue and constitutional duty 94
MARK TUSHNET

5 Positive obligations, positive rights, and constitutional amendment 109
VICKI C. JACKSON

6 Privatizing public rights: common law and state action in the United States 129
HELEN HERSHKOFF

7 Abdications of sovereignty in state action and horizontal effect jurisprudence 149
JOHAN VAN DER WALT

8 Hybrid state accountability and hybrid rights: positive rights, exclusion, and state action in Canada 173
TSVI KAHANA

9  Human rights and derivative rights: the European Convention on Human Rights and the rights of corporations  194
ANAT SCOLNICOV

10  Judicial review and *Human Rights Act* review in contracted-out public services: options for litigation in English law  215
A.C.L. DAVIES

11  Privatization and human rights in the United Kingdom  233
STEPHANIE PALMER

12  Principles of public fiduciary administration  251
PAUL B. MILLER

13  Human rights indicators and boundaries of accountability and opportunity  271
MEGAN DERSNAH AND RON LEVI

*Bibliography*  290
*Index*  324

CONTRIBUTORS

JOSÉ E. ALVAREZ, Herbert and Rose Rubin Professor of International Law, New York University School of Law.

A.C.L. DAVIES, Professor of Law and Public Policy, University of Oxford; Garrick Fellow and Tutor in Law, Brasenose College, Oxford.

MEGAN DERSNAH, PhD candidate, Political Science, University of Toronto.

HELEN HERSHKOFF, Herbert M. and Svetlana Wachtell Professor of Constitutional Law and Civil Liberties, New York University School of Law.

VICKI C. JACKSON, Thurgood Marshall Professor of Constitutional Law, Harvard Law School.

TSVI KAHANA, Associate Professor, Queen's University Faculty of Law.

RON LEVI, George Ignatieff Chair of Peace and Conflict Studies; Associate Professor, Munk School of Global Affairs and Department of Sociology, University of Toronto.

PAUL B. MILLER, Associate Professor, McGill University Faculty of Law.

STEPHANIE PALMER, University Senior Lecturer, University of Cambridge Faculty of Law.

DAVID SCHNEIDERMAN, Professor of Law and Political Science, University of Toronto Faculty of Law.

ANAT SCOLNICOV, Professor of Law, University of Winchester.

JEAN THOMAS, Assistant Professor, Queen's University Faculty of Law.

MARK TUSHNET, William Nelson Cromwell Professor of Law, Harvard Law School.

JOHAN VAN DER WALT, Professor of Philosophy of Law, University of Luxembourg.

# Introduction

A chance post-conference meeting in Jerusalem led to a realization that international lawyers, constitutional lawyers, private lawyers and legal theorists on both sides of the Atlantic were all concerned with the same overriding question: Where does the state begin and where does it end? Consequently, how should we conceptualize legal personality, state action, rights and their bearers and correlative duty-bearers? The result was a conference which took place in Cambridge, England in 2011. The papers delivered at that conference, and the discussions which they precipitated, form the nucleus of the present volume.

In this volume, the relation between two legal and political phenomena is examined: The first is the shrinking of the state as a monopoly of power in favour of the expansion of power over individuals in private hands, and the second is the change in the nature of rights.

Existing works on these two phenomena have often emanated either from a perspective of political philosophy or from the perspective of constitutional law or international law. This volume seeks to broaden, but also focus the discussion, by bringing together the disciplines of political philosophy, international studies, constitutional law, administrative law and international law, to examine the shrinking of the state and the change in nature of rights in a more integrated fashion.

While the topics covered in this book have aroused interest in the different fields, they are considered in this volume in conjunction with one another. We particularly find that international law,[1] private law[2] and constitutional law[3] are converging towards each other, but we should

---

[1] See NON-STATE ACTORS AND HUMAN RIGHTS (Philip Alston ed. 2005) (for a recent discussion of the topic in international law).

[2] See RIGHTS AND PRIVATE LAW (Donal Nolan & Andrew Robertson eds., 2011) (for the discussion within private law).

[3] See ALLAN R. BREWER-CARÍAS, CONSTITUTIONAL COURTS AS POSITIVE LEGISLATORS: A COMPARATIVE LAW STUDY (2011) (for a recent book on constitutional law in this area).

also consider them together with the examination of rights in the private sphere.[4] The role of state constitutional law within the individual states of a federal state is also considered; in particular, the role of state constitutional law in upholding human rights in the private sphere,[5] international investment law[6] and the law of international organizations.[7]

The changes and legal responses by international law and by domestic legal systems should be viewed not as discrete systems but as legal solutions to the same problems. The political fact is the changing boundary state power, and the legal responses are varied as seen in this volume: from restriction of privatization to direct application of positive rights by the state to private parties. A reconceptualization of public life is in order, one that includes within its realm the structure of society and the structure of the economy within the state. This reconceptualization is included both within the political discussion and the legal discussion.

Several sub-questions arise out of this discussion, which cut vertically across the different legal disciplines and the chapters in this volume:

(1) *The question of symmetry between the capability of having rights and the capability of having obligations under human rights law*: Some contributors have noted that this is a worrying trend in the development of human rights law. Indeed, as Schneidermann shows, it is multinational corporations who have most successfully made use of international human rights provisions – such as protection of property and due process provisions – in international litigation, particularly in investment arbitration proceedings. Alvarez warns human rights advocates that recognizing corporations as legal persons capable of having obligations in international law will mean that they will also be able to claim rights in international human rights law. Scolnicov argues, however, that there is nothing inevitable about such symmetry of rights, neither in the conceptual analysis nor in the ability to recognize such a separation between being a rights bearer and an obligation bearer in an actual legal system, such as that of the European Convention on Human Rights.

(2) *The question of the change in the nature of rights*: Does the change in the nature of the state, associated with the rise of public power, mean

---

[4] This volume also connects these to positive obligations. Amongst the recent literature on this topic see SANDRA FREDMAN, HUMAN RIGHTS TRANSFORMED: POSITIVE RIGHTS AND POSITIVE DUTIES (2008).
[5] Hershkoff in this volume.   [6] Schneiderann in this volume.
[7] Alvarez in this volume.

that we need to recognize or underscore different substantive rights than those previously recognized? Kahana suggests that it is perhaps not the nature of rights that should change, but that "low intensity" breaches of two or more combined rights – particularly positive rights – may be sufficient to warrant the same protection accorded when "high intensity" breaches of one right occurs. Examining the experience of Canada, he suggests that such adding-up of rights infringements can protect positive rights effectively. Hershkoff shows that positive obligations are not absent from United States (US) constitutional law either, as is often perceived. She argues that their existence in state constitutions and the influence of common law doctrines can lead to further extension of their applicability in US constitutional law beyond the common perception of the state action doctrine. Van der Walt shows that, surprisingly, a new constitutional court unencumbered by the past – the South African Constitutional Court – took a rather restrictive view to the application of constitutional rights to private law. The Court did not view constitutional rights as applying to the common law by virtue of the court's own involvement in the act of adjudication, and held that the application of constitutional law only applied when the state was otherwise directly involved. He sees this as an "abdication of sovereignty" by the Court, and suggests a bolder step could have been taken, especially through use of comparative law, particularly that of the German Constitutional Court.

Jackson argues that state obligations, rather than social and economic rights, should be the concern of state constitutions. This will allow flexibility to amend constitutions in times of economic downturn, without the risk that courts will view the amendments as unconstitutional – as some state constitutional courts have done with constitutional amendments detracting from enshrined social rights.

(3) *The theoretical and practical usefulness of the distinction between public and private is itself questioned*: Thomas argues that the distinction between positive and negative rights – and between rights against state actors and against non-state actors – should be abandoned, and instead the particular relationships in which they arise should be taken into account. Miller proposes that fiduciary duties in private law and in public administrative law should be viewed in tandem.

Not all the writers in this volume agree that the public/private boundary should be crossed. Alvarez warns against such boundary crossing and against the application of public law principles (however these may be defined and incorporated within public international law) to such international law regimes as treaty arbitration or the application of the Alien Tort Claim Act in US law. These serve different purposes and principles from one side and should not blindly be transposed to the other.

Stephanie Palmer and Anne Davies both examine the phenomenon of transfer of public functions to private bodies, and the response to it in law in the United Kingdom (UK). Davies argues that contracting out should mandate, rather than negate, the applicability of both public law and human rights law. Palmer, looking at responses of the UK Supreme Court to the question of applicability of human rights argues that the concept of hybrid public bodies, introduced in the Human Rights Act, can be developed and interpreted in a way that will enhance the applicability of human rights rather than constrain it.

(4) *The question of contextualization of human rights in the new private sphere*: Several papers from different disciplines show that this cannot be done in the abstract but must take into account the position of weaker and disenfranchized members of society. Indeed, this is one of the reasons prompting us to edit this volume. We perceive a need for human rights law to address a gap in the protection of the rights of those most vulnerable – arising out of the "new boundaries" of the state. Kahana notes that the Supreme Court of Canada has stepped away from its usual practice regarding positive state obligations where the rights of employees who lack union organization are infringed.

Mesnah and Levi point to the tension created by the introduction of performance indicators borrowed from the private sector to measure the efficacy of international human rights protection as well as foreign aid. They show that this, born of a neo-liberal mindset, promoted the role of the private sector, creating inherent tension with the ideals behind these rights.

The questions raised by the chapters in this collection should offer avenues for further research. Should international law concern itself with legal persons in a way substantively different from how they have been conceived before? Can global public law provide a coherent basis for analysis of actions of states in both public law and international law? Are there other legal concepts like fiduciary duties which should be defined similarly across the public/private divide? Should different jurisdictions strive towards one state action doctrine? How can rights be best protected in a global culture of privatization? All these we are sure will be discussed in academe and legal practice in years to come.

Finally, it is our great pleasure to thank the Centre for Public Law at Cambridge University and its director at the time, Christopher Forsyth, and Queen's University Law Faculty for hosting and funding the conference which led to this volume and John Berger of Cambridge University Press for seeing it to publication.

*Tsvi Kahana, Kingston, Canada*
*Anat Scolnicov, Winchester, UK*

# 1

## Our rights, but whose duties? Re-conceptualizing rights in the era of globalization

JEAN THOMAS

### Introduction

It has become commonplace to note that one effect of the horrors perpetrated by states and individuals in the twentieth century was the flourishing of rights-recognition. Recognizing individual rights was thought – hoped, perhaps – to provide a bulwark against the capacity of states for violence, cruelty, and inhumanity.[1]

In one way, this trend of rights recognition seems to extend the long-standing movement toward individualism in the liberal tradition. The idea of individualism has gotten bad press in rights scholarship and political philosophy: community, affiliation, benevolence, responsibility, difference, cultural particularity, and political reasoning have all been claimed as potential victims of the idolatry of rights-thinking.[2] Rights are faulted for perpetuating the idea that the individual is the moral locus of politics, advocacy, and philosophy. So it is worth clarifying here that the rights-bearing individual in the long history of rights recognition has a particular antagonist: the state. More specifically, the individual, in the early rights tradition, was increasingly recognized not in contradistinction to the groups, families, affiliative bonds, and community structures

---

[1] This effect has been recognized by countless scholars of rights, of state obligations, and of political morality. See Michael J. Perry, *The Morality of Human Rights*, 50 SAN DIEGO L. REV. 775 (2013), for a specific discussion of this evolution.

[2] See MARY ANN GLENDON, RIGHTS TALK: THE IMPOVERISHMENT OF POLITICAL DISCOURSE 109 (1991) (rights as destructive of moral values); MICHAEL SANDEL, DEMOCRACY'S DISCONTENT: AMERICA IN SEARCH OF A PUBLIC PHILOSOPHY (1996) (liberal rights as destructive of political discourse); Mark Tushnet, *An Essay on Rights*, 62 TEX. L. REV. 1363 (1984) (arguing that rights are indeterminate); Tracy E. Higgins, *Anti-Essentialism, Relativism, and Human Rights*, 19 HARV. WOMEN'S L.J. 89 (1996); MICHAEL IGNATIEFF, HUMAN RIGHTS AS POLITICS AND IDOLATRY (2003); Rhoda Howard, *Dignity, Community and Human Rights*, in HUMAN RIGHTS IN CROSS-CULTURAL PERSPECTIVES: A QUEST FOR CONSENSUS 81 (Abdullahi Ahmed An-Na'im ed., 1992).

to which he or she belonged, but rather in clear contradistinction to another individual, namely, the sovereign or King. The type of power that individual rights were born to counterbalance was not that of a state acting on the basis of the overlapping consensus of a reasonable public, but rather that of a state embodying an individual will – the monarch's.

Seen through the lens of feminist jurisprudence, of cultural studies, even of political philosophy in general, this particular antagonist of individualism embodied in the individual ruler might seem antiquated to the point of irrelevance – and in those contexts, it may indeed be so. But in the ongoing philosophy about and conceptualization of rights, the location of the rights-bearing subject – as she has come to be in the liberal tradition – as the protagonist in a particular kind of drama in which the monarch was the original villain; this *location* of the individual in relation to a particular type of other is extremely important.

It is important because moral rights as we have come to know them have been *conceptualized* within the context of that antagonistic relationship of individual and ruler. The social contract tradition, from Hobbes, Locke, Kant, and Rousseau to Rawls has conceived of the human universe as bifurcated: one is either *in* the state or *out* of it. The significance of the ruler in relation to the individual was conceived by Hobbes, in particular, to be so central to the human experience that the heuristic of the state of nature was spawned out of it. And the modern "right," as it has come to be conceptualized over the 600 years since the English civil war, is the chief offspring of that bifurcated worldview.

The title of this chapter calls for re-conceptualizing rights with general reference to the context of globalization. Yet the latter is one of those ideas so capacious as to be insignificant: since *homo sapiens* began crossing from one continent to another our species has been a global one. Colonization, war, trade, piracy, science, and even gastronomy have been global phenomena since early human history. So let me be clear: what the idea of globalization means, here, is the breaking down of that exclusive bifurcation of the human drama – its drama of power and morality and politics, in particular – into the antagonism of the individual and ruler.

Since individuals are affected by powerful actors other than the government of the state to which they belong, many have argued that their rights ought also to apply more broadly than against that government. And this may be so. Yet the social, economic, and institutional facts we now think of as contemporary 'globalization' call not only, not even chiefly, for the *application* of our rights in the received liberal tradition to actors outside the state, or for the recognition that the modern state has obligations to support individuals as well as to refrain from violence against them, but for a conceptual reconsideration of those rights.

In what follows I will begin to sketch such a reconsideration: I will ask what the rights that we have received in the liberal tradition *are* in a fundamental sense. This does not mean writing rights off, or starting from a different set of moral first principles. That would also be a re-conceptualization of rights but not of *those* rights – of that particular set of rights that have been most commonly recognized, made positive in law and entrenched in social practice. I will take those rights, received through the liberal tradition, at face value, as it were, but ask what they are if we remove them from the (partially) outdated context of Hobbes' bifurcated world, in which the King figures as the individual's sole antagonist.

The re-conceptualization has several implications. First, it shows that – contrary to the conventional ruler-ruled dichotomy – public law rights are best understood as entitlements that, by their moral logic, could and should apply more broadly than only against the state. Second, the reconceptualization shows that the other conventional distinction that operates in rights discourse – that between negative and positive rights – should not be taken as categorical. That is, my argument will show that negative and positive freedom, as Isaiah Berlin introduced those ideas, are better conceived of, where rights are concerned, in terms of different forms of interaction between two parties. Negative rights are not, on the account of public law rights I will set out, different *kinds of things* from positive rights. Rather, all public law rights are conceptually united and morally justified in the same way. In sum, I argue that what matters about public law rights, both conceptually and in terms of their moral justification, is the fact that they operate between an individual and a powerful other party. Whether that other party is the state or some other powerful actor is of no conceptual or moral import.

## I The evolution of rights in the liberal tradition: why reconsider them?

The emphasis on the years since the Second World War in the development of liberal rights – the current loosely overlapping set of constitutional and human rights – reflects something morally and conceptually significant about the way those rights evolved in the mid-twentieth Century. While it is certainly true that the Magna Carta, the Declaration

I. THE EVOLUTION OF RIGHTS IN THE LIBERAL TRADITION  9

of the Rights of Man (1789),[3] and the Declaration of Independence (US 1776), for example, articulate certain interests for protection on behalf of individuals against their rulers, one central unifying feature of these articulations is that they are primarily concerned with constraining the power of the state. They declare moral entitlements that appear as limits on the way states can go about whatever business they may have.[4]

It is not novel to suggest that the documents that began and developed the liberal rights tradition[5] were products of particular historical and social contexts, and thus in many ways reflect particular bargains reached by given individual rulers and those over whom they held power. Yet this point bears repeating in the present context: we have expansively interpreted the moral epiphanies recorded in these documents, but within the documents themselves they represent only the seeds of moral discovery, planted within the text of political compromises.

The Magna Carta is entirely clear in this respect: it is a deal brokered between King John and his barons. The terms of his concessions – what is granted as rights – represent exceptions from his general absolute powers over their execution of their duties to him. The barons were allowed to have leaseholds on their lands, and were made small-scale sovereigns within those lands, on condition of owing certain clearly defined duties to him. The Magna Carta is essentially a limitation only on the *ways* those duties will be enforced by the King and his representatives. This is not to diminish its moral importance either in general or with respect to the most famous clauses laying out certain aspects of procedural justice. It is only to be clear that the significance of those

---

[3] 1789 CONST. Déclaration des Droits de l'Homme et du Citoyen [Declaration of the Rights of Man and the Citizen] (Fr.) [hereinafter Declaration of the Rights of Man 1789].
[4] Magna Carta, 1215, 17 John, (Eng.), translated in ENGLISH TRANSLATION OF MAGNA CARTA (British Library), *available at* www.bl.uk/magna-carta/articles/magna-carta-english-translation [hereinafter Magna Carta of 1215]. The Magna Carta, for instance, is written in the first person plural of the particular reigning monarch – the royal "we." The concessions and rights it grants, therefore, are presented as personal obligations taken on by King John. For example, "[n]either we nor our officials will seize any land or rent in payment of a debt," *id.* cl. 9.
[5] Chiefly, I take these documents to be the Magna Carta of 1215, *supra* note 4, the Magna Carta, 1225, 9 Hen. 3, (Eng.) [hereinafter Magna Carta of 1225], the Declaration of the Rights of Man 1789, *supra* note 3, THE DECLARATION OF INDEPENDENCE (U.S. 1776), *available at* www.archives.gov/exhibits/charters/declaration_transcript.html. [hereinafter THE DECLARATION OF INDEPENDENCE], and the many sets of rights enumerated with the onset of international institutions from the League of Nations to the United Nations following the First and Second World Wars.

moral aspects for the development of natural or moral rights as a moral idea only became apparent to later generations rather than being evident on the face of the document.

By 1789, the moral imagination of the Western cultures had evolved considerably, and both the Declaration of the Rights of Man and the Declaration of Independence clearly articulate the idea, as well as the language, of individual rights outside the political state.[6] At the same time, these two documents explicitly tie the business of the state to these rights in some way.[7] And both documents set out certain interests – life, liberty, and certain procedural safeguards being the ones shared by both – as the *contents* of those extra-political rights. But of course, while those rights are stated in abstract terms, the dominant *political* purpose in each case is clear. In the case of the Declaration of Independence, the enumeration of the extra-political rights is only a kind of preamble to the bulk of the clauses, which lay out the ways in which the British government has behaved badly toward its North American subjects. The rights are set out for the explicit purpose of justifying the severing of political association with the British.

The array of rights set out in more contemporary constitutions and in the international covenants, by contrast, have a more specifically individualistic purpose – they, like the earlier articulations of rights, are products of oppression and mistreatment of persons, and thus are in that sense also products of history. But the focus on the moral or extra-political dimension of rights had by then become paramount, and although the state is the enforcer of international human rights, this is partly a function of the structure of international law and relations, in which the state as an actor plays an almost exclusive role. But in fact the preamble of the United Nations Universal Declaration of Human Rights (UDHR) conveys quite clearly the idea that even if their *legal* duties will fall only on states, the articulated rights are intended to have moral

---

[6] See THE DECLARATION OF INDEPENDENCE. Unlike the Magna Carta of 1215, *supra* note 4, and the Magna Carta of 1225, *supra* note 5, The Declaration of Independence (U.S. 1776) speaks in a neutral third person plural, expressing a view: "We hold these truths to be self-evident, that all men are created equal, that they are endowed by their Creator with certain unalienable Rights, that among these are Life, Liberty and the pursuit of Happiness." A similar voice is employed in the Declaration of the Rights of Man 1789, *supra* note 3.

[7] The preamble to THE DECLARATION OF INDEPENDENCE, *supra* note 6, prescribes "[t]hat to secure these rights, Governments are instituted among Men, deriving their just powers from the consent of the governed, That whenever any Form of Government becomes destructive of these ends, it is the Right of the People to alter or to abolish it. . . ."

# I. THE EVOLUTION OF RIGHTS IN THE LIBERAL TRADITION 11

implications for everyone: in that sense, they are portrayed as fully universal for both rights subjects and duty bearers.[8]

The discursive and moral thrust of the evolution of rights consciousness, in other words, has been from a clear orientation toward particular rulers, and the preservation of particular political and legal orders, toward the articulation of and call for protection of the rights of individuals everywhere. This shift in orientation toward individuals as rights-bearers is the first feature toward which I will turn in considering what these rights, historically received as they have been, are *like*, conceptually speaking. As I argue, however, this shift is also a central reason why we must reconsider them. This is because the development of rights thinking that is reflected in these constitutive documents articulating sets of rights has not been entirely matched by a political philosophy that has attempted to understand the deeper moral basis and nature of these rights. The philosophical understanding of what rights are and what justifies them has essentially remained tied to the social contract tradition.[9] And in that tradition, the moral universe is defined by the relationship between a single ruler and the ruled. The 'state of nature' serves mainly as a negative foil; it is more important for what it is not – that is, governed or controlled by an authority – rather than for what it is.

But that bifurcated paradigm of human existence has simply been made obsolete. States are clearly no longer the sole potential agent who can oppress and control individuals. In fact the condition of statelessness, now, looks nothing like life in the heuristic of the state of nature because even repressive modern states occupy the terrain of international legal status, and thus having the protection of a legal order has become necessary to even basic survival. To be stateless, now, is not to be free; it is to be vulnerable and quintessentially violable.

---

[8] G.A. Res. 217 (III) A, U.N. Doc. A/RES/217(III) (Dec. 10, 1948), *available at* http://daccess-dds-ny.un.org/doc/RESOLUTION/GEN/NR0/043/88/IMG/NR004388.pdf?OpenElement. The final paragraph of the preamble is general in this way:

> Now, therefore The General Assembly Proclaims this Universal Declaration of Human Rights as a common standard of achievement for all peoples and all nations, *to the end that every individual and every organ of society*, keeping this Declaration constantly in mind, shall strive by teaching and education to promote respect for these rights and freedoms and by progressive measures, national and international, to secure their universal and effective recognition and observance, both among the peoples of Member States themselves and among the peoples of territories under their jurisdiction.

*Id.* 72 (emphasis added).

[9] See JAMES GRIFFIN, ON HUMAN RIGHTS (2008) (Griffin claims that the philosophy of rights has not advanced substantially since the eighteenth century).

And of course violability, in the first instance, not necessarily the ruler, is the underlying or *implicit* antagonist of the individual even in the social contract tradition. Hobbes was concerned about political power because he had seen what the world was like in the absence of it – famously, "nasty, brutish, and short." Locke, too, took civic association to mean the protection of persons by rules – in his case, socially respected moral rules – that prevent people from being brutalized by one another. The underlying, implicit antagonist in the social contract tradition, we might conclude, is not in fact the state itself, but the *violability* that characterizes human experience, and the way in which that violability is detrimental to our well-being. Belonging to a state, now, has become a precondition for any kind of flourishing, while the power to oppress, mistreat, and violate has become diffuse among transnational actors, non-state actors, international actors; it is no longer the near-exclusive domain of the King.

Although this worldview – in which the central human drama giving rise to rights is the antagonism of the individual and the ruler – has become outdated, the rights themselves remain relevant as expressions of our moral commitments to individuals. If we strip constitutional and human rights, the currency of so much of our moral, political, and legal thought and discourse, of their formal association with the state as a political entity, how can we understand them and explain them? If they are not justified as constraints on political power, what justifies them?

## II  What are public law rights?

The account of public law rights that I will sketch is both explanatory and justificatory. I will argue that public law rights are best understood in terms of three distinct dimensions. While none of these dimensions refers to their being held against states or rulers, or to their being compacts between individuals and sovereigns, I argue that the characterization I set out accounts fully, conceptually or morally, for public law rights as we have come to understand them.

### a) *Public law rights are constraints, conceptually and morally oriented to the individual subject*

Public law rights have individuals as their subjects and are morally oriented to individual persons.[10] What does it mean to say that public

---

[10] This is not to say that groups are conceptually excluded from holding rights – that is another question altogether. Rather, that if rights are held by groups it is because the

law rights are oriented toward individuals? Chiefly, it means that they protect individuals' inviolability. They are constraints on the ways in which others can treat us. That much is uncontroversial even on the conventional way of thinking about public law rights as constraints against the state. But what does inviolability, conceived as formal constraint, mean in the absence of the state's power as antagonist?

First, the idea of *con*straint is distinct from that of *re*straint. A restraint holds something back; it prevents one from doing things. And of course some public law rights do have this function. Constraints, by contrast, are better understood as structuring the *way* in which a duty-bearer interacts with a right-holder in respect of the right. Constraints are, in a sense, restraints on choice, but not necessarily on action.

There are several clear illustrations of the fact that characterizing public law rights only as restraints on government action is simply wrong. Constitutional and human rights also impose obligations on governments in many ways. They require, that is, that governments *do* things in respect of them. This is not a novel point: protecting individuals' negative rights, for example, is now widely recognized to require actions and the expenditure of resources on the part of governments.[11] This is so in two ways. First, because the state itself must invest in adjudicative and coercive resources to vindicate and enforce individuals' rights even against the state itself, and of course must invest in the resources of policing, adjudicative institutions, and so on, to protect individuals' rights against one another. Second, procedural rights, conventionally taken to be 'negative' ones, also explicitly set out certain things that the state and its representatives *must do* that they might otherwise not do. In the treatment of criminals, for instance, the state is required to inform individuals of their rights. It is required to enable them to contact a lawyer if they choose to; it is required to clothe and feed them, to provide them with certain basic amenities, and to show them the details of the case against them.

The 'negative' right to equality, too, may mean that, when the government engages in the provision of certain resources, it must do so fairly and taking into consideration the ability of all individuals to access and benefit from those resources.[12] At the most basic level, this means only formally equal treatment before the law: the government cannot decide

---

groups consist of individuals who in some instances require protection *as* group members in order to be fully respected by others.

[11] See CASS R. SUNSTEIN and STEPHEN HOLMES, THE COST OF RIGHTS (1999).
[12] Eldridge v. B.C. (Att'y Gen.), [1997] 3 S.C.R. 624 (Can.).

to provide education as a service but then only do so for white people. It cannot decide to provide racially segregated education, or, if it chooses to provide these services, racially segregated health care, clean water, public roads, and so on. This formal equality requirement indicates that even in the case of 'negative' rights to equal treatment, the *choices* the state can make are constrained by rights, and in some cases the state may be required to do things it would not otherwise do. Public law rights limit not only *what* the state can do, as they would if they were only restraints, but also the *way* the state can go about its business.

So rights are constraints, understood as limiting the choices of others. The implication of their taking the form of constraints is that public law rights manifest some kind of inviolability. The idea of inviolability I want to invoke here is a common-sense one rather than a full-scale moral one, and it means only that if you have a right, you are inviolable in respect of the interest that the right reflects. It represents some way in which the content of that right – speech, religion, health, education – has been given a certain place in the practical reasoning of others. This inviolability is obvious in the case of negative rights, but it is also an implication of the constraints associated with all rights. If I have a contractual right that you mow my lawn, then if you do not mow it you fail to be appropriately constrained by my right and you infringe my inviolability accordingly – in other words, you violate me in that particular respect.

The inviolability associated with constraint is what we mean when we speak of rights being peremptory.[13] This peremptoriness of the reasons associated with rights is often described by reference to the way that having a duty in virtue of a right makes that duty directed to the right-holder. It imbues the right-holder with a high level of entitlement in relation to the duty. The example that is often used to illustrate this point refers to the difference between an obligation or duty to give to charity and an obligation or duty that one may have in virtue of a right. Although the duty-holder may experience both obligations as equally important, there is a kind of priority associated with the right.

The directedness of an obligation, its specificity to a particular claimant, makes that obligation enforceable in a way that obligations expressed in general terms – say, to give to charity – are not. Legal duties, in particular, commonly have this characteristic of directedness and

---

[13] See, for example, John Tasioulas, *Taking Rights out of Human Rights*, 120 ETHICS 647 (2010), on rights having this kind of quality.

enforceability. Even rights that do not seem associated with inviolability in the deeply moral sense of the term, such as the right of an administrative agency to take certain actions on behalf of the state, still reflect functional inviolability in the sense that they prohibit others from interfering with those actions for any reason except, arguably, for the weight of conflicting rights.

Of course, in the case of all legal rights that are democratically enacted, the constraint-based character of a rights-framework in general also carries a moral priority associated with the democratic process by which the right was created. If I have a right to health care, then, that right directs others to prioritize actions taken in respect of that interest rather than others. It is precisely this priority associated with the directed obligations embodied by rights that gives them their anti-maximizing character – that makes them 'trumps' over social goals – because they are meant to indicate a certain *prima facie* inviolability of interests against the choices certain others might otherwise take in pursuit of their goals and desires.

Having shown that public law rights take the form of constraints and thus manifest an idea of individual inviolability, I now want to briefly indicate the way in which human rights, in particular, illustrate the way rights conventionally addressed to the state-as-antagonist are nonetheless conceptually oriented to the individual person as subject. In the human rights context, rights protections are deliberately universal in their application, and human rights documents are heavily oriented to the subjects of rights. Article 2 of the UDHR establishes the universality of the declaration's protections:

> Everyone is entitled to all the rights and freedoms set forth in this Declaration, without distinction of any kind, such as race, colour, sex, language, religion, political or other opinion, national or social origin, property, birth or other status. Furthermore, no distinction shall be made on the basis of the political, jurisdictional or international status of the country or territory to which a person belongs, whether it be independent, trust, non-self-governing or under any other limitation of sovereignty.[14]

The declaration is therefore clear that all persons are the subjects of these rights. On the respondent side, the declaration is equally universal. These rights are simply enumerated on behalf of everyone; no particular antagonist is specified for any given right. In its preamble, the universality of

---

[14] G.A. Res. 217, *supra* note 8, at 72 art. 2.

the rights-respondent envisioned by the framers in principle is clear: "every individual and every organ of society"[15] is intended to take heed of the declaration's injunctions.

So while it is very explicit about rights' protection of each individual, the UDHR does not emphasize *who* is obligated to fulfill the entitlements set out; its focus is therefore very heavily on the entitlements themselves. Because they do not describe duties, but only rights, they can be seen as delineating a sphere of importance and protection around each individual. This is not necessarily a sphere of strict non-invasion, but it is a sphere that has moral importance and that can constrain the actions of others nonetheless.

The other human rights instruments, being treaties among member parties, enumerate more specific obligations of those parties. Yet even in these documents, each part normally describes a set of entitlements and legal measures in respect of a particular interest, and the first section of each part sets out the right by reference to the individuals that hold it. So, for instance, Article 6 of the International Covenant on Civil and Political Rights describes the right to life. Section 1 declares: Every human being has the inherent right to life. This right shall be protected by law. No one shall be arbitrarily deprived of his life. Section 1 of Article 8, describing the right against slavery, declares: No one shall be held in slavery; slavery and the slave-trade in all their forms shall be prohibited. Section 1 of Article 19 declares: Everyone shall have the right to hold opinions without interference.[16] The language in the treaties regarding the state's role has evolved from describing the state as antagonist to calling on it as protector: the state must "ensure" the rights articulated in the covenants, "promote" them as well as "protect" them. In the International Covenant on Economic, Social and Cultural Rights, states declare not that, or not, implicitly, *only* that, they will refrain from violations but that they *recognize* the rights enumerated. Article 7 declares that the states party recognize, for instance, the "right of everyone to the enjoyment of just and favourable conditions of work"; Article 11 declares that states party recognize "the right of everyone to an adequate standard of living."[17] What the contemporary human rights instruments do, then, is to tie each of the interests they set out to the right-subjects, recognizing that they

---

[15] *Id.* at 72 (pmbl.).
[16] International Covenant on Civil and Political Rights, (Dec. 16, 1966), 999 U.N.T.S. 171.
[17] International Covenant on Economic, Social and Cultural Rights, (Dec. 16 1966), 993 U.N.T.S. 3.

belong, fundamentally *to* him or her. All the moral weight, then, is placed on the importance of every individual: *her* safety, *her* well-being, and *her* thriving are of paramount importance.

### b) Public law rights articulate important interests

So public law rights are oriented toward the moral importance of individuals. They are, in this respect, uncontroversially justifiable by the moral principle of the equal status of persons. But concepts of rights that are affiliated with that moral principle have conventionally emphasized a certain conception of personhood – one characterized more by agency than by need, more by separateness than by affiliation, more by choice than by well-being. And this conceptualization of rights in general, and of justifiable and thus 'real' moral public law rights in particular, has tended to prioritize the 'negative' rights over the 'positive' ones. Socioeconomic rights, on this kind of view, are not real rights at all, but rather are aspirational statements of policy and good governance: real rights are ones that *protect* individuals against *intrusions* by others. Mistreatment, on a status-based conception of rights, refers to interferences, failures of respect, rather than failures to promote and protect individual interests.

But public law rights simply do not bear out this one-dimensional status-based conception of either personhood or rights. This is because these rights, whatever else they do, articulate the importance of the *interests* they enumerate. 'Interests', on this account, refers to aspects of well-being that have or are judged to have a certain degree of moral importance.[18] The fact that rights enumerate valuable interests, and can thus be taken to be statements of moral facts or judgments about value, is clear from the fact that human rights, at least, and the fundamental rights enumerated in many constitutions, take both negative and positive forms.

Negative rights characteristically describe a certain form of relation; in their most central case, a negative form of interaction is one in which we do not interact – in which we leave each other alone. A positive form of interaction is one in which we come into contact; positive rights normally take this form because my right to education, for example, requires that you *give* or *transfer* to me some resource involving my education. But, famously, public law rights specify certain single interests that give rise to

---

[18] JOSEPH RAZ, THE MORALITY OF FREEDOM 166 (1986).

various duties taking different forms.[19] My right to security of the person, for instance, will require that you do not assault me, and it will require that the state create a police force, legislation, and other institutional mechanisms to protect that interest. It may also require that those educating children, for instance, teach the importance of respect for others. The formal character of the rights themselves, therefore, do not map onto the negative and positive forms of interaction they normatively give rise to.

If we accept that socio-economic rights are real public law rights and thus at least partly moral rights, we *must* accept that rights are partly constituted and justified by the articulation and protection of value in the form of interests. But my argument is that all public law rights have the same conceptual structure and moral justification, and thus that there is no meaningful conceptual distinction between negative and positive rights. If that argument is to succeed, then the picture of rights I want to paint must be accurate for negative rights taken on their own as well as viewed in conjunction with positive ones.

This requires that I show that negative public law rights consist of, and are justifiable by, not only the moral status of persons but also the importance of the interest each one articulates for protection. Theories of rights that attempt to explain the interests protected by the array of public law rights by reference to the equal status of the person can usefully be called 'formal' theories, for my purpose, because they emphasize the constraining form of rights. But rights cannot be formal all the way down, in the sense that the interests they protect can be conceptually derived and morally justified exclusively by reference to the moral status of personhood.

For Nozick and others in the formalist tradition, the selection of interests can be inferred from the importance of individual agents making choices in pursuit of their goals and going about their business.[20] But rights express a hierarchy of value that is manifested in the ways we evaluate rights when they come into conflict. We do not have rights to personal space and privacy beyond a certain rather limited point, for example. And where rights conflict, where we must violate one or another, some things are clearly more important than others. The idea

---

[19] See, for example, Jeremy Waldron, *Rights in Conflict, in* LIBERAL RIGHTS: COLLECTED PAPERS 1981–1991 203 (1993) for his discussion on "waves of duties."

[20] See Hillel Steiner, *Working Rights, in* A DEBATE OVER RIGHTS: PHILOSOPHICAL ENQUIRIES 233 (Mathew H. Kramer, Nigel E. Simmons and Hillel Steiner eds., 1998).

of equal status suggests that harming people is prohibited and that all persons have an equal right to be free from harm, but in practice some harms are worse than others, and violations of the rights that protect those more valuable interests will attract more severe sanctions than others. If I negligently cut off your toe, for example, I will be sanctioned in some way; but if I negligently cut off your head, the sanction will be more severe.

Even if we limit the ambit of the interests rights protect to purely negative ones, so that they are framed, for example, in terms of freedom from being killed rather than a right to life, the fact of relative value – that some things are worse than others – is unavoidable. Suppose, for example, that I am driving a bus down a steep hill and cannot stop. I come to a narrow pass. On one side I see that the road abuts someone's house, and on the other side is a crowd of people. No matter what I do I will be violating someone's rights. Depending on the circumstances, I may be excused if the bus's brakes are failing, or I may not be, if, for example, I am driving drunk. In either case I am forced to choose between destroying someone's dwelling and killing a number of people. In this situation, two negative rights are in conflict, and my duties to both right-holders are not both possible. If I happen to think that property, or shelter, for example, are extremely important, and I elect to crash into the group of people, I will be more severely sanctioned than if I crash into the house.

Rights therefore necessarily involve both a substantive interest and a judgment that that interest is valuable in some way. Even formal theories of rights operate within a domain of value in two ways. First, the recognition of a right reflects the value of individual choice to promote and maintain individual inviolability. Second, a right reflects the value of certain interests above others.

But the fact that human and constitutional rights protect interests is in one sense an entirely trite observation about them: of course they all do, in *fact*, protect interests – the important question from the conceptual and moral standpoint is whether rights that suggest a positive form of interaction are real moral rights, and whether rights that suggest a negative form of interaction protect interests only incidentally, by accident, as it were, or whether their protection of interests is part of what justifies them morally.

But even these questions, though more to the point from a purely academic point of view, are incidental to the really important question for an account of rights that will give us what we really need, namely, an account of rights that explains the duties associated with them. If all 'real, moral' rights are actually negative, then we can relatively easily say that all persons are morally duty-bound to respect the rights of all persons, and that states are agents in the proper vindication and enforcement of that respect, as well as being agents themselves who must not interfere with individual rights. That would at least be a clear answer about who bears duties in respect of public law rights.

If, on the other hand, rights are *only* justified by the protection of important interests, then the question of who bears duties in respect of them becomes a well-recognized problem. On this account, rights themselves give no clear answer about whom they obligate, and the decision about who will bear duties in respect of them becomes either a purely pragmatic decision,[21] or one based on principles that are, at least in some cases, external to the rights themselves.[22]

But on the account I am putting forward here, neither the orientation of rights toward individuals as the moral subject, nor the protection of interests, though these elements are jointly necessary, are sufficient to explain what public law rights are and, more importantly, whom they obligate. More precisely, these first two elements are insufficient to explain the special protection of these interests in the context of the individual-state relationship. Upon closer examination and reflection, though, public law rights entail a third element, that of relational context, which is part of the concept and justification of these rights, and that also offers a new way of thinking about the question of who is morally implicated by rights – upon whom, in other words, they appropriately impose duties.

### c) Public law rights reflect a relational context

Public law rights seem to be distinctive because they are rights against the state. But we can capture the moral salience of that fact about them without referring to the state as an institution. Rather, we can say that the concept of public law rights includes the relational context in which they arise. So on my account, what public rights *are* involves values or interests deemed to be important, the constraint associated with the form of rights, and the moral features of the relational context of individual

---

[21] See Onora O'Neill, *The Dark Side of Human Rights*, 81 INT'L AFF. 427 (2005).
[22] See Joseph Raz, *Human Rights without Foundations*, in THE PHILOSOPHY OF INTERNATIONAL LAW 321 (Samantha Besson and John Tasioulas eds., 2010).

and state. That relational context, I will suggest, can be best characterized as one of dependency.

I have argued elsewhere that dependency is the relational context underlying public law rights,[23] and for reasons of space I can only summarize that argument here. Dependency articulates a particular relation between parties rather than, as power and vulnerability each are, simply an abstract description of a relational concept. In order to amount to a relation of dependency, then, both the parties to it – the controlling and the depending party – must be involved in the relation in a particular way. Dependency thus links parties specifically to one another in a way that is especially important for constructing a moral framework for interpersonal obligations.

First, dependency consists of agency and control over, second, the depending party's enjoyment of some good or interest. It obtains or occurs, third, within the context of an undertaking by the controlling party – an undertaking that includes the good or interest of the depending party in its scope. The state has a monopoly on the legal use of force. This immediately and obviously puts the state and its citizens in a relation of control over, and vulnerability with respect to, individual interests.

Control can refer both to power – 'to have power over, to rule' – and to choose over a course of action. To be in a relation of dependency is to have some aspect of one's well-being subject to the control of another.[24] There is also an intermediate factor between power and control, on the one hand, and impact and vulnerability, on the other. That intermediary is the relevant course of action of the more powerful party that links his or her control and his or her impact on the interests of others. I will refer to this 'course of action' piece of the dependency analysis as the *undertaking*.[25]

It is important to distinguish the way in which I mean the term from the one sometimes used to signify a responsibility voluntarily undertaken, as in, 'I undertake to look after your dog for the week.' Here, I mean an undertaking to refer only to the *course of action* itself, without

---

[23] See JEAN THOMAS, PUBLIC RIGHTS, PRIVATE RELATIONS (2015).
[24] See Stephen R. Perry, *Protected Interests and Undertakings in the Law of Negligence*, 42 U. TORONTO L.J. 247 (1992), and Hugh Collins, *Ascription of Legal Responsibility to Groups in Complex Patterns of Economic Integration*, 53 MOD. L. REV. 731 (1990), for a more specific discussion on the moral significance of dependency in tort liability.
[25] *Cf.* Perry, *supra* note 24 (Perry uses the term in a related but slightly different way in the context of liability for purely economic loss).

the element of intentionally taking on the duty in respect of the interest in question. The undertaking, in the context of public law rights, is that of sovereignty and the control it implies.

In the Weberian formulation, the importance of the state is its monopoly on the *legitimate* use of coercive force.[26] If we take this point seriously, we might say that the way in which the state constitutes a concern for individuals from a relational standpoint seems to have to do not only with the state's special power to infringe interests but with the fact that the exercise of that power is in some way accepted as authorized.

It is not the moral legitimacy of the state that is relevant to its relation with individuals where rights are concerned, though, but the fact that individuals, broadly speaking, follow the rules it makes for governing their conduct. If individuals do, in general, abide by the rules the state makes, then its power over them is much more extensive than mere coercion: it would suggest that it includes the second major element of the relation of dependency, namely, that of the ability of one party to willfully guide or determine the course of the other party's life in some way. In respect of the state, this element of control is perhaps epitomized in the state's legislative function. Individuals are to some extent limited in their ability to decide for themselves what they do and what happens to them by the fact of the state and their abiding by its rules.

Even an illegitimate state is a state by virtue of the fact that it decides how conduct is to be governed by rules, and then it enforces those rules. Important interests are threatened in different ways at both stages. Acquiescence to abide by the state's rules means that we effectively relinquish the right to protect our interests. This puts the state in a position to use coercive force against us to infringe those interests – because of the general assumption that that use of force will be acquiesced in. So mere acquiescence in abiding by the state's rules (or in not exercising our force-right to protect our own interests) creates a power structure in which the state has a capacity and individuals have an incapacity in a very unqualified sense. The real problem with the state's monopoly on coercive force does not arise or derive from its *use* of that monopoly – its actual exercise of power – but from the capacity imbued in it by our acquiescence in that monopoly in such a way that it is *always* in a position to infringe our interests. It has a *de jure* capacity to infringe our interests as well as a *de facto* one. Acquiescence rather than

---

[26] Max Weber, Sociological Writings (1994).

legitimacy – a descriptive rather than a normative standard – is what gives rise to the descriptive violability of individuals by the state. That violability justifies the imposition of *de jure* constraints on the state in respect of the interests set out by the rights as warranting protection.

## III  Implications of the three-dimensional account of public law rights

If we describe public law rights in this straightforward way, noting that they take the form of constraints oriented toward individuals; that they enumerate and protect interests; and that they arise or obtain in the relational context of the individual and the state, a relational context of dependency, we have described them in a way that captures their essential features without the fact of being held against the state being entailed by the account.

The model thus set out does not distinguish, conceptually, between negative and positive. Rights to different interests may give rise to different forms of interaction, but there is no conceptual or justificatory difference between a right that protects an interest in freedom from intrusion and one that protects an interest in a good, such as health care, that will tend to give rise to a positive form of interaction.

Moreover, on this account, the human person is the rights subject, and the rights potentially address *everyone*, thus obviating the central principled reason – that being rights against the state is just what public rights *are* – for applying them only against the state. So if they could at least at some level apply against everyone, what makes the set of public law rights we have inherited in the liberal tradition distinctive? These are rights that arise within the relational context I described, namely, that of dependency. And as I pointed out at the outset, the violability associated with the human condition is the central moral problem for writers in the social contract tradition. In describing the need for protection against the state, within his bifurcated worldview, Locke put the problem for individuals this way:

> Betwixt subject and subject, they will grant there must be measures, laws and judges, for their mutual peace and security: but as for the ruler he ought to be absolute, and is above all such circumstances; because he has power to do more hurt and wrong, it is right when he does it. To ask how you may be guarded from harm, or injury, on that side where the strongest hand is to do it, is presently the voice of faction and rebellion: as if when men quitting the state of nature entered into society, they

agreed that all of them but one, should be under the restraint of laws, but that he should still retain all the liberty of the state of nature, increased with power, and made licentious by impunity. This is to think, that men are so foolish, that they take care to avoid what mischiefs may be done them by pole-cats, or foxes; but are content, nay, think it safety, to be devoured by lions.[27]

If we leave aside the formal designation of political stations and look at the situation in which individuals in the modern world find themselves, we might now identify the lions among us slightly differently: we might say that those who have the 'power to do more hurt and wrong' are the modern lions and that the kinds of constraints Locke had in mind to restrain the government ought to apply, now, so that people continue to be 'guarded from harm, or injury, on that side where the strongest hand is to do it.' The constraints Locke had in mind are rights; human violability calls for the protection of these rights where that violability is the most pronounced. If we adopt the account of them I have briefly outlined, we can take account of the moral salience of the state's violative capacity, but the rights in question will also apply wherever humans are in a relation of dependency, and thus subject to extreme violability.

---

[27] JOHN LOCKE, SECOND TREATISE OF GOVERNMENT (1690) (Crowford Brough Macpherson ed. 1980).

# 2

# On suffering and societal constitutionalism

## At the border of international investment arbitration and human rights

DAVID SCHNEIDERMAN

### I Regimes

The purported "hollowing out" of states has resulted in the redirection of their functions upward, downward, and even nowhere at all. How are national human rights norms expected to follow this dispersal of functions, particularly as matters move to transnational domains? The problem is exacerbated by the widely discussed phenomenon of the fragmentation of international law. Fragmentation, the authors of the 2006 International Law Commission report contend, has given rise to discrete specialized regimes, each giving expression to their own embedded preferences.[1] The problem of coordinating between these discrete, sometimes contradictory, regimes has precipitated calls for a "compensatory constitutionalism" at the global level.[2] Habermas' multi-level global constitutional proposal, for instance, under which the subject "human rights" would be allocated to an intermediate transnational legal authority,[3] is one such proposal for having states play "catch-up" with private power.

Short of a consensus on comprehensive global legal ordering, how might we expect discrete regimes to listen to claims touching upon human rights concerns? How might, in Baxi's terms, the "voices of suffering"

---

[1] Martti Koskenniemi, *The Fate of Public International Law: Between Technique and Politics*, 70 MOD. L. REV. 1 (2007). See also Martti Koskenniemi and Päivi Leino, *Fragmentation of International Law? Postmodern Anxieties*, 15 LEIDEN J. INT'L. L. 573 (2002).

[2] Anne Peters, *Compensatory Constitutionalism: The Function and Potential of Fundamental International Norms and Structures*, 19 LEIDEN J. INT'L. L. 570 (2006).

[3] Jürgen Habermas, *The Constitutionalization of International Law and the Legitimation Problems of a Constitution for a World Society*, 15 CONSTELLATIONS 445, 449 (2008).

be heard?[4] Systems theory, as developed by Niklas Luhmann and Gunther Teubner, provides one such account, constructed as it is upon communications between autonomous subsystems. In Luhmann's terms, subsystems are "normatively closed but cognitively open" to communications – "irritations" or "perturbations" – emanating from other subsystems.[5] This is a theoretical account entirely congenial with the fragmentation hypothesis; indeed, the International Law Commission consulted with Teubner and makes specific reference to his work in their report.[6]

I take up international investment law in order to illustrate how one such global legal regime responds to such irritations in the realm of human rights. International investment law is a legal regime that is intended to promote and protect foreign investment via standards of protection – what can be likened to a robust form of property and contractual rights – contained within some 2800 bilateral and regional investment treaties.[7] The key innovation of this regime is that its standards of protection, though the product of interstate activity, are enforced by private actors before international investment tribunals. The overriding logic of international investment law is to promote cross-border capital flows and so state policy that significantly runs against this logic is more likely than not to run afoul of investment disciplines. The focus of discussion here is on the response of international investment tribunals to the challenges of human rights concerns rather than on proposals for new Bilateral Investment Treaty (BIT) language (though the latter certainly are the most effective means of reforming the system, if such reform is needed). How well does investment law respond to claims articulated in non-investment terms, such as human rights? My conclusion is not so well. It is likely that the strategies advanced by a systems-theoretic account likely will fail in checking the supremacy of economic rationality embedded within the regime's rules and institutions.

---

[4] Upendra Baxi, The Future of Human Rights 6 (2nd ed. 2006); Upendra Baxi, *Voices of Suffering and the Future of Human Rights* (1998) 8 Transnat'l L. & Contemp. Probs. 125, 127 ("I take it as axiomatic that the historic mission of 'contemporary' human rights is *to give voice to human suffering*").
[5] Niklas Luhmann, Law as a Social System 110 (Fatima Kastner et al. eds., Klaus A. Ziegert trans., 2004).
[6] Int'l Law Comm'n, Report of the Study Group, Fragmentation of International Law: Difficulties Arising from the Diversification and Expansion of International Law (U.N. Doc A/CN.4/ L682, 2006).
[7] U.N. Conf. on Trade & Dev., World Investment Report 2013: Global Value Chains: Investment and Trade for Development 101 (2013).

## II  Theorizing borders

The principal claim advanced by systems theory is that, as society has become more complex and functionally differentiated, autonomous subsystems have emerged to perform distinct social functions. This is an ambitious, totalizing account that claims to be "a universal sociological theory."[8] Theorists are describing self-referential or *autopoietic* subsystems that police their own boundaries on their own terms.[9] As various subsystems pursue their own autonomous rationalities, they invariably run up against the operating logic of other subsystems. This causes irritations and perturbations that can be heard by the offending subsystem. This is because subsystems are open to such "communications." Subsystems are not, however, open to the commands of other operating logics; rather, they can listen and adapt, should they choose, in ways consistent with the logic and in the language of the offending sub-system.

Teubner's formulation regarding "societal constitutionalism" comprehends the emergence of autonomous legal orders proliferating at the global level. International organizations, trade unions, nongovernmental organizations (NGOs), and multinational corporations are all authors in the construction of societal constitutions[10] – a constitutionalization of separate global subsystems "without the state" as Teubner provocatively put it.[11] The constitutive rules developed autonomously by these various societal actors are increasingly, however, coming into conflict. What has sometimes been described (benignly) as "global legal pluralism" is actually "the expression of deep contradiction between colliding sectors of a global society," observe Fisher-Lescano and Teubner.[12] "It is only a matter of time," writes Teubner, "before liberated energies of *autopoietic* systems "have negative consequences of such proportions that the resulting societal conflicts push for drastic change of

---

[8] NIKLAS LUHMANN, SOCIAL SYSTEMS 15 (John Bednarz, Jr and Dirk Baecker trans., 1995). This part draws upon David Schneiderman, *Legitimacy and Reflexivity in International Investment Arbitration: A New Self-Restraint?*, 2 INT'L J. DISP. MGMT. 47 (2011).

[9] *Id.* at 17.

[10] GUNTHER TEUBNER, CONSTITUTIONAL FRAGMENTS: SOCIETAL CONSTITUTIONALISM AND GLOBALIZATION 51–53 (2012) [hereinafter TEUBNER, CONSTITUTIONAL FRAGMENTS].

[11] Gunther Teubner, *Societal Constitutionalism: Alternatives to State-Centered Constitutional Theory?*, *in* TRANSNATIONAL GOVERNANCE AND CONSTITUTIONALISM 3, 8, 15 (Christian Joerges et al. eds., 2004).

[12] Andrea Fisher-Lescano and Gunther Teubner, *Regime Collisions: The Vain Search for Legal Unity in the Fragmentation of Global Law*, 25 MICH. J. INT'L. LAW 999, 1004 (2004).

constitutional politics."[13] The task today, then, is to "identify the real structures of the existing global constitutionalism, to criticize its shortcomings and to formulate realistic proposals for limitative rules."[14] This is a strategy of devising "internal limitations" to subsystems, inhibiting their compulsion to growth.[15] They can then suitably correspond to, and then do less damage to, their social environments.[16]

A singular advantage to thinking about human rights claims in systems-theoretic terms is that it dispenses with questions about "horizontal" or "radiating" effects of national constitutional rights. Instead, one can move directly to a consideration of having human rights obligations resonate (though not "apply" in the constitutional sense) to private law domains. Much of Luhmann's work, however, is constrained by thinking about rights within a national frame. They are largely negative, "self-protective," constraints that promote functionally differentiated subsystems.[17] The "common rights of citizenship" like freedom of religions will assist, for instance, in the maintenance of religious or ethnic autonomy.[18] Teubner, by contrast, envisages the negative effects of operative subsystems in a global frame that give rise to human rights violations. According to his account, the voices of the suffering are capable of being internalized but only on the infringing subsystem's own terms.[19]

System theory's account of the individual bearer of human rights is a bit more complicated than this suggests, however. Individual "minds and bodies" are not capable of communicating with other subsystems – they are "not parts of society but insuperably separate from it." Individuals have no "forum available before which they [can] assert these rights,"

---

[13] Gunther Teubner, *Constitutionalizing Polycontexturality*, 20 Soc. & Legal Stud. 210, 223 (2011) [hereinafter Teubner, *Constitutionalizing Polycontexturality*].

[14] *Id.* at 210, 214.

[15] Gunther Teubner, *A Constitutional Moment? The Logics of "Hit the Bottom,"* in The Financial Crisis in Constitutional Perspective: The Dark Side of Functional Differentiation 3 (Poul Kjaer and Gunther Teubner eds., 2011) [hereinafter Teubner, *A Constitutional Moment?*]; Teubner, Constitutional Fragments, *supra* note 10, at 11.

[16] Gunther Teubner, *Substantive and Reflexive Elements in Modern Law*, 17 Law & Soc'y Rev 239, 273 (1982–83).

[17] Gert Verschraegen, *Human Rights and Modern Society: A Sociological Analysis from the Perspective of Systems Theory*, 29 J.L. & Soc'y 258, 269 (2002).

[18] Will Kymlicka, Multicultural Citizenship: A Liberal Theory of Minority Rights 31 (1995).

[19] Teubner, Constitutional Fragments, *supra* note 10, at 172.

claims Teubner.[20] Instead, individuals can make themselves heard as abstract "legal persons" who are the "bearers of rights." They are thereby transformed into "artefacts of communication."[21] Interfacing with the "mask" of the human rights-bearing person, "social systems [can] make contact with people" – "they can massively irritate them and in turn be irritated by them."[22]

Can the human rights of flesh-and-blood human beings, asks Teubner, "ever be asserted against the structural violence of anonymous social processes?"[23] Teubner fears not. "All the groping attempts to juridify human rights," he writes, "cannot hide the fact that this is a strictly impossible project ... one which has no prospect of resolution."[24] It is impossible, in part, because society cannot communicate with individuals "but only about them," and because there is no "paramount court" to resolve conflicts between regimes in collision.[25] This is a significant admission, as Teubner has taken a mostly benign, even positive, view of the societal constitutionalism associated with international law's fragmentation and global legal pluralism. The question remains whether a similarly pessimistic view should be taken in the context of international investment law. I take up this question in the next part.

There are a variety of problems associated with a systems-theoretic account of the global legal order. First, one might want to be cautious about analogizing legal life to cellular biology. Second, there is an undue emphasis on structure over agency – individuals virtually drop out of the picture (note the difficulty in communicating with those who are making human rights claims). Third, and critically, the absence of the state in the production of societal constitutionalism is exaggerated.[26] What is

---

[20] Gunther Teubner, *The Anonymous Matrix: Human Rights Violations by 'Private' Transnational Actors*, 69 MOD. L. REV. 327, 335 (2006) [hereinafter Teubner, *The Anonymous Matrix*].
[21] *Id.* at 337.   [22] *Id.* at 339.   [23] *Id.* at 343.   [24] *Id.* at 345.
[25] As did Luhmann, Teubner underscores the futility of attempting to unify different operative social systems. See *A Constitutional Moment?*, supra note 15, at 272, where he observes: "Centralized social integration is effectively ruled out today." See also TEUBNER, CONSTITUTIONAL FRAGMENTS, *supra* note 10, at 172.
[26] This impression is enhanced by the title of Teubner's edited book, GLOBAL LAW WITHOUT THE STATE (Gunther Teubner ed. 1997), and his contribution to the volume, GLOBAL BUKOWINA: LEGAL PLURALISM IN A WORLD SOCIETY concerning the rise of *lex mercatoria*, customary law developed by commercial arbitration and practice. The account seems extravagant. See Emily Kadens, *The Myth of Customary Law Merchant*, 90 TEX. L. REV. 1153 (2012) *and* Peer Zumbansen, *Transnational Private Regulatory Governance: Ambiguities of Public Authority and Private Power*, 76 LAW & CONTEMP. PROBS. 117 (2013). Teubner takes a more nuanced view in his recent book, CONSTITUTIONAL FRAGMENTS,

missing from this account is state agency in the structuration of the global legal order. State actors have entered into bilateral or regional treaties committing states to the special treatment of foreign investors. States continue to be key actors in perpetuating the regime's legitimacy: to the extent that the bulk of states have entered into such treaties (and most every state has) and participate in dispute settlement proceedings, one can safely predict that the regime will continue to thrive. Lastly, it is difficult to sustain the notion that international investment law is "non-national" law. After all, this is a legal order built on norms that have been advanced by principal capital-importing states for some time claiming that they articulate principles of international law and civilized justice.[27] Legal norms, after all, have distributional consequences. Achieving global take-up of specific national legal norms – securing the *imprimatur* of global law – is a significant political achievement by capital-exporting states. Any theory of the global legal order should be attentive to the fact that what constitutes the set of norms we associate with international law represent the interests of a set of actors who have privileged access to the conditions giving rise to what we label "universal."[28]

I want to suggest that there is, nevertheless, analytical utility to systems theory in this legal context. Its value concerns an ability to better comprehend the behavior of relevant actors within international investment arbitration. One can identify at least two responses arising from actors within the system to "perturbations" arising from outside of it. According to the first view, investment treaties are *lex specialis* and so confined to determinations only of whether investor rights have been violated. Other considerations, such as human rights norms unconnected to property rights or multilateral environmental commitments that go unmentioned in treaty text, cannot weigh in to that equation. Arbitrators, according to this account, simply are giving effect to international agreements, whose object and purpose are the promotion and protection of foreign investment, irrespective of their consequences for conflicting rationalities.[29] It is not that municipal law or international law does not play a role in investment treaty arbitration – they perform certain functions and on

---

*supra* note 10, at 130, where he describes "an entwinement—but not a fusion—between national and transnational legal orders."

[27] David Schneiderman, *The Global Regime of Investor Rights: Return to the Standards of Civilised Justice?* 5 TRANSNAT'L LEGAL THEORY 60 (2014).

[28] A formulation I have borrowed from PIERRE BOURDIEU, PASCALIAN MEDITATIONS 70 (Richard Nice trans. 2000).

[29] JAN PAULSSON, DENIAL OF JUSTICE IN INTERNATIONAL LAW 363 (2005).

occasion fill gaps, to be sure – but recourse to these sources of law will be sporadic. The commonly expressed concern about the fragmentation of international law generates little anxiety in this camp.

The second view is more open to influences entering into international investment treaty interpretation from outside of the regime's particular object and purpose. Campbell McLachlan, for instance, describes investment treaties not as self-contained regimes but as informed by, and in conversation with, general international law.[30] The editors of the recent volume entitled *The Backlash against Investment Arbitration* similarly describe the investment arbitration regime as "in listening mode and ready to adapt."[31] According to this view, international investment arbitration must open itself up to outside influences. This will be done, however, on international investment law's own terms using the regime's own lexicon and logic.[32] McLachlan draws on the principle of "systemic integration"[33] in treaty interpretation as a means of "taking into account" the broader normative environment in which international investment law operates.[34] Having resort to this broader normative universe performs a "systemic function ... linking specialized parts to each other and

---

[30] Campbell, McLachlin, *Investment Treaties and General International Law*, 57 INT'L & COMP. L.Q. 361, 369 (2008) [hereinafter McLachlan, *Investment Treaties*]. By general international law, McLachlan is referring to the International Law Commission Report (2006) (to which he provided assistance) which admits that general international law, though not well articulated or understood, refers to general customary international law as well as to "general principles of law recognized by civilized nations" and might also refer to "principles of international law proper and to analogies from domestic laws." INT'L LAW COMM'N, *supra* note 6, at 254. The report also develops the notion of "self-contained regimes." *Id.* at 123–37).

[31] Michael Waibel et al., *The Backlash against Investment Arbitration: Perceptions and Reality*, in THE BACKLASH AGAINST INVESTMENT ARBITRATION: PERCEPTIONS AND REALITY xxxvii, xxxix (Michael Weibel et al. eds., 2010).

[32] For example, Anne Van Aaken, *Fragmentation of International Law: The Case of International Investment Law*, 17 FIN. Y.B. INT'L INV. L. 91 (2006); Charles H Brower II, *NAFTA's Investment Chapter: Initial Thoughts about Second-Generation Rights* 36 VAND. J. TRANSNAT'L L. 1533 (2003); Pierre-Marie Dupuy, *Unification Rather than Fragmentation of International Law? The Case of International Investment Law and Human Rights Law*, in HUMAN RIGHTS IN INTERNATIONAL INVESTMENT LAW AND ARBITRATION 45 (Pierre-Marie Dupuy et al. eds., 2009).

[33] Campbell McLachlan, *The Principle of Systemic Integration and Article 31(3)(C) of the Vienna Convention*, 54 INT'L & COMP. L.Q. 279, 318 (2005) [hereinafter McLachlan, *The Principle of Systemic Integration*]. McLachlan describes the term as his contribution to the International Law Commission's report on fragmentation. INT'L LAW COMM'N, *supra* note 6.

[34] INT'L LAW COMM'N, *supra* note 6, at 415, 419.

to universal principles."[35] This is a technical interpretive device that provides no definitive answers to regime collision. Rather, it is a style of management that delegates responsibility for acknowledging and accommodating the broader environment to legal technicians operating within the sub-system's discrete domains.[36]

Both views share an insistence on structuring encounters with the outside normative universe on international investment law's own terms – the terms of their interaction cannot be dictated, in other words, by actors operating from outside of the system. On either view, then, it will be international investment lawyers, arbitrators, and scholars who will determine the extent to which conflicting, non-investment-promoting considerations get let in. States, of course, have a role to play to the extent they incorporate such concerns into treaty practice.[37] What I wish to emphasize is that both responses, as a descriptive matter, resonate in systems-theoretic terms. That is, they both comprehend international investment law as a sub-system of rules and institutions with its own logic and system of policing interactions with other competing subsystems of law – the hallmarks of legal *autopoiesis*. Common to both camps, then, is an account of international investment law as developing autonomously from (though intimately related to) other norm-producing systems, which is potentially on a collision course with other subsystems of law that are organized around logics other than that of promoting foreign investment.

## III   Border policing

Though regime collision is denied by some,[38] the logic of human rights is an exemplar of this clash of rationalities. The discourse of human rights

---

[35] *Id.* at 475.
[36] Jan Klabbers, *Reluctant Grundnormen: Articles 31(3)(C) and 42 of the Vienna Convention on the Laws of Treaties and the Fragmentation of International Law*, in TIME, HISTORY AND INTERNATIONAL LAW 141, 161 (Matthew Craven et al. eds., 2007). It should be emphasized that Koskenniemi, chair of the International Law Commission study group on fragmentation, aims to politicize international law ("giving voice to those not represented in the regime's institutions") and so move away from its penchant for expert rule and managerialism. Koskenniemi, *supra* note 1, at 29. One does not get that international law should be moving in a less technical direction from McLachlan's related contributions. See McLachlan, *Investment Treaties*, supra note 30; McLachlan, *The Principle of Systemic Integration*, supra note 33.
[37] We should not, however, overstate the capacity of states to depart from the expert advice given to them by international investment norm-entrepreneurs who have the ear of those having authority over this dossier.
[38] Peters, *supra* note 2, at 602.

has difficulty obtaining resonance within international investment domains in particular. Symptomatic is the oft-cited ruling in *Biloune and Marine Drive Complex Ltd. v. Ghana Investments Centre and the Government of Ghana*.[39] The investor there claimed an independent right to damages under treaty for being arbitrarily detained and then deported, resulting in a denial of his "fundamental human rights." It did not follow, the tribunal reasoned, that it "is competent to pass upon every type of departure from the minimum standard to which foreign nationals are entitled, or that this tribunal is authorized to deal with allegations of violations of fundamental human rights."[40]

There are a number of reasons, including procedural impediments, to explain the reluctance of tribunals to tackle human rights questions in the context of investor claims. I canvass some of these reasons later, but surely a contributing factor will be what has been called the "lack of clarity" in regard to the substance of human rights norms.[41] It does not help that the "generative grammars"[42] of human rights remain laconic, even contradictory. If Moyn is correct, a "genuine" international human rights movement only gained momentum in the 1970s and arose in the place of other failed utopias, both "state-based and internationalist."[43] It has taken on the burden of a "grand political mission of providing a global framework for the achievement of freedom, identity, and prosperity."[44]

### a) Investor grounds

The dominant understanding is well articulated by Reiner and Schreuer: references to human rights in investment arbitration are "sparse and infrequent" and, in the text of an investment treaty, "highly unlikely."[45] In "practice," Simma observes, "human rights-based claims have not overrun the dockets of foreign investment tribunals."[46] No empirical

---

[39] 95 I.L.R. 184 (1989) (award on jurisdiction and liability).   [40] *Id.* at 203.
[41] Ursula Kriebaum, *Privatizing Human Rights: The Interface between International Investment Protection and Human Rights*, in THE LAW OF INTERNATIONAL RELATIONS—LIBER AMICORUM HANSPETER NEUHOLD 165, 172 (August Reinsch and Ursula Kriebaum eds., 2007).
[42] BAXI, *supra* note 4, at xvi.
[43] SAMUEL MOYN, THE LAST UTOPIA: HUMAN RIGHTS IN HISTORY 8 (2010).   [44] *Id.* at 9.
[45] Clara Reiner and Christoph Schreuer, *Human Rights and International Investment Arbitration*, in HUMAN RIGHTS IN INTERNATIONAL INVESTMENT LAW AND ARBITRATION 82 (Pierre-Marie Dupuy et al. eds., 2009).
[46] Bruno Simma, *Foreign Investment Arbitration: A Place for Human Rights?* (2011) 60 INT'L AND COMP. L.Q. 573, 578.

evidence is offered in support of these claims, though similar observations have been made by others, including the United Nations Conference on Trade and Development (UNCTAD) International Investment Monitor.[47] It may be inaccurate to conclude that human rights have no presence in international investment disputes; rather, it is that their presence has not been fully acknowledged or well articulated.

At a very basic level, it should be acknowledged that a robust form of property right is engaged in every investment dispute.[48] Yet, investors have displayed little interest in framing claims in human rights terms.[49] This can be explained by the fact that there is no need to do so. Investor rights are expansively articulated and given latitudinarian interpretation by tribunals – precisely the type of "trade-related, market friendly human right" that Upendra Baxi has written about.[50]

Foreign investors take on no direct obligations under an investment treaty, connected to human rights or otherwise. Nor do investors typically appear to be parties bound by international human rights obligations. When they are implicated, typically this will be under soft law instruments that refer to principles and voluntary measures, as in the UN's Global Compact.[51] Nor do the obligations undertaken by states in investment treaties refer directly to international (or national) human rights obligations (other than investor property rights). Obligations, instead, are owed to foreign investors – they are not owed to nationals who might have an interest in the enforcement of international human rights obligations.

### b) State grounds

Host states may find it to their advantage to invoke international human rights obligations as a means of fending off investor claims, but rarely do so.[52] Occasionally, for instance, such claims get intermingled with

---

[47] U.N. Conf. on Trade & Dev., Selected Developments in IIA Arbitration and Human Rights IIA Monito No.2 (2009) UNCTAD/WB/DIAE/IA/2009/7.

[48] ZACHARY DOUGLAS, THE INTERNATIONAL LAW OF INVESTMENT CLAIMS 52 (2009); Reiner and Schreuer, *supra* note 45, at 83.

[49] *Id.* at 88.  [50] BAXI, *supra* note 4, at 258f.

[51] United Nations, Econ. & Soc. Council, Comm'n on Human Rights, *Promotion and Protection of Human Rights: Interim Report of the Special Representative of the Secretary-General on the Issue of Human Rights and Transnational Corporations and Other Business Enterprises*, 60, U.N. Doc. E/CN.4/2006/97 (Feb. 22, 2006).

[52] Van Aaken, *supra* note 32, at 118.

national constitutional claims or are dressed up as claims about the "sovereign right to regulate."[53] There are impediments even to these sorts of arguments arising. For one, states may not want to admit that they initially were implicated in projects that have had negative human rights consequences.[54] Nor might states wish to admit before an international tribunal that, without the impugned measure, they otherwise would be failing to live up to international minimum standards. According to arbitrators, states have not well articulated these claims. The *Suez v. Argentina* dispute is instructive in this regard.[55] One of some fifty disputes launched against Argentina as a result of measures taken in response to the economic meltdown of 2000–2001, the investor sought compensation of some US $255 million for the collapse of its investment in the provision of waste and water services in the province of Santa Fe. The impugned measures included delinking the Argentinian peso to the US dollar (pesification) and de-indexing of rates to the US purchasing price index. Argentina sought to justify the taking of such measures on the basis that it was satisfying the "right to water" which, as the tribunal disparagingly put it, "somehow trumps" obligations under the BIT and "implicitly gives Argentina the authority to take actions in disregard of its BIT obligations."[56] Investment treaty obligations could not so simply be disregarded.

### c) On the ground

The voices of the suffering, those actors within host states whose actions and behavior provide a backdrop for the dispute, or who may have helped to precipitate its occasion, typically will not be heard. States, to be sure, are expected to vindicate their interests, but the scarcity of such discussions reflects the general reluctance of states to raise international human rights norms. The filing of an amicus brief, where permitted, increasingly is the place where such discussions can be expected to take

---

[53] Howard Mann, International Investments, Business, and Human Rights: Key Issues and Opportunities 17 (2008), *available at* www.iisd.org/pdf/2008/iia_business_human_rights.pdf.

[54] Reiner and Schreuer, *supra* note 45, at 89; MUTHUCUMARASWAMY SORNARAJAH, THE INTERNATIONAL LAW ON FOREIGN INVESTMENT 228 (3rd ed. 2010).

[55] Suez, Societad General de Aguas de Barcelona S.A., and Inter Agua Servicios Integrales del Agua S.A. v. The Argentine Republic, ICSID Case No. ARB/03/17, Decision on Liability (Jul. 30, 2010) [hereinafter *Suez v. Argentina*].

[56] *Id.* at para. 240.

place. This becomes the default place for those who are claiming a place at the table on behalf of those engaging in local resistance.[57] The International Centre for Settlement of Investment Disputes has liberalized rules for filing amicus briefs but not in respect of making oral submissions. Other investor-state rules and facilities are not so permissive. The London-based International Chamber of Commerce, for instance, maintains strict confidentiality and bars nonparty participation.[58]

Even when there is discussion of local action that precipitated a dispute, tribunals tend to speak disparagingly about their conduct. Tribunals will often portray local actors in the way the tribunal in *Metalclad Corporation v. United Mexican States* did: as either paid off to foment resistance on behalf of local competitors or as dupes operating under a false consciousness and mistaken about their own self-interests.[59]

### d) The text

The principal means by which human rights will enter into international investment law will be via treaty interpretation. Though not expressly mentioned in treaty text, human rights norms can enter into tribunal consideration as a matter of applicable law. There is, at present, much ink being spilled about this phenomenon. Authors typically survey standard treaty disciplines in order to describe how, in the course of considering whether a measure is "tantamount" to expropriation or amounts to a denial of "fair and equitable treatment," international human rights obligations may have a point of entry.[60] The task, it is said, is to explore "windows for the direct application of non-investment international law," including international human rights law.[61] Others propose the rapid adoption of that proportionality analysis in respect of investment disciplines in order that state objectives, including international human

---

[57] Ibironke T. Odomusu, *The Law and Politics of Engaging Resistance in Investment Dispute Settlement*, 26 PENN ST. INT'L L. REV. 251 (2007).

[58] Int'l Chamber Commerce, *Dispute Board Rules* (2011) Articles 9, 15.3, available at www.iccwbo.org/ICCDRSRules/.

[59] Metalclad Corp. v. United Mexican States, ICSID Case No. ARB(AF)/97/1, Award (Aug. 30, 2010).

[60] Morijn, John and Jasper Krommendijk, *"Proportional" by What Measure(s)? Balancing Investor Interests and Human Rights by Way of Applying the Proportionality Principle in Investor-State Arbitration*, in HUMAN RIGHTS IN INTERNATIONAL INVESTMENT LAW AND ARBITRATION 422 (Pierre-Marie Dupuy et al. eds.,2009).

[61] *Id.*

rights obligations, are weighed into determining whether a breach of an investment treaty obligation has occurred.[62] There appears to be, in other words, increasing consensus, among scholars at least, that human rights can in these ways resonate within the borders of the investment law system.

The principal disagreement is the degree of intensity with which this will be accomplished. For one group, already described, the task is to reflect on substantive norms outside of investment law within investment law itself.[63] Pierre-Marie Dupuy describes the process best: it is a matter of the arbitrator "technically" "taking into account what could be termed the external obligation ... when interpreting investment treaty disciplines."[64] For another group, it is insufficient for human rights norms to "fulfill no more than an ancillary role."[65] The preferred course of action is to conscript Article 31(3)(c) of the Vienna Convention on the Law of Treaties (VCLT) for the purposes of "integrating" international legal obligations into investment treaty interpretation. Systemic integration in treaty interpretation, according to Campbell McLachlan, is a means of (again) "taking into account"[66] the broader normative environment in which international investment law operates.[67] Having recourse to this broader normative universe performs a "systemic function ... linking specialized parts to each other and to universal principles."[68] The consequence of failing to act in this way is underscored by Simma: an investment tribunal confronted with a human rights matter that "neglected to consider" such norms would be providing "insufficient" reasons.[69] Though systemic integration is more ambitious in scope, it remains a technical device that provides no definitive answers to regime collision.[70]

---

[62] Benedict Kingsbury and Stephan Schill, *Investor-State Arbitration as Governance: Fair and Equitable Treatment, Proportionality and the Emerging Global Administrative Law*, in EL NUEVO DERECHO ADMINISTRATIVO GLOBAL EN AMÉRICA LATINA: DESAFÍOS PARA LAS INVERSIONES EXTRANJERAS, LA REGULACIÓN NACIONAL Y EL FINANCIAMIENTO PARA ED DESARROLLO 221 (Benedict Kingsbury et al. eds., 2009).
[63] Van Aaken, *supra* note 32, at 129.      [64] Dupuy, *supra* note 32, at 54, 58.
[65] Simma, *supra* note 46, at 578.      [66] INT'L LAW COMM'N, *supra* note 6, at 415, 419.
[67] *Investment Treaties*, *supra* note 30, at 318. McLachlan describes the term as his contribution to the International Law Commission's report on fragmentation, *supra* note 6.
[68] *Id.* at 475.
[69] *Supra* note 46, at 591. Simma admittedly confines these remarks to matters arising under the International Covenant on Economic, Social and Cultural Rights. I do not think it a stretch to have expanded his directive to encompass all human rights instruments, equally.
[70] Klabbers, *supra* note 36, at 161.

It is what Koskenniemmi characterizes as "rule by experts" who "manage" those practices "into unreflective support of the structural bias within a particular expert discourse."[71]

### e) The record

It remains to consider how investment tribunals have responded to this challenge in practice. This provides the best evidence of how the regime's sensors operate when confronted with impulses associated with human rights. Luke Peterson observes that arbitrators, outside of an investor's property or due process claim, generally "have not grappled to the same extent" with claims raised by states or NGOs.[72] Moshe Hirsch, like Peterson, undertakes a qualitative analysis of some of the salient cases and concludes that tribunals consistently treat international human rights law as insignificant.[73] "They adopt quite a consistent approach," he observes, "*opposing* the incorporation of human rights law in investment disputes."[74] A review of awards by Reiner and Schreuer indicate tribunals' "reluctance" to grapple with human rights concerns, preferring to dismiss claims based upon procedural grounds.[75] Until we have in hand a study that methodically reviews all investment disputes in which human rights obligations are expressly or impliedly at play, any observations in this regard necessarily are impressionistic.

One gets the impression, and it is one consistent with that already mentioned, that tribunals prefer to elide regime conflict, that is, they usually will want to define these sorts of conflicts away. The strategy I have in mind is the one taken up by the tribunal in *CMS Gas*

---

[71] Martti Koskenniemi, *Constitutionalism as Mindset: Reflections on Kantian Themes about International Law and Globalization*, 8 THEORETICAL INQUIRIES IN L. 9, 17 (2006).

[72] Luke Eric Peterson, Human Rights and Bilateral Investment Treaties: Mapping the Role of Human Rights Law within Investor-State Arbitration 9 (2009), *available at* http://publications.gc.ca/collections/collection_2012/dd-rd/E84-36-2009-eng.pdf; U.N. Conf. on Trade & Dev., *supra* note 47. Note that Peterson was the author of the UNCTAD note.

[73] Moshe Hirsch, *Investment Tribunals and Human Rights: Divergent Paths*, *in* HUMAN RIGHTS IN INTERNATIONAL INVESTMENT LAW AND ARBITRATION 97, 106 (Pierre-Marie Dupuy et al. eds., 2009).

[74] Moshe Hirsch, *Investment Tribunals and Human Rights Treaties: A Sociological Perspective*, *in* INVESTMENT LAW WITHIN INTERNATIONAL LAW: INTEGRATIONIST PERSPECTIVES 85, 89 (Freya Baetens ed. 2013) [hereinafter Hirsch, *Investment Tribunals and Human Rights Treaties*].

[75] Reiner and Schreuer, *supra* note 45, at 90.

## III. BORDER POLICING

*Transmission Co. v. The Argentine Republic,* one of the first disputes arising out of the collapse of the Argentinian economy.[76] Argentina claimed that it acted the way it did because the economic collapse "compromised basic human rights" recognized by the Argentinian constitution.[77] The tribunal responded by finding that there was no "collision" between the Argentine-US BIT and the Argentinian constitution: "First because the Constitution carefully protects the right to property, just as the treaties on human rights do, and secondly there is no question of affecting human rights when considering the issues disputed by the parties."[78] Argentina's human rights claim, admittedly, was not firmly grounded in an international obligation though it easily could have been. It might be that the argument was not very well articulated.[79] This is curious as the constitutional argument had already been made in a law review article by Professor and Justice Minister Horacio Rosatti,[80] who appeared on behalf of Argentina in the dispute. Nor is it entirely clear that the tribunal well considered the claim about Argentinian constitutional law. Weighing into a debate on Argentina's Supreme Court about the constitutionality of pesification, the tribunal preferred a ruling by a discredited court in *Provincia de San Luis* – the court which Horacio Spector describes as resurrecting a "vested rights" doctrine associated with the discredited *Lochner* era in the late nineteenth-century United States.[81] This was despite the court's return, in *Bustos,* to earlier doctrine that had validated "the most diverse invasions of private property and contractual freedom."[82] The tribunal preferred to find that reversion to earlier and previously settled doctrine did not "overrule other decisions of the Supreme Court," namely, the case that resurrected discredited vested rights doctrine.[83]

Argentina would later take up international human rights norms in *Suez v. Argentina.* The tribunal there responded to Argentina's invocation

---

[76] ICSID Case No. ARB/01/8, Award, May 12 2005 [hereinafter CMS].   [77] *Id.* at 114.
[78] *Id.* at 121, 239.
[79] Hirsch, *Investment Tribunals and Human Rights Treaties supra* note 74, at 89. In his comments at the conference where this paper was presented, Professor José Alvarez reports that the constitutional case was poorly made in CMS, if at all.
[80] Horacio Daniel Rosatti, *Los tratados bilaterales de inversión, el arbitraje internacional obligatorio y el sistema constitucional argentine,* 198 La Ley 198 (Oct.15, 2003).
[81] Horacio Spector, *Constitutional Transplants and the Mutation Effect,* 83 Chi.-Kent L. Rev. 129, 140 (2008).
[82] *Id.* at 141.
[83] See CMS, *supra* note 76, at 216, which states: "This decision [*Bustos*] does not overrule other decisions of the Supreme Court [*Provincia de San Luis*]."

of a right to water (since given international expression in the UNGA Declaration on the Right to Water)[84] by concluding that Argentina's "international human rights obligation and its investment treaty obligations are not inconsistent, contradictory or mutually exclusive ... Argentina is subject to both international obligations, i.e. human rights *and* treaty obligations, and must respect both of them."[85] This is the approach suggested by the tribunal in *S.D. Myers v. Government of Canada*, a dispute concerning the closure of the Canadian border to the export of PCB waste.[86] Canada defended its actions, admittedly after the fact, by invoking an international obligation to dispose of its own waste within its own borders in accordance with the 1989 Basel Convention on the Control of Transboundary Movement of Hazardous Waste. Guided by the language of North Atlantic Free Trade Agreement (which mentions the Basel Convention, in Article 104, though the United States had not ratified it), the tribunal concluded that "where a state can achieve its chosen level of environmental protection through a variety of equally effective and reasonable means, it is obliged to adopt the alternative that is most consistent with open trade."[87] Hirsch interprets the ruling as restricting the "margin of discretion" available to states when faced with inconsistent obligations.[88] Only the course of action most consistent with international investment obligations will be tolerated. The "most consistent" (or least restrictive) alternative can be read quite strictly as requiring the policy path that least realizes the right at issue.

This is unlikely to satisfy actors operating within the logic of the human rights system. I take the analysis by Martin Scheinin, former member of the UN Human Rights Committee (1997–2004), as a representative viewpoint. According to Scheinin, even the human-rights-friendly approach of "systemic integration" via the VCLT is inadequate. It is the failure to distinguish between different types of treaties that renders this approach deficient. Human rights treaties, Scheinin writes, are a classic example of "law-making treaties" that "go beyond the

---

[84] G.A. Res. 64/292, U.N. Doc. A/RES/64/292 (Aug. 3, 2010.) online at www.unesco.org/water/wwap/news/archives/UNDecWaterHR_EN.pdf.

[85] CMS, *supra* note 76, at 216.

[86] S.D. Myers Inc. v. Government of Canada, UNCITRAL, Partial Award, Nov. 13 2000 [hereinafter S.D. Myers].

[87] *Id.* at 221.

[88] *Interactions between Investment and Non-Investment Obligations*, in THE OXFORD HANDBOOK OF INTERNATIONAL INVESTMENT LAW 154, 166 (Peter Muchlinski et al. eds., 2008).

reciprocal binary relationship of rights and obligations between contracting states, as they have third party beneficiaries, a high number of parties, autonomous monitoring mechanisms, and an aspiration to establish objectively binding normative international standards."[89] It should be noted that international investment law exhibits some similar features and aspirations.

Nor should human rights lawyers, Scheinin continues, "join in the chorus of singing the song of fragmentation."[90] This would reduce human rights law to one of many international law branches with an accompanying overreliance on VCLT formalities to mediate between them. Scheinin recommends the adoption, instead, of a pragmatic alternative that he calls the "reconciliation" approach. The VCLT can be expected to perform some integrative functions, as it reflects some of the rules of customary international law, while acknowledging the special place of human rights treaties and their interpretation by monitoring bodies (such as the UN Human Rights Committee). These should become evidence of "subsequent practice in the application of the treaty which establishes the agreement of the parties regarding its interpretation" within the meaning of VCLT Article 31(3)(b).[91] Scheinin recommends a reconciliation approach though he would prefer taking up what he calls a "constitutional" approach where the constitutional dimension of international human rights law, as a special set of binding substantive norms, governs the interpretation of other treaties.[92] Scheinin worries, however, that a constitutional approach may be considered too radical by scholars, judges, and governments and would have the effect of marginalizing human rights advocates. His preferred constitutional approach functions as a form of critique that resembles what Koskenniemmi describes as "constitutionalism as mindset": a constitutional vocabulary that "transforms individual suffering into an objective wrong that concerns not just the victim, but everyone."[93]

Despite the proliferation of calls for what Peters calls "compensatory constitutionalism"[94] – replacing state constitutional systems but at the global level – there is no likelihood of any consensus on such matters emerging any time soon. Indeed, Teubner envisages "no new

---

[89] Martin Scheinin, *Impact on the Law of Treaties*, in THE IMPACT OF HUMAN RIGHTS LAW ON GENERAL INTERNATIONAL LAW 23, 27–28 (Martin Scheinin and Menno T. Kamminga eds., 2009).
[90] *Id.*   [91] *Id.* at 33.   [92] *Id.* at 30.   [93] *Supra* note 71, at 35.
[94] *Supra* note 2, at 580.

compensation problem, but a basic deficiency of modern constitutionalism," that is, a failure to account for sub-systemic constitutions.[95] As there is no single interpretive means of settling intersystemic conflicts,[96] we are left with the despair expressed by Teubner about such matters: in the realm of the "strictly impossible."[97] Short of amending investment treaties so as to insert human rights obligations,[98] human rights norms will continue to perturb the investment law system and the system likely will continue to resist incursions by human rights activists and actors into its domains. The question remains whether its legitimacy can survive intact without further drastic changes – in the form of "limitative constitutional norms"[99] – imposed on the regime by states.[100] If, from a systems-theoretic perspective, this is forbidden, then it seems that, from a diagnostic perspective, systems theory will have outrun its utility.

---

[95] TEUBNER, CONSTITUTIONAL FRAGMENTS, *supra* note 10, at 5.
[96] Jan Klabbers, *Beyond the Vienna Convention: Conflicting Treaty Provisions*, in THE LAW OF TREATIES BEYOND THE VIENNA CONVENTION 193, 204 (Enzo Cannizazaro ed. 2011).
[97] Teubner, *The Anonymous Matrix, supra* note 20, at 345.
[98] See Patrick Dumberry and Gabrielle Dumas-Aubin, *How to Impose Human Rights Obligations on Corporations*, 4 Y.B. ON INT'L INVESTMENT L. & POL'Y 569 (2011–12).
[99] Teubner, *Constitutionalizing Polycontexturality, supra* note 13, at 223.
[100] See DAVID SCHNEIDERMAN, RESISTING ECONOMIC GLOBALIZATION: CRITICAL THEORY AND INTERNATIONAL INVESTMENT LAW (2013), on the difficulty of resistance in this field.

# 3

## Beware

Boundary crossings

JOSÉ E. ALVAREZ[*]

### Introduction

It has long been widely accepted that international treaty regimes, such as those governing trade, investment, or human rights, are not self-contained silos separate from the rest of international law. This is clear from the references to general international law contained in the underlying treaties that give rise to such regimes as well as from the reliance on such non-treaty sources in the adjudicative "case law" produced under many of them.

The World Trade Organization's (WTO) Dispute Settlement Understanding (DSU), for example, specifically licenses WTO panelists and Appellate Body members to consult "customary rules of interpretation of public international law."[1] Accordingly, WTO arbitral decisions have relied on Articles 31 and 32 of the Vienna Convention on the Law of Treaties (VCLT) in interpreting WTO members' treaty obligations.[2] Similarly, the roughly 3000 bilateral or regional investment protection agreements that protect foreign investors, most of which were concluded in the 1980s, often reference customary rules of considerably older vintage concerning the treatment of aliens, and the resulting investor-state arbitral jurisprudence is filled with references to that law.[3] Bilateral

---

[*] Herbert and Rose Rubin Professor of International Law, New York University School of Law. The author gratefully acknowledges the research support provided by the Fiomen D'Agostino and Max E. Greenberg Research Fund.

[1] See Understanding on Rules and Procedures Governing the Settlement of Disputes art. 3 (2), Apr. 15, 1994, Marrakesh Agreement Establishing the World Trade Organization, Annex 2, 1869 U.N.T.S. 401 [hereinafter DSU].

[2] Vienna Convention on the Law of Treaties, art. 31–32, *opened for signature* May 23, 1969, 1155 U.N.T.S. 331, 8 I.L.M. 679 (1969) [hereinafter VCLT].

[3] US bilateral investment treaties (BITs), in addition to providing numerous treaty rights to foreign investors, such as rights to be free of discrimination or to national and most favored nation treatment, also make reference to customary protections through cross-

investment treaties (BITs) usually enable foreign investors to claim the benefits of the customary "international minimum standard" and therefore include investor claims for "denial of justice" if, for example, they should fail to be treated with due process in a host state's courts. BITs may also incorporate references to another general source of international law, namely, general principles of law as reflected in the municipal laws of countries around the world.[4] Human rights treaties, such as the International Covenant on Civil and Political Rights, contain a rich interlay of open-ended treaty and customary law standards. Such treaties anticipate that their interpreters will read a guarantee such as the Covenant's insistence that the "inherent right to life" be "protected by law" and not be subject to "arbitrary" deprivation, for instance, in light of preexisting custom, namely, how state practice and *opinio juris* has generally interpreted such terms.[5] The continuous interaction between many human rights treaty instruments and customary law is reflected in the close overlap between the rights in the Covenant and those in the earlier Universal Declaration of Human Rights (many of which are widely considered to be customary and applicable to all).[6] Human rights treaties may also be interpreted in the context of general principles of law, so that, for example, the Covenant's prohibition on the "arbitrary" deprivation of life may be interpreted in light of what municipal law, general precepts of law, or natural justice would consider "arbitrary."[7]

---

references to "international law" or to terms of art that are understood to reflect such rules, such as the right to "full protection and security" or the right to prompt, adequate, and effective compensation if expropriated, for example. See JOSÉ E. ALVAREZ, THE PUBLIC INTERNATIONAL LAW REGIME GOVERNING INTERNATIONAL INVESTMENT 114-17 (2011).

[4] Thus, the US Model BIT of 2004 provides in Article 5(2) that its guarantee of "fair and equitable treatment" includes the obligation "not to deny justice in criminal, civil, or administrative adjudicatory proceedings in accordance with the principle of due process embodied in the principal legal systems of the world." See United States, Treaty Concerning the Encouragement and Reciprocal Protection of Investment, art. 30(3) (2004), *available at* www.state.gov/documents/organization/117601.pdf [hereinafter 2004 US Model BIT]. See generally, RUDOLF DOLZER and CHRISTOPH SCHREUER, PRINCIPLES OF INTERNATIONAL INVESTMENT LAW 162-66 (2008).

[5] International Covenant on Civil and Political Rights, art. 6 (1), Dec. 16, 1966, 999 U.N.T.S. 171.

[6] See, for example, PHILIP ALSTON and RYAN GOODMAN, INTERNATIONAL HUMAN RIGHTS 157-62 (3d ed. 2013).

[7] See, for example, OSCAR SCHACHTER, INTERNATIONAL LAW IN THEORY AND PRACTICE 50 (1991) (identifying five conceptions of general principles of law as invoked by international judges or lawyers: as principles drawn from a comparative survey of national law, as principles derived from the unique character of the international community, as principles intrinsic to the idea of law, as universalist principles grounded in natural law,

For these reasons, Bruno Simma, former International Court of Justice (ICJ) judge, has argued that the prospect that any international legal regime has no need to resort to non-treaty sources of international obligation – no matter how detailed its own treaty rules – is unlikely since, thus far, none of them has managed to avoid them.[8] Entirely self-sufficient treaty regimes, disconnected from, for example, the rules governing treaty interpretation – now generally codified in the VCLT – or the customary rules governing state responsibility, while conceivable, do not appear to exist. This is true because treaty negotiators find it more convenient to simply rely on existing general rules rather than seek to negotiate them from scratch, and because treaty makers cannot anticipate the future or how new facts will reveal gaps in coverage that will need to be filled.

For those charged with interpreting such treaties, whether members of the WTO's Appellate Body, investor-state arbitrators under BITs, or judges on regional human rights courts, the need to resort to non-treaty sources is further strengthened by the fundamental injunction against rendering a judgment of *non liquet*.[9] International adjudicators are discouraged (if not barred) from finding that "no law" applies to a dispute or a claim properly before them. Given the innumerable legal gaps in all treaties, their interpreters must, therefore, often reach outside their four corners to settle disputes. Such gap-filling is also required in order to *explain* or *justify* what they are doing. This is especially true of international adjudicators, from judges in the International Criminal Court (ICC) to arbitrators presiding over investor-state claims, since they operate under the equally fundamental rule requiring issuance of "reasoned" opinions. The need for reasoned opinions encourages some "boundary crossings" across international legal regimes and even the occasional comparativist foray into national legal orders (as to find general principles of law), if only under the pretense that gaps in the international rule of law do not exist. If members of the WTO Appellate Body could not resort to the customary rules of treaty interpretation, the alternatives would be limited and unattractive: they would either have

---

and as "principles of justice ... premised on the rational and social nature of human beings ... which include principles of natural justice outlined in human rights instruments and the concept of equity").

[8] Bruno Simma, *Self-Contained Regimes*, 15 NETH. Y.B. INT'L LAW 111 (1985).

[9] See, for example, Prosper Weil, *The Court Cannot Conclude Definitely ... Non Liquet Revisited*, 36 COLUM. J. TRANSNAT'L L. 109, at 110 (1997) ("the view prevailing among writers is that there is no room for non liquet in international adjudication because there are no lacunae in international law").

to refuse to settle a dispute due to the absence of such rules or make these up as they go along, thereby encouraging predictable charges of activist "lawmaking."

International adjudicators cross inter-regime boundaries, in short, because pragmatically they need to because of rudimentary or incomplete treaty regimes, a shared aversion to judicial findings of *non liquet*, and the requirement that judges explain their findings enough to satisfy litigants and other stakeholders. They engage in cross-regime pollination for more normative reasons as well. If regimes such as trade or investment were truly "self-contained," and therefore subject to gaps in coverage, this could undermine confidence in the peaceful resort to dispute settlement on which such regimes rely, while also undermining the prospects for expanding international law's reach through orderly case law development.[10]

The likelihood of "self-contained" regimes is also discouraged, at least to some extent, by the ordinary rules of treaty interpretation themselves. Those rules emphasize interpretations based on the plain meaning of treaties, including their particular "context" and their "object and purpose."[11] By emphasizing the particular texts of treaties and even their distinct negotiating histories,[12] these rules encourage interpretations that are unique to the treaty in question. But the treaty interpretation rules are Janus-faced. They go beyond the plain meaning rule to require, under VCLT Article 31(3)(c), treaty interpreters to consult "relevant rules of international law applicable among the parties."[13] This rule is admittedly vague insofar as it does not define what is "relevant," what is a "rule" (as opposed to a norm or practice), what is meant by "applicable" (as opposed to "binding"), or what is intended by allowing references to rules that apply "among" the parties (as opposed to rules that apply only "between" them). But Article 31(3)(c) clearly licenses

---

[10] See *infra* text and notes 20–34 (discussing the drivers of fears of fragmentation).

[11] VCLT, *supra* note 2, art. 31(1).

[12] *Id.* art. 32 (permitting recourse to travaux to "confirm" the meaning reached by the application of art. 31, or where such an interpretation would otherwise be absurd or unreasonable). See Julian Davis Mortenson, *The Travaux of Travaux: Is the Vienna Convention Hostile to Drafting History*, 107 AM. J. INT'L L. 780 (2013) (arguing that the negotiators of the VCLT did not intend to disfavor resort to negotiating histories of treaties).

[13] VCLT, art. 31(3)(c). The VCLT also anticipates some boundary crossings for other reasons. See VCLT, *supra* note 2, art. 30 (permitting the application of successive treaties involving the same subject).

the use of sources outside the treaty in question when its admittedly ambiguous prerequisites are satisfied.

In addition, certain canons of treaty interpretation encourage boundary crossings. This includes – the canon of interpretation that, unless a treaty expressly states otherwise, certain "fundamental" principles of international law (such as applicable remedies when wrongful acts occur) should continue to apply.[14] The rules governing *lex specialis* also encourage boundary crossings. According to the International Law Commission's (ILC) oft-cited Articles of State Responsibility (which are reportedly a codification of customary rules), general rules give way to boundary demarcating *lex specialis* only when "special rules of international law" apply.[15] *Lex specialis* does not apply merely because a treaty provision exists that deals with the same subject as one that is the concern of a general rule of custom or general principles. Treaty interpreters are not to presume that a treaty intends to cut off inquiry into those general rules only because it deals with the same subject as those rules. According to the ILC's commentaries, a treaty clause is not considered to provide for *lex specialis* unless it explicitly provides for a contrary rule or specifically indicates an intent to derogate from the presumptively applicable general rule.[16]

To be sure, these open-ended and vague rules of treaty interpretation neither ensure nor require boundary crossings. Indeed, the plain meaning rule reflected in Article 31(1) of the VCLT and its possible tool for more systemic integration included within it, Article 31(3)(c), arguably point in opposite directions. Neither the rules of treaty interpretation, given their ambiguities, nor the presumptions against interpretations in violations of "fundamental" principles lead to uniform judgments about

---

[14] For applications of this canon of construction, see, for example, Sempra Energy Int'l v. Argentine Republic, ICSID No. ARB/02/16, Award, para. 378 (Sept. 28, 2007); Elettronica Sicula S.p.A. (ELSI) (U.S. v. Italy), 1989 I.C.J. 15, para. 112 (July 20) (tacit repudiation of an "important principle of customary international law" nor favored; need words "making clear an intention to do so"). See also Amoco Int'l Fin. Corp. v. Iran, 15 Iran-U.S. Cl. Trib. Rep. 189, para. 50 (1987); Legal Consequences for States of the Continued Presence of South Africa in Namibia (South West Africa) Notwithstanding Security Council Resolution 276 (1970), Advisory Opinion, 1971 I.C.J. 16, 47, para. 96 (June 21); Loewen Group, Inc. v. United States, ICSID Case No. ARB (AF)/98/3, 42 I.L.M. 811 (2003), 7 ICSID Rep. 442 (2005), para. 160.

[15] James Crawford, The International Law Commission's Articles on State Responsibility: Introduction, Text and Commentaries, art. 55, at 306 (2002) [hereinafter Articles of State Responsibility].

[16] *Id.* commentaries to art. 55, para. 4, at 307.

whether, for example, the precautionary principle found in international environmental instruments should be applicable to the interpretation of the General Agreement on Tariffs and Trade (GATT) covered agreements.[17] Moreover, as Martti Koskenniemi has pointed out, the *lex specialis* rule is subject to a variable geometry. As he argues, there is considerable lack of clarity in the distinctions that *lex specialis* requires.[18]

As international treaty regimes have proliferated, along with adjudicative mechanisms,[19] many international lawyers have grown increasingly dissatisfied with these standard approaches to treaty interpretation, and alarmed about the "fragmented" law that these rules fail to prevent.[20] Although what is meant by the term differs, "fragmentation" generally refers to normative conflicts involving differing interpretations of general international law (such as distinct views as to the applicable rules governing state attribution), conflicts between the general law and a particular rule that claims to exist as an exception to it (such as competing views as to whether the rules governing valid treaty reservations operate differently when it comes to reservations to human rights treaties), or differences among rules generated by different legal regimes.[21]

---

[17] See, for example, European Communities—Measures Concerning Meat and Meat Products (Hormones), WTO Doc. WT/DS26/AB/R, at 41–42 (adopted Feb. 13, 1998).

[18] Martti Koskenniemi, *Fragmentation of International Law—The Function and Scope of the Lex Specialis Rule and the Question of "Self-Contained Regimes": An Outline*, 6(1) TRANSNAT'L DISP. MGMT (2009), at 5 (noting that a "rule is never 'general' or 'special' in the abstract but in relation to some other rule"). Koskenniemi also points out the relational difficulties attendant to determining whether two rules relate to the "same subject matter." *Id.* at 5–6.

[19] See, for example, Karen J. Alter, *The Multiple Roles of International Courts and Tribunals: Enforcement, Dispute Settlement, Constitutional and Administrative Review*, in INTERDISCIPLINARY PERSPECTIVES ON INTERNATIONAL LAW AND INTERNATIONAL RELATIONS 345 (Jeffrey L. Dunoff and Mark A. Pollack eds., 2013) (describing the roles of 25 permanent international courts in existence as of 2006, which had produced more than 37,000 binding legal rulings through the end of 2011).

[20] For a thoughtful examination of the connections between regime density and the fragmentation concerns of legal scholars, see Kal Raustiala, *International Proliferation and the International Legal Order*, in INTERDISCIPLINARY PERSPECTIVES ON INTERNATIONAL LAW AND INTERNATIONAL RELATIONS, *supra* note 19, at 293.

[21] See Koskenniemi, *supra* note 18. Koskenniemi cites the conflicting interpretations of state attribution provided by the ICTY (concluding that "overall control" by a state was sufficient to trigger individual international criminal responsibility) and the ICJ (concluding in more than one instance that the proper test for state responsibility requires "effective control") as an example of the first kind of normative conflict. *Id.* at 562–67. He cites the ECHR's decision in *Belilos* (concluding that despite the views of some states, the normal rules that apply to treaty reservations do not apply to reservations to human rights treaties) as an example of the second conflict. *Id.* at 567–70. He cites the WTO's

Many international lawyers fear what this may do to the perceived legitimacy of international law, or its effectiveness.

Expressions of such fears are not hard to find. More than one president of the ICJ has suggested that international tribunals have proliferated "in an anarchic manner" with unfortunate consequences, including forum-shopping, conflicting decisions, and "fragmented" law.[22] Although, as some have suggested, the complaints from ICJ judges have more than a whiff of special pleading by a court that fears losing its relevance and its control over the interpretation of international law,[23] fears of fragmentation, particularly as a result of inconsistent decisions by international adjudicators, are hardly surprising for a field that, at least since the nineteenth century, has sought to instill order within an "anarchic" system precisely by appealing to interdependence, and the harmony of interests and global values shared by a single "international community."[24] Fragmenting interpretations of international law threaten, in the words of one United Nations (UN) report, the "credibility, reliability, and consequently, the authority of international law."[25] Others, like George Downs and Eyal Benvenisti, argue that fragmented law leads to (or is the product of) inequitable law since institutional forum-shopping, entailing choices as to whether to resort to "hard" or "soft" rules or "hard" or "soft" forms of enforcement, privileges richer states with the technical and other resources to engage in it.[26]

The perceived threats posed by forum-shopping are not limited to public international lawyers. The "evils" of forum-shopping and the benefits of preventing it, namely, more predictable, stable, and harmonious rules across international regimes, have been seen self-evident to lawyers generally. They have motivated US judges and legislators (who sought to limit forum-shopping through, for example, the *Erie* doctrine requiring the application of state substantive law even when federal

---

Appellate Body's decision in *Beef Hormones* (concluding that the precautionary principle had not become a binding rule of international environmental law) as an example of the third. *Id.* at 571–74.

[22] Raustiala, *supra* note 20, at 294 (citing President Guillaume). *See also* Martti Koskenniemi and Päivi Leino, *Fragmentation of International Law? Postmodern Anxieties*, 15 LEIDEN J. INT' L L. 553, at 554–55 (2002) (citing the concerns of President Guillaume as well as his predecessors Stephen Schwebel and Sir Robert Jennings).

[23] See, for example, Koskeniemi and Leino, *supra* note 22, at 562.

[24] See, for example, id. at 556 (citing the views of Sir Hersch Lauterpacht).

[25] Raustiala, *supra* note 20, at 294.

[26] Eyal Benvenisti and George W. Downs, *The Empire's New Clothes: Political Economy and the Fragmentation of International Law*, 60 STANFORD L. REV. 595 (2007).

courts exercise diversity jurisdiction), European regulators (who sought to unify private international law by avoiding forum-shopping through certain European regulations), and private international lawyers (who sought to reduce the search for a forum with the most favorable law through certain provisions in the 1980 UN Convention on Contracts for the International Sale of Goods).[27] To the legal mind, fragmented law seems inconsistent with the rule of law itself.

Given the stakes, international lawyers have increasingly reacted to the "proliferation" of international tribunals with attempts to redress what they see as its adverse consequences, especially inconsistent rulings.[28] This has included efforts to encourage more systematic interpretations of existing international legal regimes. To many, the continued legitimacy of international law requires more boundary crossings between its regimes, including but not limited to greater efforts to use the general law to interpret the specific. Fears that the generality of the rules of treaty interpretation, including the rules governing *lex specialis*, might not be enough to stem the prospects of fragmentation help to explain the ILC's recently concluded Study on Fragmentation.[29] The ILC Study seeks to promote defragmentation by providing backdrop interpretative rules that would help prevent the further splintering of the international legal system.

The ILC Study encourages boundary crossings by deploying certain interpretative rules where possible to achieve harmonized international law across distinct sub-regimes. It urges treaty interpreters to use customary rules where possible as unifying gap-fillers where the traditional rules of treaty interpretation so permit.[30] More specifically, the study recommends three ways to engage in boundary crossings in the course of treaty interpretation. It recommends that (i) where a treaty is silent on a matter, the customary rule should presumptively apply (*fall-back*); (ii) where the treaty is not silent, but the terms used are unclear and yet have a recognized meaning in customary international law, one is encouraged to interpret the treaty rule consistently with the customary rule (*harmonized fall-back*);

---

[27] For these and other examples, see Franco Ferrari, *Forum Shopping in the International Arbitration Context: Setting the Stage*, in FRANCO FERRARI, FORUM SHOPPING IN THE INTERNATIONAL COMMERCIAL ARBITRATION CONTEXT 1 (2013).

[28] See Symposium, *The Proliferation of International Tribunals: Piercing Together the Puzzle*, 31 *N.Y.U. J. INT'L L. & POL.* 679 (1999).

[29] Martti Koskenniemi, Fragmentation of International Law: Difficulties Arising from the Diversification and Expansion of International Law 11, UN Doc. A/CN.4/L.682 (Apr. 13, 2006) (report of the study group of the International Law Commission) [hereinafter ILC Study].

[30] *Id.*

and (iii) only where the treaty is clear and leads to a different result to the customary rule should one apply the treaty rule to the exclusion of that rule (*contract-out*).[31] According to the study, these canons of treaty interpretation emerge from a faithful application of the existing interpretative principles that we have, including the requisites for applying true *lex specialis* as well as the injunction contained in Article 31(3)(c) of the VCLT.[32]

The study also indicates that it is sometimes appropriate to apply Article 31(3)(c) of the VCLT as a basis for considering other relevant treaties among the parties so as to arrive at a "consistent meaning" among them.[33] It states:

> Such other rules are of particular relevance where parties to the treaty under interpretation are also parties to the other treaty, where the treaty rule has passed into or *expresses customary international law* or where they provide evidence of the *common understanding of the parties as to the object and purpose of the treaty under interpretation* or as to the meaning of a particular term.[34]

## I  Global administrative law (GAL)

A number of contemporary frameworks for understanding international law in the age of globalization take up the theme that boundary crossings are justified under the rubric of promotion of "public" values. Thus, the

---

[31] As elaborated in rule 20 of the ILC's conclusions:
 *Application of custom and general principles of law.* Customary international law and general principles of law are of particular relevance to the interpretation of a treaty under article 31(3)( c) especially where (a) the treaty rule is unclear or open-textured; (b) the terms used in the treaty have a recognized meaning in customary international law or under general principles of law; (c) the treaty is silent on the applicable law and it is necessary for the interpreter, applying the presumption in conclusion (19)(a) above, to look for rules developed in another part of international law to resolve the point.
 *Id.* at 15. See also Javier El-Hage, *How May Tribunals Apply the Customary Necessity Rule to the Argentine Cases?*, 2011-12 Y.B. ON INT'L INVESTMENT L. & POL'Y 445, 452-54 (2011-12). In this instance, the application of all three prongs of rule 20 above ((a)-(c)) would lead to the use of CIL at least to inform the meaning of Article XI or to impose the burden of proof on a party that would argue that Article XI displaces the customary rule of necessity. See *id.* at 483 (concluding that applying the ILC's rules would put the burden on those who would argue for a contrary position).

[32] See ILC Study, *supra* note 29, at paras. 17-23. Consistent with the ILC's approach, some have seen Article 31(3)(c) of the VCLT as operating as a tool for the systemic integration of international law. See Campbell McLachlan, *The Principle of Systemic Integration and Article 31(3)(c) of the Vienna Convention*, 54 INT'L & COMP. L.Q. 279 (2005). Few would deny that the customary defense of necessity is one such "relevant" rule.

[33] ILC Study, *supra* note 29, rule 21, at 15.   [34] *Id.* (emphases added).

global administrative law (GAL) project, which originated at the New York University School of Law, describes a world of global "inter-public" law, where states are regulated outside the confines of the traditional "sources of international law," much like agencies regulate within the nation-state, whether through formal international organizations, collective action by transnational networks of government officials, hybrid public/private partnerships, or private institutions with regulatory functions.[35] The prescriptive side of GAL touts the principles shared by all "public law," namely, the values of legality, rationality, proportionality, and fundamental rights, as well as the procedural requirements associated with "rule of law," namely, transparency, participation, reason-giving, and forms of review and accountability (including judicial review). GAL stresses the need to view diverse international regimes, formal and informal, as addressing matters of common concern to the (international) society as a whole.

GAL encourages multiple boundary crossings for international regulators, treaty negotiators, and international adjudicators. GAL argues, for example, that the continued legitimacy of investment law, including investor-state arbitral case law, as a form of "global administration" requires both horizontal and vertical boundary crossings. It emphasizes that the "good governance" and "rule of law" standards that are elaborated among investor-state arbitrators need to be consistent with those applied at the WTO, at the international financial institutions, and in human rights regimes, and that these in turn should be consistent with those applied under national administrative law. The intuitions of GAL scholars are appealingly simple: *international regimes that seek to make states adhere to the "rule of law" need themselves to adhere to the rule of law.*

## II  International public authority (IPA)

A comparable effort to promote cross-regime engagement appears in the Max Planck Institute's project to examine the exercise of "international public authority" (IPA).[36] Like GAL, this project is explicitly grounded in a

---

[35] Benedict Kingsbury and Richard Stewart, *The Emergence of Global Administrative Law*, 68 LAW & CONTEMP. PROBS. 15 (2005); Benedict Kingsbury, *International Law as Inter-Public Law*, *in* NOMOS XLIX: MORAL UNIVERSALISM AND PLURALISM 167 (Henry R. Richardson and Melissa S. Williams eds., 2009).

[36] THE EXERCISE OF PUBLIC AUTHORITY BY INTERNATIONAL INSTITUTIONS (Armin von Bogdandy et al. eds., 2010).

"public law" approach. It also reacts to the diverse forms of international regulation, whether or not the products are formally legally binding or adequately described by the traditional sources of international law[37] and is concerned with the legitimacy of such efforts. But, as befits a project firmly grounded in the German public law tradition, the IPA project limits its purview to entities (from formal and informal interstate organizations to hybrid public/private institutions) that include states as actors and play "an active and often crucial role in decision making and policy implementation, sometimes even affecting individuals."[38]

The scope of IPA is wider than GAL insofar as it includes those exercises of public authority that are "intergovernmental" as well as "administrative," but narrower insofar as it only includes formal or informal institutions in which states retain a role. As with GAL, the "publicness" of the international actions examined – the fact that they may have a direct legal impact on individual rights, for example – suggests the appropriateness of certain boundary crossings. Thus, a number of the cross-cutting IPA studies identify procedural rights that presumptively apply whenever or however the exercise of "public authority" occurs.[39] IPA scholars, like those of GAL, are also very much concerned with whether the international exercises of public authority that they examine respect and abide by human rights.[40]

## III  Constitutionalization

Yet a third approach, led by mostly continental scholars, has described (and most often encouraged) international boundary crossings under the

---

[37] See, for example, Matthias Goldmann, *Inside Relative Normativity: From Sources to Standard Instruments for the Exercise of International Public Authority, in id.* at 661.

[38] Armin von Bogdandy, Philipp Dann, and Matthias Goldmann, *Developing the Publicness of Public International Law: Towards a Legal Framework for Global Governance Activities,"* in THE EXERCISE OF PUBLIC AUTHORITY BY INTERNATIONAL INSTITUTIONS, *supra* note 36, at 4.

[39] See, for example, Clemens A. Feinäugle, *The UN Security Council Al-Qaida and Taliban Sanctions Committee,* in THE EXERCISE OF PUBLIC AUTHORITY BY INTERNATIONAL INSTITUTIONS, *supra* note 36, at 101; Giacinto della Cananea, *Procedural Due Process of Law Beyond the State,* in THE EXERCISE OF PUBLIC AUTHORITY BY INTERNATIONAL INSTITUTIONS, *id.* at 965.

[40] See, for example, von Bogdandy, Dann, and Goldmann, *supra* note 38, at 13 (stressing that their understanding of public law adheres to the "liberal and democratic tradition, as a body of law to protect individual freedom and to allow for political self-determination"). See generally Richard B. Stewart, *Remedying Disregard in Global Regulatory Governance: Participation and Responsiveness,* 108 AM. J. INT'L L. 211 (2014).

label of "constitutionalization." These scholars tend to emphasize the interaction between international and national legal orders and examine the legitimacy of the former through the lens of the constitutional or "rule of law" values evident in the latter (at least within liberal states in the Western legal tradition).[41] Constitutionalists go beyond functionalist or realist explanations for international regimes to stress the importance of constitutional principles such as individual freedoms and collective self-determination.[42] While some constitutionalists use this frame to explore the extent to which international legal regimes can be described as "constitutional," others use them to propose reforms for those regimes precisely to make them more "constitutional" either in effect or in terms of procedures.[43]

## IV  A "public law" recipe book

A more recent multiauthored volume, edited by Stephan Schill, illustrates how all of these perspectives, from GAL to constitutionalization, can be deployed to promote specific prescriptions for boundary crossings within the international investment regime.[44] As does GAL, Schill's study stresses the need to distinguish "public" investor-state arbitration, for purposes of description and prescription, from "private" commercial arbitration. As do constitutionalists and IPA scholars, the authors of this work emphasize the need to treat this regime not as the product of a motley group of bilateral quid pro quo treaty-contracts, but as a multilateral system that should ideally advance the interests of the entire international community.[45] This study agrees with GAL insofar as it sees

---

[41] See generally Thomas Giegerich, *The Is and the Ought of International Constitutionalism: How Far Have We Come on Habermans's Road to a "Well-Considered Constitutionalization of International Law"?*, 10 GERMAN L. J. 31 (2009).

[42] See, for example, von Bodgandy, Dann, and Goldmann, *supra* note 38, at 22.

[43] See, for example, DEBORAH CASS, THE CONSTITUTIONALIZATION OF THE WORLD TRADE ORGANIZATION (2005); Ernst-Ulrich Petersmann, *Multilevel Trade Governance in the WTO Requires Multilevel Constitutionalism*, in CONSTITUTIONALISM, MULTILEVEL TRADE GOVERNANCE AND SOCIAL REGULATION 5 (Christian Joerges and Ernst-Ultrich Petersmann eds., 2006).

[44] THE MULTILATERALIZATION OF INTERNATIONAL INVESTMENT LAW (Stephan W. Schill, ed., 2009).

[45] *Id.* at 362 (arguing that this is true because of the multilateral treaty origins of many of the investor rights contained in it, because investment protection treaties were not negotiated on a quid pro quo basis and their contents do not reflect such bargains, but reflect standard guarantees that are intended to apply globally and all too frequently achieve that status). See generally Bruno Simma, *From Bilateralism to Community Interest in*

## IV. A "PUBLIC LAW" RECIPE BOOK

investment protection treaties and investor-state arbitration as vehicles for the regulation of states; with constitutionalists since its authors also see the treaties and investor-state arbitrations as tools for organizing state functions and defending fundamental rights as do constitutions; and with IPA scholars insofar as they also assume that the regime serves the public function of safeguarding a particular market ideology.[46] Accordingly, in the introduction to the study, Schill argues that international investment law needs to be reformed by drawing on insights from all of these jurisprudential frameworks.[47] He recommends that international investment law and particularly investor-state arbitrators should seek to produce converging – not fragmenting – law that is attentive to general international law as well as the law produced by other multilateral regimes.

The specific boundary crossings recommended in this study by some of its twenty-eight authors are consistent with those elaborated by Schill and Kingsbury under GAL.[48] A number of them recommend that investor-state arbitrators should be guided by comparable settings that engage in "international judicial review" over government action, as in the WTO and by European and inter-American judges in regional human rights courts.[49] Some recommend that investment lawyers and arbitrators take up the subject of "comparative public law," to better enable other boundary crossings – not just horizontally across international regimes – but vertically, to seek comparative law insights from the administrative and constitutional law of the states where investors are located. Schill, in his introduction, suggests that national law should be taken as an interpretive guide for the meaning of vague BIT guarantees,

---

*International Law*, 250 RECUEIL DES COURS, ACAD. DE DROIT INT'L DE LA HAYE 217 (1997); Benedict Kingsbury and Megan Donaldson, *From Bilateralism to Publicness in International Law*, in FROM BILATERALISM TO COMMUNITY INTEREST: ESSAYS IN HONOUR OF BRUNO SIMMA 79–89 (Ulrich Fastenrath et al. eds., 2011) (recasting Simma's "community" interests to emphasize "publicness" and "public values").

[46] THE MULTILATERALIZATION OF INTERNATIONAL INVESTMENT LAW, *supra* note 44, at 373.

[47] Stephan Schill, *International Investment Law and Comparative Public Law—An Introduction*, in THE MULTILATERALIZATION OF INTERNATIONAL INVESTMENT LAW, *supra* note 44, at 3.

[48] See Benedict Kingsbury and Stephan Schill, *Investor-State Arbitration as Governance: Fair and Equitable Treatment, Proportionality, and the Emerging Global Administrative Law*, in EL NUEVO DERECHO ADMINISTRATIVE GLOBAL EN AMÉRICA LATINA: DESAFÍOS PAR ALAS INVERSIONS EXTRAJERAS, LA REGULACIÓN NACIONAL Y EL FINANCIAMIENTO PARA EL DESARROLLO 221, 231 (2009).

[49] Schill, *supra* note 47, at 17.

such as bars on discrimination, guarantees of fair and equitable treatment, or rules ensuring compensation for regulatory takings.[50]

Schill argues, accordingly, that "comparative public law" (embracing both international and national public law) should become part of the "standard methodology of thinking about issues in international investment law."[51] He contends that the resulting cross-pollination among all forms of public law would produce more nuanced solutions to interpretative questions. For Schill, the crossing of inter-regime boundaries would concretize vague investment protection treaty standards, rebalance the rights of investors with the rights of host states to regulate in the public interest, affirm consistent international investment law, ensure cross-regime consistency thus mitigating the effects of fragmentation, and legitimize arbitral jurisprudence.[52]

Schill's multiauthored study also recommends that adjudicators deploy another strategy for boundary crossings: greater deployment of general principles of law. This third source of general international law, as is well known, is traditionally given little importance since the content of such "general principles" has usually been limited to a few vague injunctions drawn from the handling of tort, contract, or property claims by municipal courts. As befits a source of international obligation whose basis in the consent of states is at best tenuous[53] and whose content is

---

[50] *Id.* at 24 (indicating that national law analogies be used since the VCLT rules for treaty interpretation are insufficient and the legal framework sought to be established at the international level "is functionally comparable to constitutional guarantees and administrative law principles at the domestic level that ensure nondiscrimination, government according to the rule of law, and respect for property rights").

[51] *Id.* at 24.    [52] *Id.* at 25–26.

[53] International lawyers have long had trouble defending the validity of this source of obligation if the basis for all international obligations lies in the consent of states. As one ICJ judge put it: "general principles extend the concept of the sources of international law beyond the limits of legal positivism, according to which the States are bound only by their own will." South West Africa Case (Ethiopia v. S. Air.; Liberia v. S. Mr.), 1966 I.C.J. 4, 298 (July 18) (Tanaka J. dissenting). It is hard to see the role of state consent in Schachter's five categories of "general principles"; see *supra* note 7. If general principles are derived from, for example, common principles found in national law, this is hardly evidence that states have agreed to the transplanting of such principles to use at the international level as between states. For this reason, some jurists have preferred to argue for the validity of general principles on the basis that these are inherent in the "concept of law" or in the very nature of man. See Neha Jain, *General Principles of Law as Gap-Fillers* (forthcoming), available at www.iilj.org/courses/documents/NehaJain_GeneralPrinciplesasGapFillersJan2014.pdf.

## IV. A "PUBLIC LAW" RECIPE BOOK

necessarily limited by the differences among systems of municipal law (and indeed the reluctance of some legal systems to consider the jurisprudence of courts as a source of law at all), most international lawyers' list of applicable general principles of law is relatively short. Most identify this category as including some notion of laches, the principles of *nemo plus iuris, res judicata, lex posterior derogat priori, lex specialis derogat generalis,* estoppel, *ex injuria jus non oritur,* the duty to mitigate damages, and the general injunction against findings of *non liquet.*[54]

Schill and his coauthors encourage arbitrators to find such general principles in the law that are applied between different public authorities, between public authorities and private legal subjects, as well as those found within the very nature of the "rule of law" itself.[55] Suitably expanded beyond the narrow list of general procedural rules to include rules that determine the substance of economic disputes between the regulator and the regulated, this new and more muscular set of general principles of public law can be used "not only to develop minimum but also maximum standards of investment protection."[56] This could occur, for example, if investor-state arbitrators were to accept as a general canon of interpretation that unless a BIT were to explicitly provide to the contrary, its investor guarantees would be interpreted as imposing duties on host states that are no more onerous than those that would be applied under general principles of public law, including the host state's own public law. The emerging prescriptions would be comparable to those under GAL: public arbitral awards and briefs, as well as the acceptance of amicus briefs. However, limits on arbitral remedies, at least to the extent that national laws normally limit the scope of remedies available to

---

[54] See, for example, SCHACHTER, *supra* note 7, at 50–55 (1991). As this list suggests, the category of "general principles" overlaps ambiguously with customary international law. This confusion is sometimes suggested by the not uncommon resort, by international judges, to "general principles of customary law."

[55] To be sure Schill and his coauthors are building on long-held views of the category of "general principles" but extending these categories significantly beyond the examples enumerated earlier. *Cf. id.* (enumerating categories of general principles that had, at various times, been proposed including the principles of municipal law recognized by civilized nations, general principles "derived from the specific nature of the international community," principles "intrinsic to the idea of law and basic to all legal systems, and principles of justice founded on the "very nature of man as a rational and social being").

[56] Schill, *supra* note 47, at 34.

private parties whose contracts have been breached by government action, may also emerge.[57]

The stream of potential boundary crossings that could be generated by transforming international investment law into a species of "public law" is boundless. As Schill states:

> Once investment treaty standards are identified as specific public law concepts, a more refined comparative public law analysis can concretize the meaning of those concepts in specific contexts. This involves, for example, assessing to what extent domestic and international legal systems handle liability for representations made by government officials, what kind of limits the protection of property imposes on the tax legislator, or how the tensions between the protection of cultural heritage and the right to property are resolved in other public law systems. Ideally, this comparative public law approach results in the determination of general principles recognized in the principal public law systems that can be used as a source of international law in interpreting the standards contained in international investment treaties.[58]

Like Simma and Kill, these public law efforts are driven by a perceived need to better protect human rights.[59]

The rest of this chapter examines a few examples of boundary crossings gone awry and uses them to question many of the assumptions – and prescriptions – reached by public law scholars.

## V  Boundary crossings in international investment: Two recent decisions

The largest group of investor-state arbitral decisions issued to date concern one state, Argentina. Most of those investor claims, arising under nine different BITs concluded between Argentina and the US and various European states, emerged from measures taken by that state in the wake of its economic crisis in 2001–2002. Argentina has lost most of these claims and faced, as of 2012, over $660 million in damages after a

---

[57] See *id.* See also chapters by Chester Brown, William Burke-White and Andreas von Staden; Alessandra Asteriti and Christian J. Tams; and Irmgard Marboe, all in THE MULTILATERALIZATION OF INTERNATIONAL INVESTMENT LAW, *supra* note 44.

[58] Schill, *supra* note 47, at 36 (citations omitted).

[59] Thus, Schill repeatedly invokes the jurisprudence of the ECHR. He argues that investment law "shares core functional similarities with domestic administrative and constitutional review of government conduct at the domestic as well as international level, in particular under various human rights instruments, such as the European Convention on Human Rights." *Id.* at 35.

## V. BOUNDARY CROSSINGS IN INTERNATIONAL INVESTMENT 59

series of arbitral rulings that evinced surprising consistency with respect to the relevant law despite the fragmented nature of the investment "regime" (including differences among the BITs at issue) and "gaps" in the underlying applicable law.[60]

Disagreements among the many arbitrators who have so far considered these cases have been most apparent with respect to Argentina's defenses in these cases.[61] With respect to claims arising under the US–Argentina BIT, Argentina argued that its "crisis" measures were justified and no liability was therefore owed under that treaty's "measures not precluded" clause.[62] In addition, even when the underlying treaty had no such exceptions clause, Argentina argued that no liability was due under the customary defense of necessity, which should apply even when a BIT was silent with respect to providing any excuse from wrongfulness. Argentina's claimed necessity defense under customary law was codified as Article 25 in the ILC's Articles of State Responsibility of 2001.[63] To date, the arbitrators in these cases have not reached uniform agreement on a number of crucial issues with respect to such defenses. Some of the tribunals have suggested that liability continues to exist when these defenses apply; others have suggested that liability is temporarily suspended during the period of the state's underlying emergency or crisis, while yet others have found liability for damages incurred by the investor during the period of crisis to be permanently excused.[64]

These disagreements over the substantive law in a regime are not particularly surprising for questions that are essentially those of first

---

[60] José E. Alvarez, *The Paradoxical Argentina Crisis Cases*, 6 WORLD ARB. & MEDIATION REV. 143 (2010).

[61] See, for example, El-Hage, *supra* note 31.

[62] Article XI of that treaty provided: "This Treaty shall not preclude the application by either Party of measures necessary for the maintenance of public order, the fulfillment of its obligations with respect to the maintenance or restoration of international peace or security, or the protection of its own essential security interests." Treaty between the United States of America and the Argentine Republic Concerning the Reciprocal Encouragement and Protection of Investment, 31 I.L.M. 124 (entered into force Oct. 20, 1994) [hereinafter "US–Argentina BIT"]. For a thorough discussion of Argentina's defenses in connection with the US–Argentina BIT, see José E. Alvarez and Kathryn Khamsi, *The Argentine Crisis and Foreign Investors: A Glimpse into the Heart of the Investment Regime*, 2008-09 Y.B. ON INT'L INVESTMENT L. & POL'Y 379; José E. Alvarez and Tegan Brink, *Revisiting the Necessity Defense: Continental Casualty v. Argentina*, 2010-11 Y.B. ON INT'L INVESTMENT L. & POL'Y 319.

[63] ARTICLES OF STATE RESPONSIBILITY, *supra* note 15, art. 25 at 178 (necessity) and art. 55 at 306 (*lex specialis*).

[64] Alvarez and Khamsi, *supra* note 62, at 404–09.

impression. Serious engagement with the interpretation of BITs has occurred, after all, only since the mid-1990s when the first investor-state claims were brought, and therefore, most of the relevant "case law" is less than 20 years old. Indeed, prior to the Argentina cases, no arbitrator had had an occasion to interpret a "measures not precluded clause" in a BIT. Further, the underlying defense of necessity, at least as codified as Article 25 of the Articles of State Responsibility, had also not previously been the subject of much judicial or arbitral attention. The focus here is on two outlier decisions in the series of Argentina cases, which remain highly controversial and, in my view, drew particularly erroneous conclusions by engaging in boundary crossings inspired by "public law" rationales.

In *Continental Casualty v. Argentina* (*Continental*), the arbitrators, apparently inspired by the need to render a "systemic" interpretation of Argentina's defenses to that claim, drew directly from WTO case law in interpreting the US–Argentina BIT's "measures not precluded" clause.[65] The annulment ruling in *Enron v. Argentina*, on the other hand, while accepting, contrary to the *Continental* decision, that the same clause could be interpreted as the equivalent of the customary defense of necessity, was nonetheless inspired by the normative prescriptions of the public law approach in how it interpreted its own review powers as well as the customary defense of necessity.[66]

These decisions are problematic for many reasons. The result and rationale given in *Continental* ignores the stark differences between the investment regime (where private complaints against states are made whole when their property rights have been violated) and the trade regime (providing an interstate remedy intended to prod a state into removing protectionist measures) and between the distinct texts of the two treaties at issue (the WTO's Article XX and various provisions in the US–Argentina BIT). As is further discussed below these decisions are not necessarily consistent with the progressive, human-rights-centered goals of public law scholars. In prior work, I have extensively critiqued the numerous flaws in these decisions.[67] Here, I will only summarize some of

---

[65] Continental Casualty v. Argentine Republic, ICSID Case No. ARB/03/9, Award (Sept. 5, 2008).
[66] Enron Creditors Recovery Corp. Ponderosa Assets, L.P. v. The Argentine Republic, ICSID Case No. ARB/01/3, Decision on the Application for Annulment of the Argentine Republic (July 30, 2010) [hereinafter *Enron Annulment*].
[67] Alvarez and Khamsi, *supra* note 62; Alvarez and Brink, *supra* note 62; and José E. Alvarez, *The Return of the State*, 20 MINN. J. INT'L L. 223 (2011) [hereinafter Alvarez, *Return of the State*].

the problems to indicate the risks posed by some boundary crossings, even when undertaken for "progressive" reasons.

## VI  Continental Casualty v. Argentina

Continental Casualty, a US subsidiary of a leading financial services provider, owned and controlled CNA ART, one of Argentina's leading providers of workers' compensation insurance. CNA Art's portfolio of capital investments, including cash deposits, treasury bills, and government bonds, were adversely affected by Argentina's Capital Control Regime. Continental argued that Argentina's capital controls, introduced in the wake of Argentina's financial crisis, caused it losses in these assets totaling $46.4 million.[68] In response to Argentina's defense based on Article XI of the US–Argentina BIT, the *Continental* tribunal found that this treaty clause stated a "primary rule" that, when properly relied upon by a state, absolves it from any liability under the BIT.[69] It also found that since the text of Article XI "derives from the parallel model clause of the U.S. FCN [friendship, commerce and navigation] treaties and these treaties in turn reflect the formulation of Art. XX of GATT 1947," it was "more appropriate to refer to the GATT and WTO case law which has extensively dealt with the concept and requirements of necessity ... rather than refer to the requirement of necessity under customary international law."[70] It therefore treated Article XI of the BIT as an occasion to apply the proportionality or balancing tests used in the WTO in the course of applying GATT Article XX, such as WTO rulings in *Korea-Beef*.[71]

Consistent with the WTO rulings and some of the "public law" prescriptions noted earlier, that tribunal engaged in balancing a number of considerations, including the relative importance of the end pursued by Argentina and the contribution of the means to that end. The *Continental* tribunal determined that the BIT's Article XI should be read, as is the GATT's Article XX, as *absolving* a state from a treaty violation if the state took the "least inconsistent alternative." It found that a state would not be able to benefit from Article XI only if *the claimant* could demonstrate that the measure that it chose to take failed to make a "material or decisive contribution" to protect its essential security

---

[68] *Continental, supra* note 65, para. 19.   [69] *Id.* at para. 161.   [70] *Id.* at para. 192.
[71] *Id.* at paras. 192–93. This is broadly consistent with the recommendations of Kingsbury and Schill, *supra* note 46, at 250–62.

interests or if the claimant proved that the state had ignored a reasonably available alternative that would either have prevented the essential security threat or had yielded equivalent relief to the measures actually taken.[72] The tribunal found that Argentina's measures indeed had the genuine relationship of ends and means and that the claimant had failed to demonstrate that Argentina had reasonable alternatives to violating the BIT. Based on this reasoning, the tribunal denied the claimant all relief with the exception of actions that Argentina had taken with respect to treasury bills after its crisis had ended.[73]

*Continental* short-circuited the many difficult interpretative questions under international investment law noted earlier (which continue to divide that regime's arbitrators as well as legal scholars) by turning to WTO law instead. This is a case of regime borrowing or boundary crossing that cannot be justified by the traditional gap-filling interpretative rules in the VCLT or by the gap-filling interpretative canons outlined by the ILC's Study on Fragmentation (both discussed at the beginning of this chapter). Unlike the customary defense of necessity, the trade regime's balancing test is not a "relevant rule" that an interpreter of the BIT is entitled to consult under Article 31(3)(c) of the VCLT, nor is it a fundamental rule of international law presumed to be applicable in the absence of treaty language expressly derogating from it.[74] As *Continental* appears to acknowledge, the balancing test that it uses is drawn explicitly from WTO DSU interpretations of the GATT's unique general exceptions clause, namely, its Article XX, a provision that reflects the specific object and purpose of the trade system. But Article XX bears no resemblance to the US–Argentina BIT's Article XI. These two provisions serve radically different purposes within the context of two very different treaty regimes subject to radically different remedial schemes.[75]

---

[72] *Continental, supra* note 65, at paras. 195–219.   [73] *Id.* at paras. 205–21.
[74] As is indicated later, the multilateral interstate GATT/WTO regime differs markedly from that of bilateral investment treaties, including the US–Argentina BIT in terms of the relevant texts, context, and object and purpose. No one would suggest that Article XX of the GATT constitutes a customary rule and there is no evidence of a "common understanding" among the respective treaty parties of the GATT and those of BITs with respect to either the "object and purpose" of these treaties or the meaning of the respective treaties' exceptions clauses.
[75] Moreover, the sole reason offered in *Continental* (quoted earlier), for turning to the balancing test in WTO law is based on a serious misreading of history. While it is true that the drafters of the US Model BIT (used as the basis for the US–Argentina BIT) were aware of the exceptions clauses in FCNs and in the GATT, they intentionally departed

## VI. CONTINENTAL CASUALTY V. ARGENTINA

The only justification that can be offered for *Continental*'s leap to trade law in the interpretation of Article XI – one that had previously not been undertaken by any investor-state tribunal despite the frequent considerations of Article XI in prior Argentina cases – is that which is offered by some public law theorists: the ostensible need for cross-regime borrowings to create systemically harmonious law. This prescription ignores the fact that, as many thoughtful trade and investment lawyers have noted, WTO law cannot simply be transposed onto investment law.[76] The trade case law that inspires *Continental*'s peculiarly deferential standard of proof arose under GATT Article XX, a provision that provides, in relevant part, that so long as a state does not apply its measures as a means of arbitrary or unjustifiable discrimination, it can take "necessary" measures to protect public morals or human, animal, plant life, or health or are "necessary to secure compliance with laws or regulations ... including with respect to customs enforcement, the enforcement of monopolies ... the protection of patents, trade marks and copyrights,

---

from those clauses, and particularly from the GATT's approach to exceptions, when drafting the "measures not precluded" clause in the US BIT. The text of Article XI of the US–Argentina BIT at issue in *Continental* was not based on Article XX of the GATT, which bears no resemblance to its text and which covers entirely different subject matter. It draws from the text of only one *subpart* of the typical FCN's longer list of general exceptions, namely, Article XX(d) of the typical modern FCN. Both of those provisions address state obligations for the maintenance of international peace and security; both indicate that the underlying measures need to be shown to be "necessary" for a party to protect "its essential security interests." Those provisions resemble not the GATT's Article XX but GATT Article XXI (which is scarcely mentioned by the *Continental* ruling). GATT Article XXI, not its Article XX, deals with essential security matters, but crucially it makes essential security matters "self-judging" and not subject to any kind of balancing test at all. Of course, negotiators of BITs, and particularly the US–Argentina BIT, were well aware of GATT Article XX and the self-judging nature of GATT Article XXI chooses not to incorporate either in their BIT precisely because of the differences between the object and purpose of these two regimes. Indeed, even today, when some BIT parties are attempting to narrow the scope of their treaties, most BIT parties have not incorporated GATT Article XX into their newer model BITs but have, at most, incorporated only some of the exceptions mentioned in Article XX. For a more thorough consideration of all of these issues, see Alvarez and Brink, *supra* note 62.

[76] This is recognized even by some of the contributors to the Schill volume noted earlier. See Jürgen Kurtz, *The Merits and Limits of Comparativism: National Treatment in International Investment Law and the WTO*, in THE MULTILATERALIZATION OF INTERNATIONAL INVESTMENT LAW, *supra* note 44, at 243 (urging caution with respect to drawing from WTO law on national treatment even when seemingly comparable non-discriminatory guarantees are contained in BITs precisely because of the many differences between the two regimes).

and the prevention of deceptive practices."[77] Article XX goes on to identify other legitimate regulatory interests far afield from essential security, including state measures to protect prison labor and obligations under commodity agreements. GATT Article XX is akin to a provision authorizing GATT parties to regulate in the general public interest so long as they do not engage in trade protectionism. But BITs, by their express terms, go far beyond protecting investors from discriminatory treatment, and they (or at least those involved in the Argentina cases to date) do not include a comprehensive listing of governmental measures that, when shown to be nondiscriminatory, are presumptively legitimate.

Further, the GATT jurisprudence interpreting the "necessary" Article XX measures deployed by the *Continental* has not been concerned with the essential security measures or actions taken pursuant to a state's police powers that are the explicit subject of Article XI of the US BIT. The "least restrictive alternative" balancing test that *Continental* draws from GATT Article XX jurisprudence has nothing to do with security concerns and would not even be applied within the WTO itself to such matters since those matters are covered by the GATT's very different self-judging Article XXI.[78] Indeed, GATT or WTO jurisprudence is a singularly inappropriate place to turn for guidance on how a non-self-judging "measures not precluded" clause like the US–Argentina BIT's Article XI should be interpreted. Given the self-judging nature of essential security determinations in the GATT, there is essentially no WTO case law on what a state needs to prove when it purports to take a measure to protect its "essential security."[79]

While, as noted, some investor-state arbitrators have found that the US–Argentina BIT's Article XI and the customary defense are distinct defenses, *Continental* is the only decision rendered to date that has resorted to WTO law to interpret Article XI.[80] Presumably no prior

---

[77] General Agreement on Tariffs and Trade, Oct. 30, 1947, 61 Stat. A–11, 55 U.N.T.S. 194, art. XX [hereinafter GATT].

[78] See *supra* note 75.

[79] Prior to establishment of the GATT in 1994, only one panel was ever established to consider an Article XXI defense and it did so under specific and limited terms of reference. See United States-Trade Measures Affecting Nicaragua, Oct. 13, 1986 (unadopted), GATT Doc. L/6053.

[80] See, for example, El-Hage, *supra* note 31 (discussing the leading cases in terms of the ways that determined the interaction between Article XI of the US-Argentine BIT and the defense of necessity). See also *id.* at 476 (noting the inconsistent rationales posited in *Continental*, which found no interaction between Article XI and the customary rule while

tribunal has made this interpretative leap because it seems obvious why drafters of the US BIT consciously omitted a "general exceptions" clause like the GATT's Article XX. Unlike the GATT or even FCNs (which largely focus on trade in goods), the protections extended by US BITs extend far beyond discouraging protectionist measures that discriminate against traders of goods. By contrast, the GATT's Article XX attempts to carve out general types of non-protectionist regulation. It makes no sense, however, to have a comparable exception for public policy measures applicable to this BIT as a whole. It simply makes no sense, for example, to preclude liability for a governmental expropriation simply because a government takes a measure that is, on balance, the least restrictive measure that a government can take to serve a public purpose under Article XI when the same treaty provides that governments must pay prompt, adequate, and effective compensation even for takings that serve a public purpose.[81]

*Continental* also suggests another possible hazard of cross-regime borrowing: the risk of getting the borrowed law wrong. *Continental*'s misguided effort to apply WTO jurisprudence ignores the fact that WTO adjudicators developed their interpretation of what a "necessary" measure entails pursuant to the two-tier process anticipated by the terms of Article XX. A party invoking Article XX must prove that its measure falls within one of the enumerated exceptions of Article XX(a–j) but it must also prove that its measure is applied consistently with the chapeaux of Article XX, which requires a showing that measures are not arbitrary or discriminatory. This two-tiered standard is actually the one applied in the trade cases that *Continental* would have investor-state arbitrators apply. The single balancing test that *Continental* misleadingly draws from the trade regime does not stand alone; it is actually part of two tests that, in combination, achieve the object and purpose of the GATT, namely, to

---

noting similarities between the two rules that perhaps a "harmonized fallback" interpretation between the two would have been the more proper choice).

[81] Art. IV (1), US–Argentina BIT. For similar reasons, even commentators otherwise favorable to some forms of "balancing" in the course of resolving the Argentina cases acknowledge that any attempt to use the "measures not precluded" clause of that treaty as an exception could not apply with respect to Article IV(3) of that BIT. Article IV(3) indicates that when investors suffer losses due to a number of serious circumstances, including "state of national emergency," foreign investors cannot be discriminated against if the state offers remedies to others for such losses. See Alberto Alvarez-Jiménez, *The Interpretation of Necessity Clauses in Bilateral Investment Treaties after the Recent ICSDI Annulment Decisions*, 2010–11 Y.B. ON INT'L INVESTMENT L. & POL'Y 419, at 447–49.

discourage trade protectionism. *Continental* fails to consider how the chapeaux clause of Article XX may affect the meaning of "necessary" in that provision. For all these reasons, what *Continental* applies as "WTO law" does not even accurately reflect trade law, much less investment law.

Article XI of the US–Argentina BIT does not incorporate a "least restrictive alternative" test. It is not a provision that authorizes states to generally regulate in the public interest so long as its actions are not discriminatory. On the contrary, Article XI is part of a broader treaty that anticipates that the substantive guarantees provided to foreign investors of both state parties will continue to apply even when a state regulates in the public interest, even when its actions are nondiscriminatory, and even when it takes measures in the course of emergencies.[82] While the balancing approach foreseen under the GATT's Article XX furthers the object and purpose of that treaty insofar as trade law is concerned principally with avoiding discriminatory measures, a least restrictive alternative balancing approach applicable to all rights in the US–Argentina BIT makes no sense given a number of that treaty's other provisions, and is radically inconsistent with what those treaty parties originally intended.[83]

The effects of *Continental* are striking. By interpreting Article XI as a "primary" rule that obviates consideration of the rest of the BIT and, in addition, by transforming that narrow exception into a vehicle for deploying trade law's least restrictive alternative test, *Continental* turns a treaty originally intended to, among other things, *affirm* customary protections and provide these with an effective forum for enforcement, into a pact that provides investors with *fewer* protections than they would have enjoyed under customary international law and that accords them *less effective* protection than they would have had in the days when diplomatic espousal was the only vehicle for protecting their rights.

*Continental* never asks whether Article XI was intended to be an all-encompassing excuse from compensation, no matter what the nature of the governmental action is, so long as that action is undertaken during a

---

[82] See, for example, Articles II(2)(a) (anticipating fair and equitable treatment, full protection and security, and treatment in accordance with international law), IV(1) (anticipating compensation even when expropriations are taken in a nondiscriminatory manner and for a public purpose), and IV(3) (anticipating that investors should receive certain nondiscriminatory benefits even in the wake of certain national emergencies). See also supra note 81 (discussing Article IV(3)).

[83] See Alvarez and Khamsi, *supra* note 62, and Alvarez and Brink, *supra* note 62.

## VI. CONTINENTAL CASUALTY V. ARGENTINA

period of an economic crisis. It never considers whether such a blanket excuse was intended in the context of a treaty between a major capital exporter and a country that had repeatedly resorted to such crises to escape its obligations to foreign investors and that had indicated that it was entering into the BIT with the United States (and others) precisely to provide a credible commitment that it would no longer do so in the future.[84] Apparently intent on an interpretation that would promote (and reflect) "systemic integration," *Continental* failed to interpret the actual treaty that it was compelled to apply.

*Continental*'s reliance on WTO law also failed to consider the differing remedies of the trade and investment regimes.[85] The US–Argentina BIT, like most US BITs of the same period, focus on the rights of third parties who invest in host states in reliance on these treaties. The chief remedies they authorize are damages to third parties for past harms they incurred because of government action. BITs also authorize those third parties to bring such claims for damages themselves, thereby displacing the usual espousal practice dependent on intervention by the investor's home country. BITs turn their beneficiaries, namely, the foreign investors from the respective BIT parties, into "private attorneys general" charged with treaty enforcement.[86] The trade regime, by contrast, is more state centric. It is structured to enable prospective relief of a particular kind as between states. Its remedies are limited to authorized

---

[84] Alvarez and Khamsi, *supra* note 62, at 414–15 (arguing that the US–Argentina BIT, given Argentina's century-long penchant for proclaiming emergencies, was intended to forestall exactly the broad brush defense of necessity raised by Argentina in these cases).

[85] These same flaws undermine *Continental*'s reliance on specialized principles fashioned for use in other regimes, such as the margin of appreciation doctrine used by the European Court of Human Rights. *Cf. Continental, supra* note 65, at para. 181. The ECHR's margin of appreciation principle, like the GATT Article XX balancing test that *Continental* wrongly applied, is not a relevant general principle of law or customary law entitled to consideration for purposes of treaty interpretation under Article 31(3)(c) of the VCLT. Not surprisingly, that principle has been rejected by tribunals outside of the ECHR. *See, for example*, Oil Platforms (Iran v. U.S.), 2003 I.C.J. REP. 161, paras. 73, 76 (Nov. 6), 42 I.L.M. 1334 (2003); para. 48 (sep. op. Higgins, J.); para. 11 (sep. op. Simma, J.). Siemens A.G. v. Argentina, Award, Feb. 6, 2007, ICSID Case No. ARB/02/8, para. 354. The margin of appreciation doctrine is presumably based on the particular text of the European Convention of Human Rights, including its conditioning of rights as "necessary in a democratic society." This language, which has no equivalent in US BITs, assumes and anticipates deferring to common standards among the democratic states of Europe. See Alvarez and Khamsi, *supra* note 62, at 441–48.

[86] Indeed, some have suggested that BITs thereby "privatize" what, in the age of espousal, was a governmental function.

tariff retaliation – namely, a method of countermeasures that attempts to get states to remove their offending measures.

*Continental*'s unwarranted leap to trade jurisprudence ignores these realities. It wrongly presumes that the level of deference owed to states in an interstate dispute settlement system principally designed as a bulwark against trade protectionism should be transposed to a bilateral treaty that explicitly anticipates that nationals of both of its state parties are the intended beneficiaries, that these third party beneficiaries' reliance will result in sunk costs, and that these non-state parties will be owed compensation for past injuries.[87]

None of this suggests that it is wrong to "balance" investor and government rights in the course of interpreting a BIT. Such balancing could have been applied in *Continental* itself more narrowly – as to determine whether the substantive rights to fair and equitable treatment of the investor were indeed violated, for instance. This is a more plausible rationale that may have led to a comparable outcome in *Continental* itself, without undermining the substantive scope of the other BIT rights or precluding a more careful evaluation of the many serious interpretative questions raised by Argentina's defenses. The tribunal short-changed those substantive inquiries by turning a "measures not precluded" clause into a "deferential right to regulate" clause. The differences between the trade and investment regimes that were ignored in *Continental* serve as a cautionary note against seeing alleged "public law" general principles like proportionality balancing (or the "margin of appreciation") as all-purpose legitimating principles that can be readily applied to all parts of a BIT without adverse consequences to the legitimate expectations of a regime's stakeholders.

## VII  Enron v. Argentina (Annulment)

The annulment ruling in *Enron Annulment*, another one in the series of Argentina "crisis" cases, annulled a multi-million dollar annulment decision originally rendered in favor of Enron.[88] The basis for this annulment

---

[87] It is also striking that although *Continental* relied on a distinction between "primary" and "secondary" rules, no such distinction appears in GATT jurisprudence and indeed, the concept seems alien to its remedial scheme. This is yet another instance where the jurisprudence that *Continental* applied does not accurately reflect trade law, much less investment law.

[88] *Enron Annulment*, supra note 66.

## VII. ENRON V. ARGENTINA (ANNULMENT)

turned also on the proper application or interpretation of Article XI of the US–Argentina BIT. The International Centre for Settlement of Investment Disputes (ICSID) *Enron Annulment* committee overturned the original award on the basis that the original panel, by not addressing certain questions under the customary defense of necessity, had "failed to state the reasons on which it is based" under ICSID Convention, Article 52(1)( e).[89] It also justified annulment on the basis of ICSID Article 52(1) (b) (failure to apply the applicable law) because the panel had relied on economic experts to base a legal conclusion.

The original panel ruling in the *Enron* case had, as did a number of prior arbitral decisions, interpreted Article XI in light of the customary defense of necessity as codified under the ILC's Articles of State Responsibility, Article 25.[90] That panel had also decided, on the basis of the expert opinions of the economists presented by both Argentina and the claimant, that Argentina had failed to demonstrate that the measures it had taken that had been shown to violate the BIT did not satisfy the "only way" requirement of the customary defense, and that, therefore, Argentina had failed to substantiate its Article XI defense from liability.

The annulment committee, perhaps inspired by GAL advice that legitimate investor-state rulings need to be comprehensively and clearly reasoned, annulled this decision because the original panel had failed to address "a number of issues that are essential to the question of whether the 'only way' requirement was met."[91] The *Enron Annulment* noted that the panel had failed to consider alternatives to the literal interpretation of the "only way" requirement: namely, whether a state could satisfy the defense if it adopted a measure that involved the "least grave violation of international law."[92] It noted that the panel had also failed to address whether the "relative effectiveness of alternative measures" should be taken into account,[93] and whether this determination needs to be made at the date of the award with the benefit of hindsight, or needs to take into account the information that was available to the state at the time the measures were taken.[94] The absence of considerations of these matters led the annulment committee to conclude that the panel had

---

[89] Convention on the Settlement of Investment Disputes between States and Nationals of Other States, art. 52, Mar. 18, 1965, 17 U.S.T. 1270, 575 U.N.T.S. 159 [hereinafter ICSID Convention].
[90] Articles of State Responsibility, *supra* note 15, art. 25.
[91] *Enron Annulment*, *supra* note 66, at para. 368.   [92] *Id.* at para. 370.
[93] *Id.* at para. 371.   [94] *Id.* at para. 372.

failed to give sufficient reasons. The annulment committee also opined that since determining the application of the customary defense of necessity involved the determinations of legal questions, it was an error to rely on the testimony of economic experts to resolve such matters.[95] This failure led to its finding that the panel had failed to apply the applicable law while also failing to provide adequate reasoning for its conclusions.[96] The annulment committee found nearly identical flaws with respect to the original panel's findings with respect to the other requisites of the customary necessity defense. It found that the original panel had not adequately addressed whether Argentina's measures seriously impaired the essential interests of other states or the international community,[97] and had not answered a number of interpretative questions concerning whether Argentina had "contributed" to the underlying essential security threat.[98]

Along the way, the annulment committee had interesting things to say about what it means to issue a reasoned award:

> The Committee notes that from the material before it, the parties in their arguments before the Tribunal do not appear to have expressly identified and argued the questions set out above, which would provide an explanation for why the Tribunal did not expressly address them. A Tribunal is not required to address expressly every argument put by a party, and a Tribunal is therefore certainly not required to address arguments that have not been put by parties.

---

[95] *Id.* at para. 377.   [96] *Id.* at paras. 377–78.   [97] *Id.* at paras. 379, 384.

[98] *Id.* at paras. 386–93. The annulment ruling points out, for example, that the original panel had not realized whether the "contribution" requirement of the customary defense requires a demonstration of some kind of fault on behalf of Argentina and if so, whether recklessness, negligence, or some lesser amount of fault would do. *Id.* at paras. 388–89. It noted that, even if the parties had not argued these matters to the original panel, it was still wrong to rely on the testimony of economic experts to decide the legal question of "contribution" as well. *Id.* at paras. 391–93. On this matter as well, the annulment committee had a particular view of what a reasoned opinion should be:
  The Tribunal's process of reasoning should have been as follows. First, the Tribunal should have found the relevant facts based on all of the evidence before it, including the Edwards Report. Second, the Tribunal should have applied the legal elements of the Article 25(2)(b) to the facts as found (having if necessary made legal findings as to what those legal elements are). Third, in the light of the first two steps, the Tribunal should have concluded whether or not Argentina had "contributed to the situation of necessity" within the meaning of Article 25(2)(b). For the Tribunal to leap from the first step to the third, without undertaking the second amounts in the committee's view to a failure to apply the applicable law."
  *Id.* at para. 393.

Having said that, the Tribunal is required to apply the applicable law, and is required to state sufficient reasons for its decision. In this case, a reading of the cursory reasoning of paragraphs 300 and 308–309 of the Award clearly suggests that the Tribunal accepted the expert evidence of Professor Edwards over the conflicting expert evidence of Professor Nouriel Roubini, to the effect that Argentina had other options available to it for dealing with the economic crisis. From this, without any further analysis, the Tribunal immediately concluded, that the measures adopted by Argentina were not the "only way."[99]

The *Enron* rulings, both the original panel and the annulment ruling, are valuable examples of plausible and erroneous boundary crossings. On the one hand, both the original panel and the annulment committee plausibly engaged in a substantive boundary crossing that is consistent with some (but by no means all) prior arbitral decisions on point: both sets of arbitrators turned to the general customary defense of necessity for purposes of interpreting the "measures not precluded" clause of the US–Argentina BIT. This author has previously argued why this is consistent with the text, object and purpose, and intent of that treaty and is licensed by the ILC's suggested canons of treaty interpretation.[100] Unlike *Continental's* (over) reach to WTO law, this is not an instance where the interpretive leaps violate the ordinary rules of treaty interpretation. But the *Enron Annulment* committee drew considerable criticism from the arbitration community precisely because it stretched to the breaking point the purposely narrow rationales for annulment provided in the ICSID Convention, and did so on the basis that an arbitral decision needs to contain a particular kind of reasoning.[101] Like the *Continental* ruling, the procedural posture of the *Enron Annulment* committee ignores the wider context of the underlying investor-state system. BIT state parties and investors originally turned to investor-state arbitration at least in part because it is a party-driven adversarial process focused on solving the particular dispute. They turned to ICSID arbitration in this instance precisely because that system does not anticipate a full appellate process that would add time and expense. The *Enron Annulment* committee, effectively in thrall to GAL and IPA arguments urging exceedingly detailed plenary review because

---

[99] *Id.* at paras. 375–76.
[100] See Alvarez and Khamsi, *supra* note 62; Alvarez and Brink, *supra* note 62.
[101] ICSID Convention, *supra* note 89. See, for example, Christoph Schreuer, *From ICSID Annulment to Appeal Half Way Down the Slippery Slope*, 10 L. & PRAC. OF INT'L CTS. & TRIBUNALS 211 (2011).

these are required by the "rule of law," ignored these distinguishing features as well as the text of the ICSID Convention.[102] It engaged in arbitral activism at odds with the narrow ambit accorded to ICSID annulment committees, which are not authorized to engage in *de novo* appeals from findings of fact or law.

The *Enron Annulment* ruling on the merits reflected public law prescriptions in other ways. That tribunal rendered the customary defense of necessity unrecognizable in an apparent effort to turn that purposely dichotomous, exceedingly narrow, and hard-to-prove defense from *pacta sunt servanda* into a malleable exception that "balances" investor rights and "public values." It transformed an exceptional defense for self-preservation into a far more readily available excuse from liability that requires deference to the policy choices made by sovereigns while suggesting that a private party should have the burden of showing what those policy choices were.[103] Although coming to different conclusions from *Continental* with respect to the applicable substantive law since it read Article XI in light of customary and not trade law, the result in *Enron Annulment* was in the end similar: the state is empowered at the expense of investor rights irrespective of the text, object and purpose, and negotiating history of the treaty at issue.

The *Enron Annulment*'s suggested reformulation of the customary defense of necessity has implications for a defense from wrongfulness that, absent *lex specialis*, applies to all treaties, from those involving human rights to the protection of the environment. If other arbitrators or judges insist that Enron's unanswered questions about this defense be addressed when states seek to get out of a treaty obligation, such inquiries could license much more expansive exceptions to *pacta sunt servanda*. The suggestion in *Enron Annulment* that states might be able to assert "necessity" when this is only the least undesirable (and not the only) alternative, that they can excuse themselves from their international obligations even when they have caused the underlying crisis that provokes the state's violation of law so long as they did not do so "recklessly" or "negligently," and that those resisting such defensive claims have the burden of proof are risky steps to take for those seeking to uphold the

---

[102] ICSID Convention, *supra* note 89.
[103] *Cf.* Robert D. Sloane, *On the Use and Abuse of Necessity in the Law of State Responsibility*, 106 AM. J. INT'L L. 447 (2012) (arguing that the defense was originally an exceedingly narrow one comparable to self-defense, to be used to allow a state to preserve itself when its very existence is threatened).

international rule of law.[104] That such risks emerge from a decision ostensibly justified on the basis of the need to *promote* the protection of individual rights against state abuses is an irony that should escape no one's attention.

## VIII   "Public law" crossings via international personhood

A particularly seductive but altogether different method for engaging in boundary crossings, at least for international lawyers, is to resort to international legal personhood. The appeal of branding someone or some entity a "subject" of international law is irresistible for those invested in "public law." As is clear from the IPA project discussed earlier, such a conclusion immediately transforms the actions of such subjects to matters of "public" governance of interest to the international community. A determination of international subject-hood, while perhaps not strictly necessary for determining that "public law" is implicated, is tantamount to a finding of "publicness" triggering the GAL or "rule of law" values and prescriptions enumerated previously. For some, a determination that X is a "subject" or an "international legal person" is shorthand for concluding that X is, therefore, subject to the same set of primary and secondary rules, the same rights and obligations, as states.

As the ICJ Advisory Opinion that originated the notion that international organizations have legal personhood indicates, such a conclusion would be wrong as a matter of positive law.[105] The ICJ concluded only that the UN had, in the context of the UN Charter, the ability to pursue a claim for a mediator who had been killed in the course of his or her UN duties.[106] In so ruling, the ICJ took care to examine the specific treaty-making clauses contained in the UN Charter and other evidence that the UN's "objective" personhood, good against third parties, was intended. It noted that sending a mediator to risky places where they might be killed was indeed an anticipated task of UN agents, even though peacekeeping as such was not mentioned in the Charter. Even so, the ICJ specifically warned against concluding, from the proposition that the UN was intended to be the kind of legal person that was entitled to bring a claim on behalf of damages suffered by its deceased agent, that as a result the UN was entitled to the

---

[104] See generally Alvarez, *Return of the State, supra* note 67.
[105] Reparation for Injuries Suffered in the Service of the United Nations, Advisory Opinion, 1949 I.C.J. 174 (Apr. 11) [hereinafter Reparation Case].
[106] *Id.*

*same* kind of rights and responsibilities as apply to states. It concluded that the UN was a special kind of legal person, one whose rights and responsibilities needed to be drawn based on functional necessity and an analysis of those functions as indicated in its constituent instrument.[107] The legal personality recognized by the ICJ in that case was not intended to establish a single category of legal personhood and to preclude those further inquiries.[108] The ICJ did not suggest all international legal persons necessarily enjoy rights and duties comparable to states.

The ICJ's warnings on personhood have not always been heeded by courts, human rights advocates, or even the learned luminaries charged with the codification and progressive development of international law on the ILC. Consider claims brought under the Alien Tort Act (ATA) in US courts against corporations charged with human rights violations.[109] Among the most controversial questions posed by some of the courts considering these cases is whether corporations can be seen as "subjects" of international law, or "international legal persons." The argument that they are has normally been made by human rights advocates anxious to establish liability under that US law, which permits aliens to sue for "torts" in violations of the law of nations. The issue has been addressed in a number of US courts, countless amicus briefs, and law review articles, but has so far been deftly avoided by the US Supreme Court.[110]

It is easy to see why this argument appeals from the "public law" perspectives enumerated earlier. ATA claims appear to be the embodiment of cases brought on behalf of the international community. These human rights claims seem intended to elucidate public values (such as what human rights are and who is responsible for their violation) and, while private parties and not states are their focus, frequently the hand of the state is close by but not reachable due to sovereign immunity. What better way to conclude that corporations are liable for human rights violations than to reach for a doctrine of general international law, namely, personhood, that has been extended to other non-state actors, namely, international organizations, originally by judicial fiat?[111]

---

[107] *Id.* at 179. See also *id.* at 183 (indicating the relevance of fulfilling the UN's particular purposes).

[108] See José E. Alvarez, *Are Corporations "Subjects" of International Law*, 9 SANTA CLARA J. INT'L L. 1 (2011).

[109] For discussion of some of the cases brought under the Alien Tort Statute, 28 USC § 1350, see *id.*

[110] See, most recently, Kiobel v. Royal Dutch Petroleum Co., 133 S. Ct. 1659 (2013).

[111] See Reparation Case, *supra* note 105.

However, the attempt to use international legal personhood as a shortcut for determining the primary rules applicable to corporations is an intellectual cul-de-sac that distracts US courts from what should be the real question, namely, whether given the special nature of the corporate form (which is unlike that of individuals or states), which human rights ought to be applicable to such entities, and if so, how best to do so.[112] Those of a more positivist inclination might also ask whether any of the sources of international law (treaties, custom or general principles) make human rights applicable to such actors. These more relevant inquiries lead to more serious questions about which reasonable people may disagree, such as whether those treaties or rules of custom that enable international criminal law to apply to private actors (such as war crimes or the Genocide Convention) also apply to corporate entities (and not merely individuals who are acting in their corporate capacity) or whether general principles of private law around the world envision civil or criminal liability for corporate actors and whether such national principles can be applied with respect to international human rights violations.[113] Another relevant question, more interesting to US lawyers invested in the proper interpretation of the ATA, is whether that statute anticipates bringing corporate claims or it is enough if US tort law does so. These questions are not resolved or greatly assisted by the misleading personhood inquiry.

However, ATA advocates in US courts are not the only ones who favor international personhood as a tool for systemic integration. The ILC recently completed a set of articles on the Responsibility of International Organizations (IOs).[114] The central premise of that effort is that all interstate organizations established by treaty, from the ICC to the International Monetary Fund (IMF), are "international legal persons" and, subject to *lex specialis*, are governed by a single set of secondary rules.[115] These rules, which turn out to be remarkably similar in content and structure to those that the ILC earlier elaborated for states in its Articles of State Responsibility,[116] govern matters such as whether actions can be attributed to such organizations as well as the scope of remedies from internationally wrongful acts committed by such organizations and these

---

[112] See Alvarez, *supra* note 108.     [113] *Id.* at 31–32.

[114] Draft Articles on Responsibility of International Organizations, *Yearbook of the International Law Commission*, 2011, Vol. II, *available at* http://legal.un.org/ilc/texts/instruments/english/draft%20articles/9_11_2011.pdf [hereinafter IO Articles].

[115] See *id.* art. 2(a) (defining "international organizations" for purposes of those articles).

[116] *Cf.* Articles of State Responsibility, *supra* note 15.

organizations' defenses from wrongfulness (including – yes – the defense of necessity).[117] The Articles also purport to indicate when such organizations might be liable for the acts of other organizations,[118] as well as when state members of these organizations might also be liable for organizational acts.[119]

The IO Articles enable numerous opportunities for boundary crossings across international regimes. Thanks to the ILC, we now know, for example, that if states act jointly to "circumvent" their responsibilities by using the organizational form to commit an internationally wrongful act, they might be liable, together with the organizations in question, for the wrongful acts of any of these organizations whether the wrongful act takes the form of an IMF decision to cut off funds or a WTO Appellate Body ruling.[120]

This author has been a critic of this ILC effort.[121] Like some advocates for human rights claims in US courts, the ILC appears to have misread the ICJ's warning (in its Reparation opinion) not to assume that there is a one-size-fits-all concept of an international legal person. The ILC's Articles of IO Responsibility presume that all these international legal persons are sufficiently alike that we can assume, unless their charters or rules explicitly provide otherwise, that they are subject to the same secondary rules with respect to wrongful behavior as are states. This assumes that organizations as distinct as those establishing a mechanism for engaging in treaty making and resolving trade disputes (e.g., the WTO) share the same rules for liability as does one providing loans or technical assistance (e.g., the IMF), deciding boundary disputes (e.g., the ICJ), or enforcing international peace and security (e.g., the UN Security Council). It assumes, contrary to the insights of political scientists and others, that all organizations, charged with a remarkable diversity of tasks and with differing relationships to their respective members, nonetheless operate on a single principal/agent model – and not as trustees or independent contractors, for example.[122]

---

[117] See, for example, IO Articles, *supra* note 114, arts. 28–31, 34–40 (containing the available remedies) and 21–25 (containing the excuses of self-defense, legitimate countermeasures, *force majeure*, distress, and necessity).
[118] *Id.* arts. 14–20.   [119] *Id.* arts. 58–60, 62–63.   [120] *Id.* arts. 61 and 14.
[121] José E. Alvarez, International Organizations: Accountability or Responsibility (Oct. 27, 2006), *available at* www.asil.org/aboutasil/documents/CCILspeech061102.pdf.
[122] The ILC acknowledges these differences but insists that the residual rule of *lex specialis*, no more specific than the one contained in its Articles of State Responsibility, will take care of any difficulties. IO Articles, *supra* note 114, at para. 7.

As the ILC itself acknowledges, its IO Articles partake in more than the usual share of "progressive" development as opposed to codification of actual state or IO practice.[123] Despite what the ILC has concluded in its Articles (which were never subjected to the arduous interstate negotiating process involved in securing a multilateral convention like the VCLT), there is no clear agreement by either states or IOs that a single set of secondary rules applies to all IOs.

Whether the ILC's effort is truly progressive in the sense of advancing human rights is also a dubious proposition. As with respect to the effort to find corporations "subjects" of international law for purposes of the ATA, the ILC's effort could produce a backlash – where the ostensible new "subjects" generate *lex specialis* to the contrary, duly assisted by cooperating states that may resist being put on the same plane as either international organizations or corporations. Consider the risks posed by the example of Article 14 of the ILC's Articles of IO Responsibility. Article 14 indicates that an IO that "aids or assists" a state or another IO in the commission of an internationally wrongful act is responsible if it does so "with knowledge" but only if the act would be internationally wrongful if committed by the aiding/assisting organization.[124] That rule tracks the corresponding rule that applies with respect to states that aid or assist another state in the commission of an internationally wrongful act.[125] But is this rule really what human rights advocates would want to apply if the IMF, for example, were to extend a loan to a state with the knowledge that those funds would be used to violate a human rights treaty or to commit an international crime? I suspect that many would want to hold the IMF responsible for such an act, even if Article 14's insistence on *dual* wrongfulness by both state and organization was not satisfied because the IMF, as an organization, was not bound to any underlying treaty making it subject to human rights or culpable of an international crime. Article 14 is flawed in imposing aiding and assisting secondary liability on an entity for which there is as yet no clear consensus on the applicable primary rules to which it is subject. An insistence on dual wrongfulness, except insofar as there is no *lex specialis* to the contrary, makes no sense when the "international legal persons" in question may not share the same primary obligations. Of course, Article 14, like the other IO Articles, also ignores the huge differences *among* international organizations. When dealing with an organization as

---

[123] See *id.* at paras. 5–6.   [124] IO Articles, *supra* note 114, art. 14.
[125] *Cf.* ARTICLES OF STATE RESPONSIBILITY, *supra* note 15, art. 16.

endowed and powerful as the IMF, we might want to say that it should be held responsible with no separate requirement of dual wrongfulness, that is, merely if it engaged in certain heinous actions with knowledge. But do we want to draw the same conclusions for international courts when these issue rulings are later shown to have been legally flawed or illegal? In addition, we might have questions about whether the test of "knowledge" as applied to an organizational entity like the IMF should be the same as that applied with respect to a state or a court or other entity charged with a far more limited range of tasks. (We might, on the other hand, apply the same knowledge test where the organizational body is, in reality, the alter ego of a particular state.) For all these reasons, we should not assume that the ILC's attempt at encouraging boundary crossings across IOs will produce "progressive" results.

Consider as well the possible human rights implications if, as some advocates of boundary crossings would recommend, investor-state arbitrators were to apply the concept of international legal personality to the corporate claimants before them. The international investment regime might be seen as a mere application of traditional diplomatic espousal, where the state parties to BITs ultimately retain the discretion to waive the rights given to investors in a particular case, to withdraw from these treaties, or to issue from time to time interpretative decisions that preclude certain claims by their own nationals. Alternatively, we might regard investment protection treaties (or some of them) as breaking entirely from such state centricity by making investors third-party beneficiaries whose claims, like those of human rights claimants, are their own and should not be subordinated to the needs of states.[126] On this view, states would have no power to waive or terminate investor claims at their discretion. If US courts were to find in ATC cases that corporations are "international legal persons" or "subjects" of international law and such rulings were heeded by investor-state arbitrators, would that not encourage findings by those arbitrators that indeed states no longer retain control over these subjects' rights? Would that not also encourage, as some GAL scholars suggest, more two-way traffic between investment tribunals and human rights courts, where the investor property owner would be analogized, as for purposes of determining the scope of fair and

---

[126] See generally Anthea Roberts, *Clash of Paradigms: Actors and Analogies Shaping the Investment Treaty System*, 107 AM. J. INT'L L. 45 (2013); Martins Paparinskis, *Investment Treaty Arbitration and the (New) Law of State Responsibility*, 24 EUR. J. INT'L. 617 (2013).

equitable treatment, to a human rights claimant in the European Court of Human Rights (ECHR)? But are either of these outcomes really what human rights advocates want?

As I have suggested elsewhere, it is not at all clear that either human rights advocates or investors would be pleased by genuine two-way traffic between the investment and human rights regimes.[127] Contrary to these suggestions by some public law scholars, the fairness or other standards applied in the ECHR to individuals might not appropriately be extended to corporate investors under BITs. Nor is it clear this was what was intended by either treaty regime. (The rights to nondiscrimination enjoyed by vulnerable minority groups in Europe, for example, are hardly comparable to the nondiscrimination guarantees assured to businesses under BITs, for example.)[128] We should also worry about the subtle changes that may occur with respect to either human or investor rights if these are readily imported (and translated) by regional human rights judges, WTO adjudicators, or investor-state arbitrators – whether that translation occurs as a product of reinterpreting the relevant treaties or the underlying rules of custom or drawing upon previously unknown "general principles of public law."[129] Given the different epistemic communities from where these adjudicators come, are we sure that we want, for example, the Inter-American Court of Human Rights' case law on the duty on states to "ensure" as well as "respect" human rights to be applied (and likely transformed) by the commercial lawyers who often arbitrate investor-state claims or the trade specialists in the WTO's

---

[127] Alvarez, *supra* note 108.
[128] Indeed, it is not even clear that the nondiscrimination standards between the trade and investment regimes are comparable. *See, for example*, Jürgen Kurtz, *The Merits and Limits of Comparativism: National Treatment in International Investment Law and the WTO*, in The Multilateralization of International Investment Law, *supra* note 44, at 243.
[129] See, for example, Karen Knop, *Here and There: International Law in Domestic Courts*, 32 NYU J. Int'l L. & Politics 501 (2000) (discussing the "translation" that occurs when international law is applied by national courts); Jain, *supra* note 53. But see Alec Stone Sweet and Giacinto della Cananea, *Proportionality, General Principles of Law, and Investor-State Arbitration: A Response to Jose Alvarez*, 46 (3) N.Y.U. J. Int'l L. & Pol. 911, 940 (2014) *available at* http://papers.ssrn.com/sol3/papers.cfm?abstract_id=2435307 (arguing that the structural differences identified in this chapter between the trade and investment regimes are irrelevant since the "proportionality principle would never have spread—from Germany to the European Union to the WTO; and from civil law systems (in Europe) to common law systems (Canada, Israel, and South Africa)—had judges been placed under these strictures").

dispute settlement scheme?¹³⁰ And if WTO panelists or investment arbitrators were to suggest that some of those human rights standards were not as extensive as those applied to the rights of traders and investors, would human rights advocates welcome such interpretations back in regional human rights courts? This is what two-way traffic means, after all.¹³¹

As noted, the boundary crossings in *Continental* or the *Enron Annulment* may not produce the progressive results intended, particularly if these are treated as precedents establishing that states have a general license to engage in uncompensated takings of any and all property or denials of justice (even when it occurs by complete refusal to permit access to court), if states can just assert that they took the "least restrictive alternative" to promote the public good, and private parties arguing otherwise have to prove otherwise. More generally, why is it necessarily "progressive" to give greater deference to state courts or administrative procedures, or a government's self-interested judgments about how best to balance private versus public rights? Was not the premise of international investment law, like that of international human rights law, that governments could not be trusted to safeguard private rights and needed supranational scrutiny and supranational standards to keep them in line?

## IX  The questionable premises of "public law"

### a)  Flaw one: Presuming uniformity amidst regime complexity

As those who examine the "rational design" of international legal institutions would be the first to remind us, the design of such institutions, including the underlying treaties and the adjudicative mechanisms used to enforce them, reflects the preferences of those who design them.¹³²

---

[130] See also José E. Alvarez, *How Not to Link: Institutional Conundrums of an Expanded Trade Regime*, 7 WIDENER L. SYMP. J. 1 (2001).

[131] From the other side of the ledger, is it justifiable, as some public law scholars suggest, if ECHR jurisprudence concerning the deference owed to states when it comes to rights of "possession" is readily transferred into BITs even when the latter treaties provide that when an expropriation occurs, full compensation is due even when the government acts in the public interest? Compare US–Argentina BIT, art. IV(1) and (2) (expropriation) to European Convention for the Protection of Human Rights and Fundamental Freedoms, First Protocol, art. 1.

[132] See, for example, Barbara Koremenos and Timm Betz, *The Design of Dispute Settlement Procedures in International Agreements*, in INTERDISCIPLINARY PERSPECTIVES ON INTERNATIONAL LAW AND INTERNATIONAL RELATIONS, *supra* note 19, at 371.

## IX. THE QUESTIONABLE PREMISES OF "PUBLIC LAW"

States are responsible for the proliferation of international regimes, including courts and tribunals. They choose to make only some international obligations (e.g., trade, investment, regional human rights norms) enforceable through "hard" dispute settlement while leaving other obligations (e.g., many international environmental obligations, global human rights, and labor rights) subject to "softer" enforcement tools. They license private parties to invoke only some of these dispute settlement mechanisms and the scope of delegation accorded to either "interstate" or "transnational" adjudicators varies with the regime and the degree of precision of the standards involved.[133] Whether an adjudicatory mechanism empowers only states or private parties to invoke them, includes relatively more binding tools of enforcement, or is subject to wide or narrow state defenses from liability reflects conscious choices that needed to be respected unless we want to produce sovereign backlash. That continues to be the assumption of the traditional rules of treaty interpretation and the residual canons of defragmentation discussed at the beginning of this chapter. It is what *pacta sunt servanda* means after all. Sensitivity to context has also been the basis for proper invocation of general principles of law.[134] While adjudicators and other stakeholders of all treaty regimes engage in the continuous development of these regimes over time, the rational design of such treaty regimes is owed respect. Judges or arbitrators who get ahead of that rational design risk their own de-legitimation or even defiance of their rulings.

Respecting the rational design (including boundary demarcations) of international legal regimes may encourage forum-shopping, as states or private parties search for the best forum to negotiate or arbitrate.

---

[133] Robert O. Keohane, Andrew Moravcsik, and Anne-Marie Slaughter, *Legalized Dispute Resolution: Interstate and Transnational*, 54 INT'L ORG. 457 (2000) (distinguishing between international dispute settlement mechanisms, whether "interstate" (open only to states) or "transnational" (open to non-state parties) by access, precision, and delegation and arguing that the degree of "legalization" appears to vary along such factors).

[134] This is common ground even for Schill who acknowledges that "relevant differences between the different regimes should not be forgotten." Schill, *supra* note 47, at 35. See also *supra* note 129; Hugh Thirlway, *The Law and Procedure of the International Court of Justice 1960-1989: Part Two*, 61(1) Y.B. INT'L L. 1, 113, 129 (1990); Michael Akehurst, *Equity and General Principles of Law*, 25 INT'L & COMP. L. Q. 801, at 816 (1976). Anyone seeking to import a general principle of law into the adjudication of individuals in the ICC, for example, needs to be taken heed of that court's strict adherence to the principle of legality for such crimes. See, for example, Prosecutor v. Erdemovic, IT-96-22-A, Separate and Dissenting Opinion of Judge Stephen, paras. 64, 66.

Forum-shopping (or "regime shifting") is not inherently an evil, particularly where the designers of the regime anticipate it – as does the Law of the Sea Convention's "cafeteria" approach to dispute settlement or the numerous BITs that enable private investors to choose whether to resolve their disputes in local courts or in a number of arbitral mechanisms (including some that, by design, are neither transparent nor open to third-party participation).[135] And while the forum-shopping that continues to be permitted under the relevant regimes may indeed benefit the powerful and resourceful, the results are complex and not entirely in one direction.[136]

Investor-state dispute settlement was designed to avoid politicized espousal and the gunboat diplomacy by powerful states that often accompanied it, much as the WTO was intended to displace bilateral trade leverage with a less partial application of law.[137] Investor-state arbitration was also intended to empower less powerful smaller investors, even those whose claims would not have been espoused by home states intent on pursuing greater foreign policy concerns. Private and governmental power continues to play a role in all of these forums, including investor-state dispute settlement, but the normative consequences depend on how power is deployed and by whom. Lesser developed countries have themselves resorted to regime and dispute settlement forum-shopping – as by raising issues in the General Assembly or other forums deemed favorable to their interests, including requests for advisory opinions of the ICJ. Some governments may have entered into both investor-state and human rights regimes precisely in order to *strengthen* their hands vis-à-vis internal groups that might seek to undermine these, while also tying the hands of future governments that might seek to renege on such rights.[138] This is what "constitutionalization," after all, entails.

Both horizontal and vertical boundary crossings need to be pursued with caution less they violate the very design (and intention) of the treaty

---

[135] See, for example, art. VII(3), US–Argentina BIT (according foreign investors a number of arbitral options).

[136] For a nuanced view of how benefits from "regime shifting," see, for example, Raustiala, *supra* note 20.

[137] Whether "depoliticization" has successfully occurred is another question entirely. See David Schneiderman, *Revisiting the Depoliticization of Investment disputes*, 2010–11 Y.B. ON INT'L INVESTMENT L. & POL'Y 693.

[138] See Andrew Moravcsik, *Liberal Theories of International Law*, in INTERDISCIPLINARY PERSPECTIVES ON INTERNATIONAL LAW AND INTERNATIONAL RELATIONS, *supra* note 20, at 83.

## IX. THE QUESTIONABLE PREMISES OF "PUBLIC LAW" 83

regimes in question. *Continental* teaches us that the horizontal importation of some defenses permitted under WTO law into the investor-state regime may be inconsistent with the latter. The *Enron Annulment* tells us that it may be inappropriate to transpose the procedures and reason-giving evident in one international court to another adjudicative forum. Some vertical boundary crossings involving the import from the national to the international forum – as do some crossings premised on the application of alleged "general principles of public law" – are in tension with the goals of those who designed the underlying regimes. Some forums, such as investor-state arbitration under BITs, are intended to provide an alternative to the application of national law by national courts. Most of these treaties sought to provide investors with assurances to compensate for the "obsolescing bargains" that characterize foreign investment, where sunk costs are, once invested, subject to the whims of the host state's laws, courts, and agencies.[139] The proliferation of investment protection treaties with binding arbitration is a striking departure from the doctrine propounded by Carlos Calvo, who insisted that foreign investors should get only the treatment available to local investors under local law.[140] The suggestion by some public law scholars that national administrative or constitutional law should be reimported into the interpretation of investment treaties by, for example, looking to "general" principles of administrative law, may violate the object and purpose of such treaties by reintroducing the Calvo doctrine.[141]

---

[139] ALVAREZ, *supra* note 3, at 117–19.
[140] For an account of the historical development of BITs, *see* ANDREW NEWCOMBE and LUÍS PARADELL, LAW AND PRACTICE OF INVESTMENT TREATIES 1–73 (2009).
[141] *Cf.* for example, Schill's suggestions that a more refined comparative public law analysis, perhaps a turn to general principles of public law, can resolve interpretative questions like the scope of regulatory takings for purposes of BITs or more specifically the "kind of limits that protection of property imposes on the tax legislator." See *supra* note 47, at 33, 36. This presumes that governments or their national courts have reached a common understanding on such complex questions. The need for caution in reaching for such common principles is suggested by the current reaction by some of the "mature" legal systems that, Schill suggests, might have reached a consensus on such issues. In its latest model BIT, the United States has decided that this issue is likely to be so contentious that it has imposed a highly political limit on the bringing of such claims. See art. 21(2), 2012 US Model BIT (providing that claimants cannot present a claim that a tax measure involves an expropriation unless that claim is first presented to the competent tax authorities of both BIT state parties and those authorities fail to agree that the tax measure is not an expropriation). Or consider the conclusion, suggested by the *Continental* decision and endorsed by Sweet and Cananea, *supra* note 129, that a particular

At the same time, as is indicated at the beginning of this chapter, there is considerable scope for legitimate *and legitimating* boundary crossings. If the ILC's interpretative canons in its Study on Fragmentation are taken seriously, general international law, including carefully determined and circumscribed general principles of law, will continue to be needed in many cases to fill the inevitable gaps of specific treaties. But even such boundary crossings, as the *Enron Annulment* ruling and the ILC's efforts on the responsibility of IOs suggest, need to be undertaken with caution to prevent damage to the general law being imported as well as the regime into which the importation occurs.

It is not clear how many public law scholars would endorse the specific findings in *Continental* or *Enron Annulment* or the efforts to stretch the concept of "international legal personhood" discussed earlier.[142] Some may be horrified by the careless lawyering involved in these instances and rush to proclaim that these are not the kind of boundary crossings that they would endorse. Most public law scholars are likely to agree with Schill (along with this author) that the "relevant differences between the different regimes should not be forgotten."[143] But public law scholars cannot escape responsibility for bad boundary crossings so easily. They have elevated the threats posed by fragmentation and forum-shopping and the ostensible value of boundary crossing as a solution to such an extent that they can hardly claim surprise if judges or arbitrators take both threat and solution seriously. Public law scholars have promoted the view that international treaty regimes are not as disparate as

---

kind of proportionality balancing should be applied as a general defense to all BIT claims, including presumably direct expropriations. The current US Model BIT instead anticipates the application of more circumscribed balancing, based on US takings jurisprudence, that applies only for "indirect" takings of property achieved without formal transfer of title or outright seizure. See art. 4(a), Annex B, 2012 US Model BIT. Nondiscriminatory regulatory actions, by contrast, are treated in that treaty model as presumptively valid under its Article 4(b), Annex B. As is suggested in this chapter, it was true of the US–Argentina BIT that treaty does not appear to anticipate balancing for direct takings of property. Even the most sophisticated (or at least well-developed) national case law on what constitutes a "regulatory taking" – that of the United States – cannot be reduced to a one-size proportionality balancing scheme characterized as a "general principle of law." Of course, had the United States thought that the *Continental* decision had gotten it right, it could have simply introduced in its 2012 US Model BIT the general exceptions list of GATT Article XX in its entirety. Obviously, it did not.

[142] But see Sweet and Cananea, *supra* note 102 (defending the results and rationales in the *Continental* and *Enron Annulment cases* and suggesting that these conclusions are now widely accepted within the investment regime).

[143] Schill, *supra* note 47, at 35. But see Sweet and Cananea, *supra* note 129.

they seem but are part of a "system" of "global governance," "global administrative regulation," "IPA," or "global constitutionalism." They have encouraged expectations that these regimes reflect "common public values." They should not be surprised if their public law prescriptions as idealized in their scholarship play out in unexpected ways when deployed by litigants and arbitrators in the course of hard fought litigation.

### b) Flaw two: Euro-centric comparativism

If Schill's multiauthored study is taken as symptomatic, it is striking how narrow a slice of the world is represented by this effort to engage in "comparative public law." Virtually all the examples of "public law" in that study are taken from Organisation for Economic Co-operation and Development (OECD) countries and often, from an even narrower slice of those, such as comparisons of the laws of the United States, Germany, and France. While Schill contends that it is essential that the common principles of public law sought to be applied in investor-state disputes be "broadly recognized," he suggests that examining only a narrow slice of countries is justified because BITs assume a "rights-based approach to the relation between the state and society, which is based on the rule of law and respect or individual economic rights."[144] But treaties seeking to uphold certain economic rights for foreigners and providing an international forum to enforce them do not assume that their treaty parties share the Western rule of law tradition, nor do they seek to remake states to conform to that tradition. The global reach of the international investment regime in which some 180 countries have concluded at least one BIT exceeds that of the WTO's. Any attempt to interpret this regime through a "public law" lens or to apply "general principles" to it requires a truly global comparative exercise.[145] In a world where as many as a third of existing investment protection treaties are between developing states, and China is one of the largest signers of BITs, efforts to define the

---

[144] Schill, *supra* note 47, at 30. See also id. at 57–69 (examining administrative adjudication within the OECD).
[145] Contrary to what Sweet and Cananea suggest, see *supra* note 129, this is not a simple matter of drawing a sufficiently "representative" sample of common principles adopted in the world's legal schools, such as civil versus common law countries. See, for example, Jain, *supra* note 53 (canvassing the difficulties of various engaging in comparative law with respect to finding general principles of law).

content of "comparative public law" by looking only to a handful of Western allies is risible.

Of course, even comparisons of the public law of certain OECD countries require considerable care and judgment. It is potentially hazardous to extrapolate "general public values" from disparate practices embedded in distinct national institutions even among Western nations. While it is true, for example, that the United States, German, and European Court of Justice courts engage in "proportionality" analysis, there are considerable differences among the rational basis/intermediate/strict scrutiny categories used in US constitutional law and the doctrines of "margin of appreciation" or subsidiarity deployed in European courts. Nor is it clear that these distinct methods of "balancing" stem from comparable concerns. International courts and tribunals have been appropriately more cautious about exporting the European "margin of appreciation" principle than have many public law scholars, some of whom appear to be suggesting that this principle, which arose as a democracy-representing principle based on counting the numbers of European democracies that engage in a particular practice, is a readily transferable form of "balancing" individual versus sovereign rights that can be applied to any portion of any BIT even when these involve Cuba or China as treaty parties.[146] The suggestion that this kind of "proportionality balancing" should apply to all investor rights, from fair and equitable treatment to the right to compensation upon direct or indirect expropriation (whether or not such takings are proven to be discriminatory), as well as to a "measures not precluded" clause (irrespective of what is or is not included within that specific clause) and to the customary defense of necessity presumes a sameness among all of these – and among BITs – that does not exist. While forms of proportionality balancing are indeed common to all forms of adjudication, that fact says nothing about whether it (even assuming that we were to agree on what *it* is) should occur with respect to more dichotomous rights or defenses, such as absolute rights to compensation under certain circumstances (e.g., breaches of contract, outright seizures of property) or all the defenses from wrongfulness in the Articles of State Responsibility. National courts do not apply proportionality to any and all questions in willy-nilly fashion. They "balance" only some rights and some defenses, compare distinct values when balancing, and accord different

---

[146] Sweet and Cananea, *supra* note 129. See generally Alex Stone Sweet, *Investor-State Arbitration: Proportionality's New Frontier*, 4 L. & ETHICS OF HUM. RTS. 47 (2010).

IX. THE QUESTIONABLE PREMISES OF "PUBLIC LAW" 87

weights to what they balance.[147] Why should investor rights and state defenses in BITs be treated any differently?

c) *Flaw three: Presuming that judges should act like legislators*

Some of the public law scholars have elided another important distinction: they do not distinguish prescriptions directed at adjudicators with recommendations that might be better suited to the state treaty makers or regime designers. Public law scholars may be right that many international regimes would benefit from institutional overhaul to better accommodate the rights of sovereigns to regulate or to better protect other public values. They may be right to seek changes in the ICSID Convention, for example, to permit a full scale appellate process or amendments to specific arbitration rules to permit greater transparency and third-party participation. But the proposals for treaty or regime change discussed here are directed at the regimes' adjudicators, on the apparent assumption that these have failed to engage in the desired boundary crossings because they have not seen the underlying "public law" concerns that would be apparent if they had just searched hard enough or because the arbitrators have refused to abide by clearly established "general principles of public law" for extraneous reasons (such as bias).[148]

These contentions are in tension with the innovative nature of many of the underlying public law arguments being made as well as the constraints under which these adjudicators are working. The public law frameworks enumerated in this chapter have one common characteristic: they are all recent attempts to reframe international law in light of equally recent developments, namely, the proliferation of international dispute settlement mechanisms and forums. It seems unfair to establish a "new" conception such as "GAL" while at the same time criticizing international adjudicators for failing to apply it.

The tensions between "legislative" and "judicial" change, and the merits/demerits of "judicial activism" by national judges that have divided prominent legal philosophers like Ronald Dworkin and Jeremy Waldron, are strangely absent from most of the public law

---

[147] See *supra* note 141 (discussing the provisions of the 2012 US Model BIT).
[148] See, for example, Sweet and Cananea, *supra* note 129, at 17 (suggesting that one of the arbitrators in the Argentina cases who continues to disagree with the outcome of some of the Argentina decisions lacks impartiality).

literature discussed.[149] Even within national legal systems strengthened by hierarchical courts and established checks and balances, proponents of the rule of law differ on whether and when the legislator versus the judge should be expected to take the lead for change. Those who argue that international adjudicators – whether human rights judges or investor-state arbitrators – need to turn to GAL or IPA and engage in greater boundary crossings need to wrestle with the hard question of whether it is appropriate or legitimate to promote "progressive" change *ex post*, through judicial or arbitral processes in the course of dispute settlement, rather than *ex ante*, as through changes in the practices of host states or in changes to investment treaty standards or defenses going forward.[150] Some BIT parties, as is well known, are reacting to prior arbitral rulings by changing the investment protection treaties that they are negotiating, often by shrinking the domain of the investor rights accorded while expanding the "policy space" of sovereigns.[151] At the same time, most older BITs often containing more expansive rights to foreign investors remain in place. Other states, perhaps more anxious to signal that they remain "open" to foreign investors given their own prior histories of internal protectionist pressures, continue to negotiate more investor-protective treaties. These distinct choices by the "legislators" of the investment regime add to the complex mix that is today's investment regime. These choices may be criticized on many grounds – notably the fact that they may give rise to "inconsistent" or fragmented investment case law – but they do not raise familiar complaints against "activist" adjudicators.

Public law scholars who assume that international adjudicators should settle the many substantive differences that continue to exist among states about how to strike the proper balance between the right to regulate and the protection of property fail to consider the fact that the

---

[149] Compare Ronald Dworkin, *Political Judges and the Rule of Law*, in A MATTER OF PRINCIPLE, ch. I (1985), *with* Jeremy Waldron, *The Concept and the Rule of Law*, 43 GA. L. REV. 1, 6–8 (2008). These debates have long occurred among international law scholars. See, for example, Alvarez, *supra* note 130.

[150] See, for example, Bruno Simma, *Foreign Investment Arbitration: A Place for Human Rights*, 60 INT'L & COMP. L.Q. 573 (2011) (noting the difficulties of imposing harmonized investment law, consistent with human rights, through *ex post* interpretative changes, which may accord excessive discretion to arbitrators and proposing as an alternative *ex ante* (pre-investment) "human rights" audits).

[151] See, for example, José E. Alvarez, The Evolving BIT, *in* INVESTMENT TREATY ARBITRATION AND INTERNATIONAL LAW 1 (Ian A. Laird and Todd Weiler eds., 2010).

## IX. THE QUESTIONABLE PREMISES OF "PUBLIC LAW" 89

judges or arbitrators involved differ among themselves with respect to their perceived role.[152] Some arbitrators or judges see themselves as deciding only the narrow dispute before them and do not believe that they are authorized to serve as systemic lawmakers for the international community.[153] Most often, neither the "international rule of law" nor the specific regime under which they are operating resolves that question for them. The international rule of law offers no more specific direction than does the national rule of law (which has a longer pedigree) as to the proper demarcation of legislative versus judicial roles. Neither it nor the traditional rules of treaty interpretation requires that international adjudicators should take the lead with respect to boundary crossings not currently authorized by the treaty makers. To the contrary, it may be that the international rule of law is threatened or undermined by this kind of judicial activism, especially if one believes that "if politics becomes overly judicialized, the politicization of the judiciary likely follows."[154]

### d) Flaw four: Presuming that international regimes are subject to exclusively "public" prescriptions

IPA scholars define their domain as any international regime involving the state as participant. They study how such "public authority" is exercised, whether through instruments directly affecting individuals or states themselves, more general instruments, or public standards.[155] As IPA scholars acknowledge, their efforts presume that "global governance flattens the difference between public and private phenomena."[156] GAL and constitutionalist scholars flatten these distinctions for descriptive and prescriptive purposes as well. Because international regimes affect the public, they argue, they need to be regulated by "public values," as are national administrative agencies or other mechanisms that impose constitutional values. As applied to the international investment regime, the assumed dichotomy between "public" and "private" and the preference

---

[152] See generally Jose E. Alvarez, *What Are International Judges For? The Main Functions of International Adjudication, in* THE OXFORD HANDBOOK ON INTERNATIONAL ADJUDICATION 158 (Cesare Romano, Karen J. Alter, and Yuval Shany eds., 2013).
[153] *Id.*
[154] Erik Voeten, International Judicial Independence, (Sept. 2011) (unpublished manuscript), *at* http://ssrn.com/abstract=1936132, at 29 (citing Ferejohn). Voeten provides a valuable reminder of the "constrained independence" and "bounded discretion" under which international adjudicators operate.
[155] von Bogdandy, Dann, and Goldmann, *supra* note 38.   [156] *Id.* at 10.

for the former on normative grounds leads to the critique that investor-state arbitration is in reality "public" adjudication that has been wrongly "privatized" and needs, at a minimum, to be reformed to incorporate the public values of transparency, participation, judicial review, and greater reason-giving.[157] The premise is that recourse to the institutions, tools, and persons used to solve purely commercial disputes between private parties is not suited to a juris-generative process involving matters of "public" import. This borrows a page from critics of wrongful privatization, whether involving a government's turn to "private" prisons or its use of modern-day mercenaries to wage war. Public law scholars assume that certain governmental functions should not be delegated to private parties or to private processes, at least not without making those private persons/processes subject to forms of accountability that have been used to govern the public institutions of government.

As both the IPA and GAL projects indicate, at both the national and international levels, we see an increasing resort to diverse forms of public/private partnerships, other hybrid forms of regulation and adjudication, and even increasing delegation to entirely private juris-generative mechanisms. International governance is neither wholly private nor wholly public. Why should this hybridity of form be forced into a public/private dichotomy? Why should we presume, merely from the fact that governments remain involved in such efforts (under IPA) or from the fact that such regimes have "public" effects (under GAL), that such novel and diverse forms of regulation or adjudication must demonstrate a certain shared set of "public" characteristics? Why should hybrid public/private forms of impacting the general public or, for that matter, entirely private efforts that result in the same, all be expected to fit into preconceived molds for "public" regulation or adjudication for purposes of reform? Governments, and the demos that they serve, obviously differ on the propriety of the delegation of "public" functions, as well as on the forms of accountability that may be required once delegation occurs. As Helen Hershkoff's Chapter 6 in this volume reminds us, these differences may stem from different national histories and distinct abilities among nations to engage the government in tackling certain tasks.[158] The public law theorists described here tend to ignore such distinctions. Their resort to an either/or choice between "public" and "private" leads many to ignore very real differences among international regimes (flaw one

---

[157] Kingsbury and Schill, *supra* note 48.   [158] Helen Hershkoff in this volume.

## IX. THE QUESTIONABLE PREMISES OF "PUBLIC LAW" 91

above), but reliance on this unrealistic divide also artificially constricts the range of possibilities for forms of accountability that may be unique to hybrid forms of governance. Public law scholars are surely right to examine whether the new forms of governance that we have, including investor-state arbitration, are accountable, but why delimit the forms of accountability for that hybrid form of governance to those found in some states' administrative law or to those that can only be found supported by engaging "comparative public law"?[159]

The problematic aspects of presuming a black/white, public/private divide have been suggested by, among others, Jeremy Waldron. Waldron cautions against presuming that the "rule of law" applies at the international level, to benefit states (as opposed to people).[160] He reminds us that people, not states, are the bearers of ultimate value, and that it would be an error to accord states (or governments or legislators or international institutions) the benefit of rule-of-law values, such as transparency, that presume that they, like individuals, need be accorded the benefits of liberty or dignity.[161] Unlike those who would see only one kind of "international legal person" or public law scholars who suggest, for example, that the "rule of law" requires investor-state arbitrators to recognize an overly vague sovereign "right to regulate," Waldron points out the large (if obvious) differences between states, individuals, corporations, and international institutions – and the flaw of suggesting, for example, that the "publicness" of certain agencies requires them to be treated equally or indistinguishably.[162] "Governmental freedom," he writes, "is not the raison d'etre of the ROL [rule of law]":

> The ROL does not favour freedom or unregulated discretion for the government. Quite the opposite is true; the government is required to go out of its way to ensure that legality and the ROL are honored in its administration of society. ... If official discretion is left unregulated; if

---

[159] For a useful survey of the diverse forms of accountability now found among international organizations, see Ruth W. Grant and Robert O. Keohane, *Accountability and Abuses of Power in World Politics*, 99 AM. POL. SCI. REV. 29 (Feb. 2005). See also Hershkoff, *supra* note 158. For a useful step in the direction of searching for more diverse forms of accountability by one of the originators of GAL, see Richard B. Stewart, *Remedying Disregard in Global Regulatory Governance*, 108 AM. J. INT'L L. (2014).
[160] Jeremy Waldron, *Are Sovereigns Entitled to the Benefit of the International Rule of Law?*, 22 EUR. J. INT'L. 315 (2011).
[161] *Id.* at 325.
[162] *Id.* at 334: "There is no reason to say that the Department of Defense is to be treated as the equal of the State of Mississippi and that both are to be treated as the equals of the Federal Reserve Bank."

power exists without a process to channel and discipline its exercise; if officials are in a position to impose penalties or losses upon individuals without clear legal guidelines, then this is not an opportunity, but rather a defect, a danger, and a matter of regret so far as the ROL is concerned.[163]

Of course, the investment regime is intended to compel governments to respect the rule of law in the treatment of foreign investors – precisely in the sense that Waldron describes. Investor-state arbitrations impose financial liability for states that fail to respect the rule of law. Those who criticize those arbitrations on the premise that these violate the rule of law are motivated by the adverse consequences on the public welfare that may result from, for example, a determination that a certain environmental regulation violates a BIT. But the leap from those normative consequences to general prescriptions for change *ostensibly based on the rule of law* is a jurisprudential leap of judgment that requires distinct justification – and not a blithe assumption that everything that affects the public is subject to a set of public prescriptions of accountability.

## Conclusion

The cautionary tales of boundary crossings discussed here provide a counterpoint to the public law frameworks that are emerging to explain contemporary international law in the age of legalization cum fragmentation. Unlike many who write in the "public law" vein, from GAL to IPA, this author does not believe that boundary crossings horizontally, among international courts and tribunals, or vertically, between international and national adjudicators, are necessarily to be encouraged. But this chapter is not an argument against boundary crossings. Some boundary crossings are desirable, and others are not. The legitimacy of the "international rule of law" does not always require them. Context matters.

The failure by some international adjudicators – such as investor-state arbitrators in ICSID – to engage in boundary crossings is not always the product of careless or erroneous legal analysis or, worse still, a conscious effort to promote a (nefarious) political agenda. Further, while Downs and Benvenisti are surely correct that fragmentation and the forum-shopping that accompanies and produces it are reflections of the political choices made by states, there is doubt about whether efforts to respect the

---

[163] *Id.* at 339.

boundary demarcations of international legal regimes invariably benefit the powerful. Fragmentation and its cousin forum-shopping can be and have been used to benefit the less empowered. Forum-shopping can produce races to the top in the form of "competitive multilateralism," as well as to the bottom.[164] We should also question whether, even when fragmented international regimes benefit the strong, the remedy for that lies with *adjudicative* rulings that seek to escape such political outcomes.

What will yet emerge from the rulings in *Continental* and *Enron Annulment* remain to be seen. These decisions may remain outlier decisions that other investor-state arbitrators, unconstrained by any requirement of *stare decisis*, are free to ignore. Alternatively, they may generate either support or backlash by states – in which case we can look forward to changes in BIT practice that either affirm or reject these. It is possible that more such rulings could end up being a rather poor substitute for reforming the underlying BITs themselves, particularly if they generate perceptions that investor-state arbitrators are judicial activists unconstrained by the usual rules that govern international legal interpretation. If so, these rulings could undermine, not enhance, the legitimacy of investor-state dispute settlement. Worse still would be a scenario in which these rulings, if treated as a license to widen the exceptions that states may take in treaties far afield from investment, end up enhancing the power of states to the detriment of individual rights.

Prescriptions for boundary crossings, and jurisprudential approaches that presume that these are "progressive," should be accompanied by a warning: "beware: unintended consequences ahead." But to pursue the signage metaphor further, the message is "proceed with caution"; it is *not* "no trespassing."

---

[164] See, for example, Raustiala, *supra* note 20, at 312.

# 4

# Dialogue and constitutional duty

MARK TUSHNET[*]

Borders abound in constitutional structure and doctrine. The idea that there are political questions unsuitable for resolution by the courts requires a border between the merely political and the constitutional,[1] and within the constitutional, a border between judicial constitutionalism and political constitutionalism. Classical legal thought relied on a sharp border between powers absolute in their spheres and rights equally absolute in theirs.[2] Constitutional theory is obsessed with determining the allocation of authority between courts and legislatures.

Yet, the borders in constitutional law are at least as permeable as other borders. This chapter examines and connects two domains in which borders blur. The concept of dialogue has become a central feature in contemporary thinking about constitutional review.[3] Dialogues occur between courts and legislatures over the constitution's meaning and implementation, making less clear the line between those institutions. Constitutions typically guarantee individual rights, but modern

---

[*] William Nelson Cromwell Professor of Law, Harvard Law School. I thank Vicki Jackson, Frank Michelman, and Brian Ray for comments on an earlier version of this chapter.

[1] "[T]he mere fact that [a] suit seeks protection of a political right does not mean it presents a political question. Such an objection 'is little more than a play upon words.'" Baker v. Carr, 369 U.S. 186, 209 (1962) (internal citation omitted).

[2] DUNCAN KENNEDY, THE RISE AND FALL OF CLASSICAL LEGAL THOUGHT (2006, originally published 1975). See also G. EDWARD WHITE, THE CONSTITUTION AND THE NEW DEAL (2000) (describing the US Supreme Court's role in policing the boundaries between state and national power, and between government power and individual rights).

[3] The starting point in comparative constitutional law, I believe, was Peter Peter W. Hogg and Allison A. Bushell, *The Charter Dialogue between Courts and Legislatures (Or Perhaps the Charter of Rights Isn't Such a Bad Thing after All)*, 35 OSGOODE HALL L.J. 75 (1997). For reflections on their work, see Symposium, *Charter Dialogue: Ten Years Later*, 45 OSGOODE HALL L.J. 1 (2007). For an earlier use of the idea, see Barry Friedman, *Dialogue and Judicial Review*, 91 MICH. L. REV. 577 (1993). One can find even deeper roots, for example, in Ralph Lerner's article, *The Supreme Court as Republican Schoolmaster*, 1967 SUP. CT. REV. 127, and Eugene V. Rostow, *The Democratic Character of Judicial Review*, 66 HARV. L. REV. 193 (1952).

constitutions – and, on some interpretations, older ones as well – place duties on governments, and the line between rights and duties is unclear. This chapter links the idea of constitutional dialogue with the idea of constitutional duty, with the aim of illuminating modern constitutionalism more generally.

Scholars have examined many facets of constitutional dialogue: the relation between dialogue as usually understood – as involving interactions between legislatures and constitutional courts – and amendment processes; the timeframe within which we are to consider whether dialogue has occurred; the criteria for distinguishing between dialogic responses by legislatures and courts to judicial and legislative action and legislative and judicial capitulation to superior force; and more. In this chapter I explore another facet, by inverting the usual assumptions about who makes the first "conversational" move and who responds. In the end, this inversion may not change our understanding of constitutional dialogue, but I believe that the analysis I develop by inverting the usual assumptions brings out important features of constitutional dialogue and, ultimately, of the understandings we might have of some of a constitution's purposes.

The conventional description of constitutional dialogue is this:

(1) A legislature enacts a statute.
(2) The statute faces a constitutional challenge in court.
(3) The court invalidates the statute and in doing so (a) identifies some specific ways in which the statute violates the constitution, and (b) in the course of doing so offers its best interpretation of the relevant constitutional provisions.
(4) The legislature responds. It may (a) revise the statute by rectifying the deficiencies the court identified, drawing from the court's opinion the modifications needed to satisfy the court's objections,[4] or (b) reenact the statute unchanged (described in the literature as an "in your face" action),[5] rejecting the constitutional interpretation on which the court's decision rested.

---

[4] As I discuss below, these modifications need not be seen as legislative capitulation to the court. At least sometimes, they might occur because legislative reflection has led to agreement with the court's constitutional analysis, sometimes because the legislature had not focused on the constitutional issues earlier, sometimes because the court's analysis convinces some who previously believed the statute constitutional that they were mistaken.

[5] KENT ROACH, THE SUPREME COURT ON TRIAL: JUDICIAL ACTIVISM OR DEMOCRATIC DIALOGUE 8 (2001).

(5) The statute is again challenged.

(6) The court deals with the challenge. Where the statute was modified to meet the court's objections, the court might (a) find the modifications adequate and uphold the statute, or (b) find that the modifications fall short of what is truly required, and invalidate the statute once again. Where the legislature has enacted an "in your face" statute, the court might (a) capitulate, accepting the legislature's constitutional interpretation and repudiating its own (with or without some face-saving language by the court), or (b) stand firm and invalidate the "in your face" statute. Up to this point, there has been a dialogue, and, importantly, it has been *constitutional* – that is, about the constitution's meaning. Once this point is reached, though, the metaphor of dialogue loses its appeal and some other language – "confrontation" or "crisis" perhaps – is needed.

The legislature is the "first mover" in this account.[6] But it might be profitable to consider situations in which the constitutional court is – in some important sense – the first mover. It is relatively easy to describe the general contours of such situations, though providing details will necessarily complicate the account. Here are two analytically equivalent possibilities:

(1) The constitution imposes an affirmative duty on the legislature to enact legislation on a specific topic, and the legislature simply fails to do anything at all. These are situations described in the Constitution of Portugal as ones of "unconstitutionality by omission."[7] The constitution might impose a duty on the legislature to create a system of pensions for public employees, and the legislature may have done nothing. The Portuguese constitution says: "Whenever the Constitutional Court determines that unconstitutionality by omission exists,

---

[6] My sense of the literature, but it is only a sense, is that many writers treat the court's response to the constitutional challenge as the first move, opening the dialogue with the legislature. As I develop in this chapter, I believe that the account I offer is more perspicuous, because it makes clear the distinctions—particularly between legislative action and inaction—that we can usefully draw in thinking about constitutional dialogues.

[7] Constitution of Portugal, art. 283(1) (on request from designated officials, "the Constitutional Court shall review ... any failure to comply with this Constitution by means of the omission of legislative measures needed to make constitutional rules executable"). The translation is taken from the website of the Portuguese parliament, http://app.parlamento.pt/site_antigo/ingles/ cons_leg/Constitution_VII_revisao_definitive.pdf.

it shall notify [the] competent legislative body thereof" – expressly inscribing a judicially initiated dialogue in the constitution.[8]

(2) The court discerns what we can describe as a "condition of unconstitutionality," that is, a state of affairs resulting from the practical effects of the distribution of background legal rights of property, contract, and tort over which the legislature has exercised no control.[9]

I distinguish the two situations for expository purposes, but on a deeper level, they may be identical. Roughly, in the case of unconstitutionality by omission, the legislature might claim that its constitutional duty is satisfied by the practical effects of the background rules of contract, property, and tort. Suppose the constitutional duty is that all must have minimally adequate housing. The legislature might refrain from enacting any housing program. It faces a claim of unconstitutionality by omission. It responds by contending that the background rules operate so as to generate minimally adequate housing for all. The person claiming unconstitutionality by omission denies the legislature's assertion, but the argument has been transformed into one about whether a condition of unconstitutionality exists.

In both situations, the court moves first in identifying the legislature's failure or the unconstitutional state of affairs and opens a dialogue with the legislature by telling it that the constitution requires that the legislature take some action.[10]

Next I introduce some complexities. In case (1), the legislature may have enacted a statute dealing with the subject at issue, but the court may find that the legislature has not done enough to fulfill its constitutional duty. Consider this possibility: the constitution might impose a duty phrased in quantitative terms – "a duty to create a pension system for public employees sufficient to allow them to lead decent lives after retirement." Seeking to comply with this duty, the legislature creates a

---

[8] Constitution of Portugal, art. 283(2).
[9] Or, in the case of civilian systems, where the long-established Civil Code generates background rights with the same effects in producing an unconstitutional state of affairs. In MARK TUSHNET, WEAK COURTS, STRONG RIGHTS: JUDICIAL REVIEW AND SOCIAL WELFARE RIGHTS IN COMPARATIVE CONSTITUTIONAL LAW 156 (2008), I mention a Colombian doctrine dealing with unconstitutional "states of affairs," which appears similar to the case I consider here, but I do not know enough about the Colombian jurisprudence to use it as an example.
[10] At this point, the dialogue can follow the same course as in the account where the legislature is the first mover, and for purposes of this chapter, I will say nothing more about the succeeding stages in the dialogue.

pension system. Still, the court might conclude that pension system fails to satisfy the quantitative requirement. We might think of this as a situation in which the legislature is the first mover, when it enacts the statute. Yet, both the complete-inaction scenario and the inadequate-action one seem to involve breaches of constitutional duties, and so I think we should initially deal with them in the same category of judicial first moves.[11]

Two complications can arise in case (2), involving conditions of unconstitutionality. The first is that the condition of unconstitutionality might be rectified by either the legislature, through legislation, or the courts, through an alteration in the background rules of contract, property, or tort. Consider, for example, a constitution that imposes a duty on "the State" – without specifying that the duty is imposed specifically on the legislature – to ensure that every person have access to minimally decent housing. The nation has a large population of homeless people, and so is in a condition of unconstitutionality with respect to the duty to provide housing. Noting that condition, the constitutional court could open a dialogue with the legislature by directing that the Ministry of Housing develop a plan that promises to provide housing to this population.[12] Suppose, though, that many of the homeless have simply moved into un- or underutilized buildings owned by others. The property owners seek to evict them, and the squatters resist (physically or in court). Squatting brings into the open the role that background rules play in creating conditions of unconstitutionality. The condition of unconstitutionality with respect to housing could be rectified by changing the background property rules, by giving the homeless something like an easement over un- or underutilized buildings suitable for shelter.

Constitutional courts with authority to change the background rules can address conditions of unconstitutionality by doing so. Such actions might be said to open a dialogue with the legislature, but it is not a *constitutional* dialogue, at least in the first instance. Rather, it is a dialogic opportunity familiar to common law lawyers – the ordinary dialogue that occurs when courts modify the common law, and legislatures have the opportunity to respond. I call these "common-law dialogues" for

---

[11] I return to this later in this chapter.
[12] Or to expand existing housing programs to encompass it, on the model of the complexified case (1).

convenience, but their general description is "dialogues with respect to the background rules of contract, property, and tort."

Common-law dialogues have two important features. First, legislative responses to common-law developments might be required to preserve the "integrity" of the common-law system as a whole. In the common-law tradition, the canon of statutory construction that statutes in derogation of the common law are to be construed narrowly captures this feature. Clarifying the concept of "integrity" here is quite difficult, of course, but I think I need only flag the question here.[13]

Frank Michelman has identified the second important feature of common-law dialogues.[14] Judges on constitutional courts are typically selected because they have qualities and abilities suitable to adjudicate constitutional cases (even if they also have authority to develop the background rules). Their development of the background rules might be more likely to disrupt the integrity of the system of such rules than would either development of those rules by judges chosen for their facility with those rules[15] or – as Michelman speculates – direct invocation of the constitution and the consequent opening of a constitutional dialogue. In that case, a constitutional dialogue of the sort I have described under the heading of "case (1) complexified" might then arise, and similarly, after a legislative response in a "common-law" dialogue, if the legislature's action is challenged on constitutional grounds for failing to go far enough to fulfill a constitutional duty.

The second, distinctive complication for constitutional dialogue in cases of conditions of unconstitutionality occurs when the constitutional court lacks authority to change the background rules.[16] In such situations, the constitutional court necessarily opens a dialogue with the institutions that have the authority to change the background law. Often the partner in the dialogue will be the legislature, which always has the

---

[13] For a brief treatment, see ERNEST J. WEINRIB, THE IDEA OF PRIVATE LAW 10–13 (1995) (discussing the internal "coherence" of private law).

[14] Frank I. Michelman, *The Interplay of Constitutional and Ordinary Jurisdiction*, in COMPARATIVE CONSTITUTIONAL LAW 278 (Tom Ginsburg and Rosalind Dixon eds., 2011).

[15] For a suggestion that the US Supreme Court's decision in Snyder v. Phelps, 131 S.Ct. 1207 (2011) was flawed because justices principally oriented to public law failed to understand the private law components of the tort of intentional infliction of emotional distress, see Benjamin C. Zipursky, Snyder v. Phelps, *Outrageousness, and the Open Texture of Tort Law*, 60 DEPAUL L. REV. 473 (2011).

[16] In the United States, for example, the background rules are rules of state law, which under standard interpretations the Supreme Court must take as fixed by state courts or legislatures.

power to change the background law, but sometimes it will be with a set of courts authorized to change that law.

Constitutional systems that have the doctrine of indirect horizontal effect go some way to adopting the model of "common law" rather than constitutional dialogue.[17] Consider here the South African Constitutional Court. South Africa's constitution directs "every court" to "develop" the law to "promote the spirit, purport and objects of the Bill of Rights."[18] The usual examples come from the law of defamation and invasion of privacy. Those torts have a long lineage, extending back into an era when constitutional concerns about freedom of expression were less fully developed than they are today, or when the courts that developed them were less sensitive to constitutional concerns, or when constitutional protections of freedom of expression had not been enacted into positive law. Many constitutional systems have confronted difficulties arising from the fact that some elements of these torts seem ill suited to a world with significant protections of freedom of expression. Courts that can develop the background rules can do so sensitive to constitutional concerns without invoking the constitution directly.[19] Courts that lack that authority can instruct the courts with that authority that they must develop the background rules appropriately. In the standard case, the constitutional court holds that the ordinary courts have failed to take constitutional values sufficiently into account in applying (or developing) the background rules, and remands the case for further consideration.[20]

We can push the argument further by considering the squatters' case described earlier. Suppose an ordinary court invokes existing background property rules to uphold the squatters' evictions in the situation described earlier, in a nation with a constitutionalized duty about housing and with a jurisdictional provision like South Africa's. The squatters invoke the constitutional court's jurisdiction, arguing that the ordinary courts have failed to "develop" property law to promote the housing

---

[17] We might see the doctrine of indirect horizontal effect as allowing the courts to avoid the second complication by transforming the problem into a case described by the first one.

[18] S. AFR. CONST., 1996 § 39(2).

[19] See, for example, R.W.D.S.U., Local 558 v. Pepsi-Cola Canada Beverages (West) Ltd., 2002 SCC 8 (Can.) (developing the common law to remove the illegality under the common law of secondary labor boycotts).

[20] See, for example, BVerfGE 7 (1958) (the Lüth case). The most complete analysis of this problem of which I am aware is Frank I. Michelman, *On the Uses of Interpretive 'Charity': Some Notes on Application, Avoidance, Equality, and Objective Unconstitutionality from the 2007 Term of the Constitutional Court of South Africa*, 1 CONST. CT. REV. 1 (2008).

obligation. Were the constitutional court to agree by creating an easement in favor of the squatters, it would modify property law appropriately, thereby opening the "common-law" dialogue.[21]

Notably, nothing like that development has occurred in South Africa, whose constitution does impose a duty with respect to housing.[22] In *City of Johannesburg v. Blue Moonlight Properties*, the Constitutional Court held that the city's effort to evict squatters from unoccupied commercial property was unconstitutional.[23] Interpreting statutes regulating evictions in light of the constitutional right to housing, the Court held that the evictions were not just and equitable in the absence of a concrete plan for relocating the squatters to constitutionally acceptable housing. Blending constitutional and statutory analysis in its conclusion, the Court said:

> The City's housing policy is unconstitutional in that it excludes people evicted by a private landowner from its temporary housing programme, as opposed to those relocated by the City. Blue Moonlight cannot be expected indefinitely to provide free housing to the Occupiers, but its rights as property owner must be interpreted within the context of the requirement that eviction must be just and equitable. Eviction of the Occupiers would be just and equitable under the circumstances, if linked to the provision of temporary accommodation by the City.[24]

This effectively creates a temporary easement for the squatters' benefit, but the Court's opinion speaks only in statutory and constitutional terms.

Why does development of defamation law apparently seem within reach to many constitutional court judges but development of a constitutionally influenced easement seems not within reach?[25] I can only speculate, but I offer two possibilities. First, perhaps the background

---

[21] Or, as appears to be the usual practice in Germany, the constitutional court could find that the ordinary courts had failed to give appropriate weight in their development of the background law to constitutional values and direct them to reconsider their interpretation (or development) of that law so as to give those values appropriate weight.

[22] But see Submission on Behalf of the Amicus Curiae Inner City Resources Centre, Maphango v. Aengus Lifestyle Property, CCT Case No. 57/2011 (suggesting as an alternative to finding a constitutional violation in a decision by a private landlord or a statutory violation of the Rental Housing Act's ban on "unfair practices," the Court could develop the common law of landlord-tenant relations by "recognising an implied term in the lease" prohibiting cancelation of the lease where doing so "would cause disproportionate hardship to the lessee"). I thank Frank Michelman for providing me with a copy of this submission.

[23] [2011] ZACC 33.   [24] *Id.* 97.

[25] South Africa has a nontrivial jurisprudence about squatters and evictions, but as far as I know, it involves only statutory interpretation and direct constitutional analysis, for example, of the constitutional adequacy of eviction procedures.

right to real property seems somehow "more protected" by the constitution than the background right to reputation,[26] perhaps because rights to real property are more obviously marketizable than rights to reputation.[27] Yet, both are forms of property protected by the constitution, given the structure of private law. Second, perhaps judges have a sense – a sense that I think may be shared by constitutionalists more generally – that modifying elements of defamation law, even by creating new constitutionally influenced defenses, is a relatively small step – not different in principle from widely accepted judicial modifications of the common law for pragmatic rather than constitutional reasons – but that creating an easement on behalf of squatters is a large step.[28] The metaphor used to capture this sense is well known: common-law judges develop the law through molecular rather than molar action.[29] I confess to my inability to specify even vaguely the metric for distinguishing between small and large steps, between the molecular and the molar – and I know of no substantial progress anyone else has made in specifying such a metric.[30]

So far I have argued that constitutional duties open up the possibility for judicially initiated dialogues, using substantive duties as the central example. Constitutions typically impose another type of duty, that of equal treatment. The jurisprudence of remedies when courts find certain types of equality violations already contains something akin to judicially initiated dialogues. Suppose a legislature provides a discretionary benefit (one that the constitution does not require it to provide) to one group.[31] Members of another group claim that the failure to

---

[26] I owe this suggestion to Brian Ray.
[27] Obviously a person's reputation is marketizable, but there are few markets in *rights* to reputation, and indeed I believe that standard doctrine holds that one cannot transfer one's right to reputation to another.
[28] There may be other explanations, including a reasonably obvious ideological one, that constitutional court judges tend to favor free expression rights *and* property rights, making them amenable to developing private law causes of action implicating the former but not those implicating the latter.
[29] Southern Pacific Co. v. Jensen, 244 U.S. 205, 221 (1917) (Holmes, J., dissenting).
[30] Thomas C. Grey, *Molecular Motions: The Holmesian Judge in Theory and Practice*, 37 WM. & MARY L. REV. 19 (1995), suggests that the metric is the importance of the space left open by precedent for judicial lawmaking, where "importance" means that a decision one or way or the other will have implications for only a few closely related cases expected to arise in the future. See *id.* at 44. ("Such judicial legislation was in general appropriate, on Holmes's theory, only when it did not much matter which way the judge decided.") The issue deserves more attention than I can give it here, but a strong rule-skeptic would reject the proposition that a judge today can reasonably anticipate that his or her decision in the case at hand will have few implications for future cases.

provide the benefit to them violates constitutional equality principles.[32] The constitutional court has a choice of remedies available to it if it agrees with the claim of inequality. It can "read up" the legislation, extending the benefit to the previously excluded group, or it can read the legislation down, eliminating the benefit for all.[33]

The usual formulations of the grounds for choosing one remedy rather than the other obscure the presence of judicially initiated dialogue here, though only slightly. Courts typically try to imagine what the legislature would do faced with the choice between extending the benefit to all or denying it to all,[34] reading the statute up if they imagine that the legislature would want the benefit extended and reading it down otherwise.[35] We would observe no legislative reaction when the judges' projections of legislative desires are accurate, and so might not see this as an example of judicially initiated dialogue. Yet, two points are worth noting. First, the court might make a mistake about the legislature's wishes. If so, there will be a legislative response – after a statute is read down, the legislature might extend the benefit to all, for example. Second, and perhaps more important, the general account of constitutional dialogues, even in its familiar form, does not require that legislatures actually respond to judicial invalidation of legislation. The clearest examples are these:

(a) The court invalidates a single provision embedded in a complex statute, the provision is not important for the statute's effective functioning, and no one in the legislature paid much attention either to the provision or to its potential unconstitutionality;

(b) The legislature engaged in little reflection on a statute's constitutionality, and, when the court directs the legislature's attention to constitutional questions, the legislature agrees with the court that the

---

[31] The analysis is the same in cases of discretionary burdens, with appropriate changes in the description of reading up and reading down, and I therefore do not discuss burden cases separately.

[32] Note the structural similarity between this case and the "constitutional duty" case I have taken as the paradigm for judicially initiated dialogues: in both, the constitutional challenge arises from a legislative failure.

[33] The term "reading down" is sometimes used to refer to the practice of construing a statute narrowly to avoid finding it unconstitutional.

[34] For a discussion of the doctrine, see TUSHNET, *supra* note 9, at 155.

[35] This chapter's focus makes an extended analysis of the grounds for choice unnecessary, but I note that reading down might occur if the costs of extending the benefit are high, even though those who presently receive the benefit could be expected to provide political support in the legislature for extending the benefits to all.

statute is unconstitutional. The account of constitutional dialogues, that is, is an account of *possible* interactions between courts and legislators, not one in which any specific moves necessarily occur.

Still, even though legislatures can respond when the courts read up or read down a statute to remedy equality violations, there is an important difference between the "reading up/reading down" choice and constitutional dialogue. I have already distinguished between "common-law" dialogues between courts and legislatures and constitutional dialogues. The "reading up/reading down" choice opens up the possibility of dialogue, but one more like common-law dialogues than constitutional dialogues. The remedial choice rests on more or less pure policy judgments – should the discretionary benefit be extended or retracted? – and not on constitutional ones.[36] Further, "reading down" might sometimes be thought barred by the constitution where the subject matter is itself a constitutionally protected interest: reading down would deny the constitutional right to those who had received it as a result of legislative action.[37]

Having described the general contours of constitutional dialogues initiated by the courts, I turn to a discussion of the possible range of matters on which such dialogues might occur. I think it helpful to distinguish among several kinds of rights constitutions protect:

(1) Purely formal negative rights against the government. Constitutional rules barring the government from imprisoning those who criticize its policies – classic sedition laws – fall into this category.

---

[36] A related possibility, suggested to me by Gerald Neuman, moves beyond the domain of constitutional duty. A court might observe an ongoing constitutional discussion in the legislature, which has not yet reached a resolution. No question of constitutional duty need be involved. The legislature might be considering a statute that imposes regulations on some form of expression, with legislators debating whether that expression even qualifies for coverage under free speech principles. In the United States, recent cases of this sort have involved depictions of cruelty to animals (United States v. Stevens, 559 U.S. 460 (2010), violent video games (Brown v. Entertainment Merchants Ass'n, 131 S.Ct. 2729 (2011), and lies as such (United States v. Alvarez, 132 S.Ct. 2537 (2012). The court might use some pending case as the vehicle for expressing its views on the question being mooted legislatively, by invoking grounds that simultaneously dispose of the case before it and indicate the court's position on that question, or by overt dictum. The court's position then becomes a datum in the ongoing legislative discussion. Presumably the court's action will end a legislative discussion about what the constitutional court would do when presented with the question on which it offers its views. But the court's action need not end a discussion about the constitution's meaning, a point brought out in the literature on constitutional dialogues.

[37] Here, too, I thank Brian Ray for this observation.

(2) Negative rights against the government to which some degree of "effectiveness" is attached. In the United States, some content-neutral speech regulations (formerly described as "time, place, and manner" regulations) are unconstitutional because they deny those wishing to express themselves of the effective opportunity to do so. One reason offered for finding it unconstitutional for a government to have a flat ban on the use of streets and parks for political demonstrations is that those with few monetary resources have no other venues for expressing themselves.[38] Note that in these cases, the constitutional violation arises because of the interaction between the express government regulation and the background rules of property, contract, and tort.[39]

(3) Rights whose protection necessarily affects the protections people have against invasions of *other* constitutional rights. The tension between freedom of speech and constitutionally protected rights to informational privacy and dignity, common in most constitutional systems (though not in the United States), is a standard example. For the United States, the so-called free press/fair trial dilemma serves as an example.[40]

(4) Positive rights to resources, with some quantitative dimension to the rights. These rights can be satisfied either by direct government provision or by adjusting the background rules.

(5) Pure positive absolute rights. Were nations to recognize rights to a "minimum core" of housing, medical care, and the like, as some have urged, these rights would be positive and absolute. Again, these rights can be satisfied either by government provision or by adjusting the background rules.[41]

The discussion so far has suggested that judicially initiated constitutional dialogues might occur in all but the first category, and even there, the

---

[38] Hague v. C.I.O., 307 U.S. 496 (1939).
[39] The point is captured in A.J. Liebling's comment that the freedom of the press is available to anyone who owns one (the comment is attributed to Liebling in various forms).
[40] The dilemma is that sometimes making information available to the press for publication might have the effect of impairing a criminal defendant's ability to get a constitutionally fair trial.
[41] In the United States, an indigent criminal defendant's right to counsel provided at public expenses is often offered as an example of a pure positive right. But, of course, that a defendant is indigent results from the operation of the background rules. People who can afford to hire counsel with their own resources must do so, which shows that the right to counsel is not, as such, a pure positive absolute right.

idea of "reading down" suggests a version of a judicially initiated dialogue. Consider a statute challenged as violating a purely negative right. The court might reject the *constitutional* challenge by invoking a canon of constitutional avoidance in its so-called modern form, where the courts construe statutes to avoid ruling on difficult constitutional questions.[42] The legislature can respond by insisting that it meant what it said the first time, forcing the court to address the constitutional question on the merits.[43]

The next step develops from the observation that the government has enacted some relevant legislation in almost every case of judicially initiated dialogue.[44] This suggests the thought that, in almost every case, we could characterize the dialogue as initiated by the legislature when it enacted a statute now challenged as not going far enough to protect the rights in categories (2) through (5). That thought, as such, is relatively uninteresting, though. What *is* interesting is the idea of "enough."

That idea raises the question: "Do we think that a nation falls short of the ideal whenever it could do more to reach a maximal level of constitutional achievement?"[45] The problem of conflicting rights shows that maximal achievement does not require a single-minded focus on any individual constitutional provision. Getting "more" freedom of expression might mean getting "less" informational privacy. Nor does ensuring that a positive right – to housing or water – is maximally achieved mean that every available resource must be devoted to achieving that right before the government turns to matters of "mere" policy, such as the choice of weapons systems to defend that nation against external attack. Standard formulations of positive rights, using phrases like "within available resources," show this, and sensible constitutional interpretation would find a similar limitation implicit in constitutional provisions seeming to state positive rights in absolute terms. Yet, equally standard formulations such as "progressive realization" suggest that constitutional

---

[42] For a discussion of the modern canon, see Frederick Schauer, Ashwander *Revisited*, 1995 SUP. CT. REV. 71, 88.

[43] The resemblance to "reading down" is apparent. A similar dialogic structure could occur if the court rejected the constitutional challenge on the merits but observed in dictum that extending the statute beyond the case at hand would render it unconstitutional. For a discussion of a similar form of dialogue through dictum, see *supra* note 36.

[44] At least if the category of "relevance" is appropriately capacious.

[45] I put the question in terms of "a nation" and "achievement" to avoid prejudging the judicial role in achieving the constitutional maximum, as might be suggested for example by using the word "enforced."

compliance is incomplete until the right is fully realized.[46] Even within this framework, judicially initiated dialogue can occur.

Suppose, then, that the government has done "a lot" in devoting resources to achieving a positive right. Under what circumstances can a court reject a claim that the government has not yet done enough?[47] In general, the question is about jointly maximizing all constitutional values at once. At this point, the issues raised by category (3) claims – one right set against another right – recur, and the answer should be the same. Such claims involve provisions that, in some sense, compete with each other directly. But constitutions are complex documents, and competition among provisions is, I think, ever present even if not always direct or obvious. Certainly the standard positive rights compete against each other: the "within available resources" constraint means that a government that provides more housing is likely to have to provide less water. And, although it would take a great deal of work to develop this point precisely, it seems quite likely that the adjustments in background rules needed to maximize the effective provision of negative rights – one way of dealing with category (2) cases – will have some effect on the resources available to achieve the standard positive rights.

I offer this analysis with some diffidence. If it is accurate, I believe that it has interesting implications for the idea of constitutional dialogue. It suggests that constitutional dialogues may be the only sensible way to deal with everything other than pure negative rights. The reason is that courts are not well positioned to reject an executive or legislature's argument that it has done enough *here*, in the case at hand, because it has been doing something equally important *there*. But dialogic review can press the executive ministry or the legislature to explain itself, and experience has shown that explanations are sometimes implausible, as the South African Constitutional Court thought they were in *Minister of Health v. Treatment Action Campaign*,[48] or unavailable, as in some of the South American cases dealing with the failure to make specific medications available through national health care systems, where the failures

---

[46] For both formulations, see, for example, S. AFR. CONST., 1996 § 26(2). ("The state must take reasonable legislative and other measures, within its available resources, to achieve the progressive realisation" of the right to housing.) For a discussion of these formulations that could readily be recast in terms of dialogue, see Mazibuko v. City of Johannesburg 2010 (4) SA 1 at paras. 57–59 (S. Afr.).

[47] In addressing the claim the court would take into account the background rules that provide access through "the market" to the positive right.

[48] (2002) 5 SA 721.

result from bureaucratic inertia rather than a considered judgment about medical priorities.[49] As Justice O'Regan put it in *Mazibuko v. City of Johannesburg*:

> If government takes no steps to realise the rights, the courts will require government to take steps. If government's adopted measures are unreasonable, the courts will similarly require that they be reviewed so as to meet the constitutional standard of reasonableness.... Finally, the obligation of progressive realisation imposes a duty upon government continually to review its policies to ensure that the achievement of the right is progressively realised.[50]

I began this chapter with a simple model of constitutional dialogue in which legislatures were the first movers, and then switched the order so that courts were the first movers. Doing so brought out the connection between the ideas of dialogue and constitutional duty. Then, distinguishing among types of duty suggested that constitutions require not the maximization of any – or all – constitutional values, but joint maximization in which the constitutional system as a whole achieves as much as possible even though we can see that there is something more that the system could do to achieve any particular constitutional value. Finally, I suggested that joint maximization implies that only dialogic review is appropriate if we are interested in constitutional systems as a whole. Overall, then, the boundaries between forms of constitutional review may be as blurred as those between constitutional rights and duties.

---

[49] David Landau's argument favoring structural injunctions over dialogic review, David Landau, *The Reality of Social Rights Enforcement*, 53 HARV. INT'L L.J. 402 (2012), overlooks the fact, as I think it is, that structural injunctions are almost inevitably dialogic. For my discussion, see TUSHNET, *supra* note 9, at 248–49; Mark Tushnet, *A Response to David Landau*, 53 HARV. INT'L L.J. ONLINE 155 (2012), www.harvardilj.org/2012/04/online_53_tushnet/.

[50] Mazibuko v. City of Johannesburg 2010 (4) SA at para. 67.

# 5

## Positive obligations, positive rights, and constitutional amendment

VICKI C. JACKSON[*]

In the last several decades, positive rights and obligations with respect to social welfare rights – access to education, adequate food, housing, and health care – have become increasingly common aspects of national constitutions. Other obligations are imposed on governments by virtue of traditional civil and political rights – for example, the obligation to maintain courts, or the obligation to provide places and systems for voting. Positive obligations may be imposed on the state affirmatively to act, or – in theory – on private persons as well, through the indirect or horizontal effects of constitutional requirements, for example, on what rent may be charged by private property owners. In this chapter, I am concerned primarily with the positive obligations of states to provide minimum levels of material social welfare.

This chapter explores relations among and between the forms of positive constitutional social welfare obligations, interpretive cultures, and the legal and practical difficulties of constitutional amendment. A tentative conclusion is that in some theoretical circumstances, involving a formalist interpretive culture, and a difficult amendment process, a delinkage between government duties and justiciable individual rights may be constitutionally useful. That is, government *duties* to advance social welfare *unaccompanied* by individual justiciable rights to receive particular social welfare benefits may be the option for constitutionalizing social welfare obligations that is most consistent with constitutionalism where a constitution is difficult to amend and the legal culture is inflexible in

---

[*] With thanks to Mark Tushnet for very helpful conversations, Tsvi Kahana for helpful edits, and the Constitutional Court of Colombia, for providing an occasion, the October 2011 celebration in Bogota of the Court's twenty-fifth anniversary, to consider the relationship between unconstitutional amendments and social welfare rights.

interpretive approach.¹ The chapter also hopes to cast light on the problem of constitutional interdependencies in the comparative study of constitutional law.

Part I briefly discusses the development of positive government obligations to provide for social welfare and of individual rights to positive government action. Part II provides an overview of different approaches to constitutional amendment, with special attention to provisions for unamendable constitutional provisions or principles. Part III brings these two together, to explore the ramifications for constitutional government from their interaction, in light of different cultures of interpretation.² Part IV concludes.

## I  Positive social welfare provisions: A brief history

Although recognition of government obligations to provide aid to the needy emerged as early as the eighteenth century, the idea of the "social" state more fully emerged in the nineteenth century in Prussia.³ The first instantiation of positive social obligations of government in a written national constitution may have been in the Mexican Constitution of 1917, which set out various "social" rights including free public education, and charged the Congress with enacting labor laws protecting a wide range of workers' rights set forth in the Constitution (including maximum work hours, vacation days, minimum wages, and provisions concerning employment of women within months of childbirth (Article 123)).⁴ In the same time period, the Weimar Constitution of 1919, and

---

¹ I acknowledge but do not engage a broader debate in the literature, about whether justiciable "rights" as a strategy is likely to misallocate resources to those who are better resourced in terms of access to litigation. See, for example, Octavio Luiz Motta Ferraz, *Harming the Poor through Social Rights Litigation: Lessons from Brazil*, 89 TEX. L. REV. 1643 (2011); David Landau, *The Reality of Social Rights Enforcement*, 53 HARV. INT'L L.J. 189 (2012).

² The chapter assumes readers' familiarity with longstanding debates over general approaches to constitutional interpretation, which will be alluded to in this section.

³ Dennis M. Davis, *Socio-Economic Rights*, in THE OXFORD HANDBOOK OF COMPARATIVE CONSTITUTIONAL LAW 1020, 1021 (Michel Rosenfeld and Andras Sajo eds. 2012) (noting provision in French constitution of 1793 and of such ideas in Bavaria and Prussia); see also VICKI C. JACKSON and MARK TUSHNET, COMPARATIVE CONSTITUTIONAL LAW 1691 (3rd ed. 2014) (noting the significance of Catholic social thought as expressed in the papal encyclical *Rerum Novarum* (1891)).

⁴ These provisions may have had predecessors in the Mexican Constitution, 1857, Article 3, which provided "Instruction is free." See H. N. Branch and Leo Stanton Rowe, *The*

## I. POSITIVE SOCIAL WELFARE PROVISIONS

the Russian Constitution of 1918,[5] also included provisions on social welfare. The Weimar Constitution, for example, offered what appear as positive guarantees of social welfare, in provisions that required state protection for "motherhood," Article 119, the preconditions for equality for "illegitimate children," Article 121, as well as the protection of "youth ... [from] exploitation" (Article 122). Article 151 provided that "the economy has to be organized based on the principles of justice, with the goal of achieving life in dignity for everyone." Article 157 provided that "[l]abour enjoys the special protection" of the state, and Article 161 provided that "[i]n order to maintain health and the ability to work, in order to protect motherhood and to prevent economic consequences of age, weakness and to protect against the vicissitudes of life the Reich establishes a comprehensive system of insurances, based on the critical contribution of the insured."[6] Establishment of the International Labor Organization in 1919 helped advance legal conceptions of the positive obligations of government.[7]

In the United States, nineteenth-century enabling acts for the admissions of new states sometimes required that "provision shall be made for the establishment and maintenance of systems of public schools, which shall be open to all the children of said States, and free from sectarian control."[8] These enabling acts often resulted in state constitutional provisions providing for public education systems, as was the case in the State of Washington's 1889 Constitution.[9] State constitutions from the

---

Mexican Constitution of 1917 compared with the Constitution of 1857, 71 ANNALS AM. POL. SCI. ASS'N 1, 2 (Supp. May 1917) (translating both constitutions).

[5] For an English translation of Article 17 of the 1918 Russian constitution, providing for free public education, see www.marxists.org/history/ussr/ government/constitution/1918/. The Soviet Constitution of 1936 included more extensive social rights. Davis, *supra* note 3, at 1021.

[6] Translations are from www.zum.de/psm/weimar/weimar_vve.php#Basic%20rights%20and%20obligations%20of%20the%20Germans - visited May 5, 2014. *See also* Keith D. Ewing, *Economic Rights*, in OXFORD HANDBOOK OF COMPARATIVE CONSTITUTIONAL LAW *supra* note 3 at 1036, 1040–41.

[7] Davis, *supra* note 3, at 1021.

[8] *Supra* note 3 Enabling Act, An Act to provide for the division of Dakota into two States and to enable the people of North Dakota, South Dakota, Montana, and Washington to form constitutions and State governments and to be admitted into the Union on an equal footing with the original States, and to make donations of public lands to such States. (Approved Feb. 22, 1889.) [25 U.S. Statutes at Large, c 180 p. 676.]. *See also* EMILY ZACKIN, LOOKING FOR RIGHTS IN ALL THE WRONG PLACES: WHY STATE CONSTITUTIONS CONTAIN AMERICA'S POSITIVE RIGHTS 75–79 and n. 27 (2013).

[9] *Supra* note 3 L.K. Beale, *Charter Schools, Common Schools and the Washington State Constitution*, 72 WASH. L. REV. 535, 544 (1997) (describing how the state's "Enabling Act required the state constitution to provide for a system of public schools, open to all") .

nineteenth century through to the present have been a rich source of positive constitutional rights, notwithstanding the absence of such rights from the text of the national Constitution of the United States.[10]

The provisions for free public education in the United States state constitutions long endured; the Weimar Constitution was very short lived. But in 1937, the Constitution of Ireland provided (and still does), in Article 45, for "directive principles of social policy." These were principles declared to be "for the general guidance" of the legislature, "in the care of [the legislature] exclusively," and were declared to "not be cognisable by any Court under any of the provisions of this Constitution."[11] These principles were concerned with promoting the material welfare of the people, including "to safeguard with especial care the economic interests of the weaker sections of the community, and, where necessary, to contribute to the support of the infirm, the widow, the orphan, and the aged," and to "endeavour to ensure that the strength and health of workers, men and women and the tender age of children shall not be abused . . . " Article 45(4). In order to promote justice and equality in access to material resources, the state was to "direct its policy towards securing . . . that the citizens (all of whom, men and women equally, have the right to an adequate means of livelihood) may through their occupations find the means of making reasonable provision for their domestic needs," and that "the ownership and control of the material resources of the community may be so distributed amongst private individuals and the various classes as best to subserve the common good," Article 45(2).

After World War II, with the encouragement of ideas developed in the founding of the United Nations and the Universal Declaration of Human Rights, the idea of positive welfare rights assumed larger importance. In 1950, India adopted a constitution that included "directive principles"; the Irish Constitution (1937) is widely credited as having influenced the Indian Constitution.[12] However, the Indian Constitution has an entire Section devoted to "Directive Principles of State Policy," which includes

---

[10] See generally ZACKIN, *supra* note 8 (focusing on movements within states to provide constitutional guarantees of education, labor, and the environment); *see also, for example,* Helen Hershkoff, *Foreword: Positive Rights and State Constitutions*, 33 RUTGERS L.J. 799 (2002).

[11] On the history of the Directive Principles in the Irish Constitution, see Gerard Hogan, *Directive Principles, Socio-Economic Rights and the Constitution*, 36 IRISH JURIST 174 (2001).

[12] See, for example, Paul Gallagher, *The Irish Constitution—Its Unique Nature and the Relevance of International Jurisprudence*, 45 IRISH JURIST 22, 27 and n. 25 (2010) (noting

## I. POSITIVE SOCIAL WELFARE PROVISIONS

Articles 36–51. Article 37 states "[t]he provisions contained in this Part shall not be enforceable by any court, but the principles therein laid down are nevertheless fundamental in the governance of the country and it shall be the duty of the State to apply these principles in making laws." Several detailed provisions address, *inter alia*, issues of "equal justice" including free legal aid, a "living wage" for workers, "rights to education and public assistance," and "just and humane conditions of work and maternity relief."[13] Notwithstanding the express statement that the Directive Principles were not enforceable in any court, the Indian Supreme Court has in effect read into justiciable rights in the Constitution elements of the Directive Principles.[14]

In both India and Ireland, the essential idea of the "directive principles" could be understood to embody rights without justiciable remedies unless provided by the legislature. But they may also be understood, in some instances, as government "duties" not necessarily correlated with individual justiciable rights.

Other post–World War II Constitutions, including those of Japan and Italy, included social welfare "rights" provisions and statements of government obligations. Japan's Constitution, for example, included Articles 25–27, which among other things provided that "all people shall have the right to maintain the minimum standards of wholesome and cultured living" and that "the State shall use its endeavors for the promotion and extension of social welfare and security, and of public health." It also guarantees a free compulsory education (Article 26), and the "right and obligation to work" with the "standards for hours, wages, rest and other working conditions [to] be fixed by law" (Article 27). Although *not* set

---

influence of Irish Directive Principles on the Indian Constitution and their possible influence on the constitutions of Burma (1946), Nigeria (1989), and Namibia (1990)).

[13] See *id.* Arts. 39a, 41–43. Article 45 of the directive principles had provided from 1951 that the state should endeavor, within a period of ten years after the constitution was enacted, to provide a "free and compulsory" education to children up to age fourteen.

[14] See, for example, Unni Krishnan v. State of Andhra Pradesh, 1993 SCR (1) 594 (treating the right to a free public education to age fourteen found in Article 45 of the Directive Principles as now an aspect of Article 21's justiciable right to life). The decision was followed by constitutional amendments that, *inter alia*, established a new justiciable fundamental right to a free education for children between the ages of six and fourteen. See INDIA CONST. art. 21A. Article 45 was amended to include a directive principle that the state endeavor to provide education for children under the age of six. For further discussion, see Vijayashri Sripati and Arun K. Thiruvengedam, *India: Constitutional Amendment Making the Right to Education a Fundamental Right*, 2 INT'L. J OF CONST. L. (I•CON) 148 (2004).

forth as a nonjusticiable "directive," early interpretations of Article 25 treated its parameters as essentially for the legislature to determine.[15] Italy's 1947 Constitution includes *inter alia* a "right of all citizens to work" (Article 4), and refers to the Republic as protecting "mothers, children and the young" and as "safeguard[ing] health as a fundamental right of the individual," guaranteeing "free medical care to the indigent (Articles 4, 31, and 32).

In the wave of democratization movements in the 1980s and early 1990s, explicit provisions for justiciable social welfare rights appeared in post-democratization constitutions. The (South) Korean Constitution (1987) provides in Article 31 for a free and compulsory education, in Article 32 for the right to work, and for the state to "strive to protect ... motherhood" and the "health of all citizens" (Article 36). And, perhaps most well known, the South African Constitution protects a series of social welfare rights that are plainly made justiciable: the right to access to adequate housing (Article 26); the right to an environment that is not harmful (Article 24); and the right of access to health care, food, water, and social security (Article 27). Children have specified rights (Article 28), and Article 29 provides a right to education.

Within several of these rights provisions is language describing the state's duty, "to take reasonable legislative and other measures, within its available resources, to achieve the progressive realization of each of these rights" (Article 27(2)). Like the Canadian Charter, or the Israeli Basic Law (Human Dignity and Liberty), many of the post-democratization constitutions also include specific authorization of limitations on rights, for example, the South African Constitution, Article 36, explicitly contemplating that legislation infringing on rights may be justified and thus constitutional.[16] A number of constitutions distinguish between the

---

[15] See Asahi v. Japan [Sup. Ct.] 1967, 21 Saikō Saibansho Minji Hanreishū [Minshū] 5, 1043. English transl. available at www.courts.go.jp/english/judgments/text/1967.05.24 -1964-Gyo-Tsu-No.14.html) (stating that Article 25(a) "merely proclaims that it is the duty of the State to administer national policy to enable all the people to enjoy at least the healthy, cultural and minimum standard of living, and it does not grant the individual people any concrete rights"). The Japanese Supreme Court only rarely finds government action to be unconstitutional. See, for example, David S. Law, *The Anatomy of a Conservative Court*, 87 Tex. L. Rev. 1545 (2009); David S. Law, *Why Has Judicial Review Failed in Japan?*, 88 Wash. U. L. Rev. 1425 (2011).

[16] On the importance of such limitations clauses, see, for example, Lorraine Weinrib, *Constitutional Conceptions and Constitutional Comparativism*, in Defining the Field of Comparative Constitutional Law 3 (Vicki Jackson and Mark Tushnet eds., 2002);

derogability of different rights in time of emergency, typically allowing derogation from social welfare rights.[17]

This brief review illustrates many axes along which social welfare provisions may be compared. Three are significant for this chapter. First, there is a distinction between social welfare provisions that are nonjusticiable – as in Ireland and India – and those that are justiciable, as in South Africa. Second, justiciable social welfare provisions may be framed and understood in terms of government obligations, or in terms of individual rights, or both. Third, constitutions may conceptualize rights as categorical "trumps" or as presumptive entitlements subject to limitation for broadly specified reasons – an approach that is, in a sense, a proxy for more flexible forms of interpretation.

## II  Amendment and the idea of unconstitutional amendments

Constitutions generally provide for their own amendment, and can be amended in a wide range of ways. Although it is not uncommon for constitutions to be classified as more, or less, difficult to amend,[18] recent scholarship has begun to explore the difficulty of making this assessment, at least without knowing much more about political culture and about the organization of political parties and support.[19] The complexity of the subject is further confounded because in recent constitutions it is not uncommon to find different levels of procedures for amendment, based on subject area, in the same constitution.[20]

---

see also Etienne Mureinik, *A Bridge to Where? Introducing the Interim Bill of Rights*, (1994) 10 S. AFR. J. ON HUM. RTS. 31, 32.

[17] See, for example, S. AFR. CONST., 1996 art. 37 (making certain rights nonderogable, but not including social welfare rights such as to housing, or health care, which are derogable in time of emergency).

[18] See, for example, Donald S. Lutz, *Toward a Theory of Constitutional Amendment*, in RESPONDING TO IMPERFECTION: THE THEORY AND PRACTICE OF CONSTITUTIONAL AMENDMENT 237 (Sanford Levinson, ed., 1995).

[19] See Tom Ginsburg and James Melton, *Does the Constitutional Amendment Rule Matter at All? Amendment Cultures and the Challenges of Measuring Amendment Difficulty* (May 3, 2014), University of Chicago Coase-Sandor Institute for Law & Economics Research Paper No. 682; University of Chicago, Public Law Working Paper No. 472, *available at* SSRN: http://ssrn.com/abstract=2432520; Charles Manga Fombad, *Some Perspectives on Durability and Change under Modern African Constitutions*, 11 INT'L J. CONST. L. (I.CON) 382 (2013).

[20] See, for example, S. AFR. CONST., 1996 art. 74(1), (2), (3) (providing different procedures for amendments of different parts of the Constitution); *see also* Stephen Holmes and Cass R. Sunstein, *The Politics of Constitutional Revision in Eastern Europe*, in

In addition to procedural requirements for effecting amendments, some constitutions impose substantive limits, providing that some aspects of the constitution are not amendable at all. Article 79(3) of the German Basic Law (the so-called eternity cause) provides that "Amendments to this Basic Law affecting the division of the Federation into Länder, their participation on principle in the legislative process, or the principles laid down in Articles 1 and 20 shall be inadmissible." Article 79 thereby explicitly makes unamendable the social character of the state, as set forth in Article 20, and the protection of "human dignity," in Article 1. Together, they permanently entrench the social character of the state along with its democratic and federal character and respect for human dignity. In other constitutional systems, a doctrine of "unconstitutional constitutional amendments" has been judicially developed, as in India (the "basic structure" doctrine)[21] or Colombia (the doctrine against constitutional substitution or replacement).[22]

The *Southwest Case* in Germany was one of the first judicial decisions to suggest that a constitutional provision whose substance is inconsistent with constitutional commitments to democracy could be treated as unconstitutional.[23] Forty years later, the participants in the South African constitutional process authorized a new Constitutional Court to review the whole final Constitution for conformance to thirty-four basic principles, agreed to in the negotiations that ended the apartheid; and the

---

RESPONDING TO IMPERFECTION: THE THEORY AND PRACTICE OF CONSTITUTIONAL AMENDMENT 275 (Sanford Levinson, ed., 1995) (arguing for differing amending procedures for social welfare rights, which, they argue, should be easier to amend than traditional political rights).

[21] See, for example, SUDHIR KRISHNASWAMY, DEMOCRACY AND CONSTITUTIONALISM IN INDIA: A STUDY OF THE BASIC STRUCTURE DOCTRINE (2009); GARY JACOBSOHN, CONSTITUTIONAL IDENTITY (2010).

[22] See Carlos Bernal, *Unconstitutional Constitutional Amendments in the Case Study of Colombia: An Analysis of the Justification and Meaning of the Constitutional Replacement Doctrine*, 11 INT'L J. CONST. L. (I.CON) 339 (2013); cf. JOEL COLON-RIOS, WEAK CONSTITUTIONALISM: DEMOCRATIC LEGITIMACY AND THE QUESTION OF CONSTITUENT POWER (2012).

[23] 1 BVerfGE 14 (1951):

> That a constitutional provision itself may be null and void, is not conceptually impossible just because it is a part of the constitution. There are constitutional principles that are so fundamental and to such an extent an expression of a law that precedes even the constitution that they also bind the framer of the constitution, and other constitutional provisions that do not rank so high may be null and void because they contravene these principles.

Translated in WALTER F. MURPHY and JOSEPH T. TANENHAUS, COMPARATIVE CONSTITUTIONAL LAW: CASES AND COMMENTARIES 209 (1977).

## II. AMENDMENT

South African Constitutional Court exercised this jurisdiction three years later finding that the proposed final Constitution was deficient.[24] Between these events, the Supreme Court of India, in several cases, found procedurally properly enacted constitutional amendments to be invalid, under a judicially developed doctrine that precludes amendments that changed the constitution's "basic structure," that "damaged or destroyed" the integrity of the constitution.[25]

A substantive or procedural objection to a constitutional amendment, proposed or claimed to have been made, can be justiciable – that is, capable of being decided by a court – or it may be treated as nonjusticiable, subject to resolution only by political actors.[26] Substantive objections may be based on very concrete or general texts: for example, in Honduras, the Constitution's text specifically says, the president can serve only one term and that the one-term limit cannot be amended.[27] Proposed amendments may also be opposed, or constitutional courts also might invalidate enacted amendments on other general grounds of substance, whether because of preexisting aspects of a particular constitution's identity or because of noncompliance with what the German Constitutional Court calls "law that precedes even the Constitution."[28]

I have elsewhere suggested that judicial review of constitutional amendments puts into play at least three sets of values (or sources of legitimacy): first, that constitutions be based on popular consent and facilitate democratic self-government; second, that constitutions and judicial decisions thereunder be consistent with and promote the rule of law; and, third, that constitutions reflect or be consistent with just or good principles designed to promote a just and good society.[29]

---

[24] Certification of the Const. of the Republic of S. Afr. (1996) (10) BCLR 1253.
[25] See, for example, Kesavananda Bharati v. State of Kerala, A.I.R. 1973 S.C. 1461 (India). For discussion of the Indian doctrine, see sources cited *supra* note 21.
[26] Although in many systems claims that an amendment has not been made by the proper procedures is justiciable, in one case the US Supreme Court suggested that even procedural challenges are nonjusticiable, and committed to the Congress to decide. Coleman v. Miller, 307 U.S. 433 (1939).
[27] HOND. CONST., 1982 arts. 237, 239 & 374.
[28] Southwest Case 1 BverfGE 14 (quoting a lower court decision), translated in MURPHY AND TANENHAUS, *supra* note 23.
[29] Vicki C. Jackson, *Unconstitutional Constitutional Amendments: A Window into Constitutional Theory and Transnational Constitutionalism* in DEMOCRACY PERSPECTIVES. FESTSCHRIFT FOR BRUN-OTTO BRYDE'S 70TH BIRTHDAY (Michael Bäuerle, Philipp Dann and Astrid Wall Rabenstein eds. 2013). For a similar three-pronged argument about constitutional legitimacy, see Richard Fallon, *Legitimacy and the Constitution*, 118 HARV. L. REV. 1787 (2005).

Consent can be given at the time of the framing, or it can arise over time by acquiescence. It is importantly found both in legitimate democratic constitutions and in continuing democratic politics. But, if constitutions are based on consent, this raises a familiar dilemma, which is how to account for restricting the people's ability to act according to the normal rules of democratic politics in the future. This is the true counter-majoritarian difficulty – it is a difficulty with any entrenched constitution, much more than with judicial review. Answers have been offered, including by Bruce Ackerman, about dualist democracy.[30] One might still ask whether there is not a limit on democratic self-limitation where it completely seeks to forestall change by future generations by prohibiting amendments on substantive grounds.

A second value is the rule of law, which is implicit in adopting a written constitution. A central purpose of writing down the constitutive features of a polity is to make clear how power is organized and how it may or must be deployed: if, for example, a constitution guarantees an individual "right" to housing but many remain without shelter, that raises rule-of-law concerns. Of course, no constitutional system entirely conforms to its own written rules; there are always gaps. But the more that actual practices do not conform with the written rules, the more the rule-of-law purpose of having a written constitution is put in question.

Third, constitutions exist not only to organize power but also to advance a set of principles that involve what we might call just or good norms.[31] These norms are not necessarily universal. But the purpose of a constitution writ large is to facilitate the development of a good and just society and of a country that can be recognized by and deal with others in the world on terms of equality. A "constitution" designedly advances a kind of normative claim to be worthy of respect and often does so by advancing universalist norms.

---

[30] See Bruce Ackerman, We the People: Foundations (1991).

[31] On the relationship between morality and constitutional legitimacy, see, for example, Fallon, *supra* note 29; Joseph Raz, *On the Authority and Interpretation of Constitutions: Some Preliminaries*, in Constitutionalism: Philosophical Foundations 152, 169–73 (Larry Alexander ed., 1998) (arguing that the legitimacy of "originating constitutions" rests on moral authority); Trevor R.S. Allan, The Sovereignty of Law: Freedom, Constitution and Common Law (2013) (emphasizing role of conceptions of justice, fairness, and equality in interpretive processes of British constitutionalism). Utilitarian theories of the good might also be invoked by some as part of constitutional legitimacy. For an economic approach to constitutional design, see, for example, Robert D. Cooter, The Strategic Constitution (2002).

## II. AMENDMENT

Sometimes, these three sources of legitimacy will all work in the same direction when an issue of the constitutionality of a proposed amendment arises. For example, in the United States, the Nineteenth Amendment, to guarantee women the equal right to vote,[32] was adopted just after World War I. The amendment was proposed by both houses of Congress by a two-thirds vote and ratified by three-fourths of the States. These procedures were in conformity with the written requirements of the constitution, so democracy and rule-of-law values supported its legitimacy. At a substantive level, moreover, the amendment moved the United States closer to the value of human equality that had began to appear as one of increasing importance to the United States' ideas of a good and just society, beginning with the abolition of slavery in the Thirteenth Amendment, the Equal Protection Clause of the Fourteenth Amendment, and the guarantee of voting rights irrespective of race, color, or prior condition of servitude in the Fifteenth Amendment. Thus, in a challenge to the Nineteenth Amendment as an intrusion on state sovereignty, there was a strong argument that all three sets of values – the rule of law, democracy, and substantive justice – pointed in the same direction to support rejection of the challenge.[33]

But these values can sometimes be in tension with each other. Indeed the tensions between popular consent, on the one hand, and rule of law and just principles on the other, are sometimes captured by opposing the concepts of democracy and constitutionalism.[34] These terms bear highly contested meanings, and they overlap in meanings. Popular consent can be given in many ways and at many times. The content and criteria of democracy are highly contested, as is the role of majority rule in conceptions of democracy and terms like the rule of law and constitutionalism;

---

[32] U.S. CONST. amend. XIX.
[33] Leser v. Garnett, 258 U.S. 130, 136 (1922) (rejecting the argument that "the power of amendment conferred by the federal Constitution and sought to be exercised does not extend to this amendment because of its character ... [in] destroy[ing] [the State's] autonomy as a political body"). This case arose initially as an action in the Maryland state courts to strike from the voter rolls women who had registered to vote following enactment of the Nineteenth Amendment to the federal Constitution. The Court also rejected arguments against the constitutionality of that amendment based on alleged defects in the processes by which it was ratified. *Id.* at 137.
[34] *Cf.* Abner S. Greene, *The Irreducible Constitution*, 7 J. CONTEMP. LEGAL ISSUES 293 (1996) (rejecting constitutional theories predicated either on democracy or on rights protection standing alone); James E. Fleming, *The Missing Selves in Constitutional Self-Government*, 71 FORDHAM L. REV. 1789, 1793 (2003) (arguing that we need to "live with the tension between constitutionalism and democracy").

there are thicker and thinner versions of each; and sometimes, they are also used interchangeably. And "good and just" principles might (should) include democratic self-governance, thus complicating the supposed tension between consent and just principle. Yet tensions do exist, as illustrated in the following discussion of a recent decision holding unconstitutional statutory changes in social welfare programs.

Constitutional courts have been willing to entertain and decide claims challenging social welfare cutbacks as unconstitutional.[35] The German Constitutional Court, for example, recently held unconstitutional legislation cutting back on social assistance benefits, in part under Article 20, the social state requirement, and in part under Article I, the human dignity clause, both of which are protected by the eternity clause. In *Hartz IV* (2010),[36] the Constitutional Court of Germany found that legislation designed to reduce expenditures on social assistance benefits (for unemployment) was a violation of the German Basic Law (its constitution). Although many of the Court's reasons were procedural in nature, having to do with the adequacy of the effort the legislature made to really examine the needs of the persons affected, the Court also grounded its conclusion on Article 20 of the Basic Law and Article 1 – which, in turn, under the so-called eternity clause of Article 79, are included among the principles that are not subject to amendment. The Court spoke at times in quite absolutist terms: "The fundamental right to the guarantee of a subsistence minimum that is in line with human dignity emerges from Article 1.1 of the Basic Law in conjunction with Article 20.1 of the Basic Law.... As a guarantee right, this fundamental right from Article 1.1 takes on autonomous significance, in its conjunction with Article 20.1 of the Basic Law, in addition to the right from Article 1.1 of the Basic Law to respect for the dignity of each individual, which has an absolute effect. *Fundamentally, it is not subject to the legislature's disposal and must be honoured*...."[37]

It is possible, given the reasoning of *Hartz IV*, that subsequent legislation may be found permissible, even under Article 20's commitment to a social state. But let's just imagine that an even bigger financial crisis occurs, one that causes countries, including Germany, that have long

---

[35] See, for example, HCJ 366/03 Commitment to Peace & Social Justice Soc'y v. Minister of Fin. [2005] (Isr.); HCJ 888/03 Rubinova v. Minister of Fin. [2005] (Isr.).
[36] BVerfG, 1 BvL 1/09 vom 9.2.2010, Absatz-Nr. (1–220), www.bverfg.de/entscheidungen/ls20100209_1bvl000109en.html (official translation by the Court).
[37] *Id.* (Emphasis added).

maintained social welfare programs to conclude that they simply cannot afford to do so and that urgent and quick adjustments are required for the security of the state. Imagine that the German legislature enacts new legislation designed to prevent a sovereign default, through substantial cuts in social welfare support, including to the unemployment assistance program at issue in *Hartz IV*. Imagine that the parliament also enacts a *constitutional amendment* stating that legislation designed to respond to the national crisis is within the parliament's powers, even if it requires major cuts in social assistance benefits.

Is that hypothetical amendment permissible? Should the Court invalidate such an amendment, as inconsistent with the "social state" guarantees of Article 20, the "human dignity" clause of Article 1, and the "eternity" clause of Article 79?[38] If the Court fails to invalidate such an amendment, is that an intolerable departure from the rule of law? If the Court does invalidate the amendment and determines that the legislation is inconsistent with Germany's obligations as a social state, would that be an intolerable intrusion on democratic self-governance? Would invalidating such an amendment be inconsistent not only with democracy but also with a (sustainable) social state commitment? The possibility of substantive barriers to amendment heightens the import of the questions of how social welfare guarantees are incorporated into constitutions, to which I now return.

## III  Implications: Social welfare provisions and constitutional rigidity

Let me now try to bring some threads together. Social welfare guarantees or rights will continue to be included in many constitutions. The

---

[38] Professor Lawrence Tribe has argued that allowing the judiciary to pass on the merits of amendments to the United States Constitution would unwisely subordinate the amendment process to the legal system it is intended to override, at moments of evident legal disjuncture. See Laurence H. Tribe, *A Constitution We Are Amending: In Defense of a Restrained Judicial Role*, 97 HARV. L. REV. 433 (1983). Yet there are threats in both directions; there are always risks of error in any human process. Adding judicial review to the United States' amendment process, which is a very difficult one, involving supermajorities in Congress and in state ratifications, may risk more error in unduly restricting democratic choice than potential benefits in preventing harm to central principles. In systems where amendment is easier, as in Colombia or India, judicial review of unconstitutional amendments may, in the long run, be democracy enhancing. But surely there are reasons to hesitate to invoke purely substantive review where its exercise would, as on some views of the German eternity clause, entirely foreclose lawful democratic change.

questions that so preoccupied earlier generations of scholarship, whether there is a philosophical basis for social rights, or whether including them is consistent with the purposes and nature of constitutions,[39] are in a sense both answered and mooted by real constitutional events. As Mark Tushnet, among others, has observed, the question now is not so much whether to include social welfare provisions in constitutions, but how.[40]

For these reasons, I do not discuss here many of the objections made to "social" rights in constitutions, for example, based on judiciaries lacking competence to enforce. What I do focus on is the characteristic of social rights as being more of a demand on public resources than other rights – different not in logical character, but in scope, in a way that is qualitatively different – a difference in degree that may be viewed as a difference in kind.

Social rights are ordinarily "positive" in character. To be sure, the divide between positive and negative rights does not neatly track the divide of subject areas. Some classic liberal political and civil rights require affirmative action – and commitment of resources – by the government: for example, voting requires that a state provide the apparatus for voting, while prohibitions on extrajudicial government coercion require the establishment of courts.

But social welfare obligations or social rights impose peculiar burdens, different from those entailed in securing classic liberal rights, because of a combination of factors – most notably the *scale* of the public resource commitment required. As a share of the budget, provisions for social welfare are highly likely to dwarf, many times over, the government expenditures required to vindicate rights of judicial process, or free elections.[41] Not only do social welfare rights contemplate affirmative

---

[39] For an example of this earlier debate, compare, for example, Cass Sunstein, *Against Positive Rights*, in WESTERN RIGHTS? POST-COMMUNIST APPLICATION 225 (András Sajó ed., 1996) (arguing against positive rights in constitutions) *with* Mark Tushnet, *Civil Rights and Social Rights: The Future of the Reconstruction Amendments*, 25 LOYOLA L.A. L. REV. 1207 (1992) (arguing against distinction between affirmative and negative rights); see generally Wictor Osiatynski, *Social and Economic Rights in a New Constitution for Poland*, in WESTERN RIGHTS? POST-COMMUNIST APPLICATION 233 (András Sajó ed., 1996)

[40] See Mark, Tushnet, *A Response to David Landau*, HARV. INT'L L.J., Opinio Juris, http://opiniojuris.org/2012/01/23/hilj_tushnet-responds-to-landau/ (Jan. 23, 2012).

[41] For example, compare the expenditures for courts and federal social welfare benefits in the United States' 2012 federal budget: $2109 billion dollars in "mandatory" benefits, which include primarily Social Security, Medicare, Medicaid and a number of other smaller programs, and a request of $7.3 billion for the entire federal judiciary. For

## III. IMPLICATIONS

action, they do so in a way that is – in most if not all countries – very resource intensive and, relatedly, politically self-entrenching. Government benefits once granted may be extremely difficult, politically, to "take away,"[42] *a fortiori* so when the benefit is understood to be a "constitutional right." Provisions prohibiting amendments, or making amendments very difficult, compound the risks of constitutional or judicial delegitimation on rule-of-law grounds, when applied to social welfare rights that cannot be fulfilled.

A further complication is introduced if one takes into account the interpretive culture. The language of rights, particularly when not qualified by limitations clauses or conditional duties, might be taken to invite forms of absolutism in judicial interpretation.[43] If one has a "right" to health care, then a logical result might be the orders mandating large expenditures for individuals including experimental treatments in other countries, as have emerged for example in Brazil.[44] Or, even if the rights are interpreted more flexibly, once interpreted, there may be institutional reasons or habits for courts to adhere to their own prior rulings, even if circumstances are claimed to differ in ways that justify departures. I will

---

judiciary figures, see www.coburn.senate.gov/public/index.cfm?a=Files.Serve&File_id=24a45972-f9e6-406f-940f-dac2bbbba; for 2012 mandatory benefits payments, see www.gpo.gov/ fdsys/pkg/BUDGET-2012-BUD/pdf/BUDGET-2012-BUD-29.pdf.

[42] For an example of another politically self-entrenching constitutional provision, see INDIA CONST. arts. 330, 334 (providing for reservation of states in legislatures for members of Scheduled Castes and Scheduled Tribes and originally providing that reservations should terminate in 10 years, a time period that every 10 years since has been extended for another 10 years). For a different argument that, as a moral and constitutional matter, governments cannot retreat from the provision of existing levels of benefits, see CECILE FABRE, SOCIAL RIGHTS UNDER THE CONSTITUTION: GOVERNMENT AND THE DECENT LIFE (2000).

[43] Imagine here a stylized version of what I understand to be the Brazilian approaches to the enforcement of a right to health in its constitution: the Court has issued orders directing payment of sometimes very expensive treatments, in other countries, for a single individual. See Octavio Luiz Motta Ferraz, *Social and Economic Rights: Harming the Poor through Social Rights Litigation: Lessons from Brazil*, 59 TEX. L. REV. 1643 (2011); see also César Rodríguez-Garavito, *Beyond the Courtroom: The Impact of Judicial Activism on Socioeconomic Rights in Latin America*, 89 TEX. L. REV. 1669 (2011)

[44] See note 43. Conceptual understandings, for example, of rights as "trumps," protecting particular conduct or freedoms or activities absolutely – see, for example, RONALD DWORKIN, TAKING RIGHTS SERIOUSLY (1977) – may likewise be thought to invite a degree of absolutism in interpretation. For a different conceptual approach to understanding rights that might also be thought to require absolutism of a different sort, see Matthew D. Adler, *Rights against Rules; The Moral Structure of American Constitutional Law*, 97 MICH. L. REV. 1 (1998).

refer to both an "absolutist" view of rights and a strong sense of judicial adherence to past decisions as varieties of "formalism" in this context.[45]

If a formalist interpretive culture coexists with a difficult amendment process, the enforcement of constitutional provisions concerning social welfare benefits raises particular problems for constitutionalism. Because the government's ability to fulfill goals, or rights, of adequate levels of nutrition, housing, education, and health care are expensive, unexpected financial downturns may pose genuine obstacles to their fulfillment. If a court has developed a jurisprudence under which individuals have rights to government expenditures for health care, for example, that were tolerable in good times but impose an increasing share of a stretched national budget in hard times, the following dilemmas may arise.[46]

One possibility is that the Court might retreat from its prior position. It is no secret that constitutional courts operate within constraints and that, as the constraints change, jurisprudence shifts as well. Such a shift would be more readily accepted in a socio-legal setting in which flexibility in interpretation is well accepted. Limitations clauses, or derogability provisions, may signal – or facilitate – the development of such a socio-legal culture. But in a more formalist legal culture, retreating might place the Court in a real dilemma whether to sacrifice the appearance of the rule of law or to sacrifice general well-being (to the extent that reduction in social welfare benefits is in fact consistent with such well-being).

Another possibility is that the Court might adhere to its position, requiring expenditures on positive rights that may be out of proportion to even more basic government functions (such as protection from external attack). Such judicial action might prompt attempts at amendment. If this method of response is blocked, however, either by virtue of very difficult amending provisions or by virtue of the possibility that the Court will protect its own jurisprudence through declarations of unconstitutional amendments, then a strong degree of democratic disempowerment will have occurred.

---

[45] For other categorizations of judicial approaches to the enforcement of rights in the social welfare context, see Mark Tushnet, Weak Rights, Strong Courts (2009); Katharine Young, Constituting Economic and Social Rights (2012).

[46] It is not my claim that the presence of social rights will necessarily entail either form of behavior. Indeed, the likelihood is that most of the time it will not; most courts have a healthy sense of institutional self-preservation and find ways to avoid entering decisions that will make governance impossible or risk defiance. However, I do not think these risks are trivial.

## III. IMPLICATIONS

Under these circumstances, too, there are threats to respect for the rule of law and for the constitutional order itself.

In a more formalist legal culture operating under a constitution that is difficult (or impossible) to amend, this threat to constitutionalism can arguably be mitigated through the form of social welfare provisions that delink government duties from justiciable individual rights. In such circumstances, government duties to advance social welfare *unaccompanied* by individual justiciable rights to social welfare may be the option most consistent with the rule-of-law aspects of constitutionalism, as they may allow more flexibility to governments – consistent with rule-of-law understandings – than would justiciable individual rights.[47]

Government "duties," when phrased in general terms, are rarely understood to be absolute.[48] Traditions of interpretation do not regard them as absolute – in part, in common law systems, claims of breach of duty unaccompanied by claims of breach of right may not be deemed justiciable, leaving interpretation in the hands of political actors. Government duties are often, in effect, interpreted as carrying with them implicit constraints based on resources and deference to executives in prioritizing a range of duties; indeed, this is one of the essential tasks of a good chief executive. The idea of resource constraints as limiting rights, and as requiring prioritization among rights – though by no means unfamiliar – fit less comfortably with some socio-legal traditions.

While many accept that the existence of a "right" implies a correlative duty on some person(s),[49] the converse is not necessarily true: a duty can

---

[47] Should this flexibility be understood as diminishing the constitution's legitimacy insofar as it is grounded in its advancement of or commitment to good and/or just principles? On the one hand, foregoing constitutional articulation of justiciable individual rights to minimal subsistence may be thought a loss toward advancing a just distribution of resources and preventing human misery. On the other hand, if over the medium run, a more flexible approach makes it more likely that government and society will survive to be able to fulfill such human needs, then the more flexible approach might be seen as advancing goodness and/or justice.

[48] *Cf.* ZACKIN, *supra* note 8, at 68–74 (noting that the state constitutions of the United States tend not to provide in so many words for a *right* to public education but instead establish *duties* on the state to provide education, and arguing that these obligation-creating provisions should be regarded as establishing positive rights, albeit with an emphasis on social good rather than individual right).

[49] For a classic exposition, see Wesley Newcomb Hohfeld, *Some Fundamental Legal Conceptions as Applied to Legal Reasoning*, 23 YALE L.J. 16, 30–32 (1913) (describing a "duty" as the "correlative" of a right, in the sense that "if X has a right against Y to stay off the former's land, the correlative (and equivalent) is that Y is under a duty toward X to stay off the place"). Hohfeld's primary concern was to define the legal term "right," by

plainly exist without a correlative individual right.[50] The idea of non-justiciable "duties," as expressed, for example, in the Directive Principles of the Indian Constitution, does not accord with the *Marbury v. Madison* idea that constitutions, as law, must ordinarily be subject to interpretation and enforcement by courts. But it is plain that courts can adjudicate claims about failures to perform duties, as state courts in the United States do and as courts in other common law jurisdictions do as well. Indeed, one might think of the "rights" provisions in constitutions like South Africa's as performing the function of providing standing to sue primarily to enforce – not a breach of right – but a breach of duty. The rights provisions of the South African Constitution have been interpreted primarily as imposing on the government procedural duties of planning, justification, and/or engagement with beneficiary groups, rather than as generating judicially enforceable rights to particular forms of welfare assistance to particular beneficiaries even if it is plain that they do not have access as an individual to means of improving their health,[51] or housing.[52]

The claim I am making is not one, in general, about "rights" as opposed to "duties." It is, rather, a claim about the constitutional valences of "rights" and "duties" in at least some systems, and about the possible effects of a particular form of legal culture in constitutional systems that include justiciable welfare "rights." The suggestion is that, in some legal

---

reference to its "invariable correlative," a duty. *Id.* at 31. Hohfeld suggests that the legal term "right" might be better understood by the word "claim."

[50] An example: the President of the United States has a duty to "take care" that the laws are faithfully executed; yet individuals do not have a claim against the President to enforce this duty, just because it is a duty, unless they can show a personal injury specific to some particular protected right or interest of their own (or, possibly, a specific legislative cause of action is created that provides standing for such an action). Yet the legal duty of the President still exists. A "duty" may be a correlative of a legal "right," without implying that a justiciable "right" is a correlative of a legal duty.

[51] See Soobramoney v. Minister of Health Kwazulu-Natal (12) B.C.L.R. 1696 (S. Afr.).

[52] See Gov't of the Republic of S. Afr. v. Grootboom, (CCT11/00), [2000] ZACC 19 (S. Afr.); Occupiers of 51 Olivia Road v. City of Johannesburg, (CCT 24/07), [2008] ZACC 1 (S. Afr.). *But cf.* Minister of Health v. Treatment Action Campaign, (CCT8/02) [2002] ZACC 15 (S. Afr.) (finding that the government had acted unreasonably in not allowing the drug that prevented transmission of HIV AIDS from mothers to children at birth to be made widely available). This case involved more substantive review: the drug was being provided free of charge, so the resource demands were minimal; the health arguments for allowing the drug to be used were quite substantial; and the arguments against – based on the benefits of controlled testing and management of the drug's administration – were deemed so overwhelmed by the life-saving benefits of the drug as to render the government decision unreasonable.

cultures, certain predictable harms to the rule-of-law aspects of constitutionalism might be avoided by the articulation of those rights, not as individually justiciable "rights," but rather as duties of governments. Those "duties" can be made justiciable, with language that contemplates that the duty is to be pursued "to the extent practicable" or "realizable" consistent with the advancement of other duties and protection of rights.[53]

## Conclusion

The narrow problem under discussion arises from the justiciability of an individual right, capable of being understood in substantive (rather than processual) terms, in ways that could put formalist courts in relatively rigid constitutional systems into a bind in times of unexpected economic decline. In this context, courts may feel caught between rule-of-law demands to vindicate rights, on the one hand, and a felt obligation not to make governance impossible, on the other. Perceived adherence to the rule of law is, however, only one aspect of constitutional legitimacy. And to the extent constitutional provisions on social welfare are more freely amendable or more flexibly interpreted, the net benefit to constitutionalism, of making constitutional social welfare obligations justiciable as individually enforceable rights, may also shift.

Perhaps the most interesting aspect of this small exploration is its suggestion of how interdependent the understandings of one constitutional concept – positive social welfare obligations – may be on other elements of the system. Whether welfare provisions are expressed in terms of rights or duties may matter less than how courts or other actors interpret them. If interpreted in process terms, as in *Grootboom*,[54] "rights" may prove no more a challenge to judicial manageability and institutional legitimacy than "duties." To the extent that "rights" would be given a substantive reading, and read more absolutely, however, there

---

[53] *Cf.* MARK TUSHNET, WEAK COURTS, STRONG RIGHTS 228, 247–64 (2009) (exploring possibilities that "weaker" forms of judicial review are the best ways to protect all rights, including social welfare rights, because they acknowledge possibilities of reasonable disagreement and avoid the perils of unchecked political, or unchecked judicial power). Focusing on government duties more than on individual rights may have a similar effect, even if at times the duties are aggressively enforced, insofar as courts may be more comfortable aggressively enforcing duties, and then retrenching when necessary, than doing so with respect to "rights."

[54] (11) B.C.L.R. 1169.

are risks that may be mitigated by approaches that frame issues around government duties. What this analysis also suggests is that comparing constitutional approaches to social welfare – an area in which constitutional goals, or rights, may be more dependent on the government's resources than other areas of "rights" – must rest not only on a deep understanding of the meaning of constitutional language in practice but also on the rules for constitutional amendment, the culture of amendment, and the interpretive approaches accepted within the legal culture. The "packages" of constitutional meaning and effect are, in this area as in many others, complex and interdependent.

# 6

# Privatizing public rights

## Common law and state action in the United States

HELEN HERSHKOFF[*]

### Introduction

The chapters in this volume reflect a diversity of approaches to the question of the "boundaries of rights" and the positive obligations of state and private actors. As stated, the question appears to rest on two assumptions: that a legal system recognizes legally grounded obligations to provide goods and services – education, housing, and the like – and that these obligations extend to nongovernmental actors as well as to the state. Both of these assumptions run counter to conventional understandings of United States (US) constitutional doctrine. First, the US Supreme Court has consistently interpreted the federal Constitution as affording no right to government-provided assistance of the sort included in many national constitutions adopted after World War II.[1] Second, constitutional rights in the US (other than the right not to be enslaved by another individual)[2] by their terms seem to extend vertically only against "state action" and not horizontally against

---

[*] Herbert M. and Svetlana Wachtell Professor of Constitutional Law and Civil Liberties, New York University School of Law. The Filomen D'Agostino and Max E. Greenberg Research Fund of New York University School of Law provided financial support for this project. The author is grateful to Ioana Bala, Jeffrey R. Bengel, Anthony Mohen, Katherine Elizabeth (Katie) Poor, Annie Vodhanel Preis, Eleanor (Ella) Spottswood, Gregory O. Tuttle, and Ellison Sylvina (Nelly) Ward for research assistance while they were students at New York University School of Law; to Gretchen Feltes and Linda Ramsingh for library research; to Dante DelGiacco for administrative support; and to José Alvarez, Mattias Kumm, Stephen Loffredo, and Ruth Rubio Marin for comments.

[1] See Helen Hershkoff and Stephen Loffredo, *State Courts and Constitutional Socio-Economic Rights: Exploring the Underutilization Thesis*, 115 PENN ST. L. REV. 923, 924–27 (2011).

[2] See U.S. CONST. amend. XIII (abolishing slavery).

private action.³ Although political analysts see sovereignty as dispersed between private and public actors – and so fragmented, diffuse, outsourced, and hybrid⁴ – the US Supreme Court persists in maintaining an "essential dichotomy" between the wrongdoing of government and that of nongovernmental actors, locating the latter outside the boundary of federal-constitutional enforcement.⁵ The state-action divide is pervasive throughout federal-constitutional law and applies not only to individuals deciding whether to invite someone for dinner,⁶ but also to "Alpha Institutions" – Bayless Manning's provocative term⁷ – carrying out government-authorized programs that affect individuals even in intimate matters such as health care.⁸ From the US perspective, it thus seems odd to talk about the boundary of a positive constitutional obligation that does not exist within a legal system that does not recognize constitutional rights outside a narrow sphere of public activity.

Nevertheless, locating the boundaries of rights, especially positive constitutional rights, holds theoretical and practical significance for US law.⁹ The boundary question is particularly important when the government contracts with private companies for the planning, production, and delivery of social goods – a practice known as privatization or outsourcing.¹⁰ In a familiar argument, the public sector enlists privatization because it promises benefits such as efficiency and innovation that are said to be stifled by regulation.¹¹ On the other hand, privatization also creates opportunities for rent seeking that, unchecked, allow private

---

³ See Helen Hershkoff, *"Just Words": Common Law and the Enforcement of State Constitutional Social and Economic Rights*, 62 STAN. L. REV. 1521, 1524 (2010) [hereinafter Hershkoff, "Just Words"].
⁴ See Margherita Poto, *The Principle of Proportionality in Comparative Perspective*, 8 GERMAN L.J. 835, 836 (2007).
⁵ Jackson v. Metro. Edison Co., 419 U.S. 345, 349 (1974).
⁶ See G. Sidney Buchanan, *A Conceptual History of the State Action Doctrine: The Search for Governmental Responsibility*, 34 HOUS. L. REV. 333, 424 & n. 611 (1997).
⁷ Bayless Manning, *Corporate Power and Individual Freedom: Some General Analysis and Particular Reservations*, 55 NW. U. L. REV. 38, 43 (1960) (ascribing to "Alpha Institutions" the features of "centralized control, large scale organization, substantial capital resources and relative independence of formally constituted government").
⁸ See, for example, Blum v. Yaretsky, 457 U.S. 991 (1982).
⁹ See Al Katz, *Studies in Boundary Theory: Three Essays in Adjudication and Politics*, 28 BUFF. L. REV. 383 (1978).
¹⁰ See Mark Aronson, *A Public Lawyer's Responses to Privatisation and Outsourcing*, in THE PROVINCE OF ADMINISTRATIVE LAW 40, 41 (Michael Taggart ed., 1997).
¹¹ See Jack M. Beermann, *Administrative-Law-Like Obligations on Private[ized] Entities*, 49 UCLA L. REV. 1717 (2002).

companies to misuse public power in ways that threaten to dilute service quality, subvert individual rights, and undermine constitutional norms.[12] Even if outsourcing involves goods and services that are not of constitutional dimension, their distribution nevertheless raises questions about procedural regularity and fair treatment that are encompassed within the public-law requirements of due process and equal protection. By placing the activity of government contractors outside the sphere of "state actions,"[13] privatization effectively eliminates constitutional constraints in settings where administrative or common-law remedies may be insufficient to ensure respect for democratic norms.

I approach the boundary question as a matter of US constitutional law, asking whether constitutional norms can play a role in regulating privatization without transforming all private action into state action. I do so from the perspective of subsidiarity and proportionality, two concepts said to be somewhat alien to US legal discourse,[14] and, instead, are associated with judicial practices within the European Union and its relation to member states.[15] By subsidiarity I mean the principle that collective activities should be undertaken, when feasible, through mediating structures that often are located at the local level, with the aim of nourishing democratic politics and preventing "an overcentralization of power."[16] The principle as used here embraces not only local deference but also a "positive dimension" intended to ensure "that the body assigned a particular function be able to carry it out effectively."[17] By proportionality I adopt the definition associated with Robert Alexy of rights conceptualized as "optimization" principles,[18] requiring "the realization of something to the greatest extent possible, given

---

[12] See Warren L. Ratliff, *The Due Process Failure of America's Prison Privatization Statutes*, 21 SETON HALL LEGIS. J. 371, 381 (1997).

[13] See Daphne Barak-Erez, *A State Action Doctrine for an Age of Privatization*, 45 SYRACUSE L. REV. 1169, 1183 (1995).

[14] See George Bermann, *Taking Subsidiarity Seriously: Federalism in the European Community and the United States*, 94 COLUM. L. REV. 331, 403 (1994).

[15] See Treaty on European Union art. 3b, Feb. 7, 1992, 1992 OJ (191) 1.

[16] Reimer von Borries and Malte Hauschild, *Implementing the Subsidiarity Principle*, 5 COLUM. J. EUR. L. 369, 369 (1999); see also Robert K. Vischer, *Subsidiarity as a Principle of Governance: Beyond Devolution*, 35 IND. L. REV. 103, 116 (2001).

[17] Vishcher, *supra* note 16, at 139–40 & n. 148 (quoting Philip J. Chmielewski, *Workers' Participation in the United States: Catholic Social Teaching and Democratic Theory*, 55 REV. SOC. ECON. 487, 498 (1997)).

[18] ROBERT ALEXY, A THEORY OF CONSTITUTIONAL RIGHTS 47 (Julian Rivers trans., 2002).

countervailing concerns."[19] Alexy's definition pitches proportionality at a high level of abstraction, but for present purposes, it has the advantage of subsuming the different versions of proportionality analysis applied by judicial systems around the world,[20] including the specific form of review practiced by the European Court of Human Rights.[21]

Of course, transporting foreign concepts into a domestic legal system inevitably poses danger.[22] Subsidiarity remains an elusive term even outside the US.[23] Moreover, it is easy for a US lawyer to treat subsidiarity simply as an exotic version of the more familiar principle of devolution so that it sounds like US-style federalism and loses its critical bite.[24] Similarly, proportionality analysis sometimes is rendered as a form of balancing no different from that of US interest analysis.[25] However, ignoring commonalities between US and foreign concepts also creates mischief, for it heightens a sense of "American exceptionalism" that may cut off possibilities for reform.[26]

With these disclaimers in hand, I argue that subsidiarity and proportionality add to our understanding of the boundary question in two important but overlooked ways. Above all, subsidiarity shifts the analysis from the center to the periphery, from the preoccupation of US scholars with the federal Constitution to the constitutions of the fifty states that make up "Our Federalism."[27] This change in focus allows for a thicker description of American constitutionalism: we see that positive obligations exist in US law – in state constitutions even if not in

---

[19] Mattias Kumm, *Political Liberalism and the Structure of Rights: On the Place and Limits of the Proportionality Requirement*, in LAW, RIGHTS AND DISCOURSE: THEMES FROM THE LEGAL PHILOSOPHY OF ROBERT ALEXY 7 (G. Pavlakos ed., 2006).

[20] See Vicki C. Jackson, *Being Proportional about Proportionality*, 21 CONST. COMMENT. 803, 806 (2004).

[21] See YUTAKA ARAI-TAKAHASHI, THE MARGIN OF APPRECIATION DOCTRINE AND THE PRINCIPLE OF PROPORTIONALITY IN THE JURISPRUDENCE OF THE ECHR 14–15 (2002).

[22] See, for example, Gunther Teubner, *Legal Irritants: Good Faith in British Law or How Unifying Law Ends Up in New Divergences*, 61 MOD. L. REV. 11, 12 (1998).

[23] See Yishai Blank, *Federalism, Subsidiarity, and the Role of Local Governments in an Age of Global Multilevel Governance*, 37 FORDHAM URB. L.J. 509, 532–48 (2010).

[24] See Thomas C. Fischer, *"Federalism" in the European Community and the United States: A Rose by Any Other Name ...*, 17 FORDHAM INT'L L.J. 389, 424 (1994).

[25] But see Jackson, *supra* note 20, at 833 (distinguishing proportionality analysis from "the crude balancing of costs and benefits associated, unfavorably, with balancing in the U.S. tradition").

[26] See Helen Hershkoff, *Horizontality and the "Spooky" Doctrines of American Law*, 59 BUFF. L. REV. 455, 506 (2011) [hereinafter Hershkoff, *Horizontality and the "Spooky" Doctrines*].

[27] Younger v. Harris, 401 U.S. 37, 44 (1971) (internal quotation marks deleted).

the federal.[28] In addition, proportionality likewise brings new possibilities into view. By treating rights as optimization principles, proportionality analysis enables courts to extend public norms into nongovernmental settings by reorienting discrete social relations in the light of constitutional values. In contrast, the federal Constitution's state-action doctrine takes an "all-or-nothing" approach to constitutional enforcement,[29] applying constitutional obligations "full-blast" to government actors or not at all.[30] Not surprisingly, many commentators oppose expanding the federal state-action doctrine to reach private law out of concern that constitutionalization will undermine private autonomy and dilute public rights.[31] In contrast, far from maintaining a strict separation of common-law doctrines from constitutional norms, some state courts in the US enlist constitutional provisions – even state-constitutional positive-rights provisions – when deciding disputes involving nongovernmental actors; they do so by applying an interpretive process that comports with the principle of proportionality and achieves constitutional enforcement indirectly in the horizontal position.[32]

To preview, my proposal builds on a concept of shared responsibility and assumes that constitutional requirements apply to the outsourcing relationship, but that their content and scope differ depending on whether public or private actors are in play. Within the scheme that I put forward, both the public and the private actors have constitutional obligations, but of differing scope and to different extent. Relative to the status quo and to other reforms that have been proposed in the literature

---

[28] See Hershkoff and Loffredo, *supra* note 1, at 924.
[29] Gillian E. Metzger, *Private Delegations, Due Process, and the Duty to Supervise*, in GOVERNMENT BY CONTRACT: OUTSOURCING AND AMERICAN DEMOCRACY 291, 296 (Jody Freeman and Martha Minow eds., 2009).
[30] Frank I. Michelman, *The Bill of Rights, the Common Law, and the Freedom-Friendly State*, 58 U. MIAMI L. REV. 401, 429 (2003); *see* Barbara Kritchevsky, *Civil Rights Liability of Private Entities*, 26 CARDOZO L. REV. 35, 36 (2004).
[31] See, for example, Lillian BeVier and John Harrison, *The State Action Principle and Its Critics*, 96 VA. L. REV. 1767, 1785 (2010); *but see* Du Plessis v. De Klerk 1996 (5) BCLR 658 at para 120 (S. Afr.) (characterizing as "nonsense" the view "that so-called direct horizontality will result in an Orwellian society in which the all-powerful state will control all private relationships") (Kriegler, J., dissenting).
[32] See Helen Hershkoff, Lecture, *The Private Life of Public Rights: State Constitutions and the Common Law*, 88 N.Y.U. L. REV. ONLINE 1 (2013) [hereinafter, Hershkoff, *The Private Life*]; *see also* Helen Hershkoff, *State Common Law and the Dual Enforcement of Constitutional Norms*, in NEW FRONTIERS OF STATE CONSTITUTIONAL LAW: DUAL ENFORCEMENT OF NORMS 151, 151 (James A. Gardner and Jim Rossi eds., 2011) [hereinafter, Hershkoff, *State Common Law*].

about state action, the liability scheme has the advantage of encouraging transparency, promoting accountability, and nourishing constitutional norms while nevertheless remaining sensitive to private interests. Admittedly, the US Supreme Court is not likely to embrace the proposal. Yet the ideas could have traction in encouraging the adoption of discrete contractual terms or the enactment of administrative regulations for particular outsourced relations. Facilitating normative "boundary crossing" between the private and the public in nonjudicial settings is an attractive feature of the proposal.

## I  Positive obligations and American law: Subsidiarity and state constitutions

The standard account of American constitutionalism emphasizes the almost total absence of socioeconomic rights from US law, a view that focuses exclusively – even obsessively – on the federal Constitution. Justice William O. Douglas stated the principle in its broadest terms: "[t]he Bill of Rights does not say ... what government must give, but rather what it may not take away."[33] On this view, American constitutionalism is neutral with respect to substantive policy: the federal Constitution sets out the machinery of governance and identifies a handful of "negative" rights that provide individuals with shields against government overreaching, but leaves to ordinary politics such questions as whether to provide individuals with health insurance, public schooling, or income support during old age. Despite President Franklin Delano Roosevelt's call for a Second Bill of Rights that would guarantee the right to a job, to a decent home, to adequate medical care, and to a good education,[34] federal-constitutional law protects property and the right to contract, but otherwise excludes rights to socioeconomic goods, and the US Supreme Court so far has declined to impose affirmative obligations on the states and national government.[35]

Commentators thus locate the federal Constitution ideologically among those libertarian documents that emphasize negative liberty and

---

[33] Barsky v. Bd. of Regents, 347 U.S. 422, 472–73 (1954).
[34] See Franklin D. Roosevelt, "Unless There is Security Here at Home, There Cannot Be Lasting Peace in the World"—Message to the Congress on the State of the Union, 13 Pub. Papers 32, 41 (Jan. 11, 1944).
[35] See Stephen Loffredo, *Poverty, Inequality, and Class in the Structural Constitutional Law Course*, 34 FORDHAM URB. L.J. 1239, 1243 (2007).

an anti-statist approach to government responsibility.[36] However, describing American constitutionalism as devoid of affirmative commitment rests on an incomplete version of US law. From the perspective of subsidiarity, the legal scene is understood to be much more complex, for it includes the constitutional values of the centralized authority as well as those of the peripheral states. The federal Constitution comprises only a part of the American constitutional system; every state in the US has its own constitution and many of these state constitutions, even those adopted in the eighteenth century, include provisions that deal with socioeconomic obligations such as free public schools and public hospitals.[37] Although state constitutions differ one from the other, some generalizations are possible. Every state constitution refers to public education.[38] Some regulate occupational safety and welfare payments, the right to join a union or not to join a union, child labor, and conditions in mines and other dangerous occupations.[39] Some state courts treat state-constitutional socioeconomic provisions as justiciable claims; in these systems, courts deploy forms of judicial review that differ from those of the federal courts but share similarities with those of courts abroad that likewise function within a constitutional framework of affirmative obligation.[40] Still other state-constitutional provisions clarify that the common law is subject to state-constitutional constraint – reversing the "Lochnerian" view that the state constitution is subordinate to the common law.[41] The presence of these socioeconomic provisions has led some commentators to argue that state constitutions not only complement but also "complete" the federal Constitution by extending affirmative rights and imposing correlative duties

---

[36] See, for example, David S. Law and Mila Versteeg, *The Evolution and Ideology of Global Constitutionalism*, 99 CAL. L. REV. 1163, 1170, 1230 (2011).
[37] See generally Helen Hershkoff, *Positive Rights and State Constitutions: The Limits of Federal Rationality Review*, 112 HARV. L. REV. 1131 (1999).
[38] See Shannon K. McGovern, Note, *A New Model for States as Laboratories for Reform: How Federalism Informs Education Policy*, 86 N.Y.U. L. REV. 1519, 1529–30 (2011).
[39] See Hershkoff, *"Just Words," supra* note 3, at 1524. See also Helen Hershkoff, *Transforming Legal Theory in the Light of Practice: The Judicial Application of Social and Economic Rights to Private Orderings*, in COURTING SOCIAL JUSTICE: JUDICIAL ENFORCEMENT OF SOCIAL AND ECONOMIC RIGHTS IN THE DEVELOPING WORLD 268 (Varun Gauri and Daniel M. Brinks eds., 2008); Malcolm Langford, *The Justiciability of Social Rights: From Practice to Theory*, in SOCIAL RIGHTS JURISPRUDENCE: EMERGING TRENDS IN INTERNATIONAL AND COMPARATIVE LAW 3, 17–21 (Malcolm Langford ed., 2009).
[40] See Hershkoff and Loffredo, *supra* note 1, 945–55.
[41] See Lochner v. New York, 198 U.S. 45 (1905).

on government.⁴² At the least, they motivate questions about the scope of US constitutionalism and the location of socioeconomic commitments in the legal system as a whole.

Subsidiarity thus draws attention to aspects of the American constitutional tradition that frequently are eclipsed by federal doctrine. Still, one might question whether introducing subsidiarity into the discussion adds anything; US-style federalism, whether cast as "dual,"⁴³ "cooperative,"⁴⁴ or "polyphonic,"⁴⁵ already stands for a devolutionary principle that invites us to "think local" and protects states and localities as distinct spaces for innovative policy and lawmaking.⁴⁶ Subsidiarity differs from conventional understandings of federalism that make it significant to the argument of this chapter.⁴⁷ Many commentators view US federalism as something of an empty vessel: it assumes the existence of states, but imposes few obligations on them outside the federal negative-rights framework. From this perspective, nothing in the federal Constitution obligates states to undertake socioeconomic commitments, and no principle of federalism requires that power be devolved for welfarist purposes. Nor is there a constitutional requirement that states use their power to meet the socioeconomic needs of state residents. To the contrary, US federalism, like the national Constitution, protects only what one commentator has called the states' "negative autonomy" against federal encroachment.⁴⁸

This is where subsidiarity alters the focus and puts forward somewhat different normative demands. By contrast to US federalism, subsidiarity introduces a "positive" dimension into the story, for it assumes not only the devolution of responsibility to constitutive units but also cooperation

---

⁴² See Donald S. Lutz, *The United States Constitution as an Incomplete Text*, 496 ANNALS AM. ACAD. POL. & SOC. SCI. 23 (1988); *but see* Daniel B. Rodriguez, *State Constitutional Failure*, 2011 U. ILL. L. REV. 1243, 1254 (2011).

⁴³ See, for example, United States v. Lopez, 514 U.S. 549, 567–68 (1995).

⁴⁴ See, for example, John Kincaid, *From Cooperative to Coercive Federalism*, 509 ANNALS AM. ACAD. POL. & SOC. SCI. 139 (1990).

⁴⁵ See, for example, ROBERT A. SCHAPIRO, POLYPHONIC FEDERALISM: TOWARD THE PROTECTION OF FUNDAMENTAL RIGHTS (2009).

⁴⁶ See Helen Hershkoff, *Welfare Devolution and State Constitutions*, 67 FORDHAM L. REV. 1403, 1405 (1999); *see* New State Ice Co. v. Liebmann, 285 U.S. 262, 311 (1932) (Brandeis, J., dissenting).

⁴⁷ Whether one can speak of a conventional approach to federalism is itself contested. See, for example, Denis J. Edwards, *Fearing Federalism's Failure: Subsidiarity in the European Union*, 44 AM. J. COMP. L. 537, 539 (1996).

⁴⁸ Blank, *supra* note 23, at 526.

among the constitutive parts if devolved units are not able to produce the benefits that the theory assumes.[49] Just as the centralized authority cannot usurp functions that are assigned to states and localities, so the centralized authority cannot abstain from action when devolved units are unable to achieve assigned goals. Paolo G. Carozza thus calls subsidiarity "a somewhat paradoxical principle. It limits the state, yet empowers and justifies it. It limits intervention, yet requires it."[50] On this view, subsidiarity not only encourages a thicker description of American constitutional law by including state positive obligations in the picture but also raises normative questions about the obligations of the national government if the states or smaller entities are not able or are unwilling to meet positive obligations. I do not mean to suggest that subsidiarity introduces normative demands that could not also be supported by federalism – only that the US Supreme Court overall does not yet share this vision.[51]

## II  Proportionality and common-law decision making

The standard account of American constitutionalism further assumes that the federal Constitution reaches only state action, not private action, so that common-law doctrines are beyond constitutional reach. Although there are exceptions – most notably the Court's treatment of the judicial enforcement of racial covenants in *Shelley v. Kraemer* and of libel actions in *New York Times v. Sullivan*[52] – the general rule has been a staple of federal-constitutional law at least since the *Civil Rights Cases*,[53] involving Congress's power to enact the Civil Rights of 1875.[54] Invalidating the statute as outside the enforcement power of the Fourteenth Amendment,

---

[49] *Id.* at 542.
[50] Paolo G. Carozza, *Subsidiarity as a Structural Principle of International Human Rights Law*, 97 AM. J. INT'L L. 38, 44 (2003).
[51] The argument resembles Laurence H. Tribe's attempt to incorporate affirmative rights within the US Supreme Court's federalism jurisprudence. See Laurence H. Tribe, *Unraveling National League of Cities: The New Federalism and Affirmative Rights to Essential Government Services*, 90 HARV. L. REV. 1065, 1076 (1977). For an associated view of federalism as a doctrine of government empowerment, see the writings of Erwin Chemerinsky, including *The Assumptions of Federalism*, 58 STAN. L. REV. 1763 (2006); *Reconceptualizing Federalism*, 50 N.Y.L. SCH. L. REV. 729 (2006); *Empowering States When It Matters*, 69 BROOK. L. REV. 1313 (2004); and *The Values of Federalism*, 47 FLA. L. REV. 499 (1995).
[52] See Shelley v. Kraemer, 334 U.S. 1 (1948); New York Times v. Sullivan, 376 U.S. 254 (1964).
[53] 109 U.S. 3 (1883).   [54] 8 Stat. 335 (1875).

the Court explained that the "[i]ndividual invasion of individual rights" is not subject to the amendment, which was interpreted as only "prohibitory upon the States."[55] Private wrongs can be redressed by a state's common law, the Court observed, but they do not acquire a constitutional dimension unless "sanctioned in some way by the State, or ... done under State authority."[56]

Over the years, the Court has adapted the state-action doctrine to bring within the constitutional sphere certain private activity that is attributed to the government. The public-attribution test is narrow and, so far, has been applied only when the state has delegated a "traditionally exclusive government function" to the private actor,[57] or the government has participated closely with the private actor or compelled or coerced the private actor in the victim's deprivation of rights.[58] In these contexts, the Court has justified treating the private actor as public given the "sufficiently close nexus" between the challenged action and government power.[59] Although a private entity's exercise of a power or privilege conferred by law satisfies the under-color-of-law requirement for federal civil-rights statutes, it does not automatically translate into state action for constitutional purposes.[60] However, once private action crosses the border into that of state action, it is subject to the full force of constitutional regulation. The entrenched nature of the public-private divide in American constitutional law often is traced to the Court's unwillingness to subject private actors to constitutional enforcement on the same terms as it would government actors, out of concern that extending rights would lead to rights dilution, to a loss of individual autonomy, and to undue interference with state sovereignty.[61]

The principle of proportionality points to an alternative approach to constitutional enforcement that elides the binary aspect of the state-action doctrine and avoids the problems that lifting the restriction might produce. Proportionality, as originally put forth by the German Constitutional Court, conceptualizes constitutional rights as optimization principles that are to be realized more or less, given the facts and circumstances of the dispute at hand.[62] As Robert Alexy, its chief

---

[55] The Civil Rights Cases, 109 U.S. at 10–11 (1883).   [56] *Id.* at 17.
[57] See Jackson v. Metro. Edison Co., 419 U.S. 345 (1974).
[58] See, for example, Shelley v. Kraemer, 334 U.S. 1 (1948).
[59] American Mfrs. Mut. Ins. Co. v. Sullivan, 526 U.S. 40, 52 (1999).
[60] See Lugar v. Edmondson Oil Co., 457 U.S. 922, 935 n. 18 (1982).
[61] See Hershkoff, *"Just Words," supra* note 3, at 1571–82.
[62] See Hershkoff, *Horizontality and the "Spooky" Doctrines, supra* note 26, 467–69.

## II. PROPORTIONALITY AND COMMON-LAW DECISION MAKING 139

exponent, explains, the aim of proportionality analysis is to determine "the appropriate degree of satisfaction of one principle relative to the requirements of another principle."[63] Some US state courts use an interpretive practice in their common-law decision making that strongly resembles variations of proportionality analysis by courts abroad; even in states that formally adhere to the federal state-action doctrine,[64] these state courts rely on constitutional provisions, including state-constitutional positive-rights provisions, when deciding common-law disputes involving only nongovernmental actors and private-law relations.[65] To use the language of Alexy's proportionality analysis, these state-judicial decisions seek to optimize constitutional norms in private settings taking account of countervailing concerns associated with private life. For example, the New Jersey Supreme Court has interpreted the state's Constitution to comprise a public-policy exception to the common-law at-will employment rule, so that private employers, not covered by a statutory discrimination ban, nevertheless are barred from engaging in gender-based discrimination.[66] The decision effectively extends constitutional norms of fair and equal treatment into areas of social life considered private and beyond constitutional regulation. A focus on federal-constitutional doctrine, insisting that constitutional norms have no role to play in private-law decision making, obscures this established state-judicial practice.

Indeed, the practice of indirect constitutional enforcement is an open secret among US state-court judges who candidly acknowledge the common law as a site for the articulation and development of public norms. Judith S. Kaye, former Chief Justice of the New York Court of Appeals, has described "a common law infused with constitutional values" in which "constitutional values—especially the values so meticulously set out in our lengthy state charters— ... enrich the common law."[67]

---

[63] Robert Alexy, *The Construction of Constitutional Rights*, 4 LAW & ETHICS HUM. RTS. 20, 21–22 (2010).
[64] The federal state-action doctrine does not apply to state courts, which may, consistent with their constitutions, choose to extend constitutional provisions to the actions of nongovernmental actors. See Hershkoff, *"Just Words,"* supra note 3, at 1524.
[65] This argument has been developed in prior writings; see titles collected in Hershkoff, supra notes 3, 32, 37, and 39.
[66] See, for example, Velantzas v. Colgate-Palmolive Co., Inc., 109 N.J. 189, 536 A.2d 237 (N.J. 1988); see also Helen Hershkoff, *The New Jersey Constitution: Positive Rights, Common Law Entitlements, and State Action*, 69 ALB. L. REV. 553, 556 (2006).
[67] Judith S. Kaye, *Foreword: The Common Law and State Constitutional Law as Full Partners in the Protection of Individual Rights*, 23 RUTGERS L.J. 727, 738, 743 (1992).

A number of straightforward common-law doctrines illustrate this state-court practice, which effectively recognizes the applicability of constitutional provisions in the horizontal position. In addition to the public-policy tort, common-law doctrines such as the implied covenant of good faith, "just cause" contractual provisions, and the property-law distinction between trespasser and invited guest serve as pathways for the application of constitutional norms to private disputes. These cases involve not only "horizontal" rights, such as the jury right, affecting the relation of individual to government, but also "vertical" rights, such as the right to privacy or fair treatment, affecting the relation of individual to individual in a social space that may plausibly be understood as private.[68]

As with subsidiarity, one might ask whether introducing the "foreign" concept of proportionality adds anything to the discussion of American constitutional doctrine not otherwise available through the lens of balancing.[69] Although balancing is a recognized and pervasive feature of US constitutional practice,[70] commentary places proportionality analysis outside the American mainstream – in the specific sense of limiting constitutional enforcement to state action. As Moshe Cohen-Eliya and Iddo Porat explain, distinguishing American constitutional balancing from that of German proportionality analysis:

> [U]nlike the American reading of the Constitution, the German Constitutional Court has ruled that constitutional rights apply indirectly also in the context of relations between individuals; namely, the interpretation of the rules of private law should be in line with the values of the constitution—the *Drittwirkung* doctrine. The American Constitution, on the other hand, is not interpreted as granting rights protection to individuals in their relations with other individuals, but only to individuals vis-à-vis the state.[71]

The lens of proportionality analysis brings into focus a judicial practice indigenous to US law that does not simply balance interests internal to the private law, but rather explicitly interprets private-law rules in ways

---

[68] See, for example, Hershkoff, *"Just Words,"* supra note 3, at 1559–63 (discussing the tort of wrongful discharge).

[69] See, for example, Alec Stone Sweet and Jud Mathews, *Proportionality Balancing and Global Constitutionalism*, 47 COLUM. J. TRANSNAT'L L. 72, 87–96 (2008).

[70] See T. Alexander Aleinikoff, *Constitutional Law in the Age of Balancing*, 96 YALE L.J. 943, 944 (1987).

[71] Moshe Cohen-Eliya and Iddo Porat, *The Hidden Foreign Law Debate in Heller: The Proportionality Approach in American Constitutional Law*, 16 SAN DIEGO L. REV. 367, 407 (2009).

that consider and seek to optimize constitutional rights. When state courts construct "a common law infused with constitutional values," public values do not stay cabined within the constitutional sphere, as the federal state-action doctrine presumes, but instead they inform and reorient private-law doctrines to reach nongovernmental action in ways that the federal model does not predict or recognize.[72] Nevertheless, private law does not become constitutionalized or eclipsed by public-law doctrines.[73] To provide an example, state courts have considered whether a property owner's common-law right to exclude uninvited guests trumps a state-constitutional provision allowing citizens to solicit signatures for political change. Ordering a property owner to permit access for this purpose, a state judge explained that a state court is required to "observe constitutional principles as much as a legislative or administrative body," and this requirement affects common-law as well as constitutional decision making, although to different degrees and in different ways.[74] Public law thus altered the boundary of a private relationship, but the relationship remained private and subject to common-law principles, with the court treating public norms as permissible justifications in reaching a private-law decision.[75] In such cases, the rules of decision are those of the private law reoriented in the light of public values; private law does not collapse into public law.[76]

## III Outsourcing, state action, and shared responsibility

In this section, I cross the boundary from US state-court practice to US federal-court practice and try to apply the lessons of subsidiarity and proportionality to the federal doctrine of state action as it relates to government outsourcing and the problems of diffused sovereignty.

---

[72] But see Hershkoff, *Horizontality and the "Spooky" Doctrines*, supra note 26, at 457.
[73] See, for example, Potvin v. Metro. Life. Ins. Co., 997 P.2d 1153 (Cal. 2000).
[74] Lloyd Corp. v. Whiffen, 773 P.2d 1294, 1297 (Or. 1989), discussed in Hershkoff, *The Private Life*, supra note 32, at 8–10; Hershkoff, *State Common Law*, supra note 32, at 162.
[75] See Richard H. Pildes, *Avoiding Balancing: The Role of Exclusionary Reasons in Constitutional Law*, 45 HASTINGS L J. 711, 712 (1994).
[76] Olha O. Cherednychenko distinguishes between horizontal effect in which private law is subordinate to public law or complementary to it. *See* Olha O. Cherednychenko, *Fundamental Rights and Private Law: A Relationship of Subordination or Complementarity?*, 3 UTRECHT L. REV. 1, 3 (2007); see also Olha O. Cherednychenko, *Subordinating Contract Law to Fundamental Rights: Toward a Major Breakthrough or towards Walking in Circles?*, in CONSTITUTIONAL VALUES AND EUROPEAN CONTRACT LAW 35 (Stefan Grundmann ed., 2008).

Critics cast privatization as an alternative to government that undermines democratic norms and accountability; a significant question often asked is whether a particular government function, such as policing or military operations, may be given over to private actors without undermining sovereign integrity.[77] Proponents of privatization suggest that the practice not only can achieve efficiencies but also can enhance public values by facilitating their extension through contractual terms and administrative regulation.[78] From this latter perspective, the issue is how best to design accountability mechanisms that are adapted to the hybrid, collaborative nature of the outsourced relation, recognizing that the interactions do not align with the post–World War II conception of an empowered state committed to the direct provision of social goods.

The US state-action doctrine has remained largely impervious to the interactions of public and private actors carrying out regulatory programs; it persists in drawing a binary distinction between public and private. The private contractor performing an outsourced activity remains a nonstate actor and is immune from constitutional liability; the government entity is relieved of constitutional liability and is not liable for the contractor's misdeeds even if they would violate the Constitution when carried out by the government. A limited exception applies to contractors who run prisons, because the government has an affirmative obligation to provide goods and services in this setting (although even here federal-constitutional remedies do not inevitably attach to the contractor's rights violations).[79]

Commentators differ on whether the status quo is normatively attractive. The theory of privatization assumes that cost savings and innovations will be derived from the contracting out of regulatory functions; adding layers of constitutional oversight to the outsourced relation arguably removes flexibility and increases expense. However, when it comes to constitutional rights, there is no reason to assume that private contractors, subject only to market forces, will act in the public interest.[80]

---

[77] See Paul R. Verkuil, OUTSOURCING SOVEREIGNTY: WHY PRIVATIZATION OF GOVERNMENT FUNCTIONS THREATENS DEMOCRACY AND WHAT WE CAN DO ABOUT IT (2007).

[78] See, for example, Jody Freeman, *Extending Public Law Norms through Privatization*, 116 HARV. L. REV. 1285 (2003).

[79] Compare West v. Atkins, 487 U.S. 42, 50–54 (1988) (liability), *with* Correctional Services Corp. v. Malesko, 534 U.S. 61, 69–70 (2001) and Minneci v. Pollard, 132 S. Ct. 617 (2012) (no liability).

[80] See Erwin Chemerinsky, *Rethinking State Action*, 80 NW. U. L. REV. 503, 511 (1985) [hereinafter Chemerinsky, *Rethinking State Action*].

## III. OUTSOURCING

To the contrary, rights enforcement may be expensive, and outsourcing creates perverse incentives that tilt toward rights violation: even if the government monitors its contractors, its focus will be on cost control, not rights protection.[81] As one critic has explained, "the current monitoring system, rather than providing a check against private misconduct, may actually encourage it by rewarding those companies that operate on the cheap and devote fewer resources to civil rights protection."[82] Indeed, it may be politically expedient for the government to remain ignorant of its contractors' wrongdoing;[83] elected officials may choose to ignore constitutional violations if those wrongs are politically beneficial. At best, the government's response is messy.[84]

Commentators who raise concerns about privatization have offered a variety of reforms: these vary from tort and contract remedies directed against the private contractors,[85] to enhanced administrative oversight,[86] to a combination of contractual and administrative approaches.[87] Some have urged eliding the question of whether state action is present and focusing instead on balancing the interests of the parties to determine whether constitutional norms ought to apply.[88] Others would expand the government's liability under a negligence version of *respondeat superior* for the wrongful acts of private contractors; under this approach, a court would take account of the government's supervision of its employees through institutional mechanisms such as training programs and hiring

---

[81] See Lawrence Rosenthal, *A Theory of Governmental Damages Liability: Torts, Constitutional Torts, and Takings*, 9 U. PA. J. CONST. L. 797, 856 (2007).

[82] Richard Frankel, *Regulating Privatized Government through § 1983*, 76 U. CHI. L. REV. 1449, 1500 (2009); *cf.* Alan O. Sykes, *The Economics of Vicarious Liability*, 93 YALE L.J. 1231, 1246 (1984).

[83] See Frankel, *supra* note 82, at 1500.

[84] See Daryl J. Levinson, *Making Government Pay: Markets, Politics, and the Allocation of Constitutional Costs*, 67 U. CHI. L. REV. 345, 354–57 (2000).

[85] See, for example, Paul R. Verkuil, *Privatizing Due Process*, 57 ADMIN. L. REV. 963 (2005).

[86] See, for example, Michele Estrin Gilman, *Legal Accountability in an Era of Privatized Welfare*, 89 CAL. L. REV. 569, 625–31 (2001).

[87] See, for example, Laura A. Dickinson, *Public Law Values in a Privatized World*, 31 YALE J. INT'L L. 383, 401–23 (2006).

[88] See, for example, Chemerinsky, *Rethinking State Action*, *supra* note 80, at 506; Thomas G. Quinn, *State Action: A Pathology and a Proposed Cure*, 64 CAL. L. REV. 146, 155 (1976). See also Robert J. Glennon, Jr. and John E. Nowak, *A Functional Analysis of the Fourteenth Amendment "State Action" Requirement*, 1976 SUP. CT. REV. 221, 226–27 (1976); Michael L. Wells, *Identifying State Actors in Constitutional Litigation: Reviving the Role of Substantive Context*, 26 CARDOZO L. REV. 99, 100 (2004).

and firing decisions.[89] Relatedly, some urge holding the government accountable when it delegates power to private entities but fails to effectuate adequate supervision; on this view, the government's granting of a benefit to the private actor constitutes state action, but it is the absence of constraint that gives rise to the constitutional violation.[90]

Overall, the proposals attempt either to constrain ex ante the government's delegation of power to a private actor or to remediate ex post the contractor's failure to comply with public norms. But outsourcing is a hybrid; by its very design, the relationship involves a "diffusion of power [that] carries with it a diffusion of accountability" making it difficult for the public to assess performance and compliance.[91] The practice does not cleanly map onto existing doctrinal categories of public or private in US constitutional law. Treating the government as responsible for the private company's constitutional torts makes it seem as if the company is a federal agency carrying out its job, when in fact it is a private actor securing an important private benefit at public expense but acting under very different incentives. A regime of exclusive government liability, even based on a failure to supervise delegated power, shields the private contractor from public view. Similarly, treating the private company as subject only to contractual or tort liability ignores and even conceals the role of government in the outsourced relation. A change in the law that replicates the binary quality of the existing state-action doctrine by imposing public remedies on the government or private remedies on the contractor may tend inadvertently to obscure rather than to clarify, for it creates the illusion that the government is carrying out regulatory programs when in fact a private actor is doing so.

Subsidiarity and proportionality offer a perspective that helps to reframe the state-action inquiry and better meets the problems of the private contractor who may be irresponsible, inefficient, or insolvent yet

---

[89] See Larry Kramer and Alan O. Sykes, *Municipal Liability under § 1983: A Legal and Economic Analysis*, 1987 SUP. CT. REV. 249, 283.

[90] Barbara Rook Snyder, *Private Motivation, State Action and the Allocation of Responsibility for Fourteenth Amendment Violations*, 75 CORNELL L. REV. 1052, 1076 (1990). Gillian E. Metzger has further developed this approach in her discussion of privatization as delegation. See Metzger, *supra* note 29.

[91] Free Enter. Fund v. Public Co. Accounting Oversight Bd., 561 U.S. 477 (2010) (citing The Federalist No. 72, p. 487 and No. 70, at p. 487 (J. Cooke ed., 1961) (A. Hamilton)). See also Harold J. Krent, *Federal Power, Non-Federal Actors: The Ramifications of Free Enterprise Fund*, 79 FORDHAM L. REV. 2425, 2427–28 (2011); Jack M. Beermann, *Privatization and Political Accountability*, 28 FORDHAM URB. L.J. 1507, 1516 (2001).

is authorized, empowered, and implicitly encouraged to violate constitutional rights through its contractual relation with the government. My proposal assumes that both the public actor and the private actor should be on the constitutional hook but for different substantive reasons. From the public perspective, the government's failure (as Gillian Metzger has argued)[92] derives from its inadequate structuring of the delegated activity leading to negligent training, insufficient supervision, or poor controls. From the private perspective, the contractor's failure involves its misuse of power conferred – the violation of a clearly established constitutional right that forms an implicit term of any contractual relationship with the government. The proposal avoids problems that might arise from attempting to apportion responsibility between a private actor and a public actor for constitutional harm and should not be confused with a theory of proportionate liability that reduces each defendant's liability relative to the others; the proposal instead recognizes the separate responsibility of each actor for separate constitutional harms arising under different substantive theories. Nor will the proposal impose on either defendant a share of damages larger than its own fault given the public and private actors' responsibility for different constitutional harms.

Extending the reach of constitutional requirements to a private contractor in this setting will not implicate autonomy objections frequently invoked to justify a rigid division between the public and private spheres; a private company in an outsourced relation, even if not on the scale of an "Alpha Institution," is not a principal, or exclusively a principal, entitled to pursue its own interest; it is instead an agent of public power with delegated authority for a specific regulatory goal.[93] Moreover, we should not assume that imposing constitutional liability will result in a dilution of rights. To the contrary, if we regard constitutional rights as principles to be optimized in discrete settings, then it follows that the scope of the constitutional right will turn on such factors as the nature of the violator and the competing interests that are at stake. Proportionality clarifies that subjecting the private contractor to constitutional constraint does not mean treating it the same as a government agency. But it does require assigning public and not simply private-law liability when contractual agents carry out government policy.

---

[92] See generally Metzger, *supra* note 29.
[93] See BeVier and Harrison, *supra* note 31, at 1785.

Finally, the proposed reform is consistent with the Court's own reasoning in the *Civil Rights Cases*.[94] In declining to subject private actors in those cases to regulation under the Fourteenth Amendment, the Court emphasized that the barrier to relief was not the defendant's private status, but rather the limited scope of the constitutional right: the Fourteenth Amendment aims to correct state laws "*adverse* to the rights of the citizen" and no such adverse action was found to be present.[95] In other words, as Mark Tushnet has explained, whether state action exists depends on the "applicable substantive constitutional law,"[96] and not the private or public status of the defendant. My proposal thus builds on the premise that in the outsourcing relationship, a constitutional duty exists that applies to both the government and the private actor, but recognizes – consistent with the principle of proportionality – that the substantive law, say, of equal protection or of due process, differs when applied to a private contractor than when applied to a government official and turns on factors that are context specific.[97]

## Conclusion

A half century ago, Professor Wolfgang G. Friedmann of the Columbia Law School called for a "new synthesis" of public and private thinking, observing that "the jurisprudence of this country is badly lagging in the elaboration of the proper blend of public and private law principles."[98] US jurisprudence has continued to lag in developing theories of constitutional liability when governance involves the mixed activity of public agencies and private contractors. Liability for constitutional torts persists in mapping onto private-law concepts of causation and responsibility, but the Court has declined to ask whether these private-law

---

[94] 109 U.S. 3 (1883).
[95] See Harold W. Horowitz, *The Misleading Search for "State Action" under the Fourteenth Amendment*, 30 S. Cal. L. Rev. 208, 212 (1956–57), quoting The Civil Rights Cases, 109 U.S. 3, 13 (1883); *cf.* also Larry Alexander, *The Public/Private Distinction and Constitutional Limits on Private Power*, 10 Const. Comment. 361, 372 (1993).
[96] Mark Tushnet, *Shelley v. Kraemer and Theories of Equality*, 33 N.Y.L. Sch. L. Rev. 383, 383 (1988).
[97] *Cf.* Wells, *supra* note 88, at 99, 123.
[98] W.G. Friedmann, *Public and Private Law Thinking: The Need for Synthesis*, 5 Wayne L. Rev. 291, 300 (1958–59). See also Adolf A. Berle, Jr., *Constitutional Limitations on Corporate Activity—Protection of Personal Rights from Invasion through Economic Power*, 100 U. Pa. L. Rev. 933, 942 (1952).

## CONCLUSION

doctrines are suitable to the task; at the same time, the Court has effectively insulated these private-law doctrines from constitutional scrutiny. Moreover, public law has remained largely impervious to private-law developments that allow redress despite indeterminate causation or indeterminate defendants.[99] Through such approaches as market-share liability,[100] risk-contribution liability,[101] enterprise liability,[102] proportional-share liability,[103] and alternative liability,[104] tort law as applied to private-market actors has adapted to changes in social and economic conditions in ways that are nowhere evident in the law of constitutional torts.

The concepts of subsidiarity and proportionality open up new possibilities for designing a liability regime that takes account of changing notions of the state and the evolving relationship between sovereignty and private activity. Subsidiarity reminds us that there are benefits to enlisting state and private participation in regulatory schemes, and that law should attempt to capture the value-added that mediated structures offer to public life. But subsidiarity also keeps in view that not all decentralized entities are in fact mediated structures, and that not all mediated structures can achieve the goals that devolution sets for itself. Subsidiarity also emphasizes the ongoing relation of the periphery to the center – that the public, national authority retains a role in ensuring the proper functioning of localized-power spaces when devolution does not achieve its intended purpose. Proportionality similarly reminds us that constitutional rights need not be applied in binary fashion, with rights assumed to exist in some essentialized form, but rather can be enforced to the greatest extent possible given the facts and circumstances of the dispute. Although the words subsidiarity and proportionality are not current within US legal circles, they stand for ideas and practices that fit comfortably within state-judicial practice and provide a critical perspective on how US

---

[99] For a discussion of these developments, see Mark A. Geistfeld, *The Doctrinal Unity of Alternative Liability and Market-Share Liability*, 155 U. PA. L. REV. 447 (2006).
[100] See, for example, Sindell v. Abbott Laboratories, 26 Cal.3d 588, 607 P.2d 924 (Cal. 1980).
[101] See, for example, Collins v. Eli Lilly & Co., 116 Wis.2d 166, 342 N.W.2d 37 (Wis. 1984), cert. denied, 469 U.S. 826 (1984).
[102] See, for example, Hall v. E.I. Du Pont De Nemours & Co., 345 F. Supp. 353 (E.D.N.Y. 1972).
[103] See Allen Rostron, *Beyond Market Share Liability: A Theory of Proportional Share Liability for Non-Fungible Products*, 52 UCLA L. REV. 151, 174 (2004).
[104] See, for example, Summers v. Tice, 33 Cal.2d 80, 199 P.2d 1 (1948).

federal doctrine might relocate the boundary of rights without undermining important values that traditionally are associated with private life. I hope that the approach suggested in this chapter contributes to ongoing discussion about how best to develop public norms while encouraging innovation and retaining robust protections for individual autonomy.

# 7

# Abdications of sovereignty in state action and horizontal effect jurisprudence

JOHAN VAN DER WALT<sup>*</sup>

## Introduction

Attempts to come to terms with the deep tensions and paradoxes that inform state action and horizontal effect jurisprudence are largely absent in the vast literature available today on this crucial subject. Attempts to come to terms with the conceptual difficulties that attach to the state action doctrine in the United States remain stuck between acceptances and rejections of an idea that one can, following Frank Michelman, call the "simple Hohfeldian point."[1] Michelman explains the simple Hohfeldian point in terms of the rather unproblematic recognition that the state is ultimately the author of all law, irrespective of whether this law comes in the form of legislation, common law, or executive commands.[2] But this is Michelman's shorthand statement of the Hohfeldian point. The expanded or full version of the Hohfeldian point would be this: The state is ultimately the author of all law, irrespective of whether this law comes in the form of legislation, common law, or executive commands or the absence of legislation, common law, or executive commands. This expanded version of the Hohfeldian point will be explained in Section I of this chapter.

The vicissitudes of the state action doctrine in the United States are a function of judicial attitudes that either embrace or reject the Hohfeldian point. That this is so will be shown in Section II of this chapter with

---

[*] Thanks to André van der Walt for reading and commenting on an earlier draft of this chapter. Shortcomings are of course strictly my own. The articulations of a number of the passages in this chapter rely on passages from my book THE HORIZONTAL EFFECT REVOLUTION AND THE QUESTION OF SOVEREIGNTY (2014).

[1] Frank I. Michelman, *W(H)ither the Constitution?*, 21 CARDOZO L. REV. 1063, 1076 (2000) [hereinafter Michelman, *W(H)ither the Constitution?*].

[2] Frank I. Michelman, *The Bill of Rights, The Common Law, and the Freedom-Friendly State*, 58 U. MIAMI L. REV. 401, 404 (2003) [hereinafter Michelman, *The Bill of Rights*].

reference to both the shorthand and the expanded versions of the Hohfeldian point. Some American judicial decisions accept that state authorship of law also includes, alongside legislation, authorship of common law and authorship of judicial decisions. When they do, they implicitly also accept that state authorship of law includes the absence of legislation and common law (absence of judicial decisions does not constitute a plausible variation). Some judicial decisions, on the other hand, steadfastly deny that state authorship of law includes authorship of common law rules and judicial decisions. Those that do naturally also deny that authorship of law includes the absence of legislation and common law.

A dominant trend in the history of horizontal effect jurisprudence in a number of significant jurisdictions outside the United States can be read in terms of a consistent endeavor to prevent importation of those elements of the American state action doctrine that represent a judicial endorsement of the Hohfeldian point. That this is so will be shown with reference to the Canadian and South African jurisdictions in Section III of this chapter. Section IV will also highlight the irony evident in the South African resistance to the Hohfeldian point. In its fervor to keep the boundaries of South African horizontal effect Hohfeld-tight, the South African judiciary did not only rely on the quarantine to which the Hohfeldian point was subjected in Canada. The South African judiciary also called in the service of German *Drittwirkung* jurisprudence, and more specifically, the so-called indirect *Drittwirkung* approach articulated in the famous *Lüth*[3] decision of the German Federal Constitutional Court in 1958. The irony of this reliance on *Lüth* consists in the fact that *Lüth* does not at all represent a rejection of the *Hohfeldian* point. It turns, in fact, on a clear endorsement of the Hohfeldian point and its choice in favor of the indirect approach to horizontal effect or *mittelbare Drittwirkung* does not militate one millimeter against its endorsement of the Hohfeldian point. The South African judiciary's reliance on *Lüth* pivots on a fundamental misreading of *Lüth*.

Section IV subsequently turns to the reasons that inform the judicial rejection of the Hohfeldian point. It explains the judicial rejection of the Hohfeldian point in terms of an abdication of sovereignty. One might respond that the rejection of the Hohfeldian point self-evidently amounts to an abdication of sovereignty. Why the need then to go into deeper

---

[3] Bundesverfassungsgericht [BVerfG] [Federal Constitutional Court] Jan. 15, 1958, 7 ENTSCHEIDUNGEN DES BUNDESVERWALTUNGSGERICHTS [BVerfGE] 198 (Ger.) [hereinafter *Lüth*].

analyses in this regard? The point of the deeper analyses of the relation between the rejection of the Hohfeldian point and abdications of sovereignty in state action or horizontal effect jurisprudence is to highlight the deep fault line that has been destabilizing this jurisprudence from its very beginnings. Should horizontal effect jurisprudence wish to rethink itself on firmer foundations, it would first need to come to terms with this fault line.

## I  The Hohfeldian point

The crux of the Hohfeldian point is this: Law does not only consist as a set of relations between rights and duties. Law includes the correlative relations between the binary opposites of rights and duties. The legal opposite of a right is the absence of a right or a *non-right*, as Hohfeld calls it. The opposite of a duty is the absence of a duty. Hohfeld calls the absence of a duty a *liberty*. When one is not under a duty to do or not to do something, one is at liberty to do or not to do that thing; one has the liberty to do or not do it. Liberties relate to non-rights in the same way that duties relate to rights. And Hohfeld's point is this: Law consists as much in relations between non-rights and liberties as it consists in relations between rights and duties. In fact, the vast majority of legal relationships actually consist in relations between non-rights and liberties. Relations between rights and duties materialize relatively rarely in comparison to the vast spectrum of social relations, with regard to which there are no legal rules that assign rights or duties to the individuals involved.

So how do relations between non-rights and liberties attain legal significance? They do so when litigation ends with a judicial finding that the law provides no applicable remedy under the circumstances of the case that overrides all applicable defenses. In other words, non-rights and liberties materialize in a legally significant way when the claimant or plaintiff fails to make her case. When this happens, the court basically tells the claimant that she has no right (she has a non-right) to ask the defendant to do or not to do something. The defendant has the liberty to do as he pleases as far as the complaint of the plaintiff is concerned. The important point to note, however, is that this relationship between a plaintiff that has no right and a defendant that has the liberty to act freely with regard to the complaint filed is a legal relationship. It is not qualitatively different from the relations that materialize when a court finds the plaintiff has a right and the defendant has a duty to act in compliance with the plaintiff's right. Law is still very much at issue in the relation between non-rights and liberties. Law is not absent from these relations. Law just appears in the particular but pervasive mode of its presence that is marked by the absence of positive rules that assign rights and duties.[4]

What is the point of discussing the Hohfeldian point yet again, one might well ask.[5] Not only is it child's play to make the point, as Michelman writes,[6] it also makes no real headway in any direction for there are evidently as many judges and lawyers that reject the Hohfeldian point as there are ones that endorse it. This much will become clear in the next section when we turn to state action case law in the United States and horizontal effect jurisprudence outside the United States in Sections III and IV. In other words, the Hohfeldian point may well be a clever and intellectually delightful ruse that appeals to those who subscribe to an expansive understanding of constitutional law that would extend constitutional protection of the vulnerable as far as conceivably possible. The thinking of those who do this proceeds as follows: All law is in principle subject to constitutional scrutiny. If law is also present in relations between non-rights and liberties, it is present in the form of all conceivable social relationships, which means all social relationships are subject to constitutional scrutiny and protection. But again, what is the point of continuing to make the Hohfeldian point if it is clear by now that some lawyers and some judges simply meet it with flat rejection?

The point of making the Hohfeldian point again in this essay is to interpret the rejection of the Hohfeldian point as an abdication of sovereignty that frustrates – instead of advancing – the goal pursued by this deliberate abdication. This is the main point that this chapter makes in Section IV. Rejecting or endorsing the Hohfeldian point does not only concern a choice between two conceptual stances, neither of which can claim exclusive and conclusive validity, thus leaving the question regarding the reach of law and constitutional law undecided. Rather, it also concerns a deeper choice between two seemingly irreconcilable conceptions of statehood. The Hohfeldian point articulates a strong endorsement of the principle of state sovereignty. It takes to heart the principle that there is just one sovereign that authors the law. It takes to

---

[4] *Cf.* Wesley Hohfeld, *Some Fundamental Legal Conceptions as Applied in Legal Reasoning*, 23 YALE L.J. 28 (1913). See also Joseph W. Singer, *The Legal Rights Debate in Analytical Jurisprudence from Bentham to Hohfeld*, 1982 WIS. L. REV. 975, for his instructive discussion of Hohfeld's views.

[5] Especially if one has done it so many times before. *Cf.* references, *infra* note 50.

[6] Frank I. Michelman, *W(H)ither the Constitution?*, *supra* note 1, at 1076 (2000).

## I. THE HOHFELDIAN POINT

heart the idea that any political power that claims sovereignty can only be taken seriously if it can be seen to effectively pursue the expression of its political will in all walks of civil and social life. A sovereign does not leave matters to contingent or chance social developments. The sovereign responds to all such developments with decisions to make new law or decisions to refrain from making new law. Such is the nature of complete sovereignty. The idea is surely not new. The Romans already knew and accepted the maxim of *tacitus consensu populi*.[7]

Hohfeld did not apply his analysis expressly to the state action doctrine or horizontal effect jurisprudence, but many American scholars can be seen as taking a Hohfeldian approach to the state action problematic.[8] Stephen Gardbaum's instructive contribution to the state action debate suggests the whole state action doctrine can be recast in terms of the principle that the Supremacy Clause of the United States Constitution binds all judicial action in the United States, irrespective of state laws that may be at variance with the Constitution.[9] Gardbaum's is another typical Hohfeldian approach to the state action problem, which takes all law – not only legislation but also common law and judicial interpretations of common law – as state action that is subject to the Constitution. Gardbaum does not address the point expressly, but one can assume that his line of thinking also subsumes absence of legislation and common law under the law that is bound by the United States Constitution. But these scholarly endorsements of the Hohfeldian point constitute but one camp in American jurisprudence. Another line of scholars and judges simply reject the point. They do not do so because they do not grasp its logical or conceptual force. They do so, we shall see in Sections II and III, because they entertain a different conception of the

---

[7] *Cf.* Hans Kelsen, Hauptprobleme der Staatsrechtslehre 99–101 (1984) (Ger.).
[8] *Cf.* JOHAN VAN DER WALT, THE HORIZONTAL EFFECT REVOLUTION AND THE QUESTION OF SOVEREIGNTY 171–72 n. 10 (2014) [hereinafter VAN DER WALT, HORIZONTAL EFFECT REVOLUTION], for references to the many American scholars who take a Hohfeldian stance in their state action jurisprudence.
[9] U.S. CONST. art. VI, cl. 2. The Supremacy Clause reads:
This Constitution, and the Laws of the United States which shall be made in Pursuance thereof; and all Treaties made, or which shall be made, under the Authority of the United States, shall be the supreme Law of the Land; and the Judges in every State shall be bound thereby, any Thing in the Constitution or Laws of any State to the Contrary notwithstanding.
*Id.*; *cf.* Stephen Gardbaum, *The Horizontal Effect of Constitutional Rights*, 102 MICH. L. REV. 387, 414–15 (2003).

state that resists the concept of full state sovereignty and the idea that the state is the author of all positive law *and* all absences of such positive law.

## II  Vicissitudes of the American state action doctrine

The state action doctrine sprung its source in the following dictum of Justice Bradley in the *Civil Rights Cases*:

> [C]ivil rights, such as are guaranteed by the Constitution against State aggression, cannot be impaired by the wrongful acts of individuals, unsupported by the State authority in the shape of laws, customs, or judicial or executive proceedings. The wrongful act of an individual ... is simply a private wrong, or a crime of that individual.... [But an] individual cannot deprive a man of his right to vote, to hold property, to buy and sell, to sue in the courts, or to be a witness or a juror; he may, by force or fraud, interfere with the enjoyment of the right in a particular case; he may commit an assault against the person, or commit murder, or use ruffian violence at the polls, or slander the good name of a fellow citizen; but, unless protected in these wrongful acts by some shield of State law or State authority, he cannot destroy or injure the right; he will only hold himself amenable to satisfaction or punishment, and amenable therefore to the laws of the State where the wrong acts are committed. Hence, ... where the Constitution seeks to protect the rights of the citizen against discriminative and unjust laws of the State by prohibiting such laws, it is not individual offences, but abrogation and denial of rights, which it denounces and for which it clothes the Congress with power to provide a remedy. This abrogation and denial of rights for which the States alone were or could be responsible was the great ... wrong which was intended to be remedied. And the remedy to be provided must necessarily be predicated upon that wrong. It must assume that, in the cases provided for, the evil or wrong actually committed rests upon some State law or State authority for its excuse and perpetration.[10]

The key assertion of this dictum turns on the conceptual construction or definition of individual or private conduct as absolutely incapable of curtailing or violating a Fourteenth Amendment right.[11] A state can violate a constitutional right but private individual conduct cannot. The construction derives from a literal interpretation of words contained in the Fourteenth Amendment of the Constitution, which stipulates:

> *No State* shall make or enforce any law which shall abridge the privileges or immunities of citizens of the United States; nor shall any *State* deprive

[10] 109 U.S. 3, 17 (1883).   [11] U.S. CONST. amend. XIV.

any person of life, liberty, or property without the due process of law; nor deny to any person within its jurisdiction the equal protection of the laws.[12]

At issue in this literal reading of the Fourteenth Amendment is not only the origin of the state action doctrine. Justice Bradley's literal reading of the Fourteenth Amendment also suggests that there are areas of law that do not constitute state action (state authorship), or it suggests that there are areas of social life with regard to which the state has hitherto not made any law. Either some law is not state action, or all law is state action but some individual conduct is completely untouched by law. Both of these interpretations of Justice Bradley's dictum came to mark a dominant line of thinking in American state action adjudication and jurisprudence. But this line of thinking also came to be challenged, if only intermittently, in later Supreme Court decisions. The first significant challenges came from two decisions in the 1940s: *Labor v. Swing (Swing)*,[13] decided in 1941, and *Shelley v. Kraemer (Shelley)*,[14] decided in 1948.

In *Swing* the Supreme Court decided that an Illinois common law rule prohibiting secondary picketing (the picketing of any third party not directly involved as an employer in a dispute between employers and employees) constituted an unconstitutional abridgment of the freedom of expression granted by the Fourteenth Amendment. The decision thus clearly accepted the principle that common law rules constitute state action for purposes of the Fourteenth Amendment.[15] This acceptance that common law rules constitute state action would later find more illustrious endorsement in *New York Times v. Sullivan (Sullivan)*.[16] Sullivan, a commissioner of the City of Montgomery, brought a civil

---

[12] *Id.* § 1 (emphasis added).  [13] 312 U.S. 321 (1941).  [14] 334 U.S. 1 (1948).
[15] *Swing*, 312 U.S. 321.
    The scope of the Fourteenth Amendment is not confined by the notion of a particular state regarding the wise limits of an injunction in an industrial dispute, whether those limits be defined by statute or by the judicial organ of the state. A state cannot exclude workingmen from peacefully exercising the right of free communication by drawing the circle of economic competition between employers and workers so small as to contain only an employer and those directly employed by him.
    *Id.* at 325–26; Justice Frankfurter's reference in this dictum to a "judicial organ of state" might point to the possibility that his decision is actually much closer to the one in *Shelley*, 334 U.S. 1, *cf. infra* note 21. However, a reading of the whole case suggests that it was the existence of a common law rule and not just the judicial application of the rule that decided the matter for him.
[16] 376 U.S. 254 (1963).

law libel action against four Alabama clergymen and the New York Times Company for an advertisement run in the *New York Times* on 29 March 1960.[17] The Circuit Court of the County of Montgomery awarded him damages to the amount of $500,000 on the basis of the common law of Alabama.[18] The Supreme Court of Alabama upheld the judgment on appeal, but the United States Supreme Court overturned it and dismissed the claim for damages. Justice Brennan found the Alabama libel law on which the claim turned to fall foul of the First and Fourteenth Amendments.[19] The respondent claimed that his action for damages concerned a civil or private matter on which the Federal Constitution has no bearing. Justice Brennan responded as follows:

> We may dispose at the outset of [the first ground] asserted to insulate the judgment of the Alabama courts from constitutional scrutiny. [T]he proposition relied on by the State Supreme Court that "The Fourteenth Amendment is directed against State action and not private action" ... has no application to this case. Although this is a civil lawsuit between private parties, the Alabama courts have applied a state rule of law which

---

[17] The advertisement in the *New York Times* on which the claim was based did not mention Sullivan by name, but referred to "loads of police armed with shotguns and teargas" that ringed the Alabama State College Campus in order to suppress civil rights protests on the campus. The advertisement also stated, among more allegations, that "the Southern violators have answered Dr. [Martin Luther] King's peaceful protests with intimidation and violence," "have arrested him seven times for 'speeding,' 'loitering,' and similar 'offenses' [and have now] charged him with perjury." Sullivan claimed that the article implicated the police, not only in the ringing of the campus where they were expressly mentioned but also in all of the latter actions, and by thus implicating the police, also implicated him as commissioner of Montgomery.

[18] In the trial court judgment, the judge instructed the jury that the statements in the advertisement were "libellous per se" and "not privileged." In terms of the common law of Alabama, he instructed further, injury is implied by the bare fact of the per se libellous publication. Malice, falsity, and general damages are presumed and need not be alleged or proved, and punitive damages may be awarded by the jury if they found that the statements were indeed published maliciously and not just negligently or carelessly. The liability of the defendants, therefore, ultimately only turned on the questions whether the jury found the article to have been published by the defendants and whether the statements were made "of and concerning" the plaintiff. The judge rejected the defendants' contention that his rulings abridged the freedoms of speech and of the press guaranteed by the First and Fourteenth Amendments.

[19] The decision turned on the finding that common law rules that imposed the burden to prove truth and absence of malice on the defendants in a libel claim cannot be reconciled with the robust freedom of expression granted by the First and Fourteenth Amendments when criticism of public officials and personalities is at stake. The constitutional standard, Justice Brennan decided, requires that the claimant carry the burden of proof of falsity and malice. *Cf. Sullivan*, 376 U.S. at 297–98.

petitioners claim to impose invalid restrictions on their constitutional freedoms of speech and press. It matters not that that law has been applied in a civil action and that it is common law only, though supplemented by statute. The test is not the form in which state power has been applied but, whatever the form, whether such power has, in fact, been exercised.[20]

*Sullivan* basically put state action "out of business," claims Michelman. If the Constitution tolerates neither executive state administration, nor state legislation, nor state common law that falls foul of its guarantees, there is simply no basis left on which a constitutionally unsound contention can enter a court of law and exit that court triumphantly.

State action had in fact been "put out of business" twice before *Sullivan*. The first time in 1941 by Justice Frankfurter in *Swing*, as shown earlier, and the second time in 1948, in the even more dramatic judgment of Justice Vinson in *Shelley*.[21] The disputes in *Shelley* turned on the question whether the court enforcement of two restrictive covenants entered into by private individuals constituted state action that was subject to review in terms of the Fourteenth Amendment of the United States Constitution. At issue were the appeals of two Negro families against the findings of the Supreme Courts of Missouri and Michigan that restrictive covenants between private individuals in the cities of St. Louis and Detroit that prevented Negroes from occupying properties subject to the covenants did not abridge rights protected by the Fourteenth Amendment.[22] The respondents in both cases argued that there

---

[20] *Id.* at 265. See Michelman, *The Bill of Rights*, *supra* note 2, at 403 (for a similar quotation of this passage).

[21] 334 U.S. 1 (1948).

[22] The first case concerned the enforcement of a restrictive covenant between owners of property on a section of Labadie Avenue in the city of St. Louis that they will not allow their property to be occupied by people of the "Negro or Mongolian Race" for a period of fifty years. Pursuant to a contract of sale of one of the properties subject to the restrictive covenant, the Shelleys, a "Negro" couple, received the title or deed for the property purchased from the seller in August 1945. In October 1945, other owners of property subject to the covenant sought to obtain an order from the Circuit Court of St. Louis to prevent the Shelleys from occupying the purchased property. The Circuit Court refused to grant the order. The court found that the agreement had never become effective, given the failure of the participants in the covenant to obtain the signatures of all the property owners in the district as the covenant stipulated. The Supreme Court of Missouri overturned the Circuit Court's decision by finding that the covenant had become effective. By the time it did so, however, the Shelleys had already moved into the house they purchased. They now petitioned the Federal Supreme Court to obtain an order that the restrictive covenant violated the Fourteenth Amendment. The second case concerned

was no state action involved in the covenants and that the mere enforcement of the covenants by a court of law also does not constitute state action for purposes of the Fourteenth Amendment. The Federal Supreme Court dismissed this argument. Justice Vinson's opinion for the Court put the matter in no uncertain terms:

> That the action of state courts and judicial officers in their official capacities is to be regarded as action of the State within the meaning of the Fourteenth Amendment is a proposition which has long been established by decisions of this Court. That principle was given expression in the earliest cases involving the construction of the terms of the Fourteenth Amendment.[23]

Justice Vinson's opinion proceeded to trace the acceptance that adjudication constitutes state action through a long history of Supreme Court case law. The earliest cases to which the court was referring here included *Virginia v. Rives*[24] and *Ex Parte Virginia*[25], both of which were decided in 1880, as well as the *Civil Rights Cases* of 1883. With regard to the latter, Justice Vinson observed the following:

> In the Civil Rights Cases this Court pointed out that the Amendment makes void "state action of every kind" which is inconsistent with the guaranties therein contained, and extends to manifestations of "State authority in the shape of laws, customs, or judicial or executive proceedings." Language to like effect is employed no less than eighteen times during the course of that opinion.[26]

Justice Vinson could, in fact, also have gone back all the way to Chief Justice Marshall's emphatic statement that courts are also bound by

---

an essentially similar set of facts regarding property purchased in the city of Detroit. In this case, the Circuit Court of Wayne Country granted an order that the purchasers, one Ferguson and his wife, must vacate the property within 90 days. They appealed to the Supreme Court of Michigan on the ground that they had been denied the rights protected by the Fourteenth Amendment. The Supreme Court dismissed the appeal on the finding that no Fourteenth Amendment rights had been affected by any of the afore-going events.

[23] *Shelley*, 334 U.S. at 14. It is obvious that Shelley could have been decided on the same principle that common law rules constitute state action for purposes of the protection afforded by the Fourteenth Amendment. Henry Friendly suggests it was decided thus, but Frank Michelman contends more convincingly that it was not. *Cf.* Henry J. Friendly, *The Public-Private Penumbra—Fourteen Years Later*, 130 U. PA. L. REV. 1289, 1295 (1982), with Michelman, *The Bill of Rights, supra* note 2, at 406.

[24] 100 U.S. 313 (1880).   [25] 100 U.S. 339 (1880).

[26] *Cf. Shelley*, 334 U.S. at 14–15 (1948).

written constitutions in *Marbury v. Madison*.²⁷ The consistent acceptance of the Hohfeldian point in the Supreme Court's jurisprudence appears incontestable. Yet, avers Michelman, "something persists in [American] jurisprudence that walks and talks like a state action doctrine with teeth."²⁸ Why is this so?

Justice Vinson was the first to back off from his own opinion in *Shelley*. Five years after his explosive judgment in *Shelley*, Justice Vinson would argue in *Barrows v. Jackson (Barrows)*²⁹ that the principle in *Shelley* only applies when the court's order will be the direct cause of the abridgement of an individual's constitutional rights by enforcing a racially discriminatory covenant against the member of the racial minority targeted by that covenant. It does not apply, he argued, when the court only stands to enforce the covenant between the parties to the covenant. An action for damages filed by one party to the covenant against another is therefore not covered by the rule in *Shelley*.

Chief Justice Vinson's opinion in *Barrows* did not convince the majority of the court and, for this reason, had no immediate effect. But the reasoning that he employed surely opened the door for or anticipated the majority decision in *Black v. Cutter Laboratories (Cutter Laboratories)*³⁰ in which the Supreme Court enforced a collective bargaining agreement that held Communist Party membership as a just cause for dismissal. The majority held that the decision turned on nothing but the interpretation of a contract between private parties and thus rendered constitutional principles irrelevant.³¹ Chief Justice Warren and Justices Douglas and Black tried in vain to uphold the rule in *Shelley*.³²

Justice Vinson's turn in *Barrows* and the turn of the Supreme Court in *Cutter Laboratories* could not have pivoted on a failure to grasp the Hohfeldian point. It turned on willful decisions to reject it and to ignore a long history of Supreme Court decisions in which it was incontestably accepted, a history that Justice Vinson himself traced in detail in *Shelley*. The Supreme Court's decision to ignore Hohfeld is articulated in the clearest of terms in Chief Justice Rehnquist's opinion in *Flagg Brothers, Inc. v. Brooks*.³³ As Michelman puts it, Justice Rehnquist simply

---

²⁷ 5 U.S. 137 (1803) ("confirms and strengthens the principle, supposed to be essential to all written constitutions, that a law repugnant to the constitution is void; and that all *courts*, as well as other departments, are bound by that instrument"). *Id.* at 180 (emphasis Marshall, C.J.).
²⁸ Michelman, *The Bill of Rights*, *supra* note 2, at 404.    ²⁹ 346 U.S. 249 (1953).
³⁰ 351 U.S. 292 (1956).    ³¹ *Id.* at 299.    ³² *Id.* at 300, 302.    ³³ 436 U.S. 149 (1978).

"insisted ... that American constitutional-legal doctrine must pretend not to notice it."[34] According to Chief Justice Rehnquist "[i]t would intolerably broaden ... the notion of state action under the Fourteenth Amendment to hold that the mere existence of a body of property law in a State, whether decisional or statutory, itself amounted to 'state action.'"[35]

The most remarkable aspect of Chief Justice Rehnquist's articulation of the matter is the way it even excludes *statutory* private law from the scope of state action. This exclusion of statutory private law from state action either implies that a significant percentage of the sovereign's legislation is simply not subject to constitutional scrutiny or implies that a significant percentage of American legislation is not authored by the sovereign. It either implies a considerable suspension of basic principles of constitutionalism and the rule of law, or it implies a considerable denial of sovereignty.

What happens when one admits to vast enclaves of human coexistence within state boundaries that simply fall outside the reach of state sovereignty? One turns the state into an archipelago of sovereign islands within a vast wilderness of lawlessness. One draws the *Blood Meridian* just outside one's doorstep.[36] In fact, one fails to draw the *Blood Meridian*, for the wilderness ultimately does not respect doorsteps. To the contrary, one is likely to find its darkest caves inside doorsteps, as the case of *DeShaney v. Winnebago County Department of Social Services* makes abundantly clear (*DeShaney*).[37] *DeShaney* surely represents one of the American people's darkest disavowals of sovereignty. Officials of the Winnebago County Department of Social Services knew what was going on in the house where the DeShaneys lived. They knew or should have known in view of the evidence available to them that Randy DeShaney was maiming his son Joshua DeShaney for life. They stood by and did nothing until it was too late. Instead of admitting to a failure of sovereignty, a failure of state sovereignty that dismally failed the Fourteenth Amendment of the Federal Constitution, the Supreme Court preferred to read the *DeShaney* case in terms of a disavowal of sovereignty. Joshua DeShaney would have been entitled to tort compensation from the state had the people of Wisconsin passed legislation that provided for tort action in response to the state's failure

---

[34] Michelman, *W(H)ither the Constitution?*, supra note 1, at 1076.
[35] Flagg Brothers, 436 U.S. at 160 n. 10.
[36] CORMAC MCCARTHY, THE BLOOD MERIDIAN (1990).   [37] 489 U.S. 189 (1989).

to act. But Wisconsin had not passed such legislation, averred Justice Rehnquist, and that is the end of the story.[38]

Thus did Justice Rehnquist erase the *Blood Meridian*. Thus did he turn America into the American frontier. Thus did he ensure that America would be, at least as far as its legal consciousness is concerned,[39] no country for the old, for the young, or for anyone.[40]

## III  Vicissitudes of horizontal effect in Canadian, South African and German jurisprudence

The United States Supreme Court stabilized the borders of the American Republic with its decisions in *Swing*, *Shelley*, and *Sullivan*. These decisions defined a territory in which American law and the American Constitution governed, at least in principle, in no uncertain terms. This, however, was not how the Supreme Court of Canada would see the matter when it laid down its horizontal-application jurisprudence in *RWDSU v. Dolphin Delivery Ltd* (*Dolphin Delivery*),[41] taking the exact opposite position to the one taken by Justice Frankfurter in *Swing*.[42]

*Dolphin Delivery* also turned on the question whether an injunction against secondary picketing obtained under Canadian common law constituted an unconstitutional abridgment of the right to freedom of expression guaranteed by section 2(b) of the Canadian Charter of Rights and Freedoms.[43] Section 1 of the Charter makes provision for reasonable

---

[38] *Id.*
  The people of Wisconsin may well prefer a system of liability which would place upon the state and its officials the responsibility for failure to act in situations such as the present one. They may create such a system, if they do not have it already, by changing the tort law of the state in accordance with the regular lawmaking process. But they should not have it thrust upon them by this Court's expansion of the Due Process Clause of the Fourteenth Amendment.
  *Id.* at 202–03.
[39] One need not mention its infamous laws on the possession of firearms.
[40] *Cf.* CORMAC MCCARTHY, NO COUNTRY FOR OLD MEN (2005). One can also say this is the country in which Senator Rance Stoddard gets shot instead of Liberty Valance. *Cf.* John Ford, THE MAN WHO SHOT LIBERTY VALANCE (Paramount Pictures 1962).
[41] [1986] 2 S.C.R. 573 (Can.).    [42] Labor v. Swing, 312 U.S. 321 (1941).
[43] *Id.* The appellant, a workers union (Retail, Wholesale and Department Store Union) acted as bargaining agent for the locked out employees of Purolater, an Ontario-based courier. The respondent made local deliveries for Purolater in its area, at first directly and later through Supercourier, a company connected to Purolater. Appellant had approached the British Columbia Labour Relations Board for a declaration that the respondent and Supercourier were allies of Purolator. The declaration would have

limitations of the Charter rights. The respondent argued that the common law rule constituted such a reasonable limitation of the right to freedom of expression granted by section 2(b). The appellant argued that the limitation was not reasonable. The Supreme Court of Canada finally dismissed the injunction of secondary picketing granted by the trial court. The Court did so not only on the ground that the common law rule against secondary picketing constituted a reasonable limitation of the right to freedom of expression but also on the ground that the Charter did not apply to common law disputes in which the state was not a party. It is the latter ground that is of concern in what follows.

Justice McIntyre delivered the judgment for the majority of the court. His finding that the Charter does not apply to common law disputes in which the state is not a party turned on a peculiar limitation of the reasoning in *Swing* and *Sullivan* and an implied but fervent rejection of the reasoning in *Shelley*. Justice McIntyre's judgment commenced with a firm recognition that section 52(1) of the Charter nullifies all law that is inconsistent with the provisions contained in the Charter.[44] This recognition is fully consistent with the recognition that the common law constitutes state action in *Swing* and *Sullivan*, but it did not last long. Justice McIntyre almost immediately proceeded to retreat from this broad acceptance that all common law is bound by the Constitution by asserting, in view of sections 32(a) and 32(b) of the Charter, that the Constitution only binds common law that applies to governmental action. This is how he put it:

> enabled the appellant to lawfully picket the respondent's business premises. The Board declined to hear the application for want of jurisdiction. The lawfulness of the picketing now had to be determined on the basis of the Canadian common law, given the silence of the Canada Labour Code, R.S.C. 1985, c. L-2 on the matter. Under the common law, the matter turned on the rule that secondary picketing (the picketing of any third party not directly involved as an employer in a dispute between employers and employees) was unlawful. The respondent had obtained an injunction *quia timet* on the basis of this rule and the appeal against the granting of the injunction now turned on the claim that the rule constituted an unconstitutional infringement of the right to freedom of expression guaranteed by section 2(b) of the Canadian Charter of Rights and Freedoms, Part 1 of the Constitution Act, 1982, *being* Schedule B to the Canada Act, 1982, c. 11 (U.K.).

[44] Dolphin Delivery, [1986] 2 S.C.R., para. 25:
> The English text provides that "any law that is inconsistent with the provisions of the Constitution is, to the extent of the inconsistency, of no force or effect." If this language is not broad enough to include the common law, it should be observed as well that the French text adds strong support to this conclusion in its employment of the words *"elle rend inopérantes les dispositions incompatibles de tout autre règle de droit"* (emphasis added).

## III. VICISSITUDES OF HORIZONTAL EFFECT

In this way the *Charter* will apply to the common law, whether in public or private litigation. It will apply to the common law, however, only in so far as the common law is the basis of some governmental action which, it is alleged, infringes a guaranteed right or freedom.... The element of governmental intervention necessary to make the *Charter* applicable in an otherwise private action is difficult to define. We have concluded that the *Charter* applies to the common law but not between private parties.[45]

Cast in terms of *Swing* and *Sullivan*, Justice McIntyre's move essentially amounts to saying this: The fact that the common law constitutes state action is not enough for the Constitution to apply; *further* state action is required for the Constitution to apply. *Dolphin* can, in other words, be argued to have formulated a *double state action test* for constitutional application in Canada. Justice McIntyre found it necessary to make sure that *Shelley* did not find a way into Canada. He did not refer to *Shelley*, only to the "troublesome" view of Professor Hogg. Hogg wrote in the second edition of his *Constitutional Law of Canada*:

> The fact that a court order is governmental action means that the Charter will apply to a purely private arrangement, such as a contract or proprietary interest, but only to the extent that the Charter will preclude judicial enforcement of any arrangement in derogation of a guaranteed right. In a sense, the common law authorizes any private action that is not prohibited by a positive rule of law. If the Charter applied to the common law in that attenuated sense, it would apply to all private activity. But it seems more reasonable to say that the common law offends the Charter only when it crystallizes into a rule that can be enforced by the courts. Then, if an enforcement order would infringe a Charter right, the Charter will apply to preclude the order, and, by necessary implication, to modify the common law rule.[46]

Again, Justice McIntyre found this view "troublesome." As he put it:

> I find the position thus adopted troublesome ... [I]t should not be accepted as an approach to this problem ... To regard a court order as an element of governmental intervention necessary to invoke the *Charter* would ... widen the scope of *Charter* application to virtually all private litigation. All cases must end, if carried to completion, with an enforcement order and if the *Charter* precludes the making of the order, where a *Charter* right would be infringed, it would seem that all private litigation would be subject to the *Charter*. [T]his approach will not provide the

---

[45] *Id.*, paras. 34–35.
[46] *Id.*, para. 35, *quoting* PETER W. HOGG, CONSTITUTIONAL LAW OF CANADA vol. II 678 (5th ed. 2007).

answer to the question. A more direct and a more precisely defined connection between the element of government action and the claim advanced must be present before the *Charter* applies.⁴⁷

As Hogg clearly notes in his response to the decision in *Dolphin Delivery*, Justice McIntyre was exorcising the specter of *Shelley* in this passage. Having invented this doubly fortified state action jurisprudence – *state action in the form of common law is really only state action when corroborated by further state action*, and *state action in the form of law is only state action when the further state action required to make it state action is not judicial action* – the decision in *Dolphin* that the Charter does not apply to the dispute in the case could not have come as a surprise. And thus the endless American frontier – the great Wild West – swept into the vast Canadian prairielands.

And then it crossed the Atlantic and swept south, far south. One would have thought that the freshly liberated *Republic* of South Africa, with its liberation movement government and a team of constitutional judges as faithful to the new democratic Constitution as one might have wished for, would opt forcefully and unequivocally for a constitutional jurisprudence that would consolidate and strengthen the civil sovereignty for which so many had fought so hard and for which *death had undone so many*. The invocation of Eliot is deliberate here. One would have thought that no chances would be taken with the survival and return of the wastelands of the past. But this was not to be. In its landmark judgment on the horizontal effect of the constitutional rights contained in chapter 3 of the Constitution of South Africa of 1993, *Du Plessis v. De Klerk* (*Du Plessis*),⁴⁸ the South African Constitutional Court took the clearest stance imaginable in favor of *Dolphin Delivery* and against *Shelley* and, by obvious implication, also against *Swing* and *Sullivan*. And as if *Dolphin*'s doubly fortified state action jurisprudence was not sufficient for purposes of keeping *Shelley*, *Swing*, and *Sullivan* out, the South African Constitutional Court would further invoke a serious misreading of the significantly sovereignty-friendly and *Shelley*-friendly jurisprudence that the German Federal Constitutional Court articulated in its now famous *Lüth* decision in 1958. But this was not all that was remarkable about the *Du Plessis* case. As if determined to pile irony upon irony, the judge who most vociferously announced the constitutional

---

⁴⁷ Dolphin Delivery, [1986] 2 S.C.R. 573, para. 36.   ⁴⁸ 1996 (5) BCLR 658 (CC) (S. Afr.).

## III. VICISSITUDES OF HORIZONTAL EFFECT

sovereignty of the fledgling republic, Justice Kriegler, was also the one who most vociferously disavowed this sovereignty.[49]

Space constraints preclude detailed engagement with the remarkable *Du Plessis* judgment and its most remarkable dissenting and concurrent opinions.[50] Suffice it to note the clear endorsement of the insistence in *Dolphin Delivery* that constitutional rights only apply to common law disputes when the state is directly involved in the dispute and not only as the author of applicable common law rules.[51] And suffice it to note its clear rejection of *Shelley*. That judges act on behalf of or *as* the state is a fact that none of the judges sitting in the *Du Plessis* case would deny in the abstract, but those who concurred in the majority opinion all endorsed the *Dolphin Delivery* rejection of *Shelley*: However obvious it may be that regular judicial action constitutes the third branch of sovereign government, it simply does not count as state action for purposes of activating constitutional scrutiny. To state the matter properly in terms of the key clause of the 1993 Constitution on which the decision was based, the judiciary was not included in Article 7(1), which defined the scope of state action to which the Constitution applies. Article 7(1), the majority opinion in *Du Plessis* asserted, was devised in this way exactly for purposes of negating the rule in *Shelley*.[52]

Probably sensing and addressing the significant loss of sovereignty evident in this reading of Article 7(1), the South African Constitutional Assembly revised the application provisions in Article 7(1) of the Interim Constitution incisively when they drafted Article 8(1) of the 1996 Constitution. Article 8(1) now expressly listed the judiciary among the organs of state that are subject to constitutional scrutiny.[53] And the Constitutional Assembly went even further. Almost as if to make doubly sure

---

[49] See VAN DER WALT, HORIZONTAL EFFECT REVOLUTION, *supra* note 8, at 90–92, 117–19, 160, 311–12, for an extensive engagement with Justice Kriegler's "dissenting" opinion in *Du Plessis*.

[50] I have discussed the *Du Plessis* case and South African horizontal effect jurisprudence in several other articles. See Johan van der Walt, *Progressive Indirect Horizontal Effect of the Bill of Rights: Towards a Co-Operative Relation between Common–Law and Constitutional Jurisprudence*, 17 S. AFR. J. HUM. RTS. 341 (2001); Johan van der Walt, *Horizontal Effect of Fundamental Rights and the Threshold of the Law in View of the Carmichele Saga*, 19 S. AFR. J. HUM. RTS. 517 (2003).

[51] *Cf. Du Plessis*, 1996 (5) BCLR, *supra* note 48, at para. 49b.

[52] S. AFR. CONST., 1996. Article 7(1) states: "This chapter [containing the Bill of Rights] shall bind all legislative and executive organs of state at all levels of government."

[53] *Id.* art. 8(1), which reads: "The Bill of Rights applies to all law, and binds the legislature, the executive, the judiciary and all organs of state."

that the forfeiture of sovereignty performed in *Du Plessis* would not happen again, it stipulated in Article 8(2) that the Constitution also binds private individuals when appropriate.[54] The Constitutional Court, however, persisted with the application jurisprudence developed in *Du Plessis* when it commenced to apply the 1996 Constitution. It did so by constructing an intricate semantic relation between sections 8(1), 8(2), and 8 (3) to which we shall return later. Suffice it to say that it persisted with the abdication of sovereignty performed in *Du Plessis* until it finally, by implication, reappropriated this forfeited sovereignty some years later with its decision in the case of *Carmichele v. Minister of Safety and Security and Another (Carmichele)*.[55]

In the end, the majority judgment in *Du Plessis* opted for the so-called indirect horizontal effect or *mittelbare Drittwirkung* method developed in the *Lüth* judgment. The indirect method of constitutional application has become an essential ingredient of contemporary legal consciousness.[56] It turns on the principle that constitutional protections do not apply to private disputes directly. Litigants can accordingly not rely on constitutional rights for the resolution of private disputes; they must rely on private law remedies. Constitutional rights nevertheless remain relevant to private law litigation because the judicial application of private law must remain reconcilable with constitutional values and ideally promote these values. Thus do constitutional values *radiate* through the private law system, as the German Constitutional Court put the matter in *Lüth*.[57]

The method applied as articulated in *Lüth* is problematic in many respects, as has been pointed out especially well in German scholarship over the years. Suffice it to state briefly only the most problematic aspect of the indirect method: It rarely remains a matter of pure method. It invariably addresses questions of constitutional substance (questions as to *whether* the Constitution applies or not) as mere questions of form (questions as to *how* the Constitution must be applied). The *Lüth* decision made it abundantly clear that the judiciary is one of the organs of

---

[54] *Id.* art. 8(2), which reads: "A provision of the Bill of Rights binds a natural or a juristic person if, and to the extent that, it is applicable, taking into account the nature of the right and the nature of any duty imposed by the right."

[55] Carmichele v. Minister of Safety and Security and Another 2001 (4) SA 938 (CC) (S. Afr.).

[56] Compare, for example, the essays in HUMAN RIGHTS IN PRIVATE LAW (Daniel Friedman and Daphne Barak-Erez eds., 2001).

[57] *Lüth, supra* note 3, at 205–06.

## III. VICISSITUDES OF HORIZONTAL EFFECT

state sovereignty. It is, therefore, as much conditioned (burdened would be too weak an expression) by the constitutional duty to protect the constitutional rights of citizens as the executive and legislative powers of the state are.[58] The *Lüth* judgment also corroborated its unambiguous avowal of state and judicial sovereignty – and its unflinchingly positive answer to the *whether* question – with a remarkable concluding passage that would become nothing less than a formulaic maxim that it would employ consistently in future adjudication. The conclusion in *Lüth* reads as follows:

> The decision of the Regional Court failed to recognise the significance which the right to freedom of expression enjoys also in those cases where it comes into conflict with private interests. As such it fell short of constitutional criteria and must be deemed to have violated the fundamental right which the plaintiff enjoys in terms of article 5 I.[59]

A clearer restatement of the rule in *Shelley* cannot be imagined: "The decision of the Regional Court ... must be deemed to have violated the fundamental right [of] the plaintiff." Again, the German Federal Constitutional Court went on to use this formula repeatedly in future decisions.[60] Considering its misgivings vis-à-vis *Shelley*, the South African Constitutional Court had good reason to be much more apprehensive of the jurisprudence laid down in *Lüth* than it was. But it was enamored with the indirect method in *Lüth* and proceeded to sever this method from the clear avowals of judicial state sovereignty and the clear endorsements of *Shelley* that are written all over *Lüth*. It basically ignored these avowals of sovereignty and endorsements of *Shelley* in *Lüth*. That is how it managed to turn the question of method into a question of sovereignty. No longer founded and anchored by the clear substantive avowal of sovereignty in *Lüth*, the indirect method itself commenced to stand in

---

[58] *Id.* at 206–07.
[59] *Id.* at 230:
Das Bundesverfassungsgericht ist auf Grund dieser Erwägungen zu der Überzeugung gelangt, daß das Landgericht bei seiner Beurteilung des Verhaltens des Beschwerdeführers die besondere Bedeutung verkannt hat, die dem Grundrecht auf freie Meinungsäußerung auch dort zukommt, wo es mit privaten Interessen anderer in Konflikt tritt. Das Urteil des Landgerichts beruht auf diesem Verfehlen grundrechtlicher Maßstäbe *und verletzt so das Grundrecht des Beschwerdeführers* aus Art 5 Abs 1 Satz 1 GG (emphasis added).
[60] See 24 BVerfG 278; 25 BVerfG 256; 30 BVerfG 173; 34 BVerfG 35 BVerfG 202; 42 BVerfG 142; 46 BVerfG 325; 54 BVerfG 129; 54 BVerfG 148; 60 BVerfG 234; 61 BVerfG 1; 62 BVerfG 230; 66 BVerfG 116; 73 BVerfG 261 (Ger.).

for the sovereignty question in *Du Plessis*. The indirect method became a device for determining the question *whether* – and not just *how* – the Constitution applied to a private dispute.

The debate between proponents of direct and indirect horizontal effect was fuelled from its very beginnings by the contentious way in which the indirect approach bypassed and absorbed the question of sovereignty. Or, to be more precise, it was fuelled by the perception that the indirect approach bypassed the question of sovereignty by absorbing it. Had the indirect approach from the beginning been an "innocent" matter of method; had it from the beginning recognized that the Constitution applies self-evidently to all possible instances of social conflict and discontent because the state self-evidently takes responsibility for all such conflict and discontent; and had it further only added to this that it is probably better first to cast discontent between private individuals in standard terms of private law before one starts scrutinizing the impact of the Constitution on that discontent, the debate between proponents of the direct and indirect approach to horizontal effect would have been much less charged and probably rather short lived. But proponents of the direct approach sensed that the proponents of the indirect approach were up to something more. And they were right. It was clear from Günter Dürig's first contributions to the debate that the whole brouhaha about method was informed by one thing and one thing only, namely, the endeavor to reserve an a priori sphere of private freedom that is untouched or "less touched" by the sovereignty of the Constitution.[61] At issue in the indirect approach is a surreptitious resistance to sovereignty among some legal theorists and a surreptitious inclination among some judges to forfeit sovereignty.

Constitutional clauses undoubtedly do not affect private individuals and public officials in exactly the same way. This difference between the Constitution's impact on private individuals and public officials is indeed one of the key questions that the *how* question, the question of method, should be addressing. But the *whether* question became a vehicle for evading the *how* question. Simplistic and surreptitious *whether* questions should not stand in for complex *how* questions. Surreptitious replacements of *how* questions with *whether* questions amount to either outright abdications of sovereignty or obfuscated avowals of sovereignty that fail to take sovereign responsibility as constitutional democratic sovereigns

---

[61] Günter Dürig, *Grundrechte und Zivilrechtsprechung*, in Vom Bonner Grundgesetz zur gesamtdeutschen Verfassung. Festschrift zum 75. Geburtstag von Hans Nawiasky 177–82 (Theodor Maunz ed., 1956) (Ger.).

## III. VICISSITUDES OF HORIZONTAL EFFECT

would: openly, honestly, and transparently. They amount to abdications of sovereignty when the surreptitious response is negative (i.e., the Constitution does not apply to the private sphere). They amount to obfuscations of sovereignty and failures to own up to sovereignty when the surreptitious response is positive (i.e., the Constitution does apply to the private sphere, but only by influencing private law in some way or another). It is a good question which of these two responses one should dread most.

The replacement of *how* with *whether* questions and the obfuscation of sovereignty concomitant to it continued to dominate South African constitutional jurisprudence after *Du Plessis*, as the judgment in *Khumalo v. Holomisa* (*Khumalo*)[62] makes abundantly clear. In the hope of moving the court to turn the defendant's burden of disproving negligence in defamation claims against the press (the current position in South Africa[63]) into the claimant's burden of proving malicious intent (the position in *Sullivan*), the defendants requested the court to apply the constitutional protection of freedom of speech directly to the case as Article 8(2) requires and not in terms of the development of the common law that Article 8(3) requires. Dismissing this request, Justice O'Regan surreptitiously disavowed the direct application of the Constitution to the case that she herself had just affirmed in a previous paragraph of her judgment.[64] She effectively performed this disavowal by claiming that Article 8(3) would be rendered meaningless if Article 8(2) were taken to allow direct resort to constitutional rights in private law disputes.

Some might claim that there is nothing wrong with and nothing disavowing about this argument. However, the argument turns on a crucial misreading and it is this misreading that allows for the disavowal of horizontal effect and of sovereignty at issue here. Article 8(3) would indeed be rendered *pro non-scripto* if Article 8(2) suggested constitutional rights could be invoked directly in private litigation. But there is nothing in Article 8(2) that suggests this. It only stipulates that the rights in chapter 2 apply to private legal subjects and says nothing about how this application must be pleaded by litigants or articulated by courts. Article 8(3) – which can indeed be construed as dealing with (and *only* with) the question of how horizontal effect must be pleaded and articulated by litigants and courts – can therefore not affect the direct horizontal effect stipulated in Article 8(2). It only called for a *method*. It only called

---

[62] *Khumalo v. Holomisa* 2002 (5) SA 401 (CC) (S. Afr.).
[63] *National Media v. Bogoshi* 1998 (4) SA 1196 (SCA) (S. Afr.).
[64] *Khumalo v. Holomisa* 2002 (5) SA 401 (CC) at para. 30–32 (S. Afr.).

for the undeniable direct application, already called for and established under Article 8(2), to be processed *via* the regular discourse of private law.

This, however, is not quite how Justice O'Regan approached the matter. She proceeded as if the requirement to process the claim and defense through private law affected the substantive question regarding the constitutionally required burden of proof significantly. A clear avowal of the direct horizontal effect stipulated in Article 8(2) and a clear avowal of the unambiguous affirmation of constitutional sovereignty thus contained in Article 8(2) would have made it abundantly clear to the defendants that Article 8(2) affords them no advantage that Article 8(3) takes away from them. It would have made clear that Article 8(2) does not offer a stronger defense than Article 8(3) offers. But Justice O'Regan did not do this. She preferred to leave the spurious impression hanging that the method of application prescribed in Article 8(3) restricts the substance of application prescribed by Article 8(2), that is, that the development of the common law in accordance with Article 8(3) offers some shelter against the sovereign reach of the Constitution that Article 8(2) does not provide.

That this shelter does not exist was later conceded by the Constitutional Court's judgment in *Carmichele v. Minister of Safety and Security*. The concession came in the form of the recognition that Articles 8(3) and 39(2) require constitutional scrutiny of all private law causes of action. *Carmichele* is the South African equivalent of *Swing* and *Sullivan*. The decision in *Carmichele* effectively recognized that any private law cause of action that provided insufficient protection of constitutional rights undoubtedly falls foul of those rights. This means that it ultimately cannot make any difference, as regards the question whether the Constitution applies or not, whether one processes litigation in the language of private law or constitutional law.

The decision in *Carmichele* effectively confirms the substantive reality of direct horizontal effect. It effectively confirms the reality that an option to process litigation in terms of either Article 8(2) or Article 8(3), had it existed, could never have had any impact on the substantive outcome of the litigation, as the defendants claimed in *Khumalo*. By failing to tell them so clearly, Justice O'Regan avoided the express avowal of the sovereign reach of the South African Constitution embodied in Articles 8(1) and 8(2). This avowal of constitutional sovereignty can now be distilled from close readings of the *Carmichele* decision,[65] but the South

---

[65] *Cf.* VAN DER WALT, HORIZONTAL EFFECT REVOLUTION, *supra* note 8.

African judiciary has still not developed clear jurisprudence on this point. This is remarkable when one considers the actuality that the question of horizontal effect has enjoyed for such a long time. The horizontal effect question enjoyed constant attention in South Africa ever since the enactment of the 1993 Constitution. Against this background, the *implied* affirmation of constitutional sovereignty in *Carmichele* is at best a surreptitious or obfuscated affirmation of sovereignty.

## IV  Self-defeating abdications of sovereignty

In his dissent in *Du Plessis*, Justice Kriegler believed that he was proposing "direct horizontal effect" jurisprudence for South Africa that differed significantly from the "indirect horizontal effect" jurisprudence for which the majority opted.[66] This was not really the case, as I show elsewhere, but let us nevertheless look at one of the crucial statements with which he sought to justify his "direct horizontal" approach. This "direct horizontal approach," he argued, "is a far cry from the spectre of the state placing its hand on private relationships."[67] Justice Kriegler was evidently bothered by the implications of a strong avowal of sovereignty that are evident in endorsements of "direct horizontal effect." He was, as Matthias Kumm puts it, "afraid of the total constitution" and suspected that there might be something like a totalitarian state lurking in or behind it.

The perception that the strong avowal of sovereignty evident in the endorsement of direct horizontal effect is irreconcilable with concerns with liberty may well also be the source of the notorious conceptual difficulties associated with the state action doctrine. This is indeed how Louis Seidman sees the matter in a most instructive 1993 article.[68] Seidman's basic question is whether American lawyers should not simply accept the Hohfeldian point to straighten out the conceptual problems that attach to the state action doctrine. As he puts it, "Why not simply

---

[66] *Du Plessis v. De Klerk* 1996 (5) BCLR 658 (CC) at 720 D-I (Kriegler, J., dissenting) (S. Afr.).

[67] *Id.* at 720 D-I. It should be noted again here that the majority judgment in *Du Plessis* did not literally present itself as a stance in favor of indirect horizontality, nor did Justice Kriegler present his position as a stance in favor of direct horizontality. Strictly speaking, the former simply rejected horizontal effect and the latter endorsed it. However, a close reading of both opinions shows that the majority had indirect horizontal effect in mind whereas Justice Kriegler had a kind of direct horizontality in mind – even though he too ended up proposing a kind of indirect horizontality in a rather self-contradictory way.

[68] Louis Michael Seidman, *The State Action Paradox*, 10 CONST. COMMENT. 379, 397 (1993).

concede that state action is always present in some form and move directly to an analysis of whether the state action is constitutionally permissible?"[69] And he responds as follows:

> In light of the confusion produced by the state action inquiry, this approach is certainly attractive. Unfortunately, however, it only shifts the problem without really solving it, because something like the state action doctrine—together with all the uncertainty and incoherence that accompanies it—is built into how we think about constitutional rights.[70]

And how is it that Americans think about constitutional rights, according to Seidman? They think of it, on the one hand, claims Seidman, in terms of legitimate sovereign pursuits of ideals of social justice – such as the New Deal revolution – to which we subscribe unwaveringly. But they also want "to embrace," on the other hand, "a concept of a private sphere because we know that it preserves a space for individual flourishing that the state may otherwise destroy."[71] If Seidman is right, a commitment to constitutional rights is much like being lethally allergic to oxygen. Constitutional rights depend on strong sovereignty and are fatally threatened by strong sovereignty. This would surely explain the conundrum with which Justice Kriegler's dissent in *Du Plessis* leaves us. If state action and horizontal effect jurisprudence is going to make any headway out of this conundrum, it will have to come forth with an articulation of constitutional rights that does not fatally pitch constitutional sovereignty and constitutional freedoms against one another, but rather understands them as mutually sustaining one another – that is, as reinforcing one another. This is where horizontal effect and state action theory would need to pick up the debate if it is to make any significant progress.[72]

---

[69] *Id.* at 392. This is the question asked by all the authors cited, *supra* note 8.
[70] Seidman, *supra* note 68, at 392–93.   [71] *Id.* at 401.
[72] van der Walt, Horizontal Effect Revolution, *supra* note 8 (I believe I have taken some first steps in this regard).

# 8

# Hybrid state accountability and hybrid rights

## Positive rights, exclusion, and state action in Canada

TSVI KAHANA*

## Introduction

In Canada, positive rights jurisprudence is in its infancy. The fact that the Canadian Charter of Rights and Freedoms[1] is silent on the question of whether it protects only against state action, or also against state inaction,[2] coupled with the fact that it does not include specific guarantees for health, education, shelter, minimum subsistence, and the like, has resulted in the Supreme Court of Canada generally adhering to the state action doctrine – ruling that the Charter does not compel state action.

Over the years, claimants have tried to challenge this approach and have argued that positive obligations are embedded in the general Charter provisions, such as the fundamental freedoms guarantee in section 2 of the Charter,[3] and the right to life, liberty, and security of the person in section 7. The Court's responses to these claims have not been consistent, and it has

---

* I thank Kevin Banks, Chris Essert, and Michael Pratt for their helpful suggestions.
[1] Part I of the Constitution Act, 1982, *being* Schedule B to the Canada Act, 1982 c. 11 (U.K.).
[2] Most Charter provisions are worded in language that tolerates both negative and positive interpretations. For example, section 7, which protects "life, liberty, and security of the person," leaves open the question of whether it merely limits the state's ability to deprive one of life, liberty, and security, or whether it also requires the state to provide each person with life, liberty, and security. Some provisions are worded in language that clearly entails positive action. For example, section 23 provides French and English minorities, under some conditions, with the right to state-funded education in their language. In addition, some of the Charter's legal rights, such as the right to an interpreter in section 14, impose positive obligations on the state. However, those may be read as stipulations on the state's ability to infringe upon a negative right. If the state wishes, for example, to deprive a person's security, then it must provide them with an interpreter.
[3] Section 2 protects the right to freedom of conscience and religion (subsection a), the right to freedom of expression (b), freedom of assembly (c), and freedom of association (d). In this chapter, unless otherwise implied, reference to a section number denotes a section of the Charter.

never addressed the matter of positive rights in a comprehensive and coherent way. Rather, three trends may be observed in the jurisprudence.

The most common trend may be described as "perhaps one day" jurisprudence.[4] For instance, in *Haig v. Canada* (*Haig*), the Court refused to acknowledge a constitutional obligation to provide state support for freedom of expression because "the freedom of expression contained in s. 2(b) prohibits gags, but does not compel the distribution of megaphones."[5] However, the Court added that "a situation *might* arise in which, in order to make a fundamental freedom meaningful, a posture of restraint would not be enough, and positive government action might be required."[6] Similarly, in *Delisle v. Canada* (*Delisle*), the Court suggested that "*perhaps* in *exceptional* circumstances" Parliament would have a positive obligation to provide for labor relation regimes that protect employees' freedom of association.[7] Finally, in *Gosselin v. Quebec* (*Gosselin*), the Court refused to acknowledge a positive right to minimum subsistence under the section 7 right to security of the person, but added that "[o]ne day s. 7 may be interpreted to include positive obligations."[8] Cases such as these left the door open to acknowledge positive rights in the future. However, naturally, by denying the Charter's application on each set of facts, they also strengthened the rule that the Charter protects only negative entitlements.

The second approach, found in a case from 2010, seems to ignore this rule, and assumes – without any discussion – that freedom of expression includes the right to receive government information.[9] In that decision, the Court explicitly refused to address at length the doctrinal foundation of the decision, saying that "nothing will be gained" from it.[10]

The third approach, and the focus of this chapter, acknowledges positive rights claims when they also involve discrimination, and thus allows claims to cross traditional boundaries between rights. In the two cases presenting this approach, *Dunmore v. Ontario* (*Dunmore*)[11] and *Baier v. Alberta* (*Baier*),[12] the claimants were denied access to a legislative scheme. The ground for their denial, their occupation, was not a prohibited ground of discrimination under the Charter, and therefore, their equality claim

---

[4] Gosselin v. Que. (Att'y Gen.), 2002 S.C.C. 84, 82, [2002] 4 S.C.R. 429 (Can.).
[5] Haig v. Can. (Chief Electoral Officer), [1993] 2 S.C.R. 995 at 70, [1993] S.C.J. No. 84.
[6] *Id.* at 77 (emphasis added).
[7] Delisle v. Can. (Att'y Gen.), [1999] 2 S.C.R. 989 (emphasis added).
[8] Gosselin, 2002 SCC.   [9] Ont. v. Criminal Lawyers' Ass'n of Ont., 2010 SCC 23 (Can.).
[10] *Id.*, para. 31.   [11] 2001 SCC 94, [2001] 3 S.C.R. 1016 (Can.).
[12] Baier v. Alta, 2007 SCC 31, [2007] 2 S.C.R. 673 (Can.).

was doomed. Similarly, since their claim was for inclusion in a government program, and not for removal of obstacles created by legislation, their claim was for positive rights, which – according to the "perhaps one day" jurisdiction – should have failed. Nevertheless, they were successful. In *Dunmore*, the Court granted the claimants a positive remedy and ordered the government to legislate in their matter;[13] in *Baier*, the Court affirmed *Dunmore*'s holding, but ruled that the claimants failed on the facts.[14]

In Canada and abroad, specific rights have always been the building blocks of constitutional analysis. While it has always been clear that rights intertwine, intersect, and overlap, *Dunmore* was the first Canadian case in which multiple rights claims were essentially combined. The Court did not explicitly acknowledge its act of crossing the boundaries between individual and combined rights, and thus muddled the boundaries between rights. This act is the subject matter of this chapter.

Part I describes the *Dunmore* hybrid approach, and Part II seeks to explain this hybridity in two distinct ways. The first explanation is that the claim accepted in *Dunmore* represents a hybrid form of state action – or state involvement – when the state is not directly acting, but creates an environment that makes it accountable for certain results. The claim was a freedom of association claim, but the equality claim triggered this type of hybrid state involvement. The second explanation is that the hybridity rather refers to the rights involved, and not to the type of state action. The claim accepted in *Dunmore* was a cumulative equality and freedom of association claim in a situation where the claimants were unable to prove an infringement of either. While a full analysis of the hybridity implied in *Dunmore* is beyond this chapter, I offer a preliminary analysis of it in terms of constitutional theory and constitutional practice.

## I The *Dunmore* innovation

### a) *Before* Dunmore

*Dunmore* was a meeting point for equality and positive rights jurisprudence in Canada. To fully appreciate the Court's decision in this case, one must first understand the trajectory of these two jurisprudential lines.

---

[13] *Dunmore v Ontario (Attorney General)*, 2001 SCC 94, [2001] 3 SCR 1016.

[14] The three approaches described here are majority opinion approaches. Two dissenting opinions deny any distinction between positive and negative rights in Canada. See the dissenting opinion of Arbour J. in Gosselin v. Que., 2002 SCC 84 at 309 and the dissenting opinion of Fish J. in Baier 2007 SCC.

The *Dunmore* story begins with the exclusion of agricultural workers from the Ontario *Labour Relations Act, 1995* (*LRA*).[15] These employees challenged their exclusion on two grounds: that it violated the equality guarantee in section 15 of the Charter[16] and that it rendered their freedom to associate meaningless, therefore infringing their section 2(d) right to freedom of association.[17] Based on the pre-*Dunmore* jurisprudence, they were likely to lose on both fronts.

The equality argument was likely to fail because the Supreme Court of Canada had rejected – and continues to reject – the idea that *every* exclusion triggers Charter protection. There is a list of prohibited grounds upon which the distinction must have been made in order to trigger section 15 protection: those enumerated in the Charter and those considered by the judiciary to be analogous to them.[18] "Profession" had not – and has not – been recognized as an analogous ground,[19] which left the *Dunmore* petitioners no recourse under section 15.

The section 2(d) argument was also likely to fail. The impugned legislation did not prohibit the association of agricultural employees – they were still free to associate. However, their employers had no obligation to negotiate with their association. The threat to the employees' ability to associate therefore originated not from the government, but from third parties, namely, the employers. The argument was thus not against a state action in the form of a limit on freedom of association, but a state inaction in the form of a lack of state protection for agricultural employees against their private employers. The remedy sought was not a removal of a limit on the right erected by the states – the classic negative right remedy – but rather a positive creation of a state barrier against the power of private employers in the form of inclusion in the labor relations regime. Indeed, a very similar claim was rejected only two years earlier in *Delisle*.[20]

Against all odds, the *Dunmore* petitioners won. The Court essentially combined their unsuccessful equality and freedom of association arguments into one successful argument. I will now explain this in detail.

b) *The innovation: Combining equality and freedom of association*

The following Chart A clarifies the crux of the decision in *Dunmore*, and the way in which it brought equality and positive rights jurisprudence

---

[15] S.O. 1995, c. 1, Sched. A (Can.).
[16] Dunmore v. Ont., 2001 SCC 94, [2001] 3 S.C.R. 1016, para. 1 (Can.).   [17] *Id.*
[18] Andrews v. Law Soc'y of B.C., [1989] 1 S.C.R. 143 (Can.).
[19] Delisle v. Can. (Att'y Gen.), [1999] 2 S.C.R. 989, para. 44.   [20] *Id.*

## I. THE *DUNMORE* INNOVATION

Chart A Positive Rights Pre- and Post-*Dunmore*

| Type of situation/ constitutional setting | Under a full positive rights regime | Under the Charter | |
|---|---|---|---|
| | | Pre-*Dunmore* | Post-*Dunmore* |
| **Benefit not provided to any recipient** | 1<br>Positive rights claim | 4<br>No claim | 7<br>No claim |
| **Exclusion from benefit based on a unprotected ground** | 2<br>Positive rights claim | 5<br>No claim | 8<br>The *Dunmore* innovation: under certain conditions, positive rights claim |
| **Exclusion from benefit based on a protected ground** | 3<br>Positive rights claim and equality claim | 6<br>Equality claim | 9<br>Equality claim and, under certain conditions, positive rights claim |

together. It does so by comparing the state of the law in three situations, and under three different constitutional apparatuses: a hypothetical one in which positive rights are fully protected by a constitution, a second with the protection available under the Charter pre-*Dunmore*, and a third with the protection available under the Charter after *Dunmore*.

As the chart explains, *Dunmore* did not introduce protection for positive rights where the government does not provide a benefit in the first place (first row). Instead, *Dunmore* assists claimants when the government provides a benefit but excludes a person or group based on a ground of discrimination not protected by section 15, which is the case in box 8. Here, prior to *Dunmore*, the claimant would have had no Charter recourse. After *Dunmore*, an exclusion from a positive Charter entitlement grounds a constitutional claim under certain conditions. This claim would not be based on the exclusion itself – that would be the domain of section 15. Rather, this exclusion could be challenged under the relevant Charter right as a positive one. Finally, in a situation like that in box 9, in which the exclusion is based on a ground protected by section 15, *Dunmore* adds a positive rights claim to the existing equality rights claim. In practice, this is not likely to have a significant effect.[21]

One must take care not to conflate the types of situations in boxes 7 and 8. *Dunmore* did not change the general rule that the Charter does not create positive obligations. As box 7 shows, even after *Dunmore*, there is no general constitutional recourse for positive rights claims. *Dunmore* only assists a claimant in the situation underlying box 8, in which the government has provided a benefit to some but excluded others. Indeed, the centrality of the idea of exclusion in the Court's reasoning is what led me to describe *Dunmore* as an intersection between the equality and positive rights doctrines.

The mode of reasoning in *Dunmore* is worth mentioning. The Court does not positively say that under certain circumstances, a positive rights claim arises; Justice Bastarache describes the circumstances under which a positive rights claim may *not* arise. Surveying the past cases, he cites three barriers to a claimant's challenge of an exclusion from positive government protection of a fundamental freedom. Failure to surmount these barriers prevented positive rights claims in previous cases. Therefore, if a claimant wishes to succeed, according to Bastarache J., she or he must demonstrate that these barriers do not exist in her or his situation. That is, she or he must prove that:

(1) the claim is "grounded in fundamental *Charter* freedoms rather than in access to a particular statutory regime";[22]
(2) "the exclusion permits a *substantial* interference" with rights (section 2(d) rights in *Dunmore*);[23] and
(3) "the state can truly be held accountable for any inability to exercise a fundamental freedom."[24]

On the facts in *Dunmore*, Bastarache J. found that these three barriers did not exist. First, he found that the petitioners' request to be included in the labor relations regime was not merely seeking access to a statutory regime, but access to the freedom to associate itself. That is, the *LRA* instantiated

---

[21] The difference may be in the burden of proof. Generally speaking, the Court's approach to fundamental freedoms has been broad, whereas its approach to equality has been narrow. Compare R. v. Sharpe, 2001 SCC 2, [2001] 1 S.C.R. 45, paras. 143–46 (Can.), *with* Law v. Can. (Minister of Emp't and Immigration), [1989] 1 S.C.R. 143 at 168–69, 56 D.L.R. (4th) 1. The Dunmore conditions, however, significantly limit fundamental freedom claims, and offset this difference.
[22] Dunmore v. Ont., 2001 SCC 94, [2001] 3 S.C.R. 1016, para. 24 (Can.).
[23] *Id.*, para. 25 (emphasis in original).   [24] *Id.*, para. 26.

## I. THE *DUNMORE* INNOVATION

the freedom to organize, and recognized that association would otherwise be impossible.[25] Second, the evidence showed that agricultural employees lacked the status to protect their labor interests without benefiting from labor relations legislation.[26] Finally, Bastarache J. found that the state was responsible for the infringement because excluding agricultural employees from protections afforded to most other classes of employees had a chilling effect on their non-statutory union activity.[27]

Significantly, Bastarache J. did not address the question of whether the default position, in the case of exclusion, had changed such that positive rights would then be acknowledged. In other words, even after *Dunmore*, it was not clear whether surmounting the three barriers – the *Dunmore* factors – was merely *necessary* to succeed in a positive rights claim, or if it was also *sufficient*. A contextual reading of *Dunmore* does not provide an answer to this question either. On the one hand, Bastarache J. did not purport to create a test to determine positive rights claims, and acknowledged that the rule requiring a state action for Charter application remained.[28] On the other, immediately after identifying these potential barriers and discussing the facts of the case in light of them, Bastarache J. declared that the positive rights claim was successful. This implies that a lack of barriers is not only necessary, but also sufficient for a positive rights claim.[29] As we shall see in the next section, this was the approach adopted in *Baier*.

### c) The Baier *upgrade*

In *Baier*, the appellants sought to have provisions in the Alberta *Local Authorities Election Act*[30] declared unconstitutional for violating their right to freedom of expression under section 2(b) of the Charter.[31] These provisions excluded teachers from serving as school trustees.[32] Justice Rothstein, for the majority, characterized the claim as a positive rights claim because the law did not ban them from any expressive activity, but rather did not provide them the platform of school trusteeship to express themselves on education. Applying *Dunmore*, Rothstein J. rejected the

---

[25] *Id.*, para. 36.   [26] *Id.*, para. 42.   [27] *Id.*, para. 45.
[28] For examples of the language he adopts, see infra text accompanying notes 53–55.
[29] Alternatively, it may mean that the change *Dunmore* brought about is even more fundamental, and that Bastarache J. has done away with the exceptionality requirement all together, either in exclusion cases or more generally.
[30] R.S.A. 2000, c. L-2, secs. 21, 22 (Can.).
[31] Baier v. Alta, 2007 SCC 31, [2007] 2 S.C.R. 673, para. 7 (Can.).   [32] *Id.*, para. 5.

claim.³³ He explained that school trusteeship was a particular statutory platform for expression and not part of the right to freedom of expression itself, as the first *Dunmore* factor requires.³⁴ Similarly, their exclusion from eligibility to be school trustees may have substantially interfered with their ability to serve as trustees, but it did not substantially interfere with their freedom to express themselves on education matters.³⁵ This meant that the second *Dunmore* factor requiring evidence of substantial interference with the right – in this case, freedom of expression – was not met.

These findings would have sufficed to reject the claim. However, Rothstein J. went on to implicitly answer the question left open in *Dunmore*, declaring that if a positive rights claimant could demonstrate that the *Dunmore* conditions were met, a successful positive rights claim would be made.³⁶ He crystallized the *Dunmore* factors into a test, and foreclosed the possibility that other conditions may factor into the analysis of a positive rights claim.³⁷ Moreover, whereas *Dunmore* dealt with the freedom of association provision, section 2(d), the Court held in *Baier* that the same test applies to all of the section 2 guarantees, including freedom of religion and freedom of expression.³⁸ After *Baier*, therefore, the "perhaps one day" rule does not apply to exclusions from positive goods related to fundamental freedoms in Canada.

What is the theoretical basis for this exception? Seemingly, it mixed apples and oranges. If positive rights are acknowledged, why acknowledge them only in cases of under-inclusion? And if they are not to be acknowledged, why should they be acknowledged in cases of under-inclusion? This is the topic of the next part of the chapter.

## II  Hybrid state involvement and hybrid rights: Positive rights and exclusion

### a) Introduction

As explained in the previous part, the claimants in *Dunmore* only had a successful positive rights claim because they were in the type of situation

---

[33] Baier, 2007 SCC, paras. 44, 54. Justice Rothstein found it unnecessary to examine the third condition given the failure of the first two. *Id.*, para. 54.
[34] *Id.*, para. 44   [35] *Id.*, para. 48.   [36] *Id.*, para. 30.   [37] *Id.*   [38] *Id.*, para. 29.

in box 8, in which others received the good and they did not. Had they been in the type of situation found in box 7, in which no one was provided this good, they would not have had a positive rights claim.

Now, consider the following hypothetical situation. Due to an extreme financial crisis, the Government of Canada decides to abandon public health care. A claimant argues that the non-provision of health care violates section 7 of the Charter, which guarantees "life, liberty, and security" to each person because he or she cannot afford to buy health care privately.[39] According to *Dunmore*, this claim will fail because the new health care bill does not exclude anyone – it applies universally. But this makes little sense from a substantive point of view. In the *Dunmore* situation, *some people* (agricultural workers) were excluded from a *less important* positive rights good (union protection). In our hypothetical case, *everyone* is excluded from a *more important* positive rights good (health care). Why protect the lesser need and not the greater one? Of course, the answer cannot refer to the discrimination element. As explained earlier, discrimination based on profession is allowed in Canada.[40]

If we replace "exclusion" with its consequence "noninclusion," the question becomes even clearer. If there is no program to provide health care, no one is included in such a program. From the perspective of positive rights, if exclusion is a concern, noninclusion should also be one. Why does *Dunmore* only provide protection for positive rights in the type of situations when there is exclusion? In this part of the chapter, I offer two explanations for the exclusion requirement; both are based on crossing boundaries traditionally kept in constitutional doctrine.

According to the first explanation, offered in section B, the existence of the exclusion meant that even though there was no state action per se, there was a softer form described by the Court as "State Accountability." This notion challenges the traditional boundary of state action, effectively muddling it. According to the second explanation, offered in section C,

---

[39] There will be two additional hurdles that the claimant will have to overcome. First, he or she will have to argue that Dunmore also applies to section 7. This will probably not be difficult to prove as there is nothing in Dunmore that is unique to freedom of association. Indeed, as we saw in Baier, 2007 SCC, the Court applied it to the freedom of expression and stated that it applies to all of the fundamental freedoms. Second, he or she will have to demonstrate that this section 7 infringement is not done in accordance with the principles of fundamental justice, as per the wording of section 7. This may be a more difficult task. However, for the purposes of the argument, let us assume that this is possible.

[40] See *supra* text accompanying note 18.

the claim accepted in *Dunmore* was a hybrid right claim. The agricultural employees did not have either a successful freedom of association claim or a successful equality claim, but they had a successful cumulative equality and freedom of association claim. The notion of a hybrid right collapses inner rights boundaries and allows the combination of rights to be stronger than each right separately.

### b) A hybrid state involvement: Exclusion and the boundary of state action

A close reading of *Dunmore* reveals that the exclusion of agricultural employees from the labor relations regime gave their claim enough force to push it across the boundary of the state action, even though they were essentially attacking state inaction. The boundary of state action was thus slightly pushed by this case. Prior to *Dunmore*, only positive state conduct triggered Charter claims; afterward, certain types of exclusion are considered to transform cases of state inaction into state action.

It is obvious that exclusion is a state action for the purpose of the equality guarantee in section 15. However, in a case where the exclusion is not based on a forbidden ground of discrimination under section 15, this form of state action does not assist the plaintiff. The point of *Dunmore*, under this reading of the case, is that exclusion can be used as the state action *for the purpose of a freedom of association claim*.

On the surface, this seems like mixing apples and oranges. If I have a positive right to good A, I have it not because others receive it, but because the state owes it to me. If I must demonstrate that someone else receives a good in order to establish a claim to it, my claim is not about my entitlement to the good, but about my entitlement to equal state treatment. From the perspective of freedom of association, there seems to be only two options. The first is that every individual has a right to protective labor legislation. This means that we do away with the state action requirement, meaning that state inaction – the lack of the creation of labor legislation – can be challenged. The other is that we do not do away with the state action requirement, meaning that individuals do not have a right to protective labor legislation. Neither option leaves room for exclusion as a trigger for state obligation.

In order to explain how the Court made exclusion part of the positive rights analysis and created a hybrid concept of state action, we need to delve into the *Dunmore* requirements. Next, I explore each of these requirements by asking two questions. First, is the requirement an appropriate stipulation for the protection of a positive – as opposed to negative – right? Second, is the requirement related to the idea of exclusion? Answering the second question is necessary for my inquiry here, which is the search for a connection between positive rights and exclusion. Answering the first question is necessary in order to ensure that while answering the second question, we have a clear understanding of the *Dunmore* requirements themselves.[41]

### 1. The constitutional core requirement

The first requirement, which I call the "constitutional core requirement," is that the right itself, rather than a particular legislative platform for its achievement, is what is sought to be protected.[42] This has clearly not been applied by the courts to negative rights. For example, the Court made it clear that section 2(b) of the Charter protects both the core of freedom of expression (political speech, for example)[43] and the periphery of this right (child pornography, for example).[44] The question of whether the limit on the right is a limit on the core of the right is relevant for the analysis of the justification of the limit, under section 1 of the Charter, but not for the rights analysis.[45]

The constitutional core requirement is probably based on institutional considerations in relation to positive rights, and hence is applicable only to those rights. A familiar concern with positive rights is that granting all citizens the positive entitlements they seek would bankrupt the state and make it impossible to give anyone any rights at all.[46] Going back to the health care example, funding everything relating to health as opposed to

---

[41] Beyond allowing a complete inquiry, making sure that the exclusion requirement does not apply in negative rights cases gives us a check on the correctness of the analysis. Suppose that I arrive at the conclusion that a certain Dunmore requirement entails exclusion. If this requirement also exists in negative rights cases, it means that the exclusion requirement should apply in negative rights cases. However, we know that this is not the case and that negative rights claims do not require a claim of exclusion. Our analysis has thus gone awry.

[42] See *supra* text accompanying note 22.

[43] See, for example, Harper v. Can. (Att'y. Gen.), 2004 SCC 33, [2004] 1 S.C.R. 827.

[44] R. v. Sharpe, 2001 SCC 2, [2001] 1 S.C.R. 45, para. 23 (Can.).

[45] Judicial review of right infringements under the Charter takes place in two stages. At the first stage, the claimant must prove the right is infringed; at the second stage, the state must prove that the limit is "prescribed by law" and "demonstrably justified in a free and democratic society," as per section 1 of the Charter. See R. v. Oakes, [1986] 1 S.C.R. 103, 26 D.L.R. (4th) 200.

[46] See, for example, Susan A. Bandes, *The Negative Constitution: A Critique*, 88 MICH. L. REV. 8 (1990).

a minimal funding of core health services may create a significant strain on state resources. Giving citizens only the core of positive entitlements responds to this concern.

The constitutional core requirement is clearly unrelated to the notion of exclusion. A person could be excluded from a particular venue of the right, or could be excluded from the constitutional core of the right. Exclusion is neither necessary nor sufficient for the constitutional core requirement. It is not necessary because the entire population may not have access to the constitutional core of a positive right. It is not sufficient because a person could be excluded from a particular venue of the right.

### 2. The substantial interference requirement

The second *Dunmore* requirement is that there is "substantial interference" with the right.[47] The Court does not explain what makes an interference "substantial." As such, we must examine the way in which the Court applies it in *Dunmore*. Justice Bastarache asked whether agricultural workers were able to achieve the underlying goals of the freedom of association protected by the Charter, even while being excluded from the *LRA* scheme.[48] He did so after noting that in *Delisle*, which dealt with limits on association of police officers, this requirement was not met since the officers were able to achieve some association goals without legislative protection.[49] This effectively makes the second requirement a sub-requirement of the first. In *Dunmore*, for example, if the agricultural workers were able to achieve the association goals through other means, but still claimed the right to access the labor relations scheme, they would have been claiming access to the specific platform that was the act, not to the right itself. That would violate the first *Dunmore* requirement.

Like the constitutional core requirement, the substantial interference requirement is not applicable to negative rights. A business owner, for example, may decide to advertise his or her business through loudspeakers on the street[50] and that expression will be captured by section 2(b) even though they can also use the newspaper.

Like the constitutional core requirement, the substantial interference requirement is not related to the notion of exclusion. Exclusion is neither

---

[47] See *supra* text accompanying note 23.
[48] Dunmore v. Ont., 2001 SCC 94, [2001] 3 S.C.R. 1016, para. 39 (Can.).
[49] *Id.*, para. 14.
[50] See Montréal (City) v. 2952-1366 Que. Inc., 2005 SCC 62, [2005] 3 S.C.R. 141.

necessary nor sufficient for the substantial interference requirement. It is not necessary because the state may deny everyone access to the right. It is not sufficient because a person may be excluded from a right that he or she may be able to access through alternative means.

### 3. The "true accountability" requirement

The third *Dunmore* requirement is that the state be held "truly accountable" for the infringement of the right.[51] Unlike the previous two requirements – the constitutional core requirement and the substantial interference requirement – this requirement does not focus on the nature of the infringement, but on the relationship between the infringement and the state. What does "true" accountability mean?

Positive rights claims are claims of state inaction. The doctrine of state action – which *Dunmore* does not do away with – says that when the state does not act, it is not accountable. However, *Dunmore* creates a hybrid situation in which the state is inactive but still accountable. When would such hybridity occur? Bastarache J. tries to clarify:

> [A] failure to include someone in a protective regime may *affirmatively permit restraints* on the activity the regime is designed to protect. The rationale behind this is that underinclusive state action falls into suspicion to the extent it *substantially orchestrates, encourages or sustains* the violation of fundamental freedoms.[52]

Note Justice Bastarache's linguistic moves, which soften and blur the state action boundary – even at the expense of doctrinal clarity. First, note the oxymoron "affirmatively permitting restraint." "Permitting" is passive; doing something "affirmatively" is active. "Affirmatively permitting restraint" is a creative hybrid between "affirmatively restraining" and "permitting the restraint." Naturally, such a middle point will be very hard to find. Second, note the ambiguity about what Bastarache J. considers to be an adequate level of state involvement to trigger the Charter. When the state "orchestrates" something, there is certainly state action. When the state merely "sustains" something, there appears to be no state action at all, but instead what we would traditionally have viewed as state neutrality or silence. State "encouragement" seems to be somewhere between (actively) orchestrating and (passively) sustaining. So which one is the threshold for state accountability: orchestrating,

---

[51] See *supra* text accompanying note 24.
[52] Dunmore, 2001 SCC, para. 26 (italics added).

encouraging, or sustaining? To add another level of ambiguity, Bastarache J. adds the term "substantially" to qualify these verbs, which means we may need to consider the extent to which the state orchestrates, encourages, or sustains in future cases.

Like the previous two requirements, the "true accountability" requirement does not make sense for negative rights claims. Because state action is attacked in negative rights claims, the state is by definition accountable. Unlike the previous two requirements, however, this requirement does explain the relationship between positive rights and exclusion. According to Bastarache J., the answer is that it is the exclusion that *triggers* the state's true accountability in the facts of *Dunmore*:

> What the legislature has done by reviving the LRA is not *simply allow* private circumstances to subsist; it has *reinforced* those circumstances by excluding agricultural workers from the only available channel for associational activity.
>
> The most palpable effect [of the exclusion is] to *place* a *chilling effect* on non-statutory union activity. By extending statutory protection to just about every class of worker in Ontario, the legislature has *essentially discredited* the organizing efforts of agricultural workers.
>
> The exclusion *suggests* that workplace democracy has no place in the agricultural sector and, moreover, that agricultural workers' efforts to associate are illegitimate.[53]

Again, note the linguistic moves made by Bastarache J. and the way in which his language muddles the state action boundary. First, he contrasted "*simply allow*" with "reinforce" even though, in this case, the reinforcement was done by way of, simply, allowing.[54] Second, he posited that the state in fact *acted* by excluding agricultural workers from the LRA. This exclusion, which would normally be the hallmark of a *section 15* claim, had done something *active* to their *freedom of association* as well: it *discredited* the workers, it *suggested* to employers that they were not worthy of protection, and it *placed* a chilling effect on their

---

[53] *Id.*, paras. 44–45 (emphasis added).
[54] Note the use of the adverb "simply" to accentuate the contrast between the two ideas. On the one hand, there is "simply allowing"; on the other, there is more-than-simply "reinforcing."

## II. HYBRID STATE INVOLVEMENT AND HYBRID RIGHTS

efforts – all of which were actions. According to Bastarache J., the exclusion of agricultural employees affected not only their equality – which is obvious, but which cannot be constitutionally attacked – but also their freedom of association. How can this be, given that in relation to the freedom of association of agricultural employees, the state has in fact *not* acted? The answer must be that the didactic effect of the state's silence with respect to the labor relations of agricultural workers amounts to state action because it *reduces* the level of freedom of association enjoyed by such workers.

An illustration may be helpful here. Suppose the level of protection that employers would voluntarily give to agricultural employees is level 1. And suppose that the *LRA* gives most workers level 5 protection. Metaphorically, by excluding agricultural workers from the level 5 protections of the *LRA*, the state has whispered in the ears of agricultural employers: "Your workers do not deserve state protection, so do not even give them level 1 protection."

As Chart B explains, this hypothesis explains the difference between situations 7 and 8 in Chart A. In situation 7, where no one receives the benefit, there is no state involvement at all and, therefore, there is no positive rights claim. In situation 8, even though in relation to agricultural employees there is no state action – since they are not included in the legislation – their exclusion amounts to state action, because it reduces their freedom of association, as compared to a situation of no legislation at all.

What the chart shows us is that even though agricultural employees did not have an equality claim, their exclusion from the labor regime makes their situation worse than if there were no labor relations at all, and it thus affects their freedom of association claim. Their exclusion does not only mean that they are not receiving the benefit of inclusion; it also means that the state is taking away the little associational benefit they would have had but for the legislation.

Now we see why the positive right to freedom of association in *Dunmore* was based on a hybrid state involvement. The Court did not go so far as to do away with the state action requirement. However, it was comfortable creating a softer version of state action: the discouraging message did not directly change the situation of agricultural employees, but affected their situation indirectly.

A difficulty of this construction of *Dunmore* is that it does not perfectly align with the facts of the case. It assumes that in a situation with no protective labor legislation whatsoever, agricultural employees would enjoy some voluntary protection from employers – it is the

Chart B

| Type of situation in Chart A | Level of protection to all employees | Level of protection to agricultural employees |
|---|---|---|
| **No labor legislation protection** (situation 7 in Chart A) | 1 (voluntary from employers) | 1 (voluntary from employers) |
| **Protection for all employees excluding agricultural employees (Situation 8 in Chart A)** | 5 (mandated by the Constitution) | 0 (resulting from constitutional message to employers) |

diminishing of that protection that makes the state truly accountable and triggers the freedom of association claim. However, it is not obvious that this is true. With no protection guaranteed to anyone, it may make more economic sense for employers to give agricultural employees (and everyone else) no associational benefits. So the right figures on the first line in Chart B should be 0 and 0, not 1 and 1. Given this, it is not clear that the exclusion of agricultural employees from the labor relations regime makes their situation any worse than if there was no protection for anyone, which means that the state cannot be "truly accountable" for the violation of their freedom of association by employers. Of course, the state can be truly accountable for the exclusion itself, but that exclusion, as should be clear by now, cannot be challenged by the Charter since it is not based on a prohibited ground of discrimination.[55]

### c) A hybrid right: Freedom of association and equality combined

The second explanation for the *Dunmore* conflation of freedom of association and equality is simpler and makes more sense on the facts, but is more complex in terms of constitutional theory. According to this explanation, the Supreme Court joined together a partially successful equality claim and a partially successful freedom of association claim, creating one fully successful equality and freedom of association claim. It thus implicitly acknowledged a hybrid right.

---

[55] See *supra* text accompanying note 18.

## II. HYBRID STATE INVOLVEMENT AND HYBRID RIGHTS

This account holds that Bastarache J. wished to remedy the plight of the clearly disadvantaged agricultural employees. He felt that the labor status of agricultural employees deserved some protection, but he was not able to provide them a remedy under section 2(b) since the limits on their freedom of association resulted from the actions of private employers, and not from state action. He was also not able to provide them with a remedy under section 15 since profession was not a ground of discrimination. The Court could have opened the analogous grounds debate, but that would create, as Deschamps J. said in a later case, a "sea change" to the jurisprudence.[56] Rather than doing that, Bastarache J. helped agricultural employees in another way. He brought into the analysis an element of equality and an element of freedom of association, and created a cumulative right of equality-in-relation-to-freedom-of-association. The claim made by the agricultural employees contained a component of a freedom of association claim (their association would not have any power vis-à-vis employers) and a component of an equality claim (they were excluded). Even though they were not able to make either a full section 2(d) claim (because of the lack of state action), or a full section 15 claim (because their exclusion was not based on a prohibited ground), the Court thought that, given the existence of these components, it was unfair to deny them a remedy.

The structural difference between the previous explanation (hybrid state involvement) and this explanation (hybrid right) is this: under the hybrid state involvement explanation, the claim of agricultural employees was a freedom of association claim, and the equality claim – the exclusion – was a *trigger* for this claim, since it yielded the required "true" state accountability. Under the hybrid right explanation, neither rights claim is a trigger for the other. The claim is neither an equality claim nor a freedom of association claim. It is an equality and freedom of association claim.

The notion that two partial arguments, each of which does not have enough independent strength, can be considered together to be persuasive seems intuitively convincing: if one has two reasons to go to a party, neither of which is sufficient on their own, one may nevertheless decide that together the two reasons are persuasive enough to attend. However, this notion is, a priori, inconsistent with principles of constitutional adjudication and of evidence law.

---

[56] Ont. (Att'y Gen.) v. Fraser, 2011 SCC 20, para. 319.

Principles of constitutional adjudication view the analysis unit under the Charter as the single right, since "[e]ach right is distinct."[57] Two unsuccessful rights claims do not make for one successful claim. Evidence law requires a plaintiff to prove on a balance of probabilities at least one cause of action. Almost proving two causes of action is not tantamount to meeting the overall burden of proof in a case. Judicial practice reflects these notions. In Charter cases, for example, when two arguments based on two Charter rights are made, a court examines each Charter claim in turn. If both fail, judgments do not then include an additional inquiry as to whether the cumulative force of the arguments yields success in meeting the burden of proof.

In order to make the hybrid right idea conceptually viable, we need to find a way to allow accumulations of claims for different rights. Accumulations of claims about A and B may be done in legal analysis when the analysis unit is neither A nor B but rather a broader, C, in relation to which A and B are merely building blocks. For example, when a judge or a jury evaluates the weight of evidence, they often rely on their accumulation – each evidential piece of evidence would not meet the required burden, but their accumulation does. This is possible because the analysis unit is not every piece of evidence separately, but the broader question of whether the burden was met. Similarly, the Supreme Court of Canada often uses the idea of "contextual factors" in order to determine whether a certain claim has been made. The existence of one such factor may not be sufficient, but the accumulation of factors is. This is done, for example, when the Court has to decide what the standard of judicial review of administrative decisions should be.[58] Again, this is possible because the analysis unit refers to the institutional question as a whole, and not to each individual factor.

In our case, the way to make cumulative rights claims consistent with principles of constitutional adjudication is to say that the analysis unit is not a specific right but rather something that may be called a general "Charter wrong." Under this concept, it is possible to think of a general Charter violation even when no specific rights violations independently exist. According to this idea, each right of the Charter is at once an independent source for legal claims and a source for argument about a general Charter wrong. If a claimant can bring enough components of violations of rights, their accumulation creates a general

---

[57] Thomson Newspapers Co. v. Can, (Att'y Gen.), [1998] 1 S.C.R. 877, para. 80.
[58] Dunsmuir v. N.B., 2009 SCC 9, [2008] 1 S.C.R. 190, para. 64.

## II. HYBRID STATE INVOLVEMENT AND HYBRID RIGHTS 191

Charter violation, even if those components cannot yield any specific rights claim.

An illustration would be helpful here too. Let us say that each Charter right is worth, say, 10 "Charter points." In order to succeed in a Charter claim, a claimant must follow one of two routes. The conventional route is to focus on one right, and prove the full 10 points worth of the right. The optional, and less conventional, route is to show an accumulation of 10 "Charter points" from various Charter rights. Under this alternative route, Charter rights may serve as building blocks in the more general inquiry into whether there is a general Charter wrong.

A full inquiry on the promise and perils of the idea of a Charter wrong is beyond the ambit of this chapter. A few preliminary points are nevertheless worth mentioning. The notion that all Charter rights are based on the same value – be it dignity, autonomy, liberty, or other – has some support both in constitutional theory and in constitutional doctrine. In terms of theory, some constitutional theorists believe that most, or all, constitutional rights are based on common underlying values, such as autonomy, dignity, freedom, or equality.[59] If all rights protect the same values, then it makes sense to accumulate elements of partial rights claim since these components are also components of the same underlying value. Even if only some rights protect the same values, it would make sense to accumulate partial claims of these rights. In terms of constitutional practice, the Supreme Court of Canada often points to values underlying Charter rights, and often interprets rights in light of these values.[60] The Court also acknowledged unwritten constitutional principles, which are embedded in constitutional texts and constitutional structure.[61] Based on the combination of these two notions, the Supreme Court could declare an underlying, foundational, implicit value of protecting "Charter wrongs" if they relate to the underlying purposes of the Charter.

Surely, such a move brings with it a whole new host of difficulties concerning the relation between constitutional text, constitutional principles, and rights theory. More theoretical work and doctrinal work is

---

[59] See, for example, David Mullan, *Underlying Constitutional Principles: The Legacy of Justice Rand*, 34 MANITOBA. L.J. 1 (2010).
[60] See Frank Iacobucci, *The Charter: 20 Years Later*, 21 WINDSOR Y.B. ACCESS TO JUST. 3, 8–9 (2002).
[61] See, most famously, Reference re Remuneration of Judges of the Provincial Ct. of P.E.I., [1997] 3 S.C.R. 3, para. 92, 150 D.L.R. (4th) 577 and Reference re Secession of Quebec, [1998] 2 S.C.R. 217, 161 D.L.R. (4th) 385.

required to make it workable. However, if I read *Dunmore* correctly, this was already done by the Court. The novelty and peculiarity of this idea perhaps explains why *Dunmore* was the only case in which the Supreme Court actually provided a positive rights remedy in response to a violation of the Charter's fundamental freedoms.

## Conclusion

The two types of boundary crossing hybridity discussed in the previous section are not mutually exclusive. One may represent the basis for Bastarache J. desire to help agricultural employees; the other may represent the technique he used. The existence of a hybrid right explains why Bastarache J. felt that it would be unfair to deny agricultural employees a remedy: not only did they not enjoy freedom of association, but they were also discriminated against in comparison to other workers. The technique used by Bastarache J. to provide relief was the acknowledgment that even in the face of state inaction, there may be true state accountability. If indeed both types of hybridity exist together, what we have here is a hybrid of hybrids.

The Supreme Court has not been open about the conceptual moves and boundary crossing in *Dunmore*. To the contrary, the Court played it down. The Court has provided limited explanation for the true accountability requirement in *Dunmore*, claiming that the state action doctrine has already "matured" in case law and that allowing the extension into true state accountability will not be a "quantum leap" but will merely allow the notion of state action to "further mature."[62]

This rhetoric strategy seeks to downplay the extent of innovation in *Dunmore*. The idea of maturity connotes natural progress and, more importantly, inevitability. As I explain throughout this chapter, the *Dunmore* decision actually embeds a significant innovation that requires much doctrinal and theoretical elucidation.

However, even assuming that the boundary crossings depicted in this chapter are merely natural progressions of existing doctrine, there is still much theoretical and doctrinal work to be done on positive rights in Canada. Theoretically, the nature of rights and their interaction, as well as the nature of state action, will have to be revisited. Doctrinally, the Court must reconcile and consolidate the various approaches mentioned

---

[62] Dunmore v. Ont., 2001 SCC 94, [2001] 3 S.C.R. 1016, para. 26 (Can.).

at the outset of this chapter. Second, the Court must revisit the doctrine regarding specific Charter rights, created mainly for negative rights protection, and adjust it such that existing negative rights doctrine accommodates positive rights as well.[63] Finally, the Court will have to revisit section 1 doctrine, again, given that the Oakes test was created in the context of negative rights protection. Even if the specific element of state action has been maturing in Canada, positive rights jurisdiction in Canada, as the opening of this chapter indicates, is still in its infancy.

[63] For such an attempt, see Baier v. Alta, 2007 SCC 31, [2007] 2 S.C.R. 673, para. 30 (Can.).

# 9

## Human rights and derivative rights
### The European Convention on Human Rights and the rights of corporations

ANAT SCOLNICOV

... on being asked what,
on this stage, so to say, of the world,
seemed to him most evocative of wonder,
replied that there was nothing to be seen
more marvelous than man.

G. Pico della Mirandola,
Oration on the Dignity of Man (1486)

### Introduction

This volume examines the boundaries of rights, and their relationship to the changing nature of the state. The classic postulation of human rights is that they are rights of individuals with corresponding obligations of the state. The boundaries of human rights, and corresponding obligations, have shifted over the past several decades in legal discourse. Much of that discourse centers on expansion of human rights *obligations* to entities other than the state.[1] This chapter looks at the extension of *rights* to others who are not individuals.

In previous work, I have argued, in the face of mounting support for recognition of human rights of corporations, that corporations do not have human rights, as the concept of human rights cannot apply to nonhumans.[2]

Human rights are based on the inherent worth of individuals. *Any human rights are based on this inherent worth, whether these are rights*

---

[1] See ANDREW CLAPHAM, HUMAN RIGHTS OBLIGATIONS OF NON-STATE ACTORS (2006); PHILIP ALSTON, NON-STATE ACTORS AND HUMAN RIGHTS (2005).
[2] Anat Scolnicov, *Lifeless and Lifelike in Law: Do Corporations Have Human Rights?*, available at http://dx.doi.org/10.2139/ssrn.2268537.

of humans to express themselves, or rights protecting their physical and moral integrity, or other aspects of their innate personality. Such *inherent* worth does not characterize corporations, which are always a means to achieving an end, and have no inherent value themselves.

This is not to say that the external justifications for rights are not important. Reasons not internal to the rights-bearer, such as social utility, promotion of a better society, advancement of democracy, and rule of law, are persuasive and important justifications for protection of human rights. They are certainly *additional* reasons for recognizing human rights, but cannot serve in themselves as a basis for recognition of human rights. If human rights can only be justified by internal justifications, corporations cannot have rights. They have no moral integrity, autonomy, or individuality. They are means to an end. Humans are never means to an end, and therefore, all deserve protection of their rights.

The attribution of the right claims of owners or shareholders to corporations, and the equation of their right claims to a right of the corporation, is fallacious. The legal personality accorded in law to the corporation means precisely that it is legally separate from its owners. They have certain legal rights derived from their proprietorship, but not others. They *are not* the corporation and cannot claim to exercise a human right on behalf of the corporation.[3] This was the conceptual analysis I developed elsewhere from a theoretical perspective.[4]

The present chapter examines more closely specific human rights, in order to contend with possible criticism of the approach that corporations have no human rights. The main criticism which could be raised against the no-corporate-rights approach is that not all rights should be treated equally, that is, the criticism that some rights do not apply to corporations, but other rights do apply, all depending on the nature of the rights. As this chapter maintains that no human right applies to corporations, it will contend with the difficult cases of rights which seem to be most applicable to corporations. An explanation is needed as to why nevertheless the principled no-corporate-rights approach espoused here is valid in those cases as well. This thesis, that no human rights can be corporate rights, can be substantiated in the case of each individual

---

[3] See Richard Adelstein, Firms as Persons (unpublished manuscript) (on file with author), for a similar argument that acts of the firm cannot be attributed to one individual.
[4] Scolnicov, *supra* note 2.

right. The applicability of the no-corporate-rights argument to specific human rights can be tested on rights of the European Convention on Human Rights.

The question whether a right applies to corporations does not arise in regard to some rights, such as the right to marry (Article 12), freedom from slavery (Article 5), prohibition of torture and ill treatment (Article 3), or the right to life (Article 2). These rights are simply *not capable* of being applied to corporations. Those are the easy cases. There are, however, other rights which are *capable* of being applied to corporations, but this does not mean that they *should be* recognized as applying to them. This is so particularly in regard to rights of fair trial (Article 6), prohibition on retroactivity of criminal punishment (Article 7), right to property (Protocol 1 Article 1), right of free speech (Article 10), right of nondiscrimination (Article 14), and freedom of religion (Article 9).

Rights of property, fair trial, and nonretroactivity of criminal punishment are most closely associated with companies and most often relied upon by them. But, as will be seen, they should not be recognized and applied to corporations. The justifications for these rights are vastly different in regard to humans and corporations. There may be good *policy* reasons to apply the same to corporate bodies, but as rights they only belong to humans.

Other rights – free speech, discrimination, and religious freedom – pose a different challenge for the no-corporate-rights approach, as will be seen. In some cases, the only way to give meaning to the human rights of individuals is through attribution of a right to the corporation. This is to be resolved through the introduction of the concept of "derivative rights." In such cases, derivative rights will be recognized, predicated on, and justified by the rights of individuals.

In Section I, this chapter first introduces the approach of the European Court of Human Rights to the human rights of companies, and then argues that corporate human rights should not have been recognized by the Court. In Section II, the chapter proceeds to examine cases in which rights of corporations should be recognized as derivative from the rights of individuals. In Section III, the chapter then examines rights which are most often relied upon by corporations and recognized by the European Court of Human Rights, but shows that corporate rights should not have been recognized.

Throughout the discussion in this chapter, the argument that corporations have no human rights is not predicated on a commercial purpose of their activity. Commercial purpose of an activity is neither necessary nor sufficient reason for denying the application of human rights to its actor. The commercial purpose of corporations is not the decisive factor for rejecting human rights of corporations. Humans can work toward a commercial goal and will still merit the protection of human rights when doing so. Conversely, corporations might not have a commercial purpose (it is essentially possible to incorporate a charitable enterprise as a limited company), but this does not mean that they can possess human rights.

The chapter's conclusion, after examining the European Court of Human Rights case law, is that in certain cases rights of corporations should have indeed been recognized, but only because they were derivative of rights of individuals. In other cases in which corporate rights were recognized, there is no justification for the recognition. This is so as a matter of abstract principle but also as a proposed course for the application of the European Convention on Human Rights.

## I   The European Convention on Human Rights

The European Court of Human Rights has devoted little discussion to questioning whether corporations are capable of possessing human rights as a matter of principle, although it has recognized such rights in its case law. In the Convention, legal persons are explicitly mentioned in Protocol 1 Article 1 (right to property) so it is uncontroversial that the article applies to corporations. Media enterprises are also mentioned in Article 10.

However, in regard to other rights, the Convention is silent. Article 1 provides that rights must be secured to "everyone," a term which reveals nothing about whether nonnatural legal persons are included within it. The term "everyone" in Article 10 was interpreted by the Court to mean that it includes all legal persons. But this interpretation seems to presuppose its conclusion. The Court imagines this "everyone" as including nonnatural persons, even though the Convention tells us nothing about who this "everyone" is. The question whether the Convention can be applied to corporate persons remains a lacuna in the Convention text.

Article 10(1) is suffixed by a statement that "[t]his article shall not prevent States from requiring the licensing of broadcasting, television or cinema enterprises." It is possible to surmise from the inclusion of this statement that the article applies to corporations, but this does not necessarily arise from the article. The statement simply settles a substantive matter – permitting broadcast licensing schemes – and does not determine one way or another the applicability of the article or the Convention to corporations.

The Court has never discussed the possibility that corporate rights do not exist, but simply assumed that they do. The Court assumed that Convention rights apply to corporations, recognizing them on a right-by-right basis, on the different substantive articles that came before it. So, Article 8, the protection of private life, was applied to corporations in *Société Colas Est. v. France*.[5] The Court recognized that Article 6(1), containing the fair process guarantees, applies to corporations,[6] as does Article 11, which protects the freedom of association,[7] and Article 7(1), the prohibition of retroactive criminal laws.[8] Protocol 4 Article 2 of the Convention, which assures the right to freedom of movement and freedom to choose residence, was applied to a company, although with no substantive discussion by the Court and no contestation by the respondent state.[9] The assumption by the Court that corporate human rights exist is, however, far from a forgone conclusion.

### a) Symmetry between rights and obligations

Recognition of corporate human rights has been justified by the argument that symmetry exists between rights and obligations. If corporate bodies have obligations, goes this argument, then they should have rights as well. This is an argument which has been advanced in the debate in international law over recognition of legal persons.[10]

However, this symmetry is not a necessary conclusion. Indeed, this argument is flawed. Possession of legal personality does not entail possession of all the same rights and obligations as those of any other legal person. Although possessing legal personality means the ability to have

---

[5] 39 Eur. H.R. Rep. 17 (2004).
[6] Agrotexim v. Greece, 21 Eur. H.R. Rep. 250; Immobiliare Saffi v. Italy, 30 Eur. H.R. Rep. 756; Stavebná v. Slovakia, App. No.7261/06; Matos e Silva Lda v. Portugal, 24 Eur. H.R. Rep. 573. See also Marius Emberland, *The Corporate Veil in the Case Law of the European Court of Human Rights*, 63 ZaöRV 945 (2003).
[7] A and H v. Austria, App. No. 9905/82 (1984) D.R. 18; AB Kurt Kellermann v. Sweden, App. No. 41579/98 (both concerning nonnatural legal persons that were not companies).
[8] Radio France v. France, App. No. 53984/00; Yukos v. Russia. App. No. 14902/04.
[9] Eugenia Michaelidou Developments Ltd v. Turkey, App. No. 16163/90 (although for the purposes of the friendly settlement in the case – which relied on breaches of other articles of the Convention – the sole owner of the corporation was treated as an applicant).
[10] See, for example, Jose E. Alvarez, *Are Corporations "Subjects" of International Law?*, 9 SANTA CLARA J. INT'L L. 1 (2011).

rights and obligations, it does not mean that rights of a certain type, human rights, can be possessed by any and every legal personality.

A line of decisions, including *Holy Monasteries v. Greece*[11] and *Finska församlingen and Hautaniemi v. Sweden*,[12] clarify that a body can *either* be a nongovernmental organization, and have rights under the Convention and be capable of being a "victim" who can bring applications under the Convention, *or* be part of the state, and then incapable of being a "victim" or having Convention rights. A state can, of course, have obligations under the Convention. So, under the European Convention on Human Rights, a body can, indeed must, have *either* obligations or rights. Symmetry between rights and obligations simply does not exist.

In international law, there is nothing novel in the idea that the legal personality of corporations, to the extent that it exists, is different from that of both natural persons and the natural persons of international law (states). As Alvarez points out in his contribution to this collection,[13] legal personality in international law is not "one size fits all." He suggests that in each case, recognition of human rights to corporations will be based on the special nature of the corporate form and the specific right at stake.[14]

In the first case in which the International Court of Justice recognized the legal personality of an international organization (the United Nations), that recognition meant recognition of certain rights and obligations, not all the rights and obligations of a state. So an international organization is capable of having rights and obligations, though not all the rights and obligations of a state. Commercial corporations too can have limited legal personality in international law, particularly under investment treaties,[15] with a set of rights and obligations different from that of states or international organizations.[16]

### b) Coherence and divergence in the Convention

The European Court was faced with a variety of possible choices relating to recognition of corporate rights. Regarding the right to property

---

[11] App. No. 13092/87; 13984/88.   [12] App. No. 24019/94 (1996) D.R.8 5, 94.
[13] José E. Alvarez in this volume.   [14] *Id.*, sec. VIII, near n.108.
[15] See The Treaty of Canterbury (English Channel Tunnel Agreement) *and* the BTC (Baku-Tbilisi-Ceyhan) Pipeline. See also Texaco Overseas Petroleum v. Libya, 104 J. Droit Int'l 350 (1977), 17 I.L.M. 1 (1978).
[16] Usually capability of suing and being sued.

(Protocol 1 Article 1), the European Court had no choice but to apply the provision to corporations, due to the express wording of the article. But this constraint does not mean that the Court was obliged to follow the same approach, applying all other articles of the Convention to corporations.

The Convention has underlying values, emanating from human dignity and the inherent value of all people. Interpreting the Convention articles in a way commensurate with these underlying values should take precedence over interpreting these articles so that they are consistent with each other. Greater coherence is actually promoted by following the underlying values approach and treating the rest of the Convention differently from Protocol 1 Article 1.

We can compare the question of coherence regarding rights of legal persons in interpretation of the Convention, with the question of coherence in interpreting the property right itself. Thomas Allen shows that the Court has followed two different approaches in its treatment of the property article.[17] One is an integrative approach to property rights, interpreting this right in a fashion integral to the values underpinning all articles of the Convention.[18] The other approach is the comparative approach, interpreting the right to property as it is in international law. He shows that, despite rhetoric and the occasional application of the integrative approach by the Court in the matter of compensation for property appropriation, the right was generally interpreted by the Court in a comparative manner – not in a way integral to the rest of the Convention. One can learn from Allen's analysis of the property article that the property article itself, in the way it was developed and interpreted, is a foreign transplant within the integrative values of the Convention.

Therefore, in the matter of applicability of the Convention to legal persons, I suggest the Court could also have disassociated Protocol 1 Article 1 from the rest of the Convention. The approach to the European Convention on Human Right suggested in this chapter is commensurate with Allen's integral approach. Treating Protocol 1 Article 1 *differently* from other articles of the Convention actually promotes the integrity of the rest of the Convention, as the values

---

[17] Tom Allen, *Compensation for Property under the European Convention on Human Rights*, 28 MICH. J. INT'L LAW 287 (2007).
[18] Sporrong and Lönnroth v. Sweden, App. No. 7151/75.

underpinning the vast majority of Convention articles do not support its application to corporations.

## II  Derivative rights: When can rights of corporations be recognized?

The position that corporate rights do not exist in the Convention is not free from difficulties. This chapter argues for an interpretation of the Convention that denies corporate rights. However, this section will argue that the rights of corporations should be recognized where those rights are derivative from the rights of individuals. This section will demonstrate that the breach of corporate rights should only be recognized if inherent harm to *individuals'* rights can be shown.

An exception to a principle which denies corporate human rights will be justified in situations where the ostensible protection of the rights of a corporation is necessary to protect specific rights of individuals within them. In the following sections, specific rights are examined: freedom of speech, nondiscrimination, and freedom of religion.

### a)  Free speech

The protection of a human right to freedom of expression has different rationales; some are external to the right-bearer and others internal.[19] The promotion of democracy is one of the external arguments for recognition of this right, as is the pursuit of truth. The development of self, involved in expression, whether artistic, political, or of any other kind, is an internal justification.[20] The external justifications are important for explaining the *social* purpose free speech serves, but without the internal justification, they would not be a basis for a *human* right. The internal justifications only justify a right for humans. None of these can justify a corporate right.

However, in some cases, corporations are a conduit for the speech of individuals. The protection of the freedom of expression of individuals in such cases must necessitate protection of the freedom of this conduit.

The right to freedom of speech brings out sharply the need for recognition of derivative rights. These are *seeming* exceptions to the principle that only individuals have human rights, and rights of

---

[19] For a detailed discussion, see Scolnicov, *supra* note 2.
[20] See Edward J. Eberle, *The Architecture of First Amendment Free Speech*, MICH. ST. L. REV. 1191 (2011), for further discussion on core reasons for free speech.

corporations should therefore not be recognized. Newspapers and other media corporations have a right of free speech, distinct from that of their proprietors, editors, or reporters, when these media are acting as "megaphones," amplifying the speech of individuals, such as when publishing journalists' articles, but not when expressing corporate speech, such as when advertising the company or its products.

Indeed, the European Court recognized the Article 10 right of a newspaper in its pivotal decision *Sunday Times v. United Kingdom*.[21] The United Kingdom (UK) attorney general had obtained an injunction against the newspaper in the UK, preventing it from publishing an exposé on the thalidomide scandal. In this case, the decision of the European Court, recognizing the application of Article 10 and stating that the injunction breached the obligations of the UK, can be justified on individual rights grounds. It was the expressive activity of the journalists which was protected. However, it would not have been possible to protect their right without protecting a right of the newspaper, as it was the newspaper against whom the injunction was taken.[22]

In a similar vein, *News Verlag v. Austria*[23] concerned the expressive activity of a newspaper, which published pictures of an extremist who sent letter bombs to politicians. An injunction prohibiting the newspaper from publication of the pictures, awarded to the bomb sender in order to protect his privacy, was deemed by the Court an infringement of Article 10. The Court's application of Article 10 to the newspaper was tantamount to protection of the journalists' and publishers' freedom of expression, and so a justified application of Article 10.[24]

However, the situation was different in *Autronic v. Switzerland (Autronic)*,[25] where the Court had to contend with an application by a company to protect its right to receive radio signals, which it needed solely for the testing of technical equipment.[26] Though there was no expressive content

---

[21] 2 Eur. H.R. Rep. 245.
[22] See also the recent decision in Swiss Radio and Television v. Switzerland, App. No. 34124/06, where Article 10 was seen as applying to a TV station which requested access to a prison to film and interview inmates.
[23] 31 Eur. H.R. Rep. 246.
[24] Similarly, Groppera Radio v. Switzerland, App. No. 10890/84, protects the right to rebroadcast a broadcast, so it still protects the expressive activities of broadcasters, who necessarily use the broadcasting company for their expression. See also Vereinigung Soldaten Österreichs and Gubi v. Austria, App. No. 15153/89, which concerned an association rather than a company.
[25] App. No. 12726/87, Eur. Comm'n H.R. 22 May 1990.   [26] App. No. 12726/87.

at stake, the Court accorded Article 10 protection. In *Autronic*, the Court protected the free speech of a corporate commercial activity, where such speech is not reducible to the speech of any individual within the corporation. The decision of the European Court of Human Rights in *Autronic* is not justified under the analysis proposed here, and Article 10 should not have been extended to a corporation in this situation.

The proposed analysis would mandate a different result in *Autronic*. Corporate speech, such as that in *Autronic*, that is not reducible to the speech of journalists or others, should not merit human rights protection. There is no human right or derivative right to be protected in this case.

This distinction I propose between a derivative right of free speech on the one hand and corporate speech which will not fall under Article 10 on the other is similar to, but not identical to, the distinction between commercial and noncommercial speech. This last distinction was made in a number of decisions of the Court.[27] In *Markt Intern and Beerman v. Germany*,[28] a more permissive standard was set by the Court for interference of a state in pure commercial speech of a corporation than for its interference in noncommercial speech directed at an audience. The United States Supreme Court has likewise upheld a distinction between corporate commercial speech and noncommercial speech in *Nike, Inc. v Kasky*,[29] where the Court, in denying *certiorari*, maintained the position that a corporation has only a limited First Amendment right in its commercial speech.

The difference between commercial and noncommercial speech may not always be immediately discernible. In *Demuth v. Switzerland* (*Demuth*),[30] the right to obtain a broadcasting license by a company was at stake.[31] Both the majority and dissenting judges assumed that a company could, in principle, claim a free speech right. Although both *Autronic* and *Demuth* dealt with a broadcasting license, the expressive aspect rather than the commercial aspect of speech was at stake only in

---

[27] 12 Eur. H.R. Rep. 161, Groppera Radio v. Switzerland, (1990) 12 Eur. H.R. Rep. 321. The profit- or non-profit-making nature of the speech is not relevant to the protection. See Casado Coca v. Spain App. No. 15450/89. See Bruce Johnson and Kyu Ho Youm, *Commercial Speech and Free Expression: The United States and Europe Compared*, 2 J. INT'L MEDIA & ENT. L. 159 (2008), and *Commercial Speech under the European Convention on Human Rights: Subordinate or Equal?*, 6 HUM. RTS. L. REV. 53 (2006), for further discussion on commercial speech and Article 10.

[28] (1990) 12 Eur. H.R. Rep. 161.   [29] 539 U.S. 65   [30] 31 Eur. H.R. Rep. 772.

[31] As was 92.9 Hit FM Radio v. Austria, App. No. 6754/05 and RTBF v Belgium, App. No. 50084/06, reaffirmed in Krone Verlag v. Austria (No 3), App. No. 39069/97.

*Demuth*: the station was a commercial station, but the state's refusal to license it was based on the *content* of the programming. Under the analysis offered in this article, it is germane that the prevented speech in *Demuth* was that of journalists working in the station. Therefore, the station's right was justifiably protected under the Convention.

*Expressive speech* of a corporation should attract the protection of Article 10, but only when it is a "megaphone" for the speech of individuals. It is the speech of individuals – journalists and broadcasters – which is recognized and protected.

### b) Nondiscrimination and equality

Rights of nondiscrimination (such as that protected by Article 14 of the Convention) and equality, as other human rights, should not apply to corporations. The rationale of these rights, of protecting "equal concern and respect,"[32] is an internal rationale, one which does not apply to artificial persons.[33] But in some instances, corporations will have a derivative right not to be discriminated against. Such is the case where a company is discriminated against because of the race or religion of its owners, directors, or employees. If the company faces discriminatory treatment, for instance, in its ability to tender offers for contracts, because its owners are of a certain race or it has employees of a certain religion, such disparate treatment of the company goes directly against the principle of equal concern and respect of human persons. So, protecting a corporation from discrimination in such circumstances is justified as a derivative right, derived from the rights of the individuals involved. In such a case, the application of the equality provision is justified because it will protect human dignity.

### c) Freedom of religion

The application of freedom of religion to legal persons under Article 9 of the European Convention on Human Rights was tested in claims by churches (or other religious organizations). In *X and Church of Scientology v. Sweden*,[34] a church was recognized for the first time by the

---

[32] RONALD DWORKIN, SOVEREIGN VIRTUE: THE THEORY AND PRACTICE OF EQUALITY (2001). See further analysis of Dworkin's work in PHILOSOPHICAL FOUNDATIONS OF DISCRIMINATION LAW (Deborah Hellman and Sophia Moreau eds., 2013).
[33] *See* Scolnicov, *supra* note 2.    [34] X and Church of Scientology v. Sweden, 16 D.R. 68.

European Commission of Human Rights as a victim, having an Article 9 right to freedom of religion (as well as an Article 10 right).

Churches were recognized as applicants in subsequent Article 9 cases, but the rights recognized were actually those of their members. In these cases, it was precisely the denial by the state of legal personality to the applicant religious institutions which was seen by the Court as an infringement of Article 9. In *Church of Scientology Moscow v. Russia*,[35] the church was the victim as it was not permitted by the state to register as a religious organization. However, the right recognized by the Court was the right of believers to associate in exercise of their religion, including the right to register as a legal entity. In the analysis proposed here, it would be recognized as a derivative right.

In the similar case, *Moscow Branch of the Salvation Army v. Russia*,[36] again a church was recognized as a victim. This Court decided this as it determined that Article 9 (together with Article 11) includes the right to associate for the purposes of practicing a religion.[37] Under the analysis of derivative human rights I propose, all these cases would be decided similarly, as all these Article 9 cases are instances of derivative rights, rights of the corporate body that are reducible to the rights of the individuals within it.

The European Commission of Human Rights[38] has ruled that, in their commercial activities, religious organizations cannot benefit from the protection of Article 9.[39] If, under the commission's ruling, a church cannot benefit from Article 9 protection in commercial activity, then it can be assumed with certainty that a commercial corporation would not be able to do so either. In a derivative rights approach, the same result would be reached. A corporate body engaging in a commercial activity – whether a religious organization or another corporation – is not exercising any rights of religious freedom derived from the religious freedom of any individual. It is carrying out a commercial activity on behalf of the corporation itself.

However, corporations have raised claims to rights of religious freedom in the course of regular commercial activities. Recently, this issue

---

[35] App. No. 18147/02.   [36] App. No. 72881/01.
[37] *See* ANAT SCOLNICOV, RELIGIOUS FREEDOM IN INTERNATIONAL LAW: BETWEEN GROUP RIGHT AND INDIVIDUAL RIGHT (2011).
[38] The body which decided on the admissibility of claims to the Court prior to the coming into force of Protocol 11.
[39] X and Church of Scientology v. Sweden, App. No. 7805/77 16 D.R. 68 at 72 (1979).

has come to the forefront of public discussion in the United States, following the Supreme Court decision in *Burwell v. Hobby Lobby Stores Inc.* (*Hobby Lobby*).[40] Two closely held (family owned) corporations claimed religious freedom rights that are protected by the First Amendment "exercise clause." As part of their religious freedom, they demanded to be exempt – as employers – from providing a type of contraceptive care coverage to their employees within the terms of the Affordable Care Act ("Obamacare").[41] The Court was divided on the question whether corporations could claim such rights. The US Supreme Court had previously decided that *not-for-profit religious organizations* benefit from First Amendment protection of free exercise of religion.[42]

Justice Alito, speaking for the majority, concluded that protection of religious freedom could either include or exclude all artificial persons, but not distinguish between them. Therefore, the protection which already includes non-profit corporations must also include for-profit corporations.[43] For-profit corporations, he added, further individual religious freedom just as non-profit corporations do.[44] (It should be noted that he implicitly equates this individual religious freedom with the religious freedom of the owners of the corporations and not with the religious freedom of others within the corporation, such as employees.)

Justice Ginsburg (speaking on this point for the four dissenting Justices) opined: "[T]he exercise of religion is characteristic of natural persons, not artificial legal entities," citing Justice Stevens in *Citizens United v. Federal Election Commission*[45] that corporations "have no consciences, no beliefs, no feelings, no thoughts, no desires."[46] Commercial corporations, she reasoned, should be viewed differently from religious ones, as "religious organizations exist to foster the interests of persons subscribing to the same religious faith. Not so for-profit corporations. Workers who sustain the operations of those corporations commonly are not drawn from one religious community."[47]

---

[40] Burwell v. Hobby Lobby Stores, Inc., 573 U.S. ___ (2014) Docket No. 13-354, 20.
[41] Under the federal Religious Freedom Restoration Act, 42 U.S.C. §§2000bb–2000bb-4 and therefore under U.S. Const. amend I.
[42] Hosanna-Tabor Evangelical Lutheran Church and School v. EEOC, 565 U.S. ___, (2012), Docket No. 10-553.
[43] Walz v. Tax Comm'n of the City of New York, 397 U.S. 664 (1970).
[44] *Hobby Lobby*, 573 U.S. at 21.   [45] *Hobby Lobby*, 573 U.S. at 14 (Ginsburg J.).
[46] Citizens United v. Fed. Election Comm'n, 558 U.S. 310, 466 (2010).
[47] *Hobby Lobby*, 573 U.S. at 16 (Ginsburg J.).

III. WHEN SHOULD CORPORATE HUMAN RIGHTS NOT BE RECOGNIZED? 207

However, even within religions and religious organizations, persons may have differing religious views. The religious rights of dissenters within their organizations are just as valid as those of employees in for-profit corporations. For instance, female members may have views at odds with the entrenched position of the religious leaders on the role and position of women within the religious group. The dissenters within the religion and the leadership of the religion have a priori equally valid rights claims. The same should be true of employees in for-profit corporations. Their human rights claims within the organization (corporation) are as valid as those of managers or owners.

The religious owners of closely held corporations were behind the *Hobby Lobby* lawsuit, equating the corporations' exercise of religious freedom with their own. But the semblance of a derivative right here is misleading. There is no reason to presuppose that the owners can exercise religious freedom on behalf of the corporation. Owners' religious freedom is in potential conflict with the religious freedom of employees (whose beliefs and choices regarding contraception methods might be different), and indeed their freedom from religion.

There is no principled reason to distinguish between for-profit and not-for-profit corporate entities. The commercial purpose is not the distinguishing factor between right-bearers and non-right-bearers. Rather, corporate legal persons should not be bearers of human rights. An individual benefitting financially from an activity (such as a journalist receiving payment for his writing) possesses human rights. A non-profit corporate body in its activities, just as a for-profit body, does not. This position should not be essentially different between different rights. Employees and other members, whether of for-profit or not-for-profit corporate bodies, retain their human rights, regardless of their membership.

Religious freedom of the corporation cannot be equated with one individual, both in for-profit and not-for-profit corporate bodies. A commercial corporation is not synonymous with its owners. A religious organization is not necessarily synonymous with its leadership.

### III  When should corporate human rights not be recognized?: The hard cases

This chapter has maintained that human rights, as a category, are not applicable to corporations. In the present section, some of the most difficult cases, the rights most closely associated with corporations and most often relied upon by them, will be examined. Although each of these rights is predicated on values that might be upheld independently of the right, it will be seen that in all of these rights, there is a divergence in the implications of the right for individuals and for corporate bodies, justifying these rights for individuals only.

### a) Fair trial

Fair trial or due process rights are, together with property rights, those human rights which are most obviously useful for corporations. Subsequently, corporations most frequently rely upon these rights. However, examination of the justifications given for the right to fair trial shows that there is a reason for differentiating between natural persons and legal persons in according this right. Of the reasons which have been given for fair process in civil proceedings, some are internal: maintaining dignity and enhancing participation of the litigants,[48] and maintaining equality between them.[49] Some are external; among these are appearance of fairness, efficiency, and independence of the judiciary.[50] Some are both internal and external, such as impartiality,[51] which underscores both the equal worth and respect accorded to each litigant (internal), and the value to the judicial system of achieving correct results (external). In civil proceedings – as with criminal proceedings – minimization of anxiety and undue concern to the litigant are unifying reasons behind the internal justifications for the right. These can be applicable only to human beings. It is only these justifications which can be a basis for the right, rather than the external, system-enhancing reasons, which can only be additional reasons for the right.

The European Court decisions are based on the implied assumption that companies have the same rights under Article 6(1) as individuals.[52]

---

[48] Frank I. Michelman, *The Supreme Court and Litigation Access Fees: The Right to Protect One's Rights—Part I*, DUKE L.J. 1153 (1973).

[49] W.B. Rubenstein, *The Concept of Equality in Civil Procedure* (UCLA Research Paper Series, Research Paper No. 01-18).

[50] See C. Rozakis, *The Right to a Fair Trial in Civil Cases*, 4 JUD. STUD. INST. J. 96 (2004).

[51] Martin H. Redish and Lawrence C. Marshall, *Adjudicatory Independence and the Values of Procedural Due Process*, 95 YALE L. J. 455 (1986).

[52] See Agrotexim v. Greece, App. No. 14807/89. Because of this assumption, the Court went on to discuss the cases in which a shareholder could be seen as a "victim" of the Convention when it was the company that was party to the proceedings. See GJ v. Luxembourg, 36 Eur. H.R. Rep. 40 (2003); Credit and Industrial Bank v. Czech Republic, 26 Eur. H.R. Rep. 88 (1998).

## III. WHEN SHOULD CORPORATE HUMAN RIGHTS NOT BE RECOGNIZED?

Article 6(1) of the Convention guarantees the right to determination of civil rights and obligations fairly and publicly, by an impartial tribunal within a reasonable time. The Court had suggested, in *Fayed v. United Kingdom*,[53] that the state has a responsibility to regulate public companies and, therefore, might have greater scope for legitimately interfering with access to the courts. But the point of departure in the Court's decision, as ever, was that the right of the company exists, and it is this assumption that should be questioned.

Although the European Court has applied Article 6 to companies, and the United States Supreme Court has applied the Due Process Clause of the Fourteenth Amendment to corporations,[54] an approach that denies corporations a human right of fair trial has been recognized elsewhere. The American Convention on Human Rights, which protects a right to fair trial,[55] protects only natural persons. The International Covenant on Civil and Political Rights also includes a right to fair trial[56] and mandates that state parties guarantee the right to "individuals."[57]

There are good reasons to demand that states maintain fair procedure in all legal proceedings: proper and fair procedure promotes judicial independence and maintains public trust in the judiciary. This justification applies whether the litigants are human or legal persons. There are sound utilitarian reasons why every legal system should adopt fair legal procedures.

However, the recognition of fair procedure as a human right should be for humans only. The implications for humans when their rights and obligations are not determined fairly, publicly, impartially, and promptly are very different from the implications for legal persons. While a corporation might suffer economically from a procedure that is not compliant with due process, it is only individuals whose human autonomy can be affected by curtailment of rights of fair trial.

The right to fair trial in the criminal process – even more so than the right in the civil process – is premised on respect for the humanity of the person subject to it. An individual who is subjected to criminal proceedings, whether ultimately found guilty or not guilty, undergoes a difficult, stressful, potentially harmful process undertaken by the power of the state. A corporation subject to criminal proceedings undergoes nothing of that sort. In Baron Thurlow's often-quoted words, it has "no soul to be

---

[53] 18 Eur. H.R. Rep. 393 (1994).
[54] Minneapolis & St. Louis Railway v. Beckwith, 129 U.S. 26 (1889)
[55] Art. 8, Nov. 22, 1969, 1144 U.N.T.S. 123.   [56] *Id.* art. 14.   [57] *Id.* art. 2.

damned and no body to be kicked."[58] As the United States Supreme Court has suggested in regard to one aspect of this right, speedy trial, the reason for protection of this right is "to minimize anxiety and concern accompanying public accusation and to limit the possibility that long delay will impair the ability of an accused to defend himself."[59] These are personal afflictions. Anxiety and concern do not bear on corporations. A similar analysis could be undertaken of other aspects of this right. Such is the right against self-incrimination. (This right, although not mentioned explicitly in Article 6 of the European Convention on Human Rights, was read by the European Court into Article 6 in *Saunders v. United Kingdom*.)[60] The United States Supreme Court in *Bellis v. U.S.*[61] decided that the Fifth Amendment right against self-incrimination should not be applied to corporate entities, as the right is intended to prevent coercion of confessions and maintain the dignity of the accused. The rationale of this decision should equally apply to the Article 6 right.

Criminal charges, to which Article 6(1) but also Articles 6(2) and 6(3) apply, are usually less relevant to corporations. But when corporations were subject to criminal proceedings, the Court has applied these provisions to them.[62] The argument for not applying Article 6 to corporations is even stronger in the criminal process than in the determination of civil rights. The rights included therein are the presumption of innocence in Article 6(2) and the list of rights in Article 6(3): to be informed of accusations, have a free interpreter, be able to question witnesses, be represented, and have access to legal assistance (including, when the interests of justice demand it, the right to free legal assistance). All these are rights which are capable of being applied to legal persons, but the reasons these have the elevated status of human rights are relevant only to humans. The procedural rights exist to allow the individual to participate in, and maintain his humanity during, criminal proceedings. Corporations do not merit the same rights.

### b) *Retroactivity of criminalization*

The prohibition on retroactive criminal punishment (Article 7(1) of the European Convention)[63] might appear to require an exception to a principle that corporations do not have human rights, but it does not.

---

[58] 1 John Poynder, Literary Extracts 268 (1844).
[59] U.S. v. Ewell, 383 U.S. 116, 120 (1966).   [60] 23 Eur. H.R. Rep. 313 (1996).
[61] 417 U.S. 85 (1974), applying U.S. v. White, 322 U.S. 694 (1944).
[62] See Yukos v. Russia, App. No. 14902/04.   [63] *Id.*

## III. WHEN SHOULD CORPORATE HUMAN RIGHTS NOT BE RECOGNIZED?

Although there are good reasons to prohibit retroactive criminalization of behavior both in relation to individuals and to corporations, only in relation to individuals do these reasons justify recognition of a human right. The effect of retroactive criminal prohibition on a human person is vastly and qualitatively different from its effect on a nonhuman person. Both humans and corporations are harmed by retroactive punishment in some ways: their plans are frustrated in ways they could not foresee; their prudent planning is not rewarded but rather sanctioned. However, only humans can suffer a sense that their worth is discounted, that their *autonomy* is interfered with. These much deeper harms cannot be suffered by a corporation.

So there are good reasons for a prohibition on retroactive criminal punishment for both human and nonhuman persons. But, as a matter of human rights, there is a difference between the justification of the applicability of this right to humans and its applicability to corporations. It should only be considered a human right in respect of natural persons.

### c) Freedom of association

Freedom of association as a human right has different rationales: it can be predicated on its value to democracy,[64] or on its protection of close or intimate relationships. Such intimate relationships are essential to the person in a way second only to his or her self-expression.[65] Such expressions of intimate relationships are spiritual congregation, camaraderie, or fulfillment of types of self-expression possible only in tandem.[66] The core value at the basis of this right, personal intimacy[67], suggests that the right applies to humans, not corporate entities. All these are internal justifications of the right. However, even grounding the right in its value to democracy, an external justification, would likewise steer the application of this right away from associations of companies and restrict it to associations of individuals.

Individuals have a right of association, meaning that they have a right to do together with others what they have a right to do alone.[68] But this

---

[64] As postulated most famously by ALEXIS DE TOCQUEVILLE in DEMOCRACY IN AMERICA (Harvey Mansfield and Delba Winthrop, trans. and ed., 2000).
[65] See Scolnicov, *supra* note 2, for a discussion of rationales of these rights.
[66] Amy Gutmann, *Freedom of Association, in* FREEDOM OF ASSOCIATION 3 (A. Gutmann ed., 1998).
[67] George Kateb, *The Value of Associations, in* FREEDOM OF ASSOCIATION, *supra* note 67, at 35.
[68] See Church of Scientology v. France, App. No. 1950/, in relation to Article 9.

should not mean that corporations should have the same human right to associate with each other as individuals have. The European Court applied the right of association to corporate employers in *AB Kurt Kellermann v. Sweden*.[69] That decision on Article 11 dealt with the right of employers to associate or not within the context of collective bargaining in labor relations. But, as a matter of principle, corporations should not have a right of association any more than other human rights. There may be good reasons for a state to foster associations of corporations or to limit them (to maintain free competition or for other reasons), but these do not give rise to a human right. Therefore, this should not be considered an exception to the principle that corporations have no human rights (although they may, of course, have other legal rights and capacities in law that are not human rights).

### d) Right to property

The right to property, although it appears in the European Convention on Human Rights, is not a right which is universally accepted in international human rights law, and is missing, for instance, from the International Covenant on Civil and Political Rights.[70] It is also a matter of longstanding philosophical controversy whether and why a right of property should exist. The text of Protocol 1 Article 1 (right to property) of the European Convention explicitly includes legal persons. So the lack of the discussion by the European Court of the application of this right to corporations was to be expected.[71] But this does not mean that there is a principled reason to accept that corporations do have a human right to property.

Although there are consequentialist writers who have sought to justify the right of private property based on the utility to society,[72] such an external justification has been shown here to be an insufficient basis for a human right. Of the justifications given for this right, particularly pertinent is that given by Georg Hegel. As Jeremy Waldron explains, "G.W.F. Hegel's account of property centers on the contribution property makes to the development of the self, 'superseding and replacing the subjective

---

[69] App. No.41579/98.
[70] 999 UNTS 171 and 1057 UNTS 407 / [1980] ATS 23 / 6 ILM 368 (1967).
[71] The provision is, of course, very substantially relied upon by companies. *See* App. No. 14902/04 *Yukos v. Russia*.
[72] *See* Jeremy Waldron, *Property, Justification and Need*, 6 CAN. J. L. AND JURISPRUDENCE 185 (1993).

## III. WHEN SHOULD CORPORATE HUMAN RIGHTS NOT BE RECOGNIZED?

phase of personality.'"[73] By this, Hegel means that property objectifies and stabilizes personal ambition and action. This is precisely a rationale which can justify a human right of a human person, but not of a corporation. Similarly pertinent is Locke's justification of primary private property, which is the mixing of one's labor with the object acted upon.[74] Neither of these justifications can be maintained of a right of property of corporate bodies.

It can be doubted whether the right to property is a human right at all. It is not recognized in the International Covenant on Civil and Political Rights, although it is recognized in regional human rights treaties.[75] The property provision was a subject of controversy in the drafting of the European Convention. It was therefore added only at a later stage, in the first protocol to the Convention.[76] The meaning of the provision was later developed by the Court, particularly in the matter of compensation, in ways which often veered from the core values of the Convention. The Court determined compensation by weighing interference with property in economic terms, rather than by assessing the personal value and meaning the property holds for its owner.[77]

The text of the protocol mandates its applicability to legal persons. Had it not been so, the applicability to legal persons of the right should have been questioned as a matter of principle.[78] Had Protocol 1 Article 1 not explicitly mentioned "legal persons," it could be said, for instance, that "peaceful enjoyment of possessions" (the first of the provision's rules) does not apply to companies because they cannot "enjoy" possessions, the wording of the rule pointing precisely to the personal aspect of

---

[73] Jeremy Waldron, *Property and Ownership, in* THE STANFORD ENCYCLOPEDIA OF PHILOSOPHY (Edward N Zalta ed., 2012 ed.), *available at* http://plato.stanford.edu/archives/spr2012/entries/property/). The internal quote is from GEORG W.F. HEGEL, THE PHILOSOPHY OF RIGHT para. 41a (Sir Thomas Malcolm Knox trans., 1967). *See also* JEREMY WALDRON, THE RIGHT TO PRIVATE PROPERTY (1988).

[74] John Locke, *Second Treatise, in* TWO TREATISES OF GOVERNMENT SECOND TREATISE, ch. 5 (Peter Laslett ed., 1988).

[75] See Article 21 of the American Convention on Human Rights, Article 14 of the African Charter on Human and Peoples' Rights and also Article 17 of the (not legally binding) 1948 Universal Declaration of Human Rights.

[76] Allen, *supra* note 17, at 291.

[77] *Id.* at 316; Tom Allen, *Liberalism, Social Democracy and the Value of Property Under the European Convention on Human Rights*, 59 INT'L & COMP. L.Q. 1055 (2010) (see examples there, such as Pincová and Pinc v. Czech Republic, App. No. 36548/97).

[78] In which case, shareholders could also not be able to claim infringement of their own property rights when a state interferes with the company's property. That would not change from the current position as in Agrotexim v. Greece, 21 Eur. H.R. Rep. 250 (1996).

property ownership. The two other rules in the provision, regarding deprivation and control of property, should also be understood as pertaining to the personal aspect of property, in light of the first rule.[79] Under the European Convention, the right must necessarily apply to corporations. However, there is no principled reason to accept the application to corporations of that this.

## Conclusion

This chapter has examined the approach that corporations have no human rights. It has shown that even those rights which present the strongest case for applicability to corporations should nevertheless be applicable to humans only. Therefore, an approach which treats each human right differently, deciding on the suitability of each right to corporations, should be rejected. An approach which denies all corporate human rights should be preferred, not just because it is more conceptually rigorous, but also because it withstands close scrutiny across the spectrum of rights. The conceptual analysis that corporations are not legal persons capable of possessing human rights was tested on rights of the European Convention on Human Rights. The European Convention and its protocols impose certain textual constraints on the Court's freedom to determine whether there are corporate rights. But there are policy reasons, as well as reasons of principle, that stand against recognition of corporate human rights.

Because of the financial ability of corporations to bring claims, there is a danger that peripheral issues relevant to corporations will become more prominent in the Court's docket, obfuscating the original view of human rights that guided the framers of the Convention. This is true of the European Convention on Human Rights as it is true of other human rights treaties and instruments.

The inquiry into justifications of human rights goes to a much broader concern than the question whether corporations have rights. The principled analysis of the justification of rights has implications for many practical and theoretical questions: who has human rights, how human rights can be justified, and when, if ever, these rights can be supplanted. It is important that this conceptual analysis pertains to rights of corporations. In reflecting on the boundaries, indeed existence, of corporate rights, we might better address the legitimate role of corporations in society and within the state.

---

[79] On the significance of the first rule, see James v. United Kingdom, 8 Eur. H.R. Rep. 123 (1986).

# 10

## Judicial review and *Human Rights Act* review in contracted-out public services

### Options for litigation in English law

A.C.L. DAVIES[*]

### Introduction

On a simple level, government contracts do not raise any difficult questions about the public/private divide. The government purchaser is clearly public and the contractor is clearly private. However, the shift from simple procurement to more complex and long-term contractual arrangements has made this analysis difficult to sustain. Under traditional procurement, the government purchaser would engage a contractor to build a public building, for example, a prison. The contractor would have no direct contact with prisoners. Under a public-private partnership arrangement, a private firm would be engaged by the government purchaser to build and run the prison. That private firm does not lose its status as a private firm. But it performs tasks that private firms cannot normally perform: most obviously, detaining people against their will. If a private firm performs public functions, surely it should comply with public law standards in relation to those functions. But this statement is fraught with difficulty. How are public functions to be defined? The prison example is relatively uncontroversial but others, such as the provision of residential accommodation, have given rise to difficulties in the courts. And how should the standards be enforced against the private firm? Should aggrieved individuals be able to take action in the courts directly against the private firm, or should their

---

[*] Professor of Law and Public Policy, Faculty of Law, University of Oxford. This chapter draws on chapter 8 of my book THE PUBLIC LAW OF GOVERNMENT CONTRACTS (2008) and material from that chapter is reproduced by kind permission of Oxford University Press. This chapter states the law up to September 2014.

claims lie solely against the government purchaser? This chapter will attempt to answer some of these questions.

We will begin by examining the current state of English law on contractors' liability in judicial review and under the *Human Rights Act*, 1998 (HRA). It will be argued that the courts' current approach to the definition of 'public functions' for these purposes is too narrow to capture the range of contractor activities that ought to be subject to public law standards, and too uncertain. We will suggest an alternative test that meets these criticisms. In the second part of the chapter, we will turn to two other options for litigation: using the law of contract to sue the contractor or the public authority, and bringing an application for judicial review or a claim under the *HRA* directly against the public authority in respect of the contracted-out service. We will suggest that the former is not particularly promising but that the latter has much more to offer than is sometimes supposed. While this would not obviate the need for contractor liability in all cases, it would provide a much neater and more satisfactory solution to the problems posed by outsourcing.

Although the chapter will explore different ways of ensuring that there is accountability for the delivery of public services (whether via actions against contractors or public authorities), we will work throughout on the premise that the outsourcing process was not intended to lead to a diminution of accountability for the services in question. Space precludes a full defence of this widely held assumption.[1] In contrast to privatisation, in which services are transferred from the public to the private sector, contracting out retains services within the public sector – they are designed and paid for by public authorities – whilst using private (or voluntary) bodies as the mechanism for delivery. This ongoing public responsibility for the services suggests that public law and human rights norms continue to offer the most appropriate regulatory framework. Indeed, successive governments have claimed that outsourcing will enhance, not diminish, accountability.

## I  Contractors' liability in public law

The courts have considered the meaning of 'public function' in two main settings. One is in relation to section 6 of the *HRA*, which subjects private

---

[1] See A.C.L. DAVIES, THE PUBLIC LAW OF GOVERNMENT CONTRACTS (2008).

firms to human rights where they are performing public functions. The other is in relation to the application for judicial review. Here, the courts have had to consider whether private firms and other non-statutory bodies can be subject to judicial review and hence to public law norms. This section will offer a critical examination of the courts' approach and will propose an alternative.[2]

## II  Judicial review

The leading judicial review cases are *R v. Servite Houses, ex parte Goldsmith* (*Servite*)[3] and *R (A) v. Partnerships in Care Ltd.* (*Partnerships in Care*).[4] Both cases require the claimant to show something more than just the presence of a contract with a public body in order to bring the contractor's activities within the scope of public law. This is often expressed in the phrase 'statutory underpinning'. The facts of the two cases help to illuminate this concept.

In *Servite*, Wandsworth LBC placed a contract with Servite, a housing association, to run a residential home for the elderly.[5] Servite wished to close the home because it was not profitable. The claimants were residents of the home who believed that they had been promised a home for life. They sought to bring judicial review against Servite for breach of their legitimate expectation that they could stay in the home for life.[6] The court held that section 26 of the National Assistance Act, 1948 only governed the local authority's activities. It did not provide Servite with any special statutory powers or duties. There was no 'statutory penetration' sufficient to make Servite amenable to judicial review.[7]

In *Partnerships in Care*, by contrast, the firm was the provider of a hospital.[8] The claimant was compulsorily detained under the Mental Health Act, 1983 in the hospital while she received treatment for a personality disorder. It was accepted that the treatment for personality

---

[2] See Paul Craig, *Contracting Out, the Human Rights Act and the Scope of Judicial Review*, 118 L. Q. Rev. 551 (2002), and Catherine M. Donnelly, Delegation of Governmental Power to Private Parties: A Comparative Perspective (2007), for a detailed analysis of the material discussed in this section.
[3] [2000] EWHC (Admin) 338, (2001), 33 H.L.R. 35 (Q.B.).
[4] [2002] EWHC (Admin) 529, [2002] 1 W.L.R. 2610.
[5] Servite, [2000] EWHC (Admin).
[6] R v. N. & E. Devon Health Authority, *ex parte* Coughlan, [1999] EWCA (Civ) 1871, [2001] Q.B. 213 (CA).
[7] Servite, [2000] EWHC (Admin) [76].   [8] P'ships in Care Ltd., [2002] EWHC (Admin).

disorder differed from the treatment for mental illness, but managers at the hospital proposed to treat more mentally ill patients on the ward in which the claimant was being treated. This would have left the claimant without appropriate care. It was held that:

> Whether facilities can and should be provided, and adequate staff made available, to enable the treatment which the psychiatrists say should take place ... is the subject of specific statutory underpinning directed at the hospital: the statutory duty imposed by regulation 12(1) of the [Nursing Homes and Mental Nursing Homes Regulations 1984] on the hospital to provide adequate professional staff and adequate treatment facilities was cast directly on the hospital as the registered person under the Registered Homes Act 1984.[9]

In this case, the hospital was under a direct statutory duty to provide adequate care. Breaches of this duty could be challenged by the claimant through judicial review.

These two cases do, of course, form part of a long-running line of litigation about the availability of judicial review. The 'statutory underpinning' test has developed from older cases not concerned with contractors. In the well-known *R v. Panel on Takeovers & Mergers, ex parte Datafin* case, the City Takeover Panel was a body which lacked 'visible means of legal support'.[10] Thus, the question facing the court was whether a non-statutory body could be subject to judicial review. Although the phrase 'statutory underpinning' does not feature in the judgements, the concept clearly played a role. The Court of Appeal was heavily influenced by the fact that the panel fitted into a scheme of statutory regulation even though it had not been set up by statute itself. In subsequent cases concerning regulatory bodies for sport, notably the Jockey Club, the 'statutory underpinning' test or some version of it formed part of the courts' reasons for excluding such bodies from the scope of judicial review.[11] The Jockey Club was not a statutory body, nor did it fit into any kind of statutory scheme. It was a private organisation based on a series of contractual relationships with its members.

The statutory underpinning test thus performs two roles. On the one hand, it allows bodies to be subject to judicial review even where they are not, in themselves, statutory. On the other hand, it controls contractors'

---

[9] *Id.* at 24.  [10] [1987] Q.B. 815 (CA) 824 (Sir John Donaldson M.R.).
[11] *For example,* R v. Disciplinary Comm. of the Jockey Club, *ex parte* Aga Khan, [1993] 1 W.L.R. 909 (CA); R (Mullins) v. Jockey Club App. Bd. (No.1), [2005] EWHC (Admin) 2197, [2006] A.C.D. 2.

susceptibility to judicial review by requiring claimants to show that any particular contractor has public powers or is responsible for public duties and is not just in a contractual relationship with a public body. Before examining the criticisms that have been made of this test, we will consider the position under the *HRA*.

## III HRA cases

As is well known, while section 3 of the *HRA* has horizontal effect, applying in wholly private cases, section 6 of the *HRA* draws a distinction between 'pure' public authorities and 'hybrid' public authorities. The former are caught by the *HRA* in respect of all their activities. The latter group is made up of non-public bodies which perform some public functions, and they are subject to the *HRA* in respect of their public functions only. Contractors have the potential to fall within the hybrid group. As in the judicial review decisions, the courts have taken the view that not all government contractors are hybrid public authorities and that some additional public element must be shown to make them so.[12]

In *Donoghue v. Poplar Housing* (*Poplar Housing*), the claimant was seeking to challenge her eviction from social housing.[13] The housing was provided by Poplar, a housing association, under contract to a local authority. Here, the court held that there was a sufficient public element to bring the housing association within the scope of the *HRA*. This was because the housing association had played a major role in assessing the claimant's housing needs and, at a later date, in evicting her from the property.[14] The housing association would not have been able to do what it was doing without exercising the local authority's public powers. This was enough to bring it within the scope of the *HRA*. A similar result was reached in the more recent *R (Weaver) v. London & Quadrant Housing Trust* (*Weaver*) case.[15]

However, where there is no element of coercion or determination of entitlements in the contractor's activities, the courts have tended to hold that there is no case for subjecting the contractor to *HRA* liability. The leading case is the decision of the House of Lords in *YL v. Birmingham*

---

[12] R (Heather) v. Leonard Cheshire Found., [2002] EWCA (Civ) 366, [2002] 2 All E.R. 936, [15] (Lord Woolf C.J.).
[13] Donoghue v. Poplar Housing, [2001] EWCA (Civ) 595, [2002] Q.B. 48.
[14] *Id.* at 70 (Lord Woolf, C.J.).   [15] [2009] EWCA (Civ) 587, [2010] 1 W.L.R. 363.

*City Council (YL)*.¹⁶ The claimant had been placed in a privately run care home by Birmingham City Council. She was threatened with eviction from her care home because the owner of the home took exception to her family's conduct during visits. She sought to assert Article 8 rights against the private provider of the home. A majority in the House of Lords held that the private provider was not subject to the *HRA*. Their Lordships emphasised the fact that the care home had no special statutory powers and argued that the functions would not be regarded as 'governmental' in nature.¹⁷ They argued that the care was not 'publicly funded' because although it was paid for by the council, it was obtained by contract rather than by any more general subsidy of the care home's activities.¹⁸ They considered the argument that this created a gap in protection in that those who benefited from 'in-house' services were better protected than those who benefited from contracted-out services. But they rejected this, largely on the ground that to hold the care home liable under the *HRA* would create another kind of unfairness as between those whose care was paid for by the local council and those who could afford to pay for their own care.¹⁹ The decision in *YL* has since been reversed by statute in respect of care homes.²⁰

There are obvious similarities between the *HRA* approach and the judicial review cases, although judges have differed as to the precedential value of the judicial review case-law under the *HRA*.²¹ Something more than just a contract with a public body is required in order to bring the contractor within the scope of the *HRA*. The contractor must itself be exercising public powers or performing public duties. This requires a close examination of the statutory framework governing the activity in question.

## IV  Critique

The problem with both these lines of case-law is that, in deciding whether a contractor should be subject to judicial review or the *HRA*, the courts are making a policy choice, but disguising that choice as the application

---

[16] [2007] UKHL 27, [2007] 3 W.L.R. 112.  [17] *Id*. at 115 (Lord Mance, concurring).
[18] *Id*. at 142 (Lord Neuberger, concurring).  [19] *Id*. at 119 (Lord Mance, concurring).
[20] Health and Social Care Act, 2008, c. 14, § 145 (U.K).
[21] For example, Aston Cantlow v. Wallbank, [2003] UKHL 37, [52], [2004] 1 A.C. 546 (Lord Hope).

## IV. CRITIQUE

of a legal test.[22] It will be argued in this section that their policy choice is difficult to defend and an alternative will be proposed.

The underlying policy choice is apparent when we compare the opinions of the three judges in the majority in *YL* with those of the two dissentients.[23] All five judges focused on the same set of issues, but drew radically different conclusions from them. For example, the fact that the care home was in receipt of public funds was regarded by the dissenting judges as an element of 'publicness' whereas (as we saw above) for the majority it was not relevant because the funding was provided under contract.[24] The fact that the council could have provided the care itself in its own homes was regarded by the minority as an element of 'publicness' but by the majority as a sign that the contractual arrangements were a contrasting policy option and should be regarded as private.[25] The differences between their lordships can only be explained by different policy choices about the proper scope of the *HRA* in contracting-out cases, as frankly admitted by Lord Neuberger:

> The centrally relevant words, "functions of a public nature", are so imprecise in their meaning that one searches for a policy as an aid to interpretation. The identification of the policy is almost inevitably governed, at least to some extent, by one's notions of what the policy should be, and the policy so identified is then used to justify one's conclusion.[26]

This 'policy choice disguised as legal test' is problematic. As *YL* demonstrates, the bulk of discussion in judgements is about the 'application' of the supposed legal test. The crucial issue – the underlying policy choice – is rarely explained or justified.

This means that we have to work a bit harder to discern what the judges' policy concerns are. They seem to be twofold. First, the courts are concerned about the commercial expectations of contractors. This is apparent from Lord Woolf C.J.'s judgement in the *Poplar* case:

> Section 6 should not be applied so that if a private body provides [services under contract to a public authority], the nature of the functions are inevitably public. If this were to be the position, then when a small hotel provides bed and breakfast accommodation as a temporary measure, at the request of a housing authority that is under a duty to provide that

---

[22] For example, PETER CANE, ADMINISTRATIVE LAW 43 (4th ed. 2004).
[23] YL v. Birmingham City Council, [2007] UKHL 27, [2007] 3 W.L.R. 112.
[24] *Id.* at 18 (Lord Bingham, dissenting). [25] *Id.* at 16.
[26] *Id.* at 128 (Lord Neuberger, concurring).

accommodation, the small hotel would be performing public functions and required to comply with the HRA.[27]

He clearly regards it as in some sense unfair that a small business providing simple services should be subject to unfamiliar and unexpected *HRA* liability. Second, the courts are concerned about the costs to the public purse of extending *HRA* liability to contractors. Although Lord Neuberger did not base his decision in *YL* on this ground, he noted that 'unattractive though it may be to some people, one of the purposes of contracting-out at least certain services previously performed by local authorities may be to avoid some of the legal constraints and disadvantages which apply to local authorities but not to private operators'.[28] On this view, the point of contracting out as a policy is to 'escape' liability in public law and the *HRA*, and thus to cut the cost of public service provision.

With respect, both of these reasons for permitting contractor liability only in exceptional cases are fundamentally flawed. If contractor liability were to be expanded, the first objection would fall away once contractors knew about the potential for judicial review or *HRA* actions. They would be able to take steps to familiarise themselves with the law, thus avoiding infringing people's rights, and to factor the risk of liability into the contract price. The second objection is circular: it only works if the courts hold that contractors are not normally liable in judicial review or under the *HRA*.

Most worryingly, the key policy consideration in any public law or *HRA* case – ensuring respect for public law and human rights norms and accountability for any breaches – is wholly absent from this reasoning. While it is clearly desirable that public services should be delivered at the lowest possible cost, the idea that public services should be made cheaper by reducing or eliminating the rights of service users is – when stated in blunt terms – very difficult to defend. Indeed, successive governments have suggested that the policy of contracting out would enhance rather than reduce accountability, because it would add various contractual and market mechanisms of accountability to existing techniques. A much broader view of contractor liability is therefore required.

How might this be translated into an approach to be applied by the courts? One option would be to say that all government contractors should be subject to judicial review and to *HRA* liability. This view has

---

[27] Donoghue v. Poplar Housing, [2001] EWCA (Civ) 595, [67], [2002] Q.B. 48.
[28] YL, [2007] UKHL [152].

## IV. CRITIQUE

been advanced most strongly by Craig.[29] It has the merit of simplicity, setting a 'bright line' for all contractors. However, the disadvantage of this approach is that it would make public law an issue for all government contractors, even those supplying 'back office' or support services to a public authority and having no direct contact with the public. Craig's answer is simply to say that in these cases, a contractor would be unlikely to infringe any public law or human rights norms, so that its liability in principle would not translate into liability in practice. Instead of having a test for contractor liability, we should simply allow the doctrines themselves to do the work of controlling the scope of liability.

The difficulty with this approach is that it 'flags' public law and the *HRA* to contractors as potential causes of concern in any government contract even when the prospect of liability is extremely remote. There is a small but significant difference between 'no liability' and 'remote prospect of liability', since contractors will still have to investigate the potential for liability and may increase their contract price accordingly, to the detriment of the public purse.

It is submitted that the best solution would be to adopt a rule that all contractors engaged in customer-facing activities should be potentially directly liable for the infringement of human rights and public law norms.[30] This would be significantly broader than the current case law, and would ensure that contracting out does not lead to a diminution in accountability, thus meeting the policy objectives identified earlier. Service users would have the same rights whether the relevant service was provided directly by the public authority or via a contractor. The rule would force contractors to learn about human rights and public law norms, thereby increasing compliance. For example, the owner of a bed and breakfast who was planning to evict a client would need to think about potential Article 8 issues under the *HRA* and procedural fairness and legitimate expectations in public law. Contractors could also factor the potential for liability into their contract pricing. The proposed rule has two further advantages. First, it is predictable. Contractors would be able to tell quite easily whether or not their contract would involve direct contact with members of the public from the initial invitation to tender. Second, it is not unnecessarily broad. Contractors whose job is simply to provide the public authority with the means to perform their public functions behind the scenes

---

[29] *Supra* note 2, at 557–59. See also DONNELLY, *supra* note 2, at 283.  [30] *Cf. id.* at 5.

would not be caught and would be able to exclude the potential for public law and *HRA* liability from their contract pricing.

## V Alternative solutions

In this section, we will consider two other options for ensuring that public services delivered by contractors are accountable to service users. One – which has received some attention in the literature – is to use the law of contract. This is thought to be attractive by some commentators because it avoids the need to subject contractors to unfamiliar causes of action in judicial review or under the *HRA* and instead maintains the contractual framework throughout. However, the proposed solution suffers from a number of defects. The other, which has received less attention, is to explore the public authority's own liability for contracted-out services. This would potentially avoid the need for the service user to bring proceedings against the contractor altogether. This option has been neglected because of the particular facts of the cases that have so far come to court. But it offers an interesting avenue for future litigation.

## VI Contract claims

There are two possible ways in which contract law might help the recipient of public services provided by a private contractor.[31] One is where the service user has a contract with the private firm. The other is where the service user is able to rely on the contract between the government and the private firm. We will examine each in turn.

In some cases, those who use public services may enter into a contractual relationship with the contractor. This is true of 'concession' contracts in which the government selects a contractor to perform a service but allows the contractor to charge those who use it. In *YL* itself, the claimant was in a contractual relationship with the care home.[32] The contract with the claimant in *YL* contained an express term requiring the contractor to respect the claimant's human rights. The courts will clearly enforce these standards in an action on the contract. However, this solution cannot be relied upon in every case. The contract between the

---

[31] See Catherine M. Donnelly *Leonard Cheshire again and beyond: private contractors, contract and s 6(3)(b) of the Human Rights Act*, 2005 Pub. L. 785 (2005), for a detailed analysis.
[32] YL, [2007] UKHL.

service user and the service provider may not contain a human rights clause. And in many cases, there is no contract at all between the service user and the private provider.

Lord Woolf C.J. suggested in *R (Heather) v. Leonard Cheshire Foundation* (*Leonard Cheshire*) that in cases in which the service user does not contract with the private provider, the service user might still be able to bring a contract claim based on the terms of the government's contract with the private provider.[33] Thus, if the government's contract with the provider contained a human rights clause, the claimant would be able to enforce it. This solution obviously encounters difficulties with the doctrine of privity. Under the Contracts (Rights of Third Parties) Act, 1999, a third party beneficiary would be able to enforce the contract either because the contract explicitly said that he or she could or because the contract 'purport[ed] to confer a benefit' on him or her.[34] But the major difficulty here is that government contracts standardly exclude the operation of the Act.[35]

Of course, a further possibility is that the public authority might sue the contractor. This option would only be available where terms of the contract were such that the contractor's infringement of service users' rights in public law or under the *HRA* was also a breach of its contract with the public authority. As I have argued elsewhere, this situation can give rise to difficulties in terms of damages.[36] Normally, an award of damages is designed to compensate the contracting party for its loss, but the infringement of service users' rights may not necessarily cause any loss to the public authority. Nor would there be any obligation on the public authority to pass on any damages thus obtained to the affected service users.

To sum up, the difficulty with contractual solutions is that contract drafting is largely a matter for the government. There is no guarantee that the contract in any particular case will support any or all of the suggested avenues of redress.

## VII  The public authority's liability

In this section, we will consider another option for litigants: bringing proceedings against the public authority. There is sometimes a

---

[33] R (Heather) v. Leonard Cheshire Found., [2002] EWCA (Civ) 366, [34], [2002] 2 All E.R. 936 (Lord Woolf C.J.).
[34] Contracts (Rights of Third Parties) Act, 1999, c. 31, § 1 (U.K.).
[35] For example, HM Treasury, Standardisation of PF2 Contracts, 2012, (U.K.) (draft).
[36] DAVIES, *supra* note 1, ch. 7.

perception that a public authority divests itself of responsibility when it contracts a service out. We will question that perception in this section, looking first at the position under the Deregulation and Contracting Out Act, 1994, and then at the position outside the framework of the Act. It will be argued that there is ample scope for making public authorities accountable for contracted-out public services.

### a) The Deregulation and Contracting Out Act, 1994

For some services to be contracted out, it is clear that the contractor will be unable to act unless it is formally empowered to exercise public powers. Privately run prisons are an obvious example. This formal empowerment may take place through specific legislation or through a general mechanism provided by the Deregulation and Contracting Out Act, 1994. What is interesting for our purposes is that the 1994 Act makes the public authority liable for the acts of its delegate.

A brief outline of the Act – which is not well known – may be helpful.[37] In central government, section 69 of the Act allows a minister to delegate by order any ministerial functions or functions of an office-holder which can be exercised by civil servants in accordance with the *Carltona* principle.[38] Under section 70, a minister may make an order allowing local authorities to delegate any statutory functions which may be exercised on their behalf by their officers. Authorisations under the Act may be subject to limitations and conditions.[39] They cannot be given for more than 10 years and may be revoked by the relevant minister at any time.[40] Thus, the aim of the Act – in both central and local government – is to promote contracting out by facilitating the delegation of public power to contractors.

In both cases, the 1994 Act imposes procedural and substantive controls on the process of delegation. On a substantive level, there are some statutory functions to which the 1994 Act does not apply. These have clearly been chosen for their constitutional significance:

> Subject to subsections (2) and (3) below, a function is excluded from sections 69 and 70 above if—

---

[37] See Mark Freedland, *Privatising* Carltona: *Part II of the* Deregulation and Contracting Out Act 1994, 1995 Pub. L. 21 (1995), for discussion.
[38] Carltona Ltd v. Comm'rs of Works, [1943] 2 All E.R. 560 (CA).
[39] Deregulation and Contracting Out Act, 1994, c. 40, §§ 69(4), 70(4).
[40] *Id.* §§ 69(5), 70(4).

(a) its exercise would constitute the exercise of jurisdiction of any court or of any tribunal which exercises the judicial power of the State; or
(b) its exercise, or a failure to exercise it, would necessarily interfere with or otherwise affect the liberty of any individual; or
(c) it is a power or right of entry, search or seizure into or of any property; or
(d) it is a power or duty to make subordinate legislation.[41]

The procedural control is a duty to consult the relevant officeholder (under section 69(3)) or the representatives of local government (under section 70(3)). This is also a narrow provision in the sense that there are various other potentially interested parties that could be consulted, notably citizens and service users.

The Act treats the activities of the contractor or other delegate as the activities of the minister or local authority.[42] Thus, there is no transfer of power from the public authority to the delegate. They exercise power concurrently and the public authority always remains liable for the delegate's actions as well as its own. In effect, this imposes a form of strict liability on the public authority: it may have selected a highly qualified contractor and supervised its activities with great care, but if the contractor infringes someone's Convention rights, for example, it will remain possible to bring an action against the public authority.

Thus, where contracting out has taken place within the framework of the 1994 Act, aggrieved service users clearly have rights against the public authority. Donnelly notes the apparent harshness of this rule and questions whether it would be enforced in practice.[43] However, a number of possible justifications can be offered for the Act's approach. First, it reflects the public authority's constitutional responsibility for statutory powers granted to it, or duties placed upon it, by statute, a point we will return to later. Second, it is always possible for the public authority to use the contract to protect itself where it makes economic sense to do so, for example, by imposing human rights or other relevant requirements on the contractor and seeking an indemnity from the contractor to cover situations in which it faces judicial review or *HRA* review because of the contractor's actions.

### b) Outside the Act

Of course, not all contracting out takes place within the 1994 Act. It is generally accepted that the Act is facilitative rather than

---

[41] *Id.* § 71(1).   [42] *Id.* § 72.   [43] *Supra* note 2, at 205.

mandatory.[44] Is there any scope for arguing that public authorities should be held liable for the acts of contractors outside the Act? There are two options here. The most radical would be to argue for the imposition of 'vicarious' public law liability on public authorities for contractors' actions at common law. The less radical – but equally significant – option would be to argue for a broad interpretation of public authorities' own duties when a service is contracted out.

In the ordinary law of tort, while an employer is vicariously liable for the actions of its employees (or similar[45]) acting within the course of their employment, we would not expect it to be vicariously liable for torts committed by an independent contractor hired to do a particular task. However, one way in which a defendant can be liable for the actions of an independent contractor is via the concept of 'non-delegable duties'. In these cases, which commonly arise where the defendant is under a statutory duty of some kind, the statutory language requires that the defendant remains liable regardless of the means it has chosen to fulfil the duty in question. The performance of the task may be delegable but the duty of care towards the claimant is not.

The case law on this issue was recently reviewed by the Supreme Court in the *Woodland v. Swimming Teachers Association* (*Woodland*) case.[46] In that case, a school pupil suffered a serious brain injury during a swimming lesson provided by an instructor who was an independent contractor. Lord Sumption J.S.C. held that the local authority owed a non-delegable duty towards the pupil because she was in a situation of vulnerability, she was in a prior relationship with the authority (as a school pupil) and in its care, and she had no choice over how the authority chose to perform its duties towards her.[47] Lord Sumption noted that the same principles might apply to other public bodies, such as care homes, hospitals and prisons, and that it was particularly important to develop this form of liability given the increasing use of outsourcing to provide public services.[48] However, there are limits to the principle, because liability in negligence remains primarily fault based: these limits

---

[44] See DAVIES, *supra* note 1, at 251–53, for a discussion of the permissibility of delegation without statutory authority.
[45] Various Claimants v. Inst. of the Bros. of the Christian Sch., [2012] UKSC 56, [2013] 2 A.C. 1.
[46] [2013] UKSC 66, [2014] A.C. 537.
[47] *Id.* at 23. However, Baroness Hale noted that this should not be treated as 'set in stone', *id.* at 38.
[48] *Id.* at 25.

are provided through the requirements set out earlier and the construction of the relevant statutory provisions.[49]

Although the *Woodland* case is concerned with non-delegable duties to take reasonable care in the law of negligence, it is not such a big leap to suggest that, at least in some cases, public authorities should not be able to 'lose' their duties in public law or under the *HRA* by employing an independent contractor to carry out the work.[50] Of course, this would depend on the construction of the relevant statutory provisions. A possible example of this in the *HRA* setting was offered by Buxton LJ in the Court of Appeal in *R (Johnson) v. Havering LBC*, a case joined with *YL*.[51] He suggested that if a private care home breached residents' Article 3 rights by subjecting them to inhumane treatment, the public authority would be liable because the duty to provide care under section 21 of the National Assistance Act, 1948 includes a duty to have regard to the residents' welfare.

Even if this argument fails, and we cannot establish that a public authority is liable for a wrong committed by a contractor, it is important to remember that public authorities themselves may owe continuing, direct duties to claimants in respect of contracted-out services. This was acknowledged by Lord Woolf C.J. in the *Leonard Cheshire* case (as a reason against contractor liability):

> If this were a situation where a local authority could divest itself of its Article 8 obligations by contracting out to a voluntary sector provider its obligations under section 21 of the [National Assistance Act], then there would be a responsibility on the court to approach the interpretation of section 6 (3) (b) [HRA] in a way which ensures, so far as this is a [sic] possible that the rights under Article 8 of persons in the position of the appellants are protected. This is not, however, the situation. The local authority remains under an obligation under section 21 of the NAA and retains an obligation under Article 8 to the appellants even though it has used its powers under section 26 to use LCF as a provider.[52]

A broad interpretation of the public authority's responsibilities would solve many of our problems.

---

[49] See, for example, Farraj v. King's Healthcare NHS Trust, [2009] EWCA (Civ) 1203, [2010] 1 W.L.R. 2139, for a case in which no non-delegable duty arose.

[50] It might also be possible to invoke the state's positive obligations under the European Convention on Human Rights. See Catherine Donnelly, *Positive Obligations and Privatisation*, 61 N. IR. LEGAL Q, 209 (2010), for discussion.

[51] [2007] EWCA (Civ) 26, [2008] Q.B. 1, [11].

[52] R (Heather) v. Leonard Cheshire Found., [2002] EWCA (Civ) 366, [33], [2002] 2 All E.R. 936 (Lord Woolf C.J.).

If we assume that the public authority has a statutory duty to 'provide or arrange to provide' care in a residential home,[53] what does that entail if the authority decides to contract the service out? It is sometimes suggested that it includes no more than taking care over the choice of contractor and finding alternative provision if the contractor defaults. But, on reflection, this seems overly simplistic. The process adopted by the authority involves a number of decisions and tasks: deciding the nature of the service to be provided, selecting the contractor, drafting the contract, monitoring the contractor's provision of the service and, in particular, its compliance with quality standards, and deciding to terminate the contract and replace the contractor. Although some of these decisions involve duties towards the contractor, there is no reason why they should not also be subject to judicial review or *HRA* review where they affect the rights of service users. For example, if the decision to terminate the contract will involve moving the residents to another home, it seems clear that the public authority is bound to respect the residents' Article 8 rights and legitimate expectations when making that decision. Similarly, if the contractor fails to respect the residents' privacy (again in breach of Article 8), it would be worth considering whether the public authority had shown sufficient respect for the residents' rights when designing the service, drafting the quality standards in the contract or monitoring the contractor's performance.

All of this begs the obvious question: if there is scope for litigation against public bodies, why have so many claimants pursued the contractor instead? One answer might be that the liability of public bodies is so uncertain that litigants have preferred the marginally less uncertain strategy of suing the contractor. A more plausible answer is to do with remedies.[54] In a claim under the *HRA*, it is possible to seek damages, and it is therefore relatively straightforward to order the public authority to pay for a breach caused by a contractor (and to recover the cost from the contractor, as discussed earlier). In an application for judicial review, the court may choose to award one of a number of remedies which require specific action on the part of the decision-maker. Inevitably, the court will consider the practicalities in exercising its discretion on this issue. If the contractor is running a residential home and seeks to close it in breach of the residents' legitimate expectations, the court might wish to

---

[53] *Id.* at 27; R v. Servite Houses, *ex parte* Goldsmith, [2000] EWHC (Admin) 338, (2001), 33 H.L.R. 35 (Q.B.) [44].

[54] See also Craig, *supra* note 2, at 554; DONNELLY, *supra* note 2, at 231.

issue an injunction to stop the closure. But this cannot readily be issued against the public authority because it does not own the home, nor is it likely to have any power to stop the contractor from terminating the contract (or just breaching it).[55] For practical reasons, then, the remedy against the public body in this situation is likely to be confined to a declaration. This may explain why contractors have been the focus of litigation.

### c) Conclusion

To sum up, there is ample scope for arguing that the public authority is accountable for the contractor's actions, either under the 1994 Act or because it cannot delegate its statutory duties, and that the public body is liable for a variety of decisions during the process of contracting out, broadly defined. This does not mean that contractor liability is unnecessary. As we have seen, in some cases, an action against the public authority may not give the claimants the remedies they are seeking. For outsourced public services to remain fully accountable, both options are required.

## Conclusion

Most of the case law on liability to users of public services in judicial review or under the *HRA* has focused on making contractors liable, using the argument that they are performing 'public functions'. This 'test' disguises a policy choice about what should be regarded as public and what should be regarded as private. In order that contracting out should not involve a considerable diminution in the accountability of public services to their users of the kind that no government would openly propose, the only defensible position is to make it clear that contractors performing public-facing services (as opposed to those simply providing the public authority with the means of performance) are potentially liable under the *HRA* and in public law.

More importantly, this chapter has argued that there is more scope for litigation against public authorities in respect of contracted-out services than is sometimes supposed. The Deregulation and Contracting Out Act, 1994 imposes a form of vicarious liability on public authorities for the

---

[55] Servite, [2000] EWHC (Admin) [44–45].

actions of contractors to whom they delegate public power under the Act. It is arguable that, even outside the Act, at least some statutory duties could be construed, for public law and *HRA* purposes, as 'non-delegable'. This would not prevent public authorities from hiring contractors to perform the relevant tasks, but it would mean that they would remain liable for the proper performance of the duties even if the contractor was immediately responsible for the commission of a particular wrong. Finally, a broad understanding of the public authority's decisions and actions within the process of contracting out might also provide avenues for judicial review or *HRA* review against the public authority in respect of its own failings. Unfortunately, the quirks of litigation have so far left these options largely unexplored.

While both contractor liability and public authority liability are necessary to ensure that there is a comprehensive scheme of legal accountability for outsourced public services, it would be desirable for there to be a greater development of public authority liability in future litigation, for two main reasons. First, the 'usual' defendant in judicial review or under the *HRA* is a public authority. The courts would be able to focus on the substance of claims rather than getting distracted by sterile debates about the nature of the defendant. Second, this would give public authorities a much stronger incentive to address the *HRA* and public law norms in their relationships with contractors, by including appropriate standards in the contract and the right to recover from the contractor in the event of a breach leading to litigation against the public authority. In turn, this should improve compliance with the *HRA* and with public law doctrines in outsourced public services. Although accountability may seem only to be about providing redress when things go wrong, it is important to remember its broader objective: to promote good government.

# 11

# Privatization and human rights in the United Kingdom

STEPHANIE PALMER

## Introduction

This chapter looks at the protection of human rights in the United Kingdom (UK) in the context of the privatization of activities formally carried out by public bodies. As the application of private-market ideas to public authorities has increased, the delegation of governmental power to private parties has become a common method of governance. The performance of important governmental functions and essential public services are increasingly trusted to private actors such as charities, corporations and associations. This policy of using private actors to deliver public services has transcended political divisions in the UK.

The central features of these policies of privatization pose challenges for public law. Can human rights be adequately protected in this new era of 'private' public services? How can we ensure that privatized governance does not undermine accountability? Can human rights operate to strengthen 'public law' values in the face of new arrangements to deliver public services? A further issue is whether the decision to privatize and the manner of privatization can be affected by positive obligations, as developed by the European Court of Human Rights.

The UK law and the adequacy of its legal response are assessed. In particular, this chapter analyses the process of assimilating human rights norms within an existing structure of private law rules. It argues that human rights guarantees should not be sidestepped because a government has chosen to contract out or privatize public functions formerly unambiguously assumed by the state.

## I Privatization and the public-private boundary

A discussion of the public-private boundary inevitably raises the question: 'what is "public" or "private"' and what does that distinction mean?

For jurists, the boundary traditionally provides the framework for organizing the various categories of law and the distinct remedies flowing from this binary notion. Private law traditionally regulates the relationship between individuals through the law of contract, torts and property. In very broad terms, public law is inseparable from government. Yet even here the concepts are elusive: what are the core activities of a government? Are they linked primarily to security, defence, liberty, the supply of public goods and the use of coercive force? And should it include the notion of the welfare state?

Another way of thinking about the divide is through the legitimacy of the exercise of public powers or the imposition of duties. Cane observes that:

> The law utilizes a complex set of public/private distinctions for two broad purposes: to justify the existence and exercise of powers to interfere with the freedom and autonomy of individuals in order to protect and promote social interests ('public powers'); and to justify the imposition of distinctive duties and obligations on public functionaries in order to protect the interests of individuals, groups within society, and society as a whole.[1]

In other words, private law could be perceived as primarily economic in nature and protecting individuals as economic actors and as consumers. Public law has distinctive features. The government does not exercise power in its own self-interest. In a democracy, the government must be held to account for the exercise of public power.[2]

In the nineteenth century, Dicey famously insisted that there was no substantive distinction between public and private law. He was reacting against the creation of legal privileges and immunities that could operate outside of 'the ordinary law of the land'.[3] Given the growth of judicial review, the European Union (EU) and human rights law, his account fails to portray the complexity of the contemporary world.

The combination of globalization, privatization and regulation has posed challenges for the traditional understanding of the public-private relationship. Since 1979, the UK has witnessed the tangled inter-

---

[1] Peter Cane, *Theory and Values in Public Law*, in LAW AND ADMINISTRATION IN EUROPE: ESSAYS IN HONOUR OF CAROL HARLOW 15 (Paul Craig and Richard Rawlings eds., 2003). See also William Lucy, *Private and Public: Some Banalities about a Platitude*, in AFTER PUBLIC LAW 56 (Cormac Mac Amhlaigh, Claudio Michelon and Neil Walker eds., 2013).
[2] See Anne C.L. Davies, *Ultra Vires problems in Government Contracts*, 122 L.Q. REV. 98–99 (2006).
[3] ALBERT DICEY, INTRODUCTION TO THE STUDY OF THE LAW OF THE CONSTITUTION 202–03 (10th ed. 1959).

relationship between public and private bodies through contracting out, public-private partnerships and corporatization to name but a few. These new complex arrangements call into question the role of government and the adequacy of accountability and oversight of these new ventures. Are these transformations a threat to public law or is it an opportunity for a new way of thinking about the future of public law values and, in particular, human rights protections?

There are different viewpoints on the usefulness of the public-private divide. According to Harlow, the distinction serves to conceal political issues behind a façade.[4] Oliver suggests that its contemporary significance is no longer helpful in understanding the operation of public law controls.[5] For others, the challenge lies in where the line should be drawn in various circumstances. As economic and policy choices have fundamentally altered the way in which a government operates to deliver its obligations, a reconsideration of the relationship has been called for. According to Freedland, public law needs to redefine itself in relation to this new reality 'if it is to resist the highly sophisticated project of transferring that [public service] sector largely into the domain of private law'.[6]

Is the law then lagging behind political developments or out of step with the way the world works? Is the public-private distinction an outmoded way of understanding our new 'privatized' 'regulatory' state? In spite of questions asked about the contemporary significance of the distinction in domestic law, the *Human Rights Act*, 1998 (HRA)[7] has encouraged a substantive public-private boundary by imposing on public authorities specific human rights obligations. Oliver reasons that differences between public and private bodies are not a critical factor for the purpose of legal governance. Both are concerned with the control of power and the protection of individuals against its abuse. 'Common values' operate across both spheres and principles of 'good administration' – legality, fairness and rationality – can also be grounded in private

---

[4] Carol Harlow, *'Public' and 'Private' Law: Definition without Distinction*, 43 MOD. L. REV. 241 (1980).
[5] DAWN OLIVER, COMMON VALUES AND THE PUBLIC-PRIVATE DIVIDE (1999).
[6] Mark Freedland, *Law, Public Services, and Citizenship—New Domains, New Regimes?*, in PUBLIC SERVICE AND CITIZENSHIP IN EUROPEAN LAW—PUBLIC AND LABOUR LAW PERSPECTIVES (Mark Freedland and Silvana Sciarra eds., 1998). *See also* Mark Freedland, *Public Law and Private Finance: Placing the Private Finance Initiative in a Public Law Frame*, PUB. L. 288 (1998).
[7] 1998 c. 42.

law, including contract.[8] Oliver's conclusion that the differences are not significant gives insufficient weight to the fact that certain values are distinctively public: the government does not act in its own self-interest. In contrast, private power is individualistic and primarily economic in nature. Oliver would not deny this but it undermines her argument that there is no substantive public or private law divide.[9] Jody Freeman suggests that while 'we might talk in terms of "public" and "private" actors, the reader should not conclude that there is such a thing as a purely private or purely public realm'.[10] Institutional arrangements may be public or private but functions are defined as either public or private only because we define them as such for particular purposes in a particular context.[11]

The transfer of public functions and services traditionally carried out by public bodies to the private sector continues apace in the UK.[12] The shrinking of government in favour of the private sphere has been a feature of most developed Western states. This chapter assumes that 'privatization' should be given a broad definition to include any policy that results in a reduction of government 'involvement' in economic and social life, thus including public-private partnerships.[13]

The shift away from spheres of traditional government action is supported primarily for instrumental reasons. It is widely assumed that the private sector will provide greater efficiency and more imaginative ways to deal with old problems. Government bureaucracies and public bodies are perceived as too cumbersome and tied down in red tape. The lack of response of government bodies makes them less suitable than private bodies in bringing about promised efficiencies, improved management and greater flexibility. The shrinking of government services also promises to reduce public spending. This has proved a powerful

---

[8] See Dawn Oliver, *Common Values in Public and Private Law and the Public/Private Divide*, (1997) PUB. L. 630; Dawn Oliver, *The Underlying Values of Public and Private Law*, in THE PROVINCE OF ADMINISTRATIVE LAW (Michael Taggart ed., 997) *and* DAWN OLIVER, COMMON VALUES AND THE PUBLIC-PRIVATE DIVIDE (1999)

[9] Peter Cane, *Accountability and the Public/Private Distinction*, in PUBLIC LAW IN A MULTI-LAYERED CONSTITUTION 247, 269 (Nicholas Bamforth and Peter Leyland eds., 2003).

[10] Jody Freeman, *The Private Role in Public Governance*, 75 N.Y.U. L. REV. 543, 551 (2000).

[11] See Leslie Turano, *Charitable Trusts and the Public Service: The Public Accountability of Private Care Providers*, 18 KING's L.J. 427 (2007).

[12] The Post Office and some parts of the National Health Service are recent examples.

[13] Daphne Barak-Erez, *The Private Prison Controversy and the Privatization Continuum*, 5 L. & ETHICS OF HUM. RTS. 138 (2011).

argument in favour of privatization given the high national debt of the UK and other public bodies.

Privatization takes many different forms. A common form of privatization in the UK is the transfer of government assets to private companies or actors.[14] In other circumstances, privatization is achieved through outsourcing by the government of certain functions, although the responsibility for the delivery of those functions is maintained. Outsourcing is common in the UK. Examples include residential care for the elderly, foster placements of children and adoption agencies. Private security companies rather than the armed forces carry out certain defence activities. In spite of the coercive nature of the function, prisons and immigration centres have been privatized[15] and local authorities have contracted out the function of bringing applications for anti-social behaviour orders.[16] Former services provided by the police, such as escort services for taking prisoners to and from the court, have also been contracted out.[17]

These policies cover various activities and arrangements, but they typically share three features: the transfer of public functions, with an associated delivery risk, to private entities; the use of market-style competition to select the supplier; and a shift in the measurement of performance from the process to the output. 'Internal markets' have been introduced into the provision of such fundamental public services as health and education, organized around a separation between 'purchasers' and 'providers' and governed by sophisticated commercial contracts. For example, the *Health and Social Care Act, 2012* implements a policy – called 'corporatization' – of encouraging and compelling National Health Service (NHS) bodies to operate as autonomous market actors.[18] The Secretary of State for Health retains formal constitutional responsibility for the NHS, a traditional public service in the UK, although the structure of the Act suggests that ministerial accountability may be eroded.[19]

---

[14] Utilities, such as gas and electricity, have been transferred to private companies and competition between them is encouraged and regulatory oversight has been established.

[15] Martin Gosling, *The Global Trend towards Private Prisons*, 170 JUST. OF THE PEACE & LOC. GOV'T L. 892 (2006).

[16] Police and Justice Act, 2006, c. 48, § 25.   [17] *Id.*, § 39.

[18] Health and Social Care Act, 2008, c. 14, § 145 (U.K); J. Salmon, *A Perspective on the Corporate Transformation of Healthcare*, 25 INT'L J. HEALTH SERVICES 11-42 (1995).

[19] Anne C.L. Davies, *This Time It's for Real: The Health and Social Care Act 2012*, 76 MOD. L. REV. 564 (2013),

In order to preserve public-sector values in arrangements with private entities, there is a need to strengthen public accountability. At the very least, there must be adequate oversight, monitoring and enforcement power.[20] One method of ensuring such accountability when private organizations are used to deliver formerly public functions is to require that governments respect public law obligations, including substantive human rights guarantees, However, in the UK, this has not proved to be straightforward.

## II   The Human Rights Act and the public-private boundary

The *HRA* was intended to give effect in domestic law to the rights guaranteed in the European Convention on Human Rights (ECHR).[21] 'Fundamental human rights', as traditionally conceived, provide protection against abuse by the government or the state, and not against rights violations by other private individuals. According to this traditional view, the idea of human rights is grounded in a distinction between the 'public' and the 'private'. The ECHR was drafted just after the Second World War, at a time when the public-private distinction was understood primarily in institutional terms: governmental and public bodies carried out the vast majority of public functions. Due to the state shedding many formerly governmental functions, it is no longer feasible or even useful to conceptualize the public-private boundary in terms of an institutional distinction between state and non-state entities. In the modern state, the public and the private are enmeshed as a result of the dramatic changes to our social structures and institutions. The application of the scope of the *HRA* must be considered in the light of this international law context.

Section 6(1) of the *HRA* makes it unlawful for a 'public authority' to act incompatibly with a Convention right. The issue of whether or not a 'body' is a public authority under the *HRA* has not proved straightforward. 'Public authority' is given both institutional and functional aspects.[22] The term is a critical one as the Convention rights enshrined

---

[20] Martha Minow, *Public and Private Partnerships: Accounting for the New Religion*, 116 HARV. L. REV. 1229, 1259 (2002–03).

[21] Convention for the Protection of Human Rights and Fundamental Freedoms, Nov. 4, 1950, Europ.T.S. No. 5; 213 U.N.T.S. 221 [hereinafter ECHR]. This section draws on my previous article. Stephanie Palmer, *Public Functions and Private Services: A Gap in Human Rights Protection*, 6 INT'L J. CONST. L. 585 (2008).

[22] Aston Cantlow v. Wallbank, [2003] UKHL 37, [47] (Lord Hope) where he stated that it may not be capable of precise definition. *Cf.* the approach in the Freedom of Information

in the *HRA* are directly enforceable solely against a public authority. The effect of section 6 is to create two categories of public authority. The first comprises the 'core' or 'pure' public authorities, such as government departments, local authorities, the police and the armed forces – all their actions must be compatible with human rights.[23] The second category comprises 'hybrid' bodies that perform a mixture of public and private functions. According to section 6(3)(b), 'public authority' includes 'any person certain of whose functions are functions of a public nature'.[24] The purpose behind this section was to include, within the definition of public authority, public functions exercised by hybrid bodies, while excluding acts of a private nature. Although hybrid public authorities are institutionally private bodies, they are treated as public when carrying out a public function. In this way, the scope of the *HRA* is extended to include bodies other than the traditional core authorities by reference to the concept of 'public function', regardless of the institutional source of the provider's power. The flexible idea of hybrid public authorities alters the traditional binary understanding of either public or private.[25]

During the course of parliamentary debates on the passage of the *HRA*, it was clear that private entities delivering privatized or subcontracted public services were meant to be included within the scope of the Act through the concept of 'public function'.[26] The *HRA* thus attempted to address the reality of modern government and the increased delegation of public power to private bodies. As a consequence of the distinction it created, core public authorities are bound to act in conformity with the ECHR regardless of whether the activity in question is a public or private one. Hybrid public authorities must respect Convention rights while exercising public functions but not when performing private acts.

---

Act, 2000, c. 36 where the public authorities to which the Act applies are listed in a schedule.

[23] c. 42, § 6(1). See also HOME OFFICE, RIGHTS BROUGHT HOME: THE HUMAN RIGHTS BILL, 1997, Cm. 3782 [2.2], which lists the following as traditional public authorities: central government, including executive agencies; local government; the police; immigration; courts and tribunals. *Note also* Maric v. Thames Water Ltd., [2003] UKHL 66 (statutory sewerage undertaking); Malcolm v. Mackenzie, [2004] EWCA (Civ) 1748 (Her Majesty's Revenue and Customs); and R (on the application of Wilkinson) v. Broadmoor Special Hosp. Auth., [2001] EWCA (Civ) 1545 (NHS trusts and their staff).

[24] c. 42.

[25] Note Alexander Williams, *Public Authorities, in* THE IMPACT OF THE UK HUMAN RIGHTS ACT ON PRIVATE LAW 48 (David Hoffman ed., 2011). Williams argues that hybrid authorities do not lose their own Convention rights.

[26] See, for example, 314 Parl. Deb., H.C. (6th ser.) (1998) 409-10.

Distinguishing between a public function and a private act is not straightforward and is difficult to sustain without a contextual or principled basis upon which to make the determination.

The shift of activities and capacities of once exclusively public services to private, voluntary and charitable institutions provides a clear example of the operation of the public-private divide. Privatization and contracting out usually operate through a contractual relationship but within a framework of statutory control either by giving powers to regulators or by establishing service provider duties. The public and private systems are interwoven and each must take account of the other. In the context of the *HRA*, this does not mean that the public-private distinction is irrelevant. Rather, it is the nature of the power exercised, the function that should be the significant factor in deciding how its exercise should be controlled. In this way, the public-private distinction remains an important tool in this era of privatization. The exercise of public functions should be subject to different accountability measures than private activities, and the rights secured in the *HRA* should be directly enforceable against the hybrid body. But this solution still begs the question: 'what is a "public" function?'

Cane suggests that:

> [S]upporters and opponents of the public-private distinction are talking past each other at a normative level. Opponents are making the empirical claim that the distinction misrepresents the way in which power *is* distributed and regulated, while supporters make the normative claim that the distinction embodies an attractive theory of the way power *should be* distributed and regulated.[27]

He argues persuasively that the formulation should be a normative one. A values-based distinction would recognize that certain values are public while others such as those linked to economic self-interest and profit making are distinctly private.[28] Although this is an attractive approach which provides an explicitly open method for deciding the distinction, it does not provide the magic formula to determine where the line should be drawn in individual cases. As Cane intimates, the focus is not on an empirical search to identify the essential attribute of government or the state but a normative quest to determine

---

[27] Nicholas Bamforth and Peter Leyland, *Public Law in a Multi-Layered Constitution*, in PUBLIC LAW IN A MULTI-LAYERED CONSTITUTION, *supra* note 9, at 19.

[28] Cane, *supra* note 8, at 247, 275.

what it is that should be considered a governmental or public function in the twenty-first century.

The *HRA* does provide other mechanisms through which ECHR rights can be engaged against private parties. Courts and tribunals are specifically included as public authorities in section 6(3)(a) of the *HRA*. Some commentators had suggested that the inclusion of the courts as public authorities pursuant to section 6(1) would mean that the Convention rights would be given full horizontal effect through the *HRA* and the definitional problems could then be avoided.[29] The courts did not follow this suggestion but, instead, have adopted a system of indirect horizontal effect.[30] Existing common law causes of action have been developed in accordance with Convention rights.[31] However, where private entities are supplying services formerly provided by public bodies, indirect horizontal effect may be of no assistance, as there may be no pre-existing common law cause of action on which the victim can rely.

## III Hybridization and human rights

The courts have had a number of opportunities to consider hybrid public authorities. On the whole, the term 'functions of a public nature' under section 6(3)(b) has been given a cautious, even narrow, interpretation. In *Donoghue v. Poplar Housing (Poplar)*,[32] the issue was whether a housing association – a registered charity that had been created and assisted by a local authority to take over a publicly funded service – was carrying out a public function. The association sought to evict one of its tenants who argued that her rights under Article 8(1) of the ECHR – right to respect for private life, family and home – would be breached if she were evicted.

Lord Woolf proposed a 'generous interpretation' of the term 'public function'.[33] His proposals, however, suggested a restricted view in some important respects: in order to make an otherwise private act a public one, there must be 'a feature or a combination of features which impose a public character or stamp on the act'.[34] Such public characteristics may include statutory authority for the task carried out; the degree of control

---

[29] WADE AND FORSYTH, ADMINISTRATIVE LAW 168 (9th ed. 2004).
[30] The common law horizontal effect mechanism provides a way to hold private bodies, indirectly, to human rights standards. *See* Alison L. Young, *Mapping Horizontal Effect, in* THE IMPACT OF THE UK HUMAN RIGHTS ACT ON PRIVATE LAW, *supra* note 25, at 16.
[31] See, for example, Campbell v. MGN Ltd., [2004] UKHL 22 (development of a law of privacy pursuant to Article 8 of the ECHR from the existing breach of confidence action).
[32] [2001] EWCA (Civ) 595, [2002] Q.B. 48.   [33] *Id.* at 58.   [34] *Id.* at 65.

exercised by the public body over the exercise of the function; and how closely the acts in question are 'enmeshed in the activities of the public body'.[35] On the facts of this case, the Court found that the housing association was a public authority exercising a public function because of its close association with the local authority.

Thus, section 6(3)(b) of the *HRA* applies to private associations that are assisted by a public body in the taking over of responsibility for a public service – as was the case in *Poplar*. The courts have also found that a private entity exercising statutory coercive powers would be delivering 'functions of a public nature'.[36] However, other than in these examples, the courts have been unwilling to hold that private organizations carrying out formerly public functions are hybrid authorities. The delivery of privatized services has been held not to fall within the definition of hybrid authority.[37]

The implications of the Court's restricted reasoning were revealed in the decision of *R (Heather) v. Leonard Cheshire Foundation* (*Leonard Cheshire*).[38] The appellants were long-term residents of a private nursing home who challenged its impending closure as a violation of their right to respect for private life under Article 8(1) of the ECHR. The local authority had placed the appellants in the residential care home operated by the Leonard Cheshire Foundation. The Foundation – a charity – provided the accommodation service in fulfillment of the local authority's statutory duty. The Court of Appeal held that the Foundation was not performing a public function when delivering these services. Lord Woolf emphasized that the Foundation's functions were private: there was no special characteristic of the relationship between the local authority and the charity that would suggest that it should be considered a hybrid authority.

The decision in *Leonard Cheshire* was affirmed by the House of Lords in the similar case of *YL v. Birmingham City Council* (*YL*).[39] By a slim majority – 3–2 – the House of Lords decided that a privately owned care home, operating on a for-profit commercial basis and acting pursuant to a contract with a local authority, could not be deemed to be a hybrid

---

[35] *Id.*
[36] R (A) v. P'ships in Care Ltd., [2002] EWHC (Admin) 529, [2002] 1 W.L.R. 2610.
[37] Cameron v. Network Rail Infrastructure Ltd., [2006] EWHC 1133 (Q.B.); James v. London Elec. Plc., [2004] EWHC 3226 (Q.B.).
[38] R (Heather) v. Leonard Cheshire Found., [2002] EWCA (Civ) 366, [2002] 2 All E.R. 936.
[39] [2007] UKHL 27, [2007] 3 W.L.R. 112.

public authority under section 6(3)(b) of the *HRA*. The majority and minority judgements of the House of Lords reveal different views concerning the responsibility of government, welfare law and policy, as well as the extent of the reach of the *HRA*. The decision leaves the law in an incongruous position. If a function were considered 'public' when delivered by a local authority, it would seem logical that it still be regarded as 'public' when contracted out to a private entity on behalf of the local authority.[40]

The majority and minority judges disagreed on the nature of the function that was being performed. In determining whether a function is 'public' within the meaning of section 6(3)(b) of the *HRA*, Lord Neuberger commented that these words 'are so imprecise in their meaning that one searches for a policy as an aid to interpretation'.[41] The majority judges adopted the classical liberal distinction between public (state) and private (economically self-interested individuals). They were not persuaded by the argument that the care was being paid for out of public funds. While this might be a *necessary* condition for activities classified as public functions, it is not itself a decisive factor and can only be given limited weight.[42] Lord Mance distinguished between the statutory duty of a local authority to arrange care and accommodation and a private company delivering the services on a commercial basis after contracting with the local authority. He commented that 'the actual provision, as opposed to the arrangement, of care and accommodation' is not an inherently governmental function.

Baroness Hale described this distinction as 'artificial and legalistic', given that the state has assumed responsibility for both meeting needs and arranging care.[43] Both minority judges placed emphasis on the context and policy of social welfare in the UK: while private arrangements could be made for the delivery of care and accommodation, this function should still be considered public when 'performed pursuant to statutory arrangements'.[44] In Lord Bingham's view, the contractual arrangements between the parties are 'of little or no moment'.[45] He was in no doubt that the state had accepted the social welfare responsibility of ensuring that those in need of care would be provided for through the agency and expense of the state.[46]

---

[40] Paul Craig, *Contracting Out, the Human Rights Act and the Scope of Judicial Review*, 118 L. Q. Rev. 551, 556 (2002).
[41] YL, [2007] UKHL [141].    [42] *Id.* at 142, 148 (Lord Neuberger, concurring).
[43] *Id.* at 49–53.    [44] *Id.* at 66.    [45] *Id.* at 16.    [46] *Id.* at 72.

The majority judges in *YL* were influenced by the public-private distinction that is applied in the domestic judicial review case law. In 1987, the seminal case of *R v. Panel on Takeovers and Mergers,* ex parte *Datafin,*[47] paved the way for the courts to extend their review of jurisdiction to private bodies. Its importance lies in its having articulated an approach based on the 'true nature' of the function being exercised.[48] The Court of Appeal reformulated the public-private test in order to 'recognize the realities of executive power'.[49] The influence of the jurisprudence relating to judicial review has been used to limit the reach of the *HRA*. Traditional public law constraints have not applied to private entities exercising public functions according to contract law. In *YL*, the contractual source of the arrangement was perceived by the majority as differentiating Southern Cross from any 'function of a public nature'.[50] As contract law is the usual vehicle to achieve privatization or contracting out, the majority's conclusion dramatically limits the effect of section 6(3)(b) of the *HRA*.

The majority also emphasized the commercial motivation of the private profit-earning company.[51] Examining the motivation of a private contractor will assist in deciding whether or not the institution or actor in question is a public or private one. However, it will not clarify whether a contractor is carrying out a public function. It is becoming increasingly difficult to differentiate between the pursuit of traditional public functions and the pursuit of private commercial gain.

At the heart of the difference between the majority and minority judgments is whether social welfare is considered a responsibility of the government in the UK.[52] After separating the responsibility from the actual provision of care, Lord Neuberger was of the opinion that providing care and accommodation should not be considered a government function.[53] After considering the argument that the National Assistance Act, 1948 imposed an 'essential duty on the State to provide care and accommodation for the needy', Lord Mance could see nothing to

---

[47] [1987] Q.B. 815 (CA).
[48] Murray Hunt, *Constitutionalism and Contractualisation of Government in the United Kingdom,* in THE PROVINCE OF ADMINISTRATIVE LAW, *supra* note 8, at 29. See also R v. Chief Rabbi of the United Hebrew Congregations of Great Britain and the Commonwealth, *ex parte* Wachmann, [1992] 1 W.L.R. 1036; R v. Disciplinary Comm. of the Jockey Club, *ex parte* Aga Khan, [1993] 1 W.L.R. 909 (CA).
[49] Datafin, [1987] Q.B.    [50] YL, [2007] UKHL [120] (Lord Mance, concurring).
[51] *Id.* at 31 (Lord Scott), 116 (Lord Mance, concurring).
[52] Palmer, *supra* note 21, at 571.    [53] YL, [2007] UKHL [162].

suggest 'an inherently governmental function' in what he perceived to be a safety net 'conditional on care and attention being not otherwise available'.[54] In contrast, Baroness Hale concluded that after 60 years, social welfare law forms an intrinsic part of our government to provide care for the needy.[55] In agreement, Lord Bingham stated that the ultimate responsibility lies with the state.[56]

The government was also concerned that vulnerable members of society would be left unprotected when private entities deliver services that meet essential human needs. Under section 145 of the *Health and Social Care Act, 2008*,[57] the delivery of residential care services by private bodies on behalf of public authorities will amount to a public function under section 6(3)(b) of the *HRA*. This legislative intervention has reversed the result of the *YL* and *Leonard Cheshire* decisions but the reasoning in these decisions has been left untouched and will be applicable in other contracting-out disputes.

## IV  Positive obligations and the public-private divide

The international law obligations imposed on a state party by the ECHR includes protecting everyone within the Convention's jurisdiction. Many of the articles of the ECHR impose positive obligations on state parties to take steps to prevent a breach of an individual's human rights. Thus, positive obligations create responsibilities on the part of the state.[58] Moreover, these obligations may arise in the context of private relations. As the European Court of Human Rights has observed in relation to the right to respect for private life in Article 8, positive obligations may involve adopting measures 'even in the sphere of the relations of individuals between themselves'.[59]

While positive obligations create responsibilities on the part of the state, privatization, in contrast, is associated with the 'hollowing out of the state'. Governments are handing over responsibility for public functions to private entities and often divesting themselves of

---

[54] *Id.* at 115.   [55] *Id.* at 49–53.   [56] *Id.* at 15.   [57] 11 & 12 Geo., c. 29.
[58] See, for example, X & Y v. The Netherlands, 91 Eur. Ct. H.R. (ser. A) (1985); Airey v. Ireland, 2 Eur. H.R. Rep. 305 (1979); Z v. United Kingdom (2001) 34 E.H.R.R. 97; Osman v. United Kingdom, 29 Eur. H.R. Rep. 245 (1998); Costello-Roberts v. United Kingdom, 27-C Eur. Ct. H.R. (ser. A) (1993).
[59] See von Hannover v. Germany, 40 Eur. H.R. Rep. 1, 57 (2004).

responsibility and reducing their accountability. The two concepts do not fit together comfortably.

In the UK, the doctrine of parliamentary sovereignty means that there are no effective constitutional limits on the ability and freedom of a government to privatize or outsource its functions. The sole constraint on this policy is political. The decision to privatize is perceived as a 'high policy' issue and not a question of law. Many of the institutions in the UK that were once considered quintessentially public have been privatized or outsourced to some extent. The Post Office, prisons and the NHS are three examples of institutions that were once perceived of as the 'face' of government and which now, to some extent, have been privatized. One concern is whether private entities, whose aims are commercial and profit oriented, diminish the welfare and wider community interests that should be the focus of publicly provided services. The shifting understandings of the role of the state and its functions raises questions about whether there could be any limits to the extent and nature of privatization.

The Supreme Court in the UK addressed the issue of state responsibility under the ECHR in the *YL* decision. All the judges agreed on the relevance of the Strasbourg jurisprudence. Yet the majority and minority judges disagreed about the circumstances in which the government of the UK would be held responsible in Strasbourg for a violation of protected Convention rights stemming from the acts of a private body. In Baroness Hale's view, the decision of the European Court of Human Rights in *Storck v. Germany* (*Storck*)[60] was a compelling indication that acts of private bodies would engage state responsibility.[61] In the *Storck* decision, the Strasbourg Court found that the police had assisted in the illegal detention of the applicant in a private psychiatric clinic. The confinement was not authorized or supervised by any state entity, and the police had forced her to return after she had fled. In addition, Baroness Hale emphasized the positive obligation of the state to prevent violations. In her opinion, 'the most effective way for the UK to fulfill its positive obligations to protect individuals against violations of their rights is to give them a remedy against the violator'.[62]

Lord Mance, in the majority, adopted a narrower view of the scope of state responsibility.[63] He identified two relevant principles in the case

---

[60] 2005-V Eur. Ct. H.R.   [61] YL, [2007] UKHL [56].   [62] *Id.* at 60.   [63] *Id.* at 92.

law, although the Strasbourg court does not always clearly distinguish between them. First, in some circumstances, such as in *Storck*, the state may be responsible if it fails to regulate or control effectively the activities of private persons.[64] Second, the state may remain responsible for acts of private bodies to which it has delegated essential state or governmental functions or powers.[65] *Wos v. Poland* concerned a challenge under Article 6(1) of the ECHR.[66] The private Polish-German Reconciliation Foundation had been set up to award compensation to Poles who had been subjected to forced labour during the Second World War. The specific circumstances of the case led to the conclusion that the compensation scheme engaged the responsibility of the state. The European Court made clear that the state's choice of 'a form of delegation in which some of its powers are exercised by another body cannot be decisive for the question of state responsibility *ratione personae*'.[67] However, delegation to a body, operating under private law, of the Polish state's obligations arising out of international agreements could not 'relieve the Polish state of the responsibilities it would have incurred had it chosen to discharge these obligations itself, as it could well have'.[68] In *Sychev v. Ukraine* (*Sychev*) the private body in question was a law commission which was delegated certain state powers to execute court judgements.[69] According to the European Court, 'the exercise of state powers which affects Convention rights and freedoms raises an issue of state responsibility regardless of the form in which these powers happen to be exercised, be it for instance by a body whose activities are regulated by private law'.[70] Lord Mance distinguished these cases from the position in *YL* on the basis that, unlike the commission that was the subject of *Sychev*, a care home does not exercise any obvious state power or duty, and, in contrast to both cases, it is not established or funded by the state for state purposes.[71]

Turning to the issue of whether it may be possible to impose any limits on the UK government's privatization policies based upon the positive obligations jurisprudence, it is necessary to consider different aspects of privatization. First, a decision by a government to withdraw from

---

[64] The following examples were provided: Van der Mussele v. Belgium, 70 Eur. Ct. H.R. (ser. A) (1983); Costello-Roberts v. United Kingdom, 247-C Eur. Ct. H.R. (ser,A) (1993); Botta v. Italy 1998-I Eur. Ct. H.R.; Marzari v. Italy, App. No. 36448/97, 28 Eur. H.R. Rep. Comm'n Dec. 175 (1999); Z v. United Kingdom, 2001-IV Eur. Ct. H.R.
[65] YL, [2007] UKHL [97].   [66] 2005-IV Eur. Ct. H.R.   [67] *Id.* at 72.
[68] YL, [2007] UKHL [97].   [69] App. No. 4773/02 (2005).
[70] *Id.* at 58, cited in YL v. Birmingham City Council, at [98].   [71] *Id.* at 99.

providing some 'public' services or replacing a service by encouraging a private service provider may lead to a breach of a positive obligation. Again the issue turns on which public services formerly provided by the government should be considered a public function. The field of security provides one example where the issue of state responsibility could arise.[72] The state cannot opt out of the responsibility for doing 'all that could reasonably be expected of them, to avoid a real and immediate risk to life of which they have or ought to have knowledge'.[73] Article 2 of the ECHR – right to life – requires the state to maintain some provision even though there is nothing to prevent private security firms from taking over some of the former duties carried out by the police force. The Strasbourg jurisprudence has also made it clear that the state can never extract itself from taking reasonable steps to protect children 'from ill-treatment of which the authorities had or ought to have had knowledge'.[74] Although the state is not prohibited from privatizing elements of the adoption and foster placement services, it must retain overall responsibility.[75]

Prisons are an exercise of the coercive power of the state yet even some prisons have been privatized in the UK. Both Lords Mance and Neuberger in the *YL* decision accepted that the operation of a private prison would fall within the definition of public function under the *HRA* although such companies are profit making. Positive obligations in the Strasbourg jurisprudence may prevent a state from using privatization to withdraw from its responsibilities to protect positive obligations. It has not, however, prevented an essential component of governance from being privatized. In contrast, a decision in Israel breaks the constitutional silence on privatization.[76]

In a landmark decision, the Israeli Supreme Court objected to privatization in the prison service.[77] The Court ruled that a law transferring authority from the Israeli government to a private, commercial contractor to manage an Israeli prison was unconstitutional.[78] President

---

[72] See generally David A. Sklansky, *Private Policing and Human Rights*, 5 L. & ETHICS OF HUM. RTS. 112 (2011).
[73] Osman v. United Kingdom, 29 Eur. H.R. Rep. 245, 116 (1998).
[74] Z v. United Kingdom, 34 Eur. H.R. Rep. 97, 73 (2001).
[75] Note The Children and Families Act, 2014, c. 6.
[76] Note *also* Nandini Sundar v. Chattisgarh, (2011) 7 S.C.C. 547 (India). The Supreme Court of India decided that policing is an essential state function and could not be delegated.
[77] HCJ 2605/05 The Academic Ctr. of Law and Bus. v. The Minister of Fin.
[78] Barak Medina, *Constitutional Limits to Privatization: The Israeli Supreme Court Decision to Invalidate Prison Privatization*, 8 INT'L J. CONST. L. 690 (2010).

Beinisch stated the following: 'the very existence of a prison that operates on a profit-making basis reflects a lack of respect for the status of the inmates as human beings, and this violation of the human dignity of the inmates does not depend on the extent of the violation of human rights that actually occurs behind the prison walls'.[79] In effect, the Court held that the detainees had the right to have the state directly provide the measure that deprived them of their liberty and dignity. It was unacceptable for the state to transfer powers limiting detainees' liberty and dignity to private actors who were pursuing their own individual economic interests.[80]

Although positive obligations have never prevented a decision to privatize a public function, it may have some influence on the *manner* in which privatization is carried out. Article 5(4) of the ECHR provides that everyone deprived of liberty by arrest or detention shall be entitled to 'take proceedings by which the lawfulness of his detention shall be decided speedily by a court and his release ordered if the detention is not lawful'.[81] This article could be relevant in the context of private prisons and immigration centres. For example, if a private entity is paid according to the length of detention, a decision-maker who has no pecuniary interest in the outcome must decide whether or not early release is appropriate.

Article 6 of the ECHR demands independence and impartiality of decision-makers. These procedural protections could be relevant in many situations, particularly where the government has contracted out decision-making powers that affect civil rights to private companies.[82] Private actors may be in a position to decide whether or not individuals are entitled to certain benefits. The impartiality of the decision-maker could be compromised if a payment structure encourages him or her to act in a particular manner. The ability of private actors to influence public agendas may also raise issues under Article 6.

---

[79] The Academic Ctr. of Law and Bus., 36.
[80] Daphne Barak-Erez, *The Private Prison Controversy and the Privatisation Continuum*, 5 L. & ETHICS OF HUM. RTS. 138, 149 (2011).
[81] *Supra* note 21.
[82] The European Court of Human Rights has held that benefits such as incapacity or housing benefits are 'civil rights' which trigger Article 6 protections of independence and impartiality. See, for example, Tifoyo v. United Kingdom, 48 Eur. H.R. Rep. 18, 39 (2009).

## Conclusion

Privatization has posed challenges for our understanding of the public-private boundary. This chapter has argued that privatization should not be used as a method of avoiding or 'contracting out' of human rights obligations. Public law values should not be diluted through this new mode of governance. The notion of hybrid public authorities provides one way to bypass the binary public-private divide.

Part of the debate in the UK has centred around the question: 'what makes a particular function "of a public nature". Although there is no agreement on this issue, a compelling reason to give an expansive interpretation to public function is that public entities are acting in their capacity as representatives of the electorate when privatizing services. Thus, human rights standards can increase the accountability in relationships connecting public and private institutions and functions. Individuals should be treated as citizens and not consumers.

# 12

# Principles of public fiduciary administration

PAUL B. MILLER[*]

## Introduction

In recent years, a fiduciary theory of the authority of the state has been offered as an alternative to theories rooted in the social contract tradition. The fiduciary model provides an evocative basis for rethinking the nature and limits of state authority. Some who employ this model do so with the modest assertion that trusteeship is a more apt metaphor than contract for understanding the authority of the state. These scholars usually also make rather narrow normative claims, suggesting that public officials have loyalty obligations that approximate those owed by private fiduciaries.[1] But other theorists have made broader and more foundational claims on behalf of the fiduciary theory,[2] with the most carefully detailed analysis found in the work of Evan Fox-Decent.[3] Fox-Decent argues that state authority is actually, not merely metaphorically, fiduciary, and that public law encompasses a set of normative constraints that parallel those

---

[*] Assistant Professor, McGill University Faculty of Law. I am very grateful for comments and criticism provided by Evan Criddle, Evan Fox-Decent, Stephen Galoob, Andrew Gold, and Dan Kelly, as well as for helpful remarks provided by participants in the Fiduciary Theory Panel at the 2014 Law and Society Association Annual Meeting in Minneapolis, Minnesota.

[1] See, for example, D. Theodore Rave, *Politicians as Fiduciaries*, 126 HARV. L. REV. 671 (2013); Sung Hui Kim, *The Last Temptation of Congress: Legislator Insider Trading and the Fiduciary Norm against Corruption*, 98 CORNELL L. REV. 845 (2013).

[2] See Paul Finn, *The Forgotten 'Trust': The People and the State*, in EQUITY: ISSUES AND TRENDS 131 (Malcolm Cope ed., 1995) (suggesting decades ago that the authority of the state is fiduciary); Evan J. Criddle, *Fiduciary Administration: Rethinking Popular Representation in Agency Rulemaking*, 88 TEX. L. REV. 441 (2010) (establishing a historical basis for this view in American legal and political traditions); David L. Ponet and Ethan J. Leib, *Fiduciary Law's Lessons for Deliberative Democracy*, 91 B.U. L. REV. 1207 (2011) (Ethan Leib writing on how the fiduciary theory informs our understanding of popular representation).

[3] EVAN FOX-DECENT, SOVEREIGNTY'S PROMISE: THE STATE AS FIDUCIARY (2011) [hereinafter FOX-DECENT, SOVEREIGNTY'S PROMISE].

governing private fiduciaries. One of the distinctive features of the fiduciary theory as articulated by Fox-Decent and Criddle is their suggestion that it supports a variety of positive obligations on the state, including obligations to act on climate change[4] and to protect human rights.[5]

In other work, I have suggested that the fiduciary theory is attractive insofar as it is based on commonalities between private and public fiduciary authority.[6] Presently, I will suggest that while these commonalities are real and important, there are equally important differences. Normative commonalities are clearest at the level of general principle. When one descends from principles to particularized norms, the parallels give way to some basic differences between private and public ordering. Appreciation of these differences is as important to the vitality of the fiduciary theory as is an understanding of common features of private and public fiduciary law.

This chapter is structured as follows. In Part I, I briefly analyze differences in the bases, constitution, and objects of private and public fiduciary authority. In Part II, I suggest that these differences are reflected in the substance and structure of fiduciary accountability in private and public law. In Part III, I suggest that private and public fiduciary administration is nevertheless governed by a common set of general principles. I canvass these principles before offering some brief conclusions.

## I  Private and public fiduciary authority

In order to appreciate the extent of overlap in their normative implications, it is necessary first to consider the nature of private and public fiduciary authority respectively.

### *a)  The sources of fiduciary authority*

Fiduciary authority is a kind of agency authority; it consists in the standing to make decisions for or on behalf of another through the

---

[4] Evan Fox-Decent, *From Fiduciary States to Joint Trusteeship of the Atmosphere: The Right to a Healthy Environment through a Fiduciary Prism*, in FIDUCIARY DUTY AND THE ATMOSPHERIC TRUST 253 (Ken Coghill, Charles Sampford, and Tim Smith eds., 2012).

[5] Evan Fox-Decent and Evan J. Criddle, *The Fiduciary Constitution of Human Rights*, 15 LEGAL THEORY 301 (2009); Evan J. Criddle and Evan Fox-Decent, *Human Rights, Emergencies, and the Rule of Law*, 34 HUM. RTS. Q. 39 (2012).

[6] Paul B. Miller, *The Fiduciary Relationship*, in PHILOSOPHICAL FOUNDATIONS OF FIDUCIARY LAW 63, 86–89 (Andrew S. Gold and Paul B. Miller eds., 2014).

exercise of powers derived from the legal personality of another person. How does one come to possess fiduciary authority? This question is difficult in part because it raises questions concerning the scope of fiduciary law. To the extent that fiduciary principles partly determine the legitimate exercise of fiduciary authority, it is natural to wonder whether they are properly to be understood as a *constraint* on fiduciary authority or as a constitutive *basis* of fiduciary authority (or both).

In my view, fiduciary principles are properly to be understood as a constraint upon but not a basis of fiduciary authority. Consider recognized modes of authorization, such as consent, contract, and legislative or judicial decree. These modes of authorization (and underlying practices) suggest that a valid grant of authority from someone with the personal or fiduciary authority to make it is the sole necessary condition of rightful possession of fiduciary authority. Rarely, fiduciary authority may be conferred by law.[7] However, fiduciaries normally act under a consensual cession of authority. As is implicit in the language of conferral and cession, the power of a (corporate or natural) person to effectuate authorization is premised on that person possessing personal or fiduciary authority relative to the powers or capacities conferred upon the fiduciary.

This generates certain complexities for the fiduciary theory. A distinguishing virtue of the theory is said to be its capacity to justify state authority without resorting to the "fiction" of popular consent.[8] This enables avoidance of a problem that bedevils social contract theories; namely, explaining how individuals could authorize the state to exercise powers that they are juridically incapable of enjoying. The fiduciary theory avoids this problem by suggesting that assertion of authority by the state is legitimated by fiduciary principles.[9] This analysis is

---

[7] Consider statutes that provide for appointment of public executors, trustees, and guardians. *See* Fox-Decent, Sovereignty's Promise, *supra* note 3, at 90 (Fox-Decent suggests that fiduciary authority is always conferred by law: "In fiduciary relations, it is the law rather than the beneficiary that entrusts the fiduciary with legal powers.").

[8] *Id.* at 29. Fox-Decent frames the theory in terms of factual sovereignty:

Th[e] overarching fiduciary relationship arises from what we may think of as the fact of sovereignty.... [the] general attributes of the state point to a non-consensual relationship of proclaimed authority between state and subject, notwithstanding democratic channels (in democratic states) through which the people's voice may be heard. *Id.*

[9] Evan Fox-Decent, *Fiduciary Authority and the Service Conception*, in Philosophical Foundations of Fiduciary Law 363, 378 (Andrew S. Gold and Paul B. Miller eds., 2014) [hereinafter Fox-Decent, *Fiduciary Authority and the Service Conception*]. Fox-Decent

provocative but not convincing. It conflates the fact that *compliance* with fiduciary constraints legitimates *exercise* of fiduciary authority with the distinct (and untenable) supposition that the *existence* of fiduciary constraints can legitimate a *claim to possession* of fiduciary authority.[10]

Consider first conferral of authority through consensual cession. In fiduciary relationships ordinarily premised on consensual cession, a fiduciary could not point to his compliance with fiduciary constraints as a basis for claiming rightful possession of fiduciary authority. One cannot validly claim to be a director of a corporation, a trustee of a trust, or a lawyer of a client simply on the basis that one has acted as a fiduciary would and has consciously respected the obligations of a fiduciary. Respect for fiduciary strictures does not a fiduciary make. The same is true of nonconsensual relationships said to be the proper analogues of the state-subject relationship. Fox-Decent is right, I think, to suggest that something other than consensual cession must explain parental fiduciary authority. But that something is not the fiduciary principle. Consider the following twist on Fox-Decent's story about an officious intermeddler, Superdad. Fox-Decent relates the story when analyzing the duty to obey an authority. Imagine, he says, an absent-minded father who fails to notice that his daughter is drinking dirty water from a duck pond. Superdad orders her to stop, assuming the mantle of parental authority. The child rightly refuses to obey, Fox-Decent says, even though Superdad is genuinely concerned with her welfare and obeying him would better enable the child to comply with reasons that apply to her. The story is offered as an illustration of the limitations of Raz's service conception of authority. But it serves equally well to illustrate the limitations of the fiduciary theory. For while Superdad might not be able to legitimately claim authority by virtue of the quality of the reasons underlying his commands, neither could he legitimately claim authority by arguing that he is complying with parental fiduciary obligations. The legitimacy of a

---

says, for example, that "consent is a plausible ground of political but not legal authority. Trust and the fiduciary principle's authorization of state power best justify legal authority," see Fox-Decent, Sovereignty's Promise, *supra* note 3, at 89; that "the fiduciary principle entrusts the state to establish legal order on behalf of the people," *id.* at 106; and that "The fiduciary's authority arises ... from the obligation under which her power must be exercised," *id.* at 134. Elsewhere, he says that "duty begets authority because duty makes accountability to public standards possible." Fox-Decent, *Fiduciary Authority and the Service Conception*, *supra* note 9, at 378.

[10] See also Andrew S. Gold, *Reflections on the State as Fiduciary*, 63 U. of Toronto L.J. 655 (2013).

claim to parental authority falls to be determined by considerations other than those supplied by its fiduciary nature. An implication is that while the fiduciary theory supports recognition of fiduciary constraints on the exercise of authority by the state, the theory must be supplemented by non-fiduciary justification of the assertion of authority. So, too, accounts of the assertion of authority by private fiduciaries must be supplemented by analysis of non-fiduciary justificatory considerations.

### b) The constitution of fiduciary authority

Legal authority is inherently relational. It implies, at the very least, recognition of the authority's privileged position to make decisions, issue directives, be accountable, and hold others to account relative to the object(s) of her authority. It may also imply acceptance of, or compliance with, her decisions or directives.

Legal authority may be personal or agential. Personal authority is an incident of the legal personality of natural persons. It arises by virtue of one's legal status as a person and it is essential to the manifestation of personality through law. Fiduciary authority is different. It is never innate. It must be granted and is subject to rescission, suspension, or reclamation. This reflects the fact that fiduciary authority is agential. Being a kind of agency authority, fiduciary authority enables persons to represent each other.[11]

Private fiduciary authority is a form of standing derived from the legal personality of ordinary legal persons. Usually, it is granted directly from one person to another. But it may be conferred by a group of persons, acting jointly or severally, in and through their membership of an organization. However granted, private fiduciary authority is always wielded relative to a specific purpose or specific practical interests of a beneficiary or class of beneficiaries. Private fiduciary authority, like all forms of legal authority, is a kind of standing. But it is necessarily more limited than that entailed by personal authority. The fiduciary stands in substitution for (or, following Hobbes, *personates*)[12]

---

[11] See THOMAS HOBBES, LEVIATHAN 112 (Richard Tuck ed., 1991) ("the Right of doing any Action, is called AUTHORITY and sometimes *warrant*. So that by Authority, is always understood a Right of doing any act: and *done by Authority*, done by Commission, or Licence from him whose right it is").

[12] *Id.* ("[t]he word Person ... signifies the *disguise*, or *outward appearance* of a man ... a Person, is the same that an *Actor* is, both on the Stage and in common Conversation; and to *Personate*, is to *Act*, or Represent *himself*, or another").

the person(s) who granted him authority only to the extent provided for in the grant of authority.

Public fiduciary authority is constituted differently. It, too, is a kind of standing. Public fiduciaries engage in official acts that are recognized as such by persons subject to them. Indeed, the state, in acting through its officials, must be seen as asserting authority in its representations, decisions, and declarations for it to effectively act as such (i.e., to act as a state in and through law). As is true of ordinary persons (natural or artificial), the state sets and pursues (i.e., authors) specific ends and is taken as responsible for (i.e., as having authored) the ordinary legal consequences of its words and deeds. However, uniquely, the personality of the state implies an authority that extends further. The *public* character of the authority of the state is revealed most obviously in the assertion of standing to establish and maintain public order through the exercise of distinctively public fiduciary powers (i.e., legislative, judicial, executive, and administrative powers). As is well known, the authority of the state uniquely encompasses (a) the power to issue binding directives with which subjects are duty bound to comply and (b) to threaten direct use of coercive force to sanction or punish noncompliance.

The differences run deeper. Whereas beneficiaries or benefactors of private fiduciary mandates do (indeed, must) enjoy personal legal capacity in respect of the powers conferred on their fiduciaries, beneficiaries of public fiduciary mandates are legally incapable of personally enjoying distinctively public fiduciary powers. Public fiduciary authority and associated powers can be juridically located only in the *sui generis* legal personality of the state and can be exercised only by officials personating the state.

These constitutive differences have important normative implications, seen most clearly (if abstractly) in variation in the extent of decisional sovereignty and subjection that characterize the positions of fiduciary and beneficiary. The private fiduciary does not determine, much less dictate, ends for a beneficiary or benefactor where the latter is capable of doing so, nor can she compel compliance with her decisions. The beneficiary and the benefactor are *liable* to the exercise of power by the fiduciary but they are not *obligated* to obey the fiduciary. Indeed, ordinarily a disappointed beneficiary or benefactor can defy or depose the fiduciary, reclaim, or undertake fiduciary powers, and/or issue binding directions to the fiduciary.

This reflects the fact that private fiduciary authority is usually conditioned by beneficiary and/or benefactor codetermination. The accommodation of codetermination involves respect for rights or powers retained by the beneficiary or benefactor relative to the objects of fiduciary authority. Through the exercise of such rights or powers, the fiduciary and the beneficiary/benefactor jointly determine how the latter's ends or interests are to be served. Codetermination reflects the fact that fiduciary authority is subject to the presumption that the personal sovereignty of persons attaches to any extension or delegation of personal authority.

Public fiduciary authority, by contrast, is not conditioned by codetermination. Subjects can call upon constitutional protections, apply for judicial review, and call for prosecution of public officials when their rights are violated by the state. But they have no residual authority that would support enjoyment of rights or powers coordinate with those vested in the state by virtue of *its* authority.

### c) The objects of fiduciary authority

The objects of private fiduciary authority are either purposes that ordinary legal persons are capable of specifying or the significant practical interests of such persons. The objects of public fiduciary authority are different in respect of those powers of the state that are attributable to its *sui generis* personality. Distinctively public fiduciary powers are not held relative to the discrete interests of ordinary persons or purposes specified by them. Instead, they are held relative to the interests of the public – that is, a polis or political community – in general. Public interests are, by definition, collective interests – for example, interests in peace, order, and good government.[13] These are interests in which everyone has a stake but which depend for their security on the existence of a properly functioning state. Unlike the personal interests that ground private fiduciary authority, public interests in the authority of the state are irreducibly public. They cannot be dissolved or disaggregated and made the subject of interpersonal claim rights. As we shall see, this has profound implications for the substance and structure of public fiduciary accountability.

## II Private and public fiduciary accountability

Fiduciaries are invested with authority in order that they may exercise associated discretionary powers for or on behalf of others. The mere possession of these powers entails the risk of abuse. Various fiduciary

---

[13] Fox-Decent, Sovereignty's Promise, *supra* note 3, at 3.

accountability rules serve to check this risk. Some of these rules are expressed similarly in private and public law. But the similarities can be overstated. In what follows, I shall highlight some differences between private and public fiduciary accountability.

### a) Judicial review of fiduciary administration

Consider first judicial review of the exercise of private fiduciary powers. As has been widely noted, there are some obvious parallels in the judicial review of private and public fiduciary administration.[14] In both contexts, judicial review protects affected parties from illegality, irrationality, abuse, and procedural unfairness in the exercise of power. Access to judicial review is, however, significantly broader in public than in private law.[15] Public law requires that an applicant demonstrate a "sufficient interest."[16] "Sufficiency" does not require that one have an interest directly subject to, or right held against, a power. Instead, it can be established by showing that one has a genuine personal interest in the accountability of an official or that one's interests may be influenced by their conduct. The breadth of access to judicial review in the context of public administration makes sense given the general public interest in the proper exercise of public fiduciary powers.[17]

Access to judicial review of private fiduciary administration is far more restrictive. Generally speaking, applications can be brought only by a beneficiary, benefactor, or their surrogate. This restrictiveness is sensible in light of the distinctive bases, constitution, and objects of private fiduciary authority. Private fiduciaries ordinarily receive their powers by grant from private persons for the benefit of private persons or their purposes. Benefactors have a clear and direct interest in fiduciary powers

---

[14] Finn, *supra* note 2; Evan J. Criddle, *Fiduciary Foundations of Administrative Law*, 54 UCLA L. REV. 117 (2006); FOX-DECENT, SOVEREIGNTY'S PROMISE, *supra* note 3.

[15] SIR WILLIAM WADE, WADE AND FORSYTH ON ADMINISTRATIVE LAW 709 (7th ed. 1994) (Wade describes the doctrine of standing as "generous and public oriented").

[16] See Supreme Court Act, 1981, c. 54, Pt II, § 31(3) (U.K.), *and* R v. Inland Revenue Comm'rs, exp. National Federation of Self-Employed and Small Businesses Ltd., [1982] A.C. 617 (H.L.) (appeal taken from Eng.) (U.K.).

[17] Inland Revenue Comm'rs, [1982] A.C. 617 [644]. As Lord Diplock explained, there would be:

[A] grave lacuna in our system of public law if a pressure group ... or even a single public-spirited taxpayer, were prevented by outdated technical rules of *locus standi* from bringing the matter to the attention of the court to vindicate the rule of law and get the unlawful conduct stopped. *Id.*

being exercised as intended inasmuch as private fiduciary authority must be understood as an extension of their capacity to act purposively.[18] Likewise, beneficiaries' protected interests are located juridically in the objects of fiduciary power (including any non-fiduciary rights in those objects) and their enjoyment of primary rights relative to the powers wielded by the fiduciary.

### b) The structure of fiduciary accountability

More obvious differences are structural in nature. Ordinary persons, acting in a personal capacity, can challenge the exercise of public powers in a variety of ways, but generally speaking, they do not have personal fiduciary claim rights in distinctively public fiduciary powers.[19] The doctrine of sovereign immunity means that, in general, acts in excess or abuse of the authority of the state will not found civil liability of a public official.[20] The doctrine may be suspended only by consent of the state. Tellingly, the doctrine is thought necessary to ensure that affairs of the state can be administered in the public interest without distortion by litigation reflecting personal or factional interests.[21] Sovereign immunity implies that there is no *interpersonal* fiduciary accountability between public officials and citizens in connection with the exercise of distinctively public fiduciary powers. This makes sense insofar as these powers are derived from the *sui generis* personality of the state and are devoted to objects of public rather than private interest. Where ordinary persons act to hold public officials to account as fiduciaries, they appear to do so on the basis of collective rights (i.e., rights enjoyed by a community, or

---

[18] See generally Hanoch Dagan and Sharon Hannes, *Managing Our Money: The Law of Financial Fiduciaries as a Private Law Institution*, in PHILOSOPHICAL FOUNDATIONS OF FIDUCIARY LAW 91 (Andrew S. Gold and Paul B. Miller eds., 2014).

[19] They may, of course, have personal claim rights as provided by public law (e.g., constitutional rights).

[20] See Harold J. Krent, *Reconceptualizing Sovereign Immunity*, 45 VAND. L. REV. 1529, 1529 (1992). ("The United States generally is immune from suit without its consent. Accordingly, neither Congress nor the executive branch need pay damages for any contract breached, any tort committed, or any constitutional right violated by the federal government.") See also Jerry L. Mashaw, *Civil Liability of Government Officers: Property Rights and Official Accountability*, 42 LAW & CONTEMP. PROBS. 8 (1978); Caleb Nelson, *Sovereign Immunity as a Doctrine of Personal Jurisdiction*, 115 HARV. L. REV. 1559 (2002).

[21] Krent, *supra* note 20, at 1531 ("the prospect of market damages in a tort or contract suit might deter even the most committed government officials or legislators from pursuing initiatives that they believe are in the public interest ... it is a structural protection for democratic rule").

that may be asserted by a member of a community by virtue of her membership in the community as such)[22] and to invoke a collective form of accountability (i.e., a form of accountability in which the person held to account is deemed answerable to a community).

Private fiduciary accountability, by contrast, is interpersonal. The beneficiary (and/or the benefactor) enjoys personal claim rights directly in the powers wielded by the fiduciary. She may also enjoy personal claim rights in the objects of fiduciary authority. These rights are reflected in correlative duties which constrain the conduct of fiduciaries. In bringing a claim for breach of fiduciary duty, the beneficiary asserts a private right of action. She is claiming that she, *personally*, has suffered a civil wrong committed by the fiduciary, and that the fiduciary, *personally*, is accountable to *her* for the wrong. Private rights of action presuppose that primary rights and duties establish bilateral or interpersonal accountability relationships between persons in their individual capacities.[23] The interpersonal structure of private fiduciary accountability reflects, in turn, the fact that private fiduciaries exercise a kind of authority that is rooted in the personality of ordinary persons and is devoted to the private interests or purposes of ordinary persons.[24]

### c) *The form and substance of fiduciary accountability*

As will become evident in Part III, later, there are important parallels between private and public fiduciary accountability. But they are, for the

---

[22] See Joseph Raz, The Morality of Freedom 208 (1986), on the nature of collective rights in general:
> A collective right exists when the following three conditions are met. First, it exists because an aspect of the interest of human beings justifies holding some person(s) to be subject to a duty. Second, the interests in question are the interests of individuals as members of a group in a public good and the right is a right to that public good because it serves their interests as members of the group. Thirdly, the interest of no single member of that group in that public good is sufficient by itself to justify holding another person to be subject to a duty.

*Id.* It bears emphasis that a collective right does not depend for its existence on the capacity of a collective to be a bearer of a right in itself. Instead, collective rights can be grounded in interests of individuals that are inextricably bound up with the interests of a collective, inasmuch as pursuit of certain goods is possible only through coordinated action; *see also* Leslie Green, *Two Views of Collective Rights*, 4 Can. J. Law Jurisprudence 315, 320–21 (1991).

[23] Stephen Darwall and Julian Darwall, *Civil Recourse as Mutual Accountability*, 39 Fla. St. U. L. R. 17 (2011).

[24] Paul B. Miller, *Justifying Fiduciary Remedies*, 63 U. Toronto L.J. 570 (2013).

## II. PRIVATE AND PUBLIC FIDUCIARY ACCOUNTABILITY

most part, *not* evident at the level of right and duty or associated standards of conduct and modes of redress. Furthermore, appreciation of the function of fiduciary accountability rules gives reason to doubt the fiduciary characterization of some duties that are said to apply to public fiduciaries by virtue of their possession of fiduciary authority.

We may begin with a matter of form that also implicates the structure of accountability. This is the issue of manner in which fiduciary rights and duties are assigned within a fiduciary relationship. Many private law relationships give rise to reciprocal duties, but the private law fiduciary relationship does not. The fiduciary is subject to certain legal duties, and the beneficiary holds correlative claim rights, but the beneficiary is not subject to any corresponding duty to the fiduciary. The same is not, and cannot, be true of public fiduciary relationships. The effectiveness of distinctively public fiduciary powers is contingent on citizen-beneficiaries' recognition and abidance of a duty of obedience. Again, there is no parallel duty in private law. The private fiduciary enjoys powers correlative to which beneficiaries and/or benefactors face liabilities. But these juridical consequences of subjection to a legal power are not inescapable in the way that a duty of obedience is and they do not connote subjection in the same sense. Furthermore, the vulnerability entailed by liability to the exercise of fiduciary power is usually checked by the presence of rights or retained powers by the beneficiary or benefactor. These rights and powers are so significant that some suggest that *fiduciaries* are subject to a duty of obedience.[25]

There are other significant differences in the substance of private and public fiduciary norms. Before averting to these, however, we may first identify similarities. The most obvious of these implicate loyalty norms. The fiduciary duty of loyalty applicable to private fiduciaries encompasses two conflict rules. By virtue of these rules, fiduciaries must avoid actual or possible conflicts of interest or duty. The conflict rules protect beneficiaries and benefactors from the risk that the fiduciary will

---

[25] Rob Atkinson, *Obedience as the Foundation of Fiduciary Duty*, 34 J. Corp. L. 45, 48 (2008):
> The duty of obedience is often overlooked ... precisely because it is so basic as to be almost invisible ... The irreducible root of the fiduciary relationship is one person's acting for another. The duty of obedience derives directly from ... [this] principle. The root of the fiduciary relationship is this directive from the principal to the fiduciary: Serve the one the principal designates, as the principal designates. The fiduciary must, at the most basic level, obey that directive; that directive is the duty of obedience.
> Id.

appropriate fiduciary powers in service of his own purposes. There is an identical concern in public law.[26] A public official might exercise official powers to further his own interests or those of a person, group, or faction for whom he feels competing loyalty. The response of public law to this concern generally tracks that of the private law: public officials are required to avoid conflicts.

There are, nevertheless, important differences in the ways in which private and public law respond to the risk of appropriation of fiduciary power. Whereas private fiduciary accountability is premised on conceptualization of disloyalty as a civil wrong defined by exacting standards, public fiduciary accountability is ordinarily premised on conceptualization of disloyalty as one of several criminal wrongs reflecting less exacting standards. For private fiduciaries, the mere presence of a possible conflict may generate liability to an individual beneficiary. By contrast, for public fiduciaries, the mere presence of a possible conflict will rarely found liability, civil or criminal.[27] Instead, cases involving egregious conflict grounded in self-interest (e.g., breach of confidence for personal gain, appropriation of public monies, or acceptance of bribes) are treated as indictable corruption-based criminal offenses.[28]

---

[26] FOX-DECENT, SOVEREIGNTY'S PROMISE, *supra* note 3 at 171–74. See Paul Finn, *Fiduciary Reflections*, 88 AUSTL. L.J. 127, 128 (2014). As Finn observes, "a manifest purpose of the law was to maintain public trust and confidence in officialdom. It did this by protecting the public from neglect or misuse of official power and position, especially when for private gain," *id*. See also Lionel D. Smith, *Can We Be Obliged to Be Selfless?*, in PHILOSOPHICAL FOUNDATIONS OF FIDUCIARY LAW 141 n. 65 (Andrew S. Gold and Paul B. Miller eds., 2014). As Smith explains:

[A] judge in giving judgment is [required to act] ... in the interests of the administration of justice. Because this is a requirement to exercise judgment in an unselfish way, the law applies similar constraints to those that apply in private law; for example, judges are subject to a version of the no-conflict rule, that can make their judgments voidable.
*Id.*

[27] Of course, liability is not the only relevant legal consequence. Where an individual can show that a decision to which he was subject was tainted with bias, he can challenge it through judicial review.

[28] R v. Bembridge, (1783) 22 State Tr. 1 [155–56] (H.L.) (appeal taken from Eng.) (Gr. Brit.):
[W]here there is a breach of trust, a fraud or an imposition in a subject concerning the public, which, as between subject and subject, would only be actionable by a civil action, yet as that concerns the king and the public (I use them as synonymous terms), it is indictable.

*Id.;* Finn, *supra* note 2, at 143. ("If a wrong is committed in or under the colour of office it, in consequence, is a public wrong. And so, from medieval times the regulation of public officials was put on a course which channeled it, first and foremost, through the criminal law.")

## II. PRIVATE AND PUBLIC FIDUCIARY ACCOUNTABILITY 263

One might still suspect that there is a deeper substantive similarity in the content, if not the enforcement, of loyalty norms. However, while private and public law share certain loyalty-based standards of conduct, they are animated by different ideals of loyalty.[29]

Fiduciary loyalty in the private law context requires that the fiduciary show preference for the specified interests or purposes of the beneficiary or benefactor over the interests or purposes of others when exercising fiduciary powers. Indeed, the private law conflict rules exact a jealous form of partiality, requiring that the fiduciary consider *only* the interests or purposes to which or to whom her powers have been devoted.

Public officials are not, and cannot be, subject to *this* ideal of loyalty. Citizens do not have a presumptive claim to partial treatment of their personal interests or purposes by public officials. To the contrary, public officials must prove assiduously *impartial* in the exercise of distinctively public fiduciary powers. Where the private fiduciary is expected to show personal allegiance, the public official must rise above contending personal and factional interests in acting for the benefit of the commonwealth. The ideal of fiduciary loyalty at work in public law thus necessarily encompasses suppression of the corrupting influence of self-interest, but also supposes transcendence of the kind of blinkered partiality that is a celebrated[30] and reviled[31] feature of private fiduciary law.

Fox-Decent has suggested that these differences might be bridged in recognition that a "different" standard of loyalty applies to private fiduciaries responsible for multiple beneficiaries. According to him, when a private fiduciary is ministering to the interests of a group, conventional standards of loyalty give way to a fairness standard under which each beneficiary is entitled to no more and no less than due regard of his interests.[32] The same standard is said to apply to public fiduciaries.[33]

---

[29] See Andrew S. Gold, *The Loyalties of Fiduciary Law*, in PHILOSOPHICAL FOUNDATIONS OF FIDUCIARY LAW *176* (Andrew S. Gold and Paul B. Miller eds., 2014) (on the concept(s) of loyalty in private law).

[30] See, for example, DANIEL MARKOVITS, A MODERN LEGAL ETHICS: ADVERSARY ADVOCACY IN A DEMOCRATIC AGE (2011).

[31] See ARTHUR APPLEBAUM, ETHICS FOR ADVERSARIES (2000).

[32] SOVEREIGNTY'S PROMISE, *supra* note 3 at 34. "[T]he discrete fiduciary duty of loyalty is necessarily transformed into duties of fairness and reasonableness in private law cases with multiple beneficiaries whose interests conflict."

[33] See *Id.* at 103. "In the private sphere ... [pension] fund directors must exercise their powers fairly and reasonably, taking into account the interests of each of the funds' beneficiaries. Similar principles are at play in the public sphere," *id*; and arguing that there is a "tight analogy between, on the one hand, private law fiduciary cases with

The difficulty with this is that fairness standards are not actually a substitute for exclusive-interest standards in private law. They are supplemental standards having little to do with loyalty as such. The fairness rules require that fiduciaries treat two or more beneficiaries fairly by pursuing options that will result in equal advantage for all or – where this is not possible or where the fiduciary has discretion to choose between beneficiaries – by giving full consideration to their respective interests. The fairness rules are focused on the relationship between (i.e., the relative standing of) beneficiaries; they are not concerned with the fiduciary's loyalty to his beneficiaries. The fact that groups of beneficiaries do not have, on an *inter se* basis, exclusive claims does not mean that exclusive-interest standards of loyalty do not apply. Rather, the exclusive-interest standards secure the exclusivity of the claim of beneficiaries *as a class* over fiduciary power vis-à-vis the fiduciary and any other person or group for whom the fiduciary might presume to act in exercising the power. Groups of beneficiaries thus *do* enjoy a claim to the single-minded partiality of their fiduciary; it is only that the fiduciary's loyalty falls to be measured by the common interests of the group rather than by the disaggregated interests of its members. The state's duty of impartiality must, therefore, be understood as embodying a distinctive ideal of public fiduciary loyalty.

We may now briefly consider the extent to which reasoning from private fiduciary law supports recognition of positive fiduciary obligations on the part of the state to secure specific objects of public interest, such as protection of the environment or advancement of human rights. In my view, while fiduciary principles can readily *accommodate* obligations such as these, they cannot offer independent juridical support for them. Positive obligations to secure particular objects are best understood as entailments of independently justified binding goals of fiduciary mandates.

To appreciate why this is so, an important first step lies in clarifying the extent to which fiduciary duties are positive or prescriptive in general. While there is debate on this point,[34] there are prescriptive standards attached to certain fiduciary duties. For instance, standards of diligence

---

multiple beneficiaries, and, on the other, public law cases in which a decision-maker must act in the public interest while exercising power over a particular individual who lacks a pre-existing right to the interest at stake," *id* at 167.

[34] See Darryn Jensen, *Prescription and Proscription in Fiduciary Obligations*, 21 King's L.J. 333 (2010).

associated with the duty of care at the very least require periodic exercise of judgment. Similarly, the duty of disclosure requires fiduciaries to take positive steps to communicate information to their beneficiaries. But standards such as these prescribe the *manner* in which the fiduciary must execute her mandate without specifying the *outcomes* to be achieved. Achievement of specific outcomes is undeniably important to fiduciaries and beneficiaries in private and public law. Fiduciaries are, after all, ordinarily hired, elected, or appointed with the expectation that they will accomplish certain objectives. Indeed, these expectations are often a determining factor in the decision to vest authority in a particular fiduciary. For that reason, in the private law context, expectations relating to outcomes are often explicitly contracted for – consider the prevalence of contingency fees and performance bonuses. But the very prevalence of contracting over outcome-related expectations is telling of the fact that they are not protected by fiduciary law itself.

Fiduciaries are not subject to a general duty to secure positive outcomes, much less specific duties to secure particular outcomes. Thus, the fiduciary theory of state authority cannot provide direct support for positive obligations of the state to secure public interest objectives. As is true of private law, so in public law, fiduciary principles make an important but necessarily limited contribution to our understanding of how law and morality limit the assertion and exercise of fiduciary power.

## III Principles of (public) fiduciary administration

In what follows, I suggest that there are at least four principles common to private and public fiduciary administration: the principle of fidelity; the principle of prudence; the principle of transparency; and the principle of consensualism. The principles are offered as statements of general norms guiding fiduciary administration. Being abstract, they are susceptible of being specified in different ways in private and public law.

### a) The principle of fidelity

The agential character of fiduciary authority grounds a *principle of fidelity*. This principle requires that fiduciaries prove faithful to the general and particular objects to which their powers are devoted. In the usual case, fidelity will mean manifest commitment to the fate of the purpose or person for which or for whom fiduciary powers are held. Commitment will be shown in positive measures that are reasonably calculated to advance or protect the cause of the purpose or person(s) in question. Whereas private fiduciary powers are ordinarily devoted to specific practical interests of *persons*, public fiduciary powers are most commonly granted for pursuit of *purposes* that engage the public interest.

The principle of fidelity clearly finds specification in conflict rules in private and public law. As discussed earlier in Part II.C, the conflict rules supply default standards of loyalty of differing degrees of sensitivity. These rules are reflected in canonical statements of the private law duty of loyalty and are also embodied in corruption-based criminal offenses with which public officials may be charged.[35] Some think that the conflict rules are exhaustive of fiduciary loyalty.[36] But this is not tenable considering that alternative standard(s) of loyalty must govern the conduct of fiduciaries acting under authorized conflicts.[37] It is also called into question by jurisprudence and academic commentary that treat good faith as an element of fiduciary loyalty.[38] For present purposes, however, questions concerning how loyalty requirements are specified in private and public law are beside the point. One need only recognize that fiduciary authority entails a general principle of fidelity which may encompass a variety of standards of conduct. The principle and associated standards secure the expectation that fiduciaries exercise their powers faithfully to advance the ends to which they were devoted.

### b) The principle of prudence

Administration of a fiduciary mandate, like the fulfillment of contractual promises, calls for positive acts of performance. A *mandate* is, after all, an authorization to *act*. A fiduciary is vested with authority in the hope that she will exercise her powers to salutatory effect. However, as we have seen, fiduciary law does not subject fiduciaries to prescriptive obligations to secure outcomes. Instead, it invokes a general principle of prudence.

The principle of prudence requires that fiduciaries execute their mandates with due care. As a *fiduciary* principle, it is not concerned with care

---

[35] Finn, *supra* note 2.
[36] Matthew Conaglen, Fiduciary Loyalty: Protecting the Due Performance of Non-Fiduciary Duties (2010).
[37] Paul B. Miller, *Multiple Loyalties and the Conflicted Fiduciary*, 40 Queen's L.J. 301 (2014).
[38] See Gold, *supra* note 29; Julian Velasco, *How Many Fiduciary Duties Are There in Corporate Law*, 83 S. Cal. L. Rev. 1231 (2010); Leo Strine et al., *Loyalty's Core Demand: The Defining Role of Good Faith in Corporation Law*, 93 Geo. L.J. 629 (2010).

### III. PRINCIPLES OF (PUBLIC) FIDUCIARY ADMINISTRATION 267

or prudence *in general*. Rather, it requires that a fiduciary show due care when *acting as a fiduciary* (i.e., determining whether and how to act on fiduciary powers) in pursuing the objects which ground her authority, bearing in mind the foreseeable impact of same on *interests of the beneficiary or benefactor*. The principle requires mindfulness that fiduciary powers are to be deployed in service of another, attentiveness to the burden of performance, and a deliberative posture in decision-making.

The principle of prudence establishes deliberative and attitudinal ideals for fiduciary decision-making. It also supports a universal duty of care governing the execution of fiduciary mandates. While a duty of care is uniformly imposed on fiduciaries in private and public law, associated standards of care are highly variable. In some contexts, care is understood as merely connoting rational decision-making processes. In other circumstances, it is understood as extending to the reasonableness of decisions made. This variability is multiplied further by differences in standards of review. Then there are differences in the calibration of the reasonableness standards. Some fiduciaries (e.g., trustees) have historically been subject to objective standards of care while others have been subject to subjective or mixed standards. Notwithstanding ambivalence over the formulation and enforcement of standards of care, few would doubt that the agential character of fiduciary authority supports a general principle of prudence.

#### c) The principle of transparency

Ordinarily when we make decisions for ourselves, we do so under no legal obligation of transparency. The process by which we come to personal decisions, and the bases of the decisions we reach, are usually opaque and often considered private. It is up to us to determine whether, and if so to whom, to disclose information about our decisions. This reflects the fact that personal authority entails the standing to make decisions in exercising personal rights, powers, and privileges without liability to requirements of public or interpersonal justification. Fiduciary decision-making is categorically different. Fiduciary decisions are made for or on behalf of others. Expectations of transparency are entailed by the very idea of accountability or answerability in decision-making of this nature.

The principle of transparency requires that the fiduciary be open in her decision-making and that she be willing to provide information material to her decision-making as well as reasons for her decisions.

Private fiduciaries are not required to be *generally* transparent in their decision-making. Instead, normally only beneficiaries, benefactors, or their surrogates legitimately hold expectations of transparency.[39] A broader conception of transparency is, by contrast, appropriate to public fiduciaries. Acknowledging national security, privilege, and other public interest justifications for secrecy, generally speaking, we expect public officials to be broadly – that is, *truly publicly* – transparent in their decision-making.[40] These expectations underlie and partly explain the openness of our courts and legislatures, requirements that legislative debate, voting, and hearings be conducted publicly, and that judges and administrative officials give public reasons for their decisions.

The principle of transparency is important for reasons not fully captured in the modest literature on the subject.[41] First, transparency is the foundation of the consensual formation and termination of fiduciary relationships. Second, it is essential to monitoring and thus to accountability within fiduciary relationships. Third, the validity of *ex post* transactions between the beneficiary and the fiduciary turns on the latter having met elevated standards of transparency. Fourth, in many cases, transparency is critical to achievement of particular objects associated with a fiduciary mandate (e.g., law-giving by public fiduciaries). Fifth and finally, in private law, transparency is essential to the sound exercise of retained powers or rights held relative to fiduciary powers. In these and other ways, the principle of transparency ensures that those with salient interests understand decisions reached by a fiduciary as well as circumstances relevant to their ongoing participation in fiduciary relationships.

### d) *The principle of consensualism*

Leading accounts of fiduciary duties emphasize inequality and dependence in fiduciary relationships.[42] It is not for nothing that they do. The conferral of authority upon a fiduciary entails dependence and

---

[39] Indeed, in many circumstances, broader disclosure could expose the private fiduciary to liability for breach of confidence.

[40] FOX-DECENT, SOVEREIGNTY'S PROMISE, *supra* note 3, at 257–60.

[41] See, for example, Richard R. W. Brooks, *Knowledge in Fiduciary Relations*, in PHILOSOPHICAL FOUNDATIONS OF FIDUCIARY LAW 225 (Andrew S. Gold and Paul B. Miller eds., 2014).

[42] Tamar Frankel, *Fiduciary Law*, 71 CALIF. L. REV. 795, 809–10 (1983); Deborah A. DeMott, *Beyond Metaphor: An Analysis of Fiduciary Obligation*, 1988 DUKE L.J 879, 902 (1988).

### III. PRINCIPLES OF (PUBLIC) FIDUCIARY ADMINISTRATION

vulnerability. The manner in which a fiduciary exercises her powers is bound to influence the purposes or persons relative to which they are held, for good or for ill.

Dependence and vulnerability are nowhere more evident than in fiduciary relationships involving incapable persons. Guardianship relationships are an important subset of fiduciary relationships. But it would be a mistake to venture generalizations about fiduciary relationships based on them. More particularly, it would be a mistake to suppose, *pace* Fox-Decent, that fiduciary law generally treats beneficiaries as passive and incapable by virtue of their subjection to fiduciary authority.[43] Most fiduciary relationships are in fact mutually consensual and feature some measure of codetermination.

The principle of consensualism requires that fiduciaries respect the consensual nature of their association with beneficiaries and/or benefactors to the extent appropriate given their capacity to act independently or conjointly with the fiduciary in respect of the particular objects of fiduciary authority. More specifically, it calls first for respect for the (ordinarily) consensual basis of the conferral of fiduciary authority, including decisions made by a beneficiary and/or benefactor whether and when to enter and exit from the relationship. Second, it requires respect for the actual, lapsed, or maturing autonomy and capacity of the beneficiary and/or benefactor. How respect should be shown will vary depending on the present capacity of the beneficiary or benefactor (e.g., a parent deciding for an adolescent child may include the child in decision-making;[44] a surrogate must show respect for the now-lapsed capacity of an incapable adult by respecting previously expressed wishes). Third, in private law it entails respect for decisions made in the exercise of rights enjoyed relative to fiduciary powers or in the exercise of retained powers. Fourth and finally, in conjunction with the principle of transparency, it requires the fiduciary to support the consensual involvement of the beneficiary or benefactor in the fiduciary relationship by disclosing information material to (a) their understanding of decisions reached by the fiduciary and (b) the decisions that they have to make. In these and

---

[43] Fox-Decent, Sovereignty's Promise, *supra* note 3 at 89 (claiming that to be considered a fiduciary one "must have unilateral discretionary power to affect the legal or practical interests of a peculiarly vulnerable party ... And the beneficiary's vulnerability must arise from an incapacity on the part of the beneficiary to exercise or control the power entrusted to the fiduciary").

[44] See Ethan J. Leib and David L. Ponet, *Fiduciary Representation and Deliberative Engagement with Children*, 20 J. Pol. Phil. 178 (2012).

other ways, the law eschews the notion that fiduciary relationships are inherently paternalistic. In addition to safeguarding the purposes of benefactors and/or the interests of beneficiaries, fiduciaries must also respect their autonomy and their choices.

## Conclusion

Fiduciary theories of the state are promising. They present an important alternative to theories in the social contract tradition. The best work of fiduciary theory is premised on a finely constructed account of the authority of the state. A key insight of this account is that public and private fiduciaries are fiduciaries precisely because they enjoy a distinctive form of legal authority. I have presently sought to broaden and deepen our understanding of common properties of private and public fiduciary authority. But I have also sounded a note of caution. In searching for commonalities, we sometimes neglect differences. Close analysis reveals that there are important unrecognized differences between private and public fiduciary authority and accountability. Private and public fiduciaries equally enjoy authority derived from the legal personality of persons. But the state is no ordinary person. The *sui generis* legal personality of the state is reflected in the unique constitution and objects of public fiduciary authority. Differences in the nature of private and public fiduciary authority are, in turn, reflected in mechanisms of fiduciary accountability. Generally speaking, the interests of beneficiaries or benefactors in private fiduciary relationships are secured through individual claim rights relative to fiduciary powers enforceable by way of private rights of action. By contrast, generally speaking, the public interest in public fiduciary relationships is secured through collective rights enforceable through ordinary public law accountability mechanisms (and especially through criminal law). Direct resonance in the normative implications of private and public fiduciary authority is seen most clearly at the level of general principle. Future work might consider how fiduciary accountability understood in light of these principles is realized concretely in private and public law and the extent to which fiduciary and non-fiduciary norms interact in constituting and constraining private and public fiduciary authority.

# 13

# Human rights indicators and boundaries of accountability and opportunity

MEGAN DERSNAH AND RON LEVI

## Introduction

Over the past 20 years, indicators relating to global governance have gained massive ground.[1] The proliferation of indicators is itself part of a general rise in standardization,[2] which includes a politics that values transparency, auditability, and rankings,[3] as well as a project of commensurability for how we identify countries, their performance, and their status more generally.[4] Some of these indicator frameworks have been long known, such as World Bank "doing business" indicators or Organisation for Economic Co-operation and Development (OECD) measured credit risks. The demand for standardized indicators has, however, spread like wildfire, including into fields such as human rights where they have been conventionally resisted – so much so that, for the past several years, there has been "an emerging market in human rights indicators."[5] To take merely one data point on the rapid proliferation of these indicators, nearly 10 years ago, a United Nations Development Plan (UNDP) survey already identified 165 current indices on global governance, 83% of which were created between 1991 and 2006, and 50% between 2001 and 2006.[6]

---

[1] Kevin Davis et al., *Indicators as a Technology of Global Governance* (Global Admin. L. Series, Inst. for Int'l L. & Just., Working Paper 2010/2, 2010).
[2] Marcos Ancelovici and Jane Jenson, *La standardisation et les mécanismes du transfert transnational*, 1 REV. GOUV'T ACTION PUB. 37 (2012) (Fr.).
[3] MICHAEL POWER, THE AUDIT EXPLOSION (1994).
[4] Wendy Espeland and Mitchell L. Stevens, *Commensuration as a Social Process*, 24 ANN. REV. SOC. 313 (1998).
[5] AnnJannette Rosga and Margaret L. Satterthwaite, *The Trust in Indicators: Measuring Human Rights* 2 (Ctr. for Hum. Rts. & Global Just. Working paper, Number 20).
[6] Romina Bandura, *A Survey of Composite Indices Measuring Country Performance: 2006 Update*, (U.N.D.P/O.D.S. Working Background Paper, 2006).

Of course, the proliferation of indicators cannot be understood on its own. It is itself part of a general rise in standardization that gained ground over the course of the neoliberal era, including demands for transparency, auditability, and rankings around which states, donors, and international organizations are all converging.[7] To be sure, calculable indicators of this sort have different effects, depending on the institutional and political context in which they are deployed, yet the spread of these techniques to new domains – and in particular to conventionally public functions, domestically and internationally – stems from the broader critique of the welfare state that was formulated during the neoliberal era,[8] and with it a general critique of state bureaucracies.[9] This turn to indicators is thus part of what legal theorist Alain Supiot refers to as the dream of harmony *through* calculation: a dream in which governance by legal standards has been replaced with a logic of metrics and calculation, corresponding to an ultraliberal utopia of a total market.[10] For Supiot, this logic of calculability can run the risk of crowding out other experiential modes of governing – and, in particular, contrasts with a conventional legal mode said to be based on experience and openness to conflict.

All indicators tacitly embody theories about the appropriate standards against which to measure societies and the appropriate ways to measure compliance.[11] However, this chapter does not take up the normative claim over whether the turn to human rights indicators is better or worse for achieving human rights outcomes. Instead, we focus on how the move to human rights indicators developed over the past three decades, by situating this shift in accountability for human rights violations within historical debates and competitions over human rights indicators from the early 1970s onwards. With an increasing consensus around human rights indicators emerging over the past several years, we then turn to the case of gender equality to review

---

[7] Ancelovici and Jenson, *supra* note 2.
[8] Nikolas Rose, Powers of Freedom: Reframing Political Thought (1999).
[9] Jane Jenson and Ron Levi, *Narratives and Regimes of Social and Human Rights: The Jack Pines of the Neoliberal Era*, in Social Resilience in the Neoliberal Era 69 (Peter A. Hall and Michèle Lamont eds., 2013).
[10] Alain Supiot, *Le rêve de l'harmonie par le calcul*, Le Monde Diplomatique, Feb. 2015, at 3 (Fr.) [hereinafter Supiot, *Le rêve de l'harmonie par le calcul*]; Alain Supiot, État social et mondialisation: analyse juridique des solidarités, 2012–2013 Annuaire C. France 717 (2014) [hereinafter Supiot, *État social et mondialisation*].
[11] Davis et al., *supra* note 1.

the literature on some of the effects of the turn to indicators within and beyond the United Nations system, and we outline the polarizing normative debates that this has often produced. In so doing, we highlight how human rights indicators push multiple actors to engage with each other – states, international organizations, nongovernmental organizations (NGOs), and the private sector – on common platforms, all the while having to satisfy multiple stakeholders in the process. While these common platforms may create tensions across multiple actors, and while some welcome indicators while others resist them, the larger point is that human rights indicators have shifted from being a heterodox approach resisted by states and other actors to one that is emerging as a new human rights orthodoxy, with effects for which programs are both pursued and abandoned.

## I Human rights histories, boundary crossings, and the turn to measurement

Focusing on the expansion of human rights indicators, anthropologist Sally Engle Merry laments that "the political process of judging and evaluating is transformed into a technical issue of measurement and counting," and concludes that these techniques "developed in the economic domain move uneasily into these newer fields, promising greater specificity of human rights and definitions of compliance yet importing new ambiguities in the definition of indicators and the kinds of data they use."[12]

Nonetheless, understanding the development of human rights indicators, and the political pressures they faced and later overcame, requires attending to the context in which human rights emerged in US foreign policy throughout the 1970s and 1980s.[13] As we delineate later, this grew over several boundary crossings: some political, some substantive, and some geographic. Though we do so only telegraphically in this chapter, we emphasize that the political and cultural conjunctures of the neoliberal era are thus of particular importance to understand how indicators gained momentum, and set the stage for their later extension and framework internationally.

---

[12] Sally Engle Merry, *Measuring the World: Indicators, Human Rights, and Global Governance*, 103 AM. SOC'Y OF INT'L L. PROC. ANN. MEETING 239, 243 (2009) [hereinafter Merry, *Measuring the World* 2009].

[13] *Cf.* Samuel Moyn, *A Powerless Companion: Human Rights in the Age of Neoliberalism*, 77 LAW & CONTEMP. PROBS. 147(2015).

The momentum of human rights indicators within the era of neoliberalism is not, in and of itself, surprising. Despite early resistance to human rights, the neoliberal era coincided not only with the rise of human rights but with new cultural understandings of how to govern, including the risk of audit, transparency, risk assessments, performance indicators, and distrust of Weberian bureaucracies, that would coalesce to produce this approach to human rights.[14] As Samuel Moyn has recently argued, to merely demonstrate this coincidence is "not to say much"[15] – what we instead require is an understanding of the specific trajectory of human rights within the neoliberal era that demonstrates how this historical conjuncture framed available human rights tools.

We argue that, in contrast to reductionist views of human rights (and with them, human rights indicators) as stalking horses for neoliberal economics and market fundamentalism,[16] understanding how human rights indicators emerged and their influence on how we conceive of rights requires attending both to the political conjuncture of the neoliberal era and to the governance formats that gained prominence during neoliberalism.[17] This perspective echoes and extends Moyn's argument on human rights generally, namely, that "[i]ntellectually, international human rights were not new in the 1970s but enjoyed new practical circumstances in the middle of that decade that made them prestigious overnight."[18] As we develop later, these new circumstances were the result of political opportunities, position-takings among those investing in human rights in the United States and abroad, and new techniques of governance and measurement that proliferated across sectors throughout this era.

As Jenson and Levi[19] demonstrate, human rights indicators of various sorts had been collected and relied on since the 1970s, including by advocacy organizations and within domestic contexts, such as the Chilean Human Rights Commission.[20] Yet these were largely isolated and

---

[14] Jenson and Levi, *supra* note 9.  [15] Moyn, *supra* note 13, at 150.
[16] *For example,* DAVID HARVEY, A BRIEF HISTORY OF NEOLIBERALISM (2005); Amy Bartholomew and Jennifer Breakspear, *Human Rights as Swords of Empire?*, 40 SOCIALIST REG. 125 (2009).
[17] Jenson and Levi, *supra* note 9.  [18] Moyn, *supra* note 13, at 155.
[19] Jenson and Levi, *supra* note 9.
[20] Russel Lawrence Barsh, *Measuring Human Rights: Problems of Methodology and Purpose,* 15 HUM. RTS. Q. 87 (1993); Rajeev Malhotra and Nicolas Fasel, *Quantitative Human Rights Indicators: A Survey of Major Initiatives,* Abo Akedemi University, Expert Meeting on Human Rights Indicators, Mar. 2005 (Fin.).

small-scale efforts. This began to shift in the late 1970s, which saw a sea change in the boundaries between human rights and US foreign policy. Following Amnesty International's rise in the United Kingdom in the early 1960s and significant US investment in human rights by the Ford Foundation, President Carter relied on his 1977 inauguration address to identify human rights as a centerpiece of US foreign policy. The text of this address is important, since it argues that US foreign policy choices should be based on *selecting* states through their human rights records, rather than marshaling human rights arguments to advance otherwise strategic preferences.[21] In Carter's address, "our commitment to human rights must be absolute," since "the world itself is now dominated by a new spirit" of demanding human rights, and "our moral sense dictates a clear-cut preference for these societies which share with us an abiding respect for individual human rights." This approach led to an increased emphasis on human rights data, which generated significant research to form the basis of foreign policy efforts.[22] Indeed, the result of this selection process led to reversals in US policy for countries such as Chile, Nicaragua, and Guatemala.[23]

This emphasis on human rights data was extended in the subsequent Reagan administration. While this shift in government initially led to the view that a human rights policy should not restrict the capacity of the United States to ally itself with foreign states,[24] the Reagan administration soon turned to human rights as a mechanism for bringing Soviet Bloc practices to the attention of the world, and even more so as a tool for democracy promotion abroad, most notably by establishing the National Endowment for Democracy.[25] By crossing this new boundary of foreign policy, the new articulation of human rights as democratization led to ever-greater investment in indicator approaches, now in World Bank Reports and State Department country reports,[26] with institutions such

---

[21] Yves Dezalay, and Bryant Garth, *From the Cold War to Kosovo: The Rise and Renewal of the Field of International Human Rights*, 2 ANN. REV. L. SOC. SCI. 231 (2006).

[22] Barsh, *supra* note 20, at 98; Judith Innes de Neufville, *Social Indicators of Basic Needs: Quantitative Data for Human Rights Policy*, 11 SOC. INDICATORS RES. 383, 385 (1982).

[23] ARYEH NEIER, TAKING LIBERTIES: FOUR DECADES IN THE STRUGGLE FOR RIGHTS 174–76 (2003); KATHRYN SIKKINK, MIXED SIGNALS: US HUMAN RIGHTS POLICY AND LATIN AMERICA 121–25 (2004).

[24] SIKKINK, *supra* note 23, at 185–89; NICOLAS GUILHOT, THE DEMOCRACY MAKERS: HUMAN RIGHTS AND INTERNATIONAL ORDER 82 (2005).

[25] GUILHOT, *supra* note 24; Tamar Jacoby, *The Reagan Turnaround on Human Rights*, 64 FOREIGN AFF. 1066, 1067 (1986).

[26] de Neufville, *supra* note 22.

as Freedom House continuing and refining their research on measuring freedom and civil and political rights.[27] This newly energized link between human rights and democracy promotion spawned a new field of expertise in governance and state reform that, over time, gained ever-greater currency at institutions such as the World Bank, where, by 1989, the monetarist emphasis of the bank had given way to an emerging view that development also requires "vigorous protection" of human rights.[28]

If indicators came to be dominant in what were identified as major institutions of the neoliberal era, dominant human rights NGOs also began to rely more forcefully on human rights data around the same time period, eager to develop new and rigorous expertise on human rights – rather than seen as merely trading on the symbolic gravitas of domestic legal elites.[29] As sociologists of law Dezalay and Garth demonstrate, given the perception that neoliberal governments were deploying human rights cynically and selectively, human rights actors in the United States and the United Kingdom (in particular NGOs such as Amnesty International) turned to emphasize the production of objective data regarding human rights compliance,[30] with Amnesty International's emphasis on research reflecting a "quasi-obsessional identification with neutrality" that would provide prestige to the field by distancing itself from mere political choice.[31]

However, as these methods moved boundaries from the United States to the international human rights regime more directly, the reliance on indicators became deeply contested. Perhaps the apex of this heated debate can be traced to 1991, when the UNDP produced a "Human Freedom Index" in its Human Development Report. The UNDP had begun these reports the year prior, in an attempt to shift the conceptual boundaries of how to think about economic growth and development beyond exclusively economic indicators. This UNDP Report was followed, a few weeks later, by the World Bank's release of its World Development Report, which also relied on a human rights index to argue for a relationship between freedom, human rights, and economic growth.[32]

---

[27] HANS OTTO SANO and LONE LINDHOLT, HUMAN RIGHTS INDICATORS 2000: COUNTRY DATA AND METHODOLOGY 58 (2000).
[28] GUILHOT, *supra* note 24, at 211; Galit A. Sarfaty, *Why Culture Matters in International Institutions: The Marginality of Human Rights at the World Bank*, 103 AM. J. INT'L L. 647 (2009).
[29] Dezalay and Garth, *supra* note 21.   [30] NEIER, *supra* note 23.
[31] Dezalay and Garth, *supra* note 21.
[32] U.N. Dev. Program, Human Development Report 1991: Financing Human Development (1991); World Bank, World Development Report 1991: The Challenge of Development (1991).

These human rights and freedom indicators led to resistance among developing countries, who argued that an index of compliance with human rights treaties to rank nearly ninety countries would find the poorest countries to be the "least free" – and to draw what they regarded as political conclusions by the UNDP, including the claim that "political freedom seems to have unleashed the creative energies of the people – and lead to ever higher levels of income and social progress." With the UNDP having provided nearly 1.5 billion dollars of assistance to the Third World in the year prior to the report, the language and implications of the Human Freedom Index were not lost on observers. As an article in the *Globe and Mail* predicted, in addition to political resistance from low-ranked states across Africa and Asia, the UNDP's perspective could legitimate cutbacks in foreign aid (Canadian foreign aid was being slashed by the Conservative Mulroney government by over 1 billion at this time), so that "[v]oluntary aid agencies in the West may also protest against the report, arguing that at a time of economic recession, the UNDP is merely reflecting donor governments' preoccupation with domestic deficits and is telling needy nations to make do with less, instead of arguing against foreign aid cutbacks."[33]

Speaking on behalf of developing nations, the ambassador for Ghana railed against the UNDP's attempt to devise universal standards of human rights that were regarded as merely a Western conception of human rights.[34] The extension across boundaries – to the international and to the field of development – led to pushback, since measuring freedom in relation to development was said to suggest that "the lack of political commitment, not of financial resources, is often the real cause of human neglect."[35] In the face of heated criticism on the floor of the UN General Assembly, the UNDP Administrator defended this reliance on human rights indicators by expanding the definition of development to place a premium on individual autonomy and human freedom as the engine of economic growth, and sought to distance the question of which measurement indicator is most appropriate.[36] Faced with a critical UN General Assembly resolution, the attempt to integrate indicators into the mainstream of the international field failed, at least for the moment.

---

[33] Howard Ross, *UN Body Criticizes Development Aid: Report Urges Wealthy Countries to Divert Spending to Basic Needs*, THE GLOBE AND MAIL, May 21, 1991, at A1.
[34] Jenson and Levi, *supra* note 9.   [35] Barsh, *supra* note 20, at 88.
[36] U.N. Dev. Program, *Response by William H. Draper III Administrator of the United Nations Development Programme to the General Debate* (June 12, 1991) (William H. Draper).

Instead, the UNDP's human rights indicators were replaced by a somewhat narrower set of "political freedom indicators," and detailed rankings and scores of countries were replaced by broad aggregations of countries into groups.[37] The UNDP itself continued to defend the production of human rights indicators, though now suggesting they "may be no more than rough approximations."[38] Other institutions, such as the World Bank and Freedom House, continued to produce new measurements and rankings, but a broad international, development-rooted project of standardization for human rights indicators did not gain more traction at this time.

## II  Global indicators as persistent cultural form

While we will soon turn to the return of human rights indicators – redesigned – in more recent years, it is important to emphasize that the practice of using indicators to measure human rights evolved within the early 1990s context of the increasing strength of the Washington Consensus and the cultural emphases of the neoliberal era. Transparency as an approach to accountability gained traction over the course of this decade through a critique of the role and conception of the Keynesian state: Weberian-style state bureaucracies were to be reconfigured, with state functions privatized and overseen through audits, and with the importing of notionally private sector practices of risk management, indicators, and audit into the state itself.[39] As Nikolas Rose argues, this has profound implications, since "government by audit transforms that which is to be governed," since they "create accountability to one set of norms – transparency, observability, standardization and the like – at the expense of accountability to other sets of norms," emphasizing evaluation over other substantive goals.[40]

It is thus not surprising that, while human rights indicators may have proven highly contentious in the early 1990s, the cultural form of indicators continued to progress throughout the global system. As OECD indicator specialists Charles Oman and Christiane Arndt argue,[41] there

---

[37] Barsh, *supra* note 20, at 89–90; Jenson and Levi, *supra* note 9.
[38] U.N. Dev. Program, Human Development Report, 1992: Global Dimensions of Human Development 28 (1992).
[39] Jenson and Levi, *supra* note 9. See also Supiot, *État social et mondialisation*, *supra* note 10.
[40] ROSE, *supra* note 8, at 154.
[41] CHRISTIANE ARNDT and CHARLES OMAN, USES AND ABUSES OF GOVERNANCE INDICATORS (2006).

## II. GLOBAL INDICATORS AS PERSISTENT CULTURAL FORM 279

are four main reasons for the recent rapid increase in the use and production of governance indicators. First, the large increase in international investment in developing countries has prompted investors to seek more information to reduce investment risk. Second, the end of the Cold War and the decline of the ideological commitments that underpinned it highlighted the negative effects of weak governance on the developing world. Third, the failure of reform efforts and aid projects in the developing world during the 1980s and 1990s gave rise to donor insistence on improving (and monitoring) the efficacy of their funding. And fourth, the emerging school of new institutional economics would enter the fray to emphasize the relationship of national governance for long-term economic growth, enhanced human welfare, and societal development. Emphasizing the cultural dimensions of indicators, Oded Löwenheim goes on to add a fifth factor: the domestic move toward more transparent and accountable public policy within Western countries has similarly prompted governments to justify their foreign aid expenditures according to measurable benchmarks and standards.[42]

Indeed, within the context of development, these indicator standards gained real dominance throughout the neoliberal era. From the outset of the debt crisis in the early 1980s to the late 1990s, economic policies centered around the idea that political and social problems can be solved primarily through market-based mechanisms and the rule of law, as opposed to state intervention.[43] These quickly became the guiding principles of foreign aid donors, including international financial institutions, which established requirements for the conditional measurement of economic growth. The Washington Consensus shifted discourses of development away from modernization toward a focus on "performance" – whether economic, agricultural, fiscal, or otherwise – and, via these various standards, countries were partitioned and ranked according to their performance.[44] These assessments were further incorporated into the discourse and practice of structural adjustment, so that adjustment involved improving the performance of national economies by increasing the efficiency of resource allocation.[45] As Rose

---

[42] Oded Löwenheim, *Examining the State: A Foucauldian Perspective on International 'Governance Indicators'*, 29 THIRD WORLD Q. 255 (2008).

[43] John Williamson, *What Washington Means by Policy Reform*, in LATIN AMERICAN ADJUSTMENT: HOW MUCH HAS HAPPENED 7 (John Williamson ed., 1990).

[44] Charles Gore, *The Rise and Fall of the Washington Consensus as a Paradigm for Developing Countries*, 28 WORLD DEV. 789 (2000).

[45] *Id.*

might suggest,[46] this had the effect of also changing the criteria for success: since the central criteria used to measure performance were Gross Domestic Product growth rate and macroeconomic stability, by the 1990s, the work of development focused around short-term growth and reestablishing financial balances, rather than the long-term transformation of economies and societies.

As with human rights indicators, the backlash to this performance-based approach was significant. The discontent toward structural adjustment programs was made salient by the rising insecurity and civil conflict in the Global South throughout the 1990s, as well as the sheer failure of the development agenda to resolve the high rates of poverty and income polarization in developing countries. There was a deep and prolonged collapse in output in countries making the transition from communism to market economies; Sub-Saharan Africa failed to grow, despite significant policy reform and continued foreign aid, with market-oriented reforms proving unsuitable to deal with the growing public health emergency on the continent; and there were frequent financial crises in Latin America, East Asia, Russia, and Turkey.[47] And yet, in spite of the backlash in the field of development, the idea of indicators and the culture of standardization and transparency, promised by the Washington Consensus and neoliberal framework, became strongly rooted, persisting within the context of the global governance of development politics and also seeping into other new domains of global governance, including a return to the domain of human rights.

## III The return of human rights indicators: New boundaries to cross

Created in the crucible of the neoliberal moment, the project of human rights indicators was vociferously contested, leading to a general chill over human rights indicators for several years.[48] Yet as Davis et al. argue, indicators tend to be attractive precisely because they appear transparent, consistent, and dependable, garner high levels of trust, and command scientific authority.[49] Such interest in human rights indicators reemerged

---

[46] ROSE, *supra* note 8.
[47] Dani Rodrik, *Goodbye Washington Consensus, Hello Washington Confusion?*, XLIV J ECON. LITERATURE 973 (2006) (reviewing WORLD BANK, ECONOMIC GROWTH IN THE 1990S: LEARNING FROM A DECADE OF REFORM (2005)).
[48] Rosga and Satterthwaite, *supra* note 5.
[49] Davis et al., *supra* note 1.

in the late 1990s,[50] and has quickly risen in prominence through the coordination and research efforts of the UN Office of the High Commissioner for Human Rights (OHCHR).

When the new turn to human rights indicators reemerged, the dominant approach to human rights indicators was adapted to gain greater interest and "buy-in" from states. In contrast to the earlier approach of ranking achievements via indicators, this newer approach emphasizes benchmarking – and thus includes attention to progress and commitment to human rights, rather than exclusively focusing on outcomes.[51] This builds on the approach taken by the Committee on Economic, Social and Cultural Rights, which, throughout the 1990s, sought to promote progress on rights while avoiding charges by states over the cost of compliance.[52] The result has been an approach that emphasizes benchmarking, emphasizes an approach of progressive realization (even, implicitly, when it comes to civil and political rights), and emphasizes, within country benchmarking, the rejection of any comparison of countries on their human rights records.[53]

Since 2006, the OHCHR has, at the request of the chairs of the human rights treaty bodies, been engaged in an effort to develop international human rights indicators across civil, political, economic, social, and cultural rights.[54] The purpose of this effort was to monitor compliance with human rights treaties because, over time, the treaty bodies have taken on a more judicial role in assessing the performance of states as they report on their treaty obligations, with some – including the Committee on the Rights of the Child – regularly requesting statistics in reports from state parties. However, while treaty bodies could use these to monitor compliance, the OHCHR also stressed that "it seeks neither to prepare a common list of indicators to be applied across all countries irrespective of their social, political and economic development, nor to make a case for building a global measure for cross-country comparisons

---

[50] Sally Engle Merry, *Measuring the World: Indicators, Human Rights, and Global Governance*, 52 CURRENT ANTHROPOLOGY S83–S95 (2011) [hereinafter Merry, *Measuring the World* 2011].

[51] Rosga and Satterthwaite, *supra* note 5; U.N. Office of the High Comm'r for Human Rights, Human Rights Indicators: A Guide to Measurement and Implementation (2012), www.ohchr.org/Documents/Publications/Human_rights_indicators_en.pdf.

[52] Rosga and Satterthwaite, *supra* note 5; Merry, *Measuring the World* 2009, *supra* note 12.

[53] Jenson and Levi, *supra* note 9.    [54] *Id.*

on the realization of human rights."⁵⁵ It is instead focused on providing "structural-process-outcome indicators," so that states are measured on their commitment, on their efforts, and on the results achieved.⁵⁶ Indeed, as they have developed over time, such indicators need not be quantitative, though the majority of the emphasis continues to reflect such an approach.

Nonetheless, part of this return of human rights indicators also has to do with a continued substantive boundary-crossing between the fields of human rights and development. By the time this second wave of indicators emerged, the Cold War was over and the OHCHR was in place, with a mandate to link rights and development, so that the earlier foray of the UNDP into the human rights field had taken ever-greater hold. World summits on human rights linked the two fields through discussion of a right to development, and, under Kofi Annan, human rights were to be "mainstreamed" across UN work, including in the area of development.⁵⁷ And, of course, these global changes also paralleled the establishment of the Millennium Development Goals (MDGs), agreed to in 2000, which include indicators across a series of goals, including some that map closely to human rights achievements (such as the goal of promoting gender equality and women's empowerment).

We see these boundary-crossings most visibly in the recent OHCHR indicators.⁵⁸ Among the first quotes in the publication is attributed to Douglas Daft, the CEO of Coca-Cola – as quoted by an earlier UNDP Human Development Report – that "what gets measured gets done."⁵⁹ The Report's foreword, written by the High Commissioner Navi Pillay, explicitly invokes the importance of indicators to achieve this boundary-crossing: because of their capacity to engage different stakeholders, Pillay concludes that "[i]ndicators are in this sense a potential bridge between the human rights and the development policy discourses,"⁶⁰ with the Report later pointing to the possibility that indicators can address "skepticism among economic policymakers about working with human rights"

---

⁵⁵ U.N. Office of the High Comm'r for Human Rights, Rep. on Indicators for Promoting and Monitoring the Implementation of Human Rights, HRI/MC/2008/3, June 6, 2008, 19.
⁵⁶ Id. at 6.
⁵⁷ Craig G. Mokhiber, *Toward a Measure of Dignity: Indicators for Rights-Based Development*, 18 STAT. J. UNITED NATIONS ECON. COMMISSION EUR. 155, 156–57 (2001).
⁵⁸ Human Rights Indicators: A Guide to Measurement and Implementation, *supra* note 51.
⁵⁹ Id. at 1.  ⁶⁰ Id. at iv.

## III. THE RETURN OF HUMAN RIGHTS INDICATORS

in national development plans.[61] Indeed, in addition to the capacity for indicators to provide relevant information about state practice, in this second wave of human rights indicators, there is increased attention on the work indicators can do in bridging fields of UN practice that are mandated to mainstream human rights, including the field of development cooperation, as well as the need for transparency demanded by donors.[62]

As conceptual work on indicators would predict, what the indicator measures thus changes the very understanding of human rights. Perhaps the most apparent shift is in the historical divide between "positive" and "negative" rights. Whereas in the past civil and political rights were understood as being of a different logic than social and cultural rights – with violations of the former being explicit and binary, while the latter was subject to a logic of progressive realization – the emergence of these structural-process-outcome indicators has fundamentally shifted the debate, to emphasize commitment and conduct on the part of states to reach these goals in both cases. As the OHCHR Report indicates, these indicators thus imply "the rationale for adopting a common, practical approach" that emphasizes progress in realizing and assessing compliance with rights across the spectrum.[63] Similarly, the very indicators used then go on to provide human rights with the capacity to be further moved across fields of practice. While indicators themselves are conceived as emerging from existing human rights standards and treaty obligations, they are not only for local consumption; instead, "[h]uman rights indicators are instrumental in meeting local development and good governance goals ... by emphasizing the intrinsic importance of human rights in human well-being."[64] The hopeful and anticipated result is that human rights data will find their way into national development reports and national plans for investing in good governance and population well-being.

Where are we left? In this most recent authoritative statement from the OHCHR, we see how the bridge between human rights and development has led to a nuanced and calibrated shift in expectations over time. Indicators of result have given way to indicators that benchmark state performance, measuring commitments and efforts as well as its results, and seeking to integrate with national development and governance reforms. These metrics as developed – in reaction to earlier approaches

---

[61] *Id.* at 120.   [62] *Id.* at 19.   [63] *Id.* at 24; see also Jenson and Levi, *supra* note 9.
[64] *Id.* at 43.

that ranked and compared country performance against each other – also led to a shift in the very conceptual framework for thinking about "negative" and "positive" rights, so that crossing the boundary of human rights and development has had effects within the legal framework itself.

## IV  Indicator extensions: The case of gender, international development, and human rights indicators

Despite the flexible approach outlined in the OHCHR Report on Human Rights Indicators, concerns remain over the emergence of human rights indicators. These include a perception of increased reporting requirements, conflicts over measurement, and tensions over how to satisfy multiple stakeholders. Academic critique has followed, with some arguing that indicators inevitably enshrine some ideas over others,[65] others predicting that human rights indicators produce a world divorced of context,[66] and still others suggesting that global governance indicators narrow the space for political contestation.[67]

While we do not address these claims here, we take two examples relating to gender equality – one in the field of development, and the other in the field of human rights – to consider the effects that indicators have had on programming and institutional actors in this field. Gender is among the most prominent examples relied on in the intersection of human rights and development. And, as we see later, in both of these fields, indicators of gender equality gain momentum even in light of critique and contestation. In the case of development, critique over the choice of indicators leads to a proliferation of new indicators, and, in the case of human rights, gender indicators are now not only salient in assessing state practice but have also extended to assessing the practice of UN agencies themselves.

### a)  Gender and development

Gender equality and women's empowerment is the third of eight MDGs. These goals are deeply tied to the achievement of human rights obligations and represent the substantive bridging of the domains of development and human rights priorities. The MDGs for gender equality and women's empowerment were translated into proxy variables of

---

[65] Löwenheim, *supra* note 42.   [66] Merry, *Measuring the World* 2011, *supra* note 50.
[67] Davis et al., *supra* note 1.

education, employment, and political participation, with targets of eliminating gender disparities in education; increasing women's share of wage employment in the nonagricultural sector; and increasing the proportion of seats held by women in national parliaments.

These were seen by some to be disappointingly narrow indicators, with critics suggesting that they did not sufficiently reflect the realities of gender inequality in many countries.[68] For example, for a national government to reach a certain quota of women elected in parliament need not imply that those women have significant power, or that women across the country are any more empowered: if anything, existing research suggests that women's increased political participation has not necessarily led to greater legislative support in realizing women's rights.[69] Similarly, while many countries have succeeded in eliminating gender disparities in access to primary education, much less focus has been placed on retention rates in schools and girls remain more likely than boys to drop out of school. This is due to early pregnancy, due to cultural norms, and because young girls often bear the brunt of unpaid domestic and care work in the home.[70] And, while increasing women's employment in the nonagricultural sector has proven to be empowering, research also points to women then pooling in vulnerable and insecure work in the informal sector or only part-time work in the formal economy.[71]

As a response to this criticism and in an effort to expand the original MDG framework, many countries have begun to go beyond these variables to capture broader contours of gender inequality.[72]

---

[68] For example, Naila Kabeer, *Gender Equality and Women's Empowerment: A Critical Analysis of the Third Millennium Development Goal*, 13 GENDER & DEV. 13 (2005). A second critique is that, when faced with development indicators, states may invest mainly in improving their score in order to attract foreign aid and political capital. Studies show that in some countries such as Malawi, India, and Ethiopia, expansion in educational enrolment took place at the expense of the quality of education. Elaine Unterhalter, Expert Paper, *The MDGs, Girls' Education and Gender Equality*, U.N. Women, Expert Grp. Meeting, Oct. 21–24, 2013. Furthermore, despite greater equality in school enrolment, girls and children from the poorest quintiles continue to achieve the lowest grades, *id*.

[69] Report of the Expert Group Meeting on Envisioning Women's Rights in the Post-2015 Context, U.N. Women, Expert Grp. Meeting, Nov. 3–5, 2014.

[70] Dorrit Posit and Daniela Casale, Expert Paper, *Gender, Education and Labour Market Outcomes*, U.N. Women, Expert Grp. Meeting, Nov. 3–5, 2014.

[71] Report of the Expert Group Meeting on Envisioning Women's Rights in the Post-2015 Context, *supra* note 68.

[72] Megan Dersnah, Background Paper, *A Review of National MDG Reports from a Gender Perspective*, U.N. Women, Expert Grp. Meeting, Oct. 21–24, 2013.

Some have adopted new indicators and targets, thereby "localizing" the MDGs to meet their particular development goals and priorities – and several countries have identified that the key problems that women face pertain less to the MDG indicators than to other concerns, for example, over a discriminatory division of labor, wage gaps between women and men, and women's underrepresentation in decision-making.[73]

Thailand, for example, created a new national target for gender equality, aiming to double the proportion of women in the national parliament, sub-district administrative organizations, and executive positions in the civil service during the period of 2002–2006. Thailand thus proposed a new set of indicators that went beyond the MDGs, including the measurement of female to male students in selected fields in tertiary education; the ratio of literate women to men over 40 years old; and the share of women in executive positions in the civil service, amongst others. Jordan, on the other hand, has sought to measure women's representation in various leadership positions, including local governance, ministries, diplomatic corps, judges, and professional associations. And a number of countries, including the Seychelles, Cambodia, Kazakhstan, and Colombia, have developed indicators related to violence against women as part of their efforts to address the MDGs, focusing in particular on gender-based violence, and the percentage of ever-married women who have experienced physical violence by their husband or partner.

### b) Gender, indicators, and the international human rights regime

No longer vociferously contested by states, the turn to human rights indicators is now having effects beyond states – particularly for UN agencies themselves.

In the past few years alone, in the field of gender equality and women's rights, the UN system has advanced a minimum set of fifty-two indicators to measure gender issues; a set of indicators on violence against women; a global gender statistics program; and a set of indicators on women, peace, and security. The UNDP 2010 Human Development Report also launched the Gender Inequality Index (GII), which quantifies

---

[73] *Id.*

progress on gender inequality by bringing together indicators on labor force participation, education attainment, parliamentary representation, adolescent fertility, and maternal mortality. All of these sets of indicators demand that states be held accountable to their commitment to their women's rights obligations.

This emphasis on gender-based indicators has now been brought into the practices of the UN itself. As Löwenheim might have predicted, rather than focusing solely externally, the UN is now also increasingly being held accountable – and is holding *itself* accountable – for its human rights policies and practices through the use of indicators, targets, and scorecard programs.[74] New indicators are increasingly being developed to ensure that UN programming and practice meet strict performance standards. In the case of women's rights, for example, in 2009, the UNDP launched a new "gender marker" program modeled after the OECD Development Co-operation Directorate gender marker. The United Nations Children's Fund, the UN Peacebuilding Fund, and United Nations Population Fund also followed suit. The program keeps track of how much the UNDP and other UN organizations are spending on gender equality in all of their programming, and it requires managers to rate projects against a four-point scale indicating the project's contribution toward the achievement of gender equality. In response, some states, including Sweden, refuse to provide funding to UN programs that do not meet certain gender equality standards, as measured by the "gender marker" program.

In 2012, UN Women also launched and rolled out a program called the System-Wide Action Plan on Gender Equality and the Empowerment of Women (UN-SWAP), which monitors the gender-related work of all UN entities, through the use of performance indicators.[75] Using a framework of fifteen performance indicators, the UN-SWAP program monitors how and whether UN agencies and organizations adopt policies on gender equality and women's empowerment and, for example, ensures that corporate strategic planning documents commit to achieving at least one gender equality objective. The first results of UN-SWAP were published in 2013, providing a baseline for future measurements as the action plan continues to gain strength across the UN system.

---

[74] Löwenheim, *supra* note 42.
[75] U.N. Women, Promoting UN Accountability (UN-SWAP) (2014), www.unwomen.org/en/how-we-work/un-system-coordination/promoting-un-accountability.

## Conclusion: From past to future boundaries? – The private sector, indicators and accountability for human rights

Boundary-crossing has been central to the emergence and development of human rights indicators, from the 1970s through to the present. Human rights indicators gained prominence – along with human rights generally – throughout the neoliberal era, largely by crossing boundaries to the fields of foreign affairs, democratization, and international development, and from the US context to international organizations. Buoyed by its cultural resonance with neoliberal transformations domestically and in international governance,[76] this boundary-crossing may have led to the resistance to human rights indicators in the context of development, but also underwrote its later return: the current, second generation of human rights indicators are themselves regarded as a bridge between the human rights and development communities, providing indicators that reflect a logic of development that refracts human rights differences in a new way, while also providing an opportunity to make claims for human rights integration into national planning. And, indeed, once embedded, the logic of indicators provides an ever-greater capacity to cross into new boundaries: as the case study of gender-based indicators suggests, critique of indicators can often lead to the proliferation of new indicators, and their use externally can also lead to new indicators, such as for UN actors, to measure an ever-greater scope of activity related to this field.

The next frontier, it seems to us, may well turn to the role of the private sector in human rights. Much of the discussion of indicators to date exists with little reference to the private sector – despite the growth of an array of actors, including banks, corporations, and others that are increasingly investing in human rights promotion.[77] Nonetheless, here, too, the role of the private sector is bound to be influenced by indicator-driven development frameworks: as part of broader corporate social responsibility standards, human rights impact assessments increasingly promote attention to business and human rights, driven in large part by the International Finance Corporation in the World Bank Group.[78]

---

[76] Jenson and Levi, *supra* note 9.
[77] See, for example, Report of the Expert Group Meeting on Envisioning Women's Rights in the Post-2015 Context, *supra* note 69.
[78] International Financial Corporation, IFC Sustainability Framework: Policy and Performance Standards on Environmental and Social Sustainability Access to Information Policy (2012), www.ifc.org/wps/wcm/connect/b9dacb004a73e7a8a273fff998895a12/IFC_Sustainability_+Framework.pdf?MOD=AJPERES.

Much of this remains voluntary, though several thousand companies have at minimum signed on to the UN Global Compact's initiative to implement human rights principles in their operations. And, in 2011, the UN Human Rights Council went so far as to endorse guiding principles on business and human rights – targeting not only private actors themselves with a duty to respect human rights, but a duty of states to protect against business-related human rights abuses. While not in and of itself enforceable, the move here is precisely toward documentation and transparency: the obligation on business is to "know and show," thereby developing a due diligence approach for companies to assess actual and potential impacts, track responses, ensure appropriate human rights expertise to assess their work, and develop impact assessments with appropriate qualitative and quantitative indicators.[79] There may be a current trade-off with the extension of these indicators back across this boundary to the private sector, with this turn to transparency here arriving without an emphasis on enforceability.

We return, then, to Supiot's analysis of the dream of calculability.[80] This dream has generated a new human rights orthodoxy, with conventional and new actors alike now drawn into human rights practice not by a logic of legal standards, but one of metrics, benchmarks, and apparent legibility. As we outline – and Supiot anticipates – this can have the effect of crowding out other complexities. Yet while Supiot demonstrates that legal institutions may at times resist a turn to metrics,[81] we find that the suggestion that metrics empty legal regimes of contestation is overstated. While said to usher a dream of harmony through calculation, indicators are themselves embedded in legal politics. Indicators have been mobilized to extend human rights regimes to new fields, have provided a path for new actors to invest in human rights, have responded to political conjunctures and stakes, and have spurred redefinitions of human rights norms. Following the boundary-crossings of indicators thus provide insight into how this dream of calculability also opens new terrains of legal competition, transformation, and recreation.

---

[79] U.N. Special Representative of the Secretary-General, *Guiding Principles on Business and Human Rights: Implementing the United Nations 'Protect, Respect and Remedy' Framework*, H.R.C. Doc. A/HRC/17/31 (Mar. 21, 2011) (John Ruggie); U.N. Office of the High Comm'r for Human Rights, Frequently Asked Questions about the Guiding Principles on Business and Human Rights (2014), www.ohchr.org/Documents/Publications/FAQ_PrinciplesBussinessHR.pdf.
[80] Supiot, *Le rêve de l'harmonie par le calcul*, supra note 10.
[81] Supiot, *État social et mondialisation*, supra note 10.

# BIBLIOGRAPHY

## Books

Ackerman, Bruce, *We the People: Foundations* (Cambridge: Harvard University Press, 1991).
Adelstein, Richard, Firms as Persons (unpublished manuscript) (on file with author).
Alexy, Robert, *A Theory of Constitutional Rights* (Julian Rivers trans., New York: Oxford University Press, 2002).
Allan, Trevor R.S., *The Sovereignty of Law: Freedom, Constitution and Common Law* (Oxford, UK: Oxford University Press, 2013).
Alston, Philip, ed., *Non-State Actors and Human Rights* (Oxford, UK: Oxford University Press, 2005).
Alston, Philip & Ryan Goodman, *International Human Rights*, 3rd ed. (Oxford, UK: Oxford University Press, 2013).
Alvarez, José E., *The Public International Law Regime Governing International Investment* (The Hague, Hague Academy of International Law, 2011).
Applebaum, Arthur, *Ethics for Adversaries* (Princeton: Princeton University Press, 2000).
Arai-Takahashi, Yutaka, *The Margin of Appreciation Doctrine and the Principle of Proportionality in the Jurisprudence of the ECHR* (Antwerp: Intersentia, 2002).
Arndt, Christiane & Charles Oman, *Uses and Abuses of Governance Indicators* (Paris: Development Centre of the Organisation for Economic Co-Operation and Development, 2006).
Baxi, Upendra, *The Future of Human Rights*, 2nd ed. (New Delhi: Oxford University Press, 2006).
Bourdieu, Pierre, *Pascalian Meditations* (Richard Nice trans., Cambridge, UK: Polity Press, 2000).
Brewer-Carías, Allan R., *Constitutional Courts as Positive Legislators: A Comparative Law Study* (Cambridge, UK & New York: Cambridge University Press, 2011).
Cane, Peter, *Administrative Law*, 4th ed. (Oxford: Clarendon, 2004).
Cass, Deborah, *The Constitutionalization of the World Trade Organization* (Oxford & New York: Oxford University Press, 2005).

Clapham, Andrew, *Human Rights Obligations of Non-State Actors* (Oxford: Oxford University Press, 2006).
Colon-Rios, Joel, *Weak Constitutionalism: Democratic Legitimacy and the Question of Constituent Power* (London & New York: Routledge, 2012).
Conaglen, Matthew, *Fiduciary Loyalty: Protecting the Due Performance of Non-Fiduciary Duties* (Oxford & Portland, Oregon: Hart Publishing, 2010).
Cooter, Robert D., *The Strategic Constitution* (Princeton: Princeton University Press, 2002).
Davies, Anne C.L., *The Public Law of Government Contracts* (Oxford: Oxford University Press, 2008).
de Tocqueville, Alexis, *Democracy in America* (Harvey Mansfield & Delba Winthrop, trans. and ed., Chicago & London: University of Chicago Press, 2000).
Dicey, Albert, *Introduction to the Study of the Law of the Constitution*, 10th ed. (London: Macmillan, 1959).
Dolzer, Rudolf & Christoph Schreuer, *Principles of International Investment Law* (Oxford, Oxford University Press: 2008).
Donnelly, Catherine M., *Delegation of Governmental Power to Private Parties: A Comparative Perspective* (Oxford: Oxford University Press, 2007).
Douglas, Zachary, *The International Law of Investment Claims* (Cambridge, UK & New York: Cambridge University Press, 2009).
Dworkin, Ronald, *Sovereign Virtue: The Theory and Practice of Equality* (Cambridge, MA: Harvard University Press, 2001).
*Taking Rights Seriously* (London: Duckworth, 1977).
Fabre, Cecile, *Social Rights under the Constitution: Government and the Decent Life* (Oxford, UK: Clarendon Press & New York: Oxford University Press, 2000).
Fredman, Sandra, *Human Rights Transformed: Positive Rights and Positive Duties* (Oxford, UK & New York: Oxford University Press, 2008).
Friedman, Daniel & Daphne Barak-Erez eds., *Human Rights in Private Law* (Portland, Oregon: Hard Publishing, 2001).
Fox-Decent, Evan, *Sovereignty's Promise: The State as Fiduciary* (Oxford: Oxford University Press, 2011).
Glendon, Mary Ann, *Rights Talk: The Impoverishment of Political Discourse* (New York: Free Press & Toronto: Collier Macmillan & New York: Maxwell Macmillan, 1991).
Griffin, James, *On Human Rights* (Oxford & New York: Oxford University Press, 2008).
Guilhot, Nicolas, *The Democracy Makers: Human Rights and International Order* (New York: Columbia University Press, 2005).
Harvey, David, *A Brief History of Neoliberalism* (Oxford: Oxford University Press, 2005).
Hegel, Georg W.F., *The Philosophy of Right* (Sir Thomas Malcolm Knox trans., Lanham: Oxford University Press, 1967).

Hellman, Deborah & Sophia Moreau, eds., *Philosophical Foundations of Discrimination Law* (Oxford: Oxford University Press, 2013).
Hobbes, Thomas, *Leviathan* (Richard Tuck ed., Cambridge, UK & New York: Cambridge University Press, 1991).
Hogg, Peter W., *Constitutional Law of Canada* vol. II, 5th ed. (Toronto: Thomson Carswell, 2007).
Ignatieff, Michael, *Human Rights as Politics and Idolatry* (Princeton: Princeton University Press, 2003).
Jackson, Vicki C. & Mark Tushnet, *Comparative Constitutional Law*, 3rd ed. (St Paul, Minn: Foundation Press, 2014).
Jacobsohn, Gary, *Constitutional Identity* (Cambridge, Mass: Harvard University Press, 2010).
Kelsen, Hans, *Hauptprobleme der Staatsrechtslehre* (Aalen: Scientia, 1984) (Ger.).
Kennedy, Duncan, *The Rise and Fall of Classical Legal Thought* (Washington, DC: Beard Books, 2006, originally published 1975).
Krishnaswamy, Sudhir, *Democracy and Constitutionalism in India: A Study of the Basic Structure Doctrine* (New Delhi & Oxford: Oxford University Press, 2009).
Kymlicka, Will, *Multicultural Citizenship: A Liberal Theory of Minority Rights* (Oxford: Clarendon Press, 1995).
Locke, John, *Second Treatise of Government* (1690), (Crawford Brough Macpherson ed., Indianapolis: Hackett Publishing Company, 1980).
Luhmann, Niklas, *Law as a Social System* (Fatima Kastner, Richard Nobles, David Schiff & Rosamund Ziegert eds., Klaus A. Ziegert trans., Oxford & New York: Oxford University Press, 2004).
  *Social Systems* (John Bednarz, Jr & Dirk Baecker trans., Stanford: Stanford University Press, 1995).
Mann, Howard, International Investments, Business, and Human Rights: Key Issues and Opportunities (2008), available at www.iisd.org/pdf/2008/iia_business_human_rights.pdf.
Markovits, Daniel, *A Modern Legal Ethics: Adversary Advocacy in a Democratic Age* (Princeton: Princeton University Press, 2011).
McCarthy, Cormac, *No Country for Old Men* (New York: Alfred A. Knopf, 2005).
  *The Blood Meridian* (London: Picador, 1990).
Moyn, Samuel, *The Last Utopia: Human Rights in History* (Cambridge, Mass: Belknap Press of Harvard University Press, 2010).
Neier, Aryeh, *Taking Liberties: Four Decades in the Struggle for Rights* (New York: Public Affairs, 2003).
Newcombe, Andrew & Luís Paradell, *Law and Practice of Investment Treaties* (The Netherlands: Kluwer Law International, 2009).
Nolan, Donal & Andrew Robertson eds., *Rights and Private Law* (Oxford: Hart Publishing, 2011).

Oliver, Dawn, *Common Values and the Public-Private Divide* (London: Butttterworths, 1999).
Paulsson, Jan, *Denial of Justice in International Law* (Cambridge, UK & New York: Cambridge University Press, 2005).
Peterson, Luke Eric, Human Rights and Bilateral Investment Treaties: Mapping the Role of Human Rights Law within Investor-State Arbitration (2009), available at publications.gc.ca/collections/collection_2012/dd-rd/E84-36-2009-eng.pdf.
Power, Michael, *The Audit Explosion* (London, UK: Demos, 1994).
Poynder, John, *Literary Extracts* (London: William Edward Painter, 342, Strand, 1844).
Raz, Joseph, *The Morality of Freedom* (Oxford: Clarendon Press, 1986).
Roach, Kent, *The Supreme Court on Trial: Judicial Activism or Democratic Dialogue* (Toronto: Irwin Law, 2001).
Rose, Nikolas, *Powers of Freedom: Reframing Political Thought* (Cambridge, UK & New York: Cambridge University Press, 1999).
Sandel, Michael, *Democracy's Discontent: America in Search of a Public Philosophy* (Cambridge, Mass: Belknap Press of Harvard University Press, 1996).
Schachter, Oscar, *International Law in Theory and Practice* (Dordrecht, Boston: M. Nijhoff Publishers, 1991).
Schapiro, Robert A., *Polyphonic Federalism: Toward the Protection of Fundamental Rights* (Chicago & London: The University of Chicago Press, 2009).
Schill, Stephan W., ed., *The Multilateralization of International Investment Law* (Cambridge & New York: Cambridge University Press, 2009).
Schneiderman, David, *Resisting Economic Globalization: Critical Theory and International Investment Law* (Hampshire & New York: Palgrave Macmillan, 2013).
Scolnicov, Anat, *Religious Freedom in International Law: Between Group Right and Individual Right* (Oxon & New York: Routledge, 2011).
Sikkink, Kathryn, *Mixed Signals: US Human Rights Policy and Latin America* (Ithaca, NY & London: Cornell University Press, 2004).
Sornarajah, Muthucumaraswamy, *The International Law on Foreign Investment*, 3rd ed. (Cambridge, UK & New York: Cambridge University Press, 2010).
Sunstein, Cass R. & Stephen Holmes, *The Cost of Rights* (New York: W.W. Norton & Company, 1999).
Teubner, Gunther, *Constitutional Fragments: Societal Constitutionalism and Globalization* (Oxford: Oxford University Press, 2012).
Thomas, Jean, *Public Rights, Private Relations* (Oxford: Oxford University Press, 2015).
Tushnet, Mark, *Weak Courts, Strong Rights: Judicial Review and Social Welfare Rights in Comparative Constitutional Law* (Princeton, N.J.: Princeton University Press, 2008).

van der Walt, Johan, *The Horizontal Effect Revolution and the Question of Sovereignty* (Berlin & Boston: Walter de Gruyter GmbH, 2014).

Verkuil, Paul R., *Outsourcing Sovereignty: Why Privatization of Government Functions Threatens Democracy and What We Can Do about It* (Cambridge & New York: Cambridge University Press, 2007).

von Bogdandy, Armin, Rüdiger Wolfrum, Jochen von Bernstorff, Philipp Dann & Matthias Goldmann eds., *The Exercise of Public Authority by International Institutions* (Berlin, Heidelberg: Springer Berlin Heidelberg, 2010).

Wade, Sir William, *Wade and Forsyth on Administrative Law*, 7th ed. (Oxford: Clarendon Press, 1994).

*Wade & Forsyth, Administrative Law*, 9th ed. (Oxford & New York: Oxford University Press, 2004).

Waldron, Jeremy, *The Right to Private Property* (Oxford: Clarendon Press, 1988).

Weber, Max, *Sociological Writings* (New York: Continuum, 1994).

Weinrib, Ernest J., *The Idea of Private Law* (Cambridge, Mass: Harvard University Press, 1995).

White, G. Edward, *The Constitution and the New Deal* (Cambridge, Mass: Harvard University Press, 2000).

Young, Katherine, *Constituting Economic and Social Rights* (Oxford: Oxford University Press, 2012).

Zackin, Emily, *Looking for Rights in All the Wrong Places: Why State Constitutions Contain America's Positive Rights* (Princeton & Oxford: Princeton University Press, 2013).

## Chapters

Alter, Karen J., The Multiple Roles of International Courts and Tribunals: Enforcement, Dispute Settlement, Constitutional and Administrative Review, in *Interdisciplinary Perspectives on International Law and International Relations* 345 (Jeffrey L. Dunoff & Mark A. Pollack eds., New York: Cambridge University Press, 2013).

Alvarez, José E. in this volume.

The Evolving BIT, in *Investment Treaty Arbitration and International Law* 1 (Ian A. Laird & Todd Weiler eds., Huntington, NY: JurisNet, 2010).

What are International Judges For? The Main Functions of International Adjudication, in *The Oxford Handbook on International Adjudication* 158 (Cesare Romano, Karen J. Alter & Yuval Shany eds., Oxford: Oxford University Press, 2013).

Aronson, Mark, A Public Lawyer's Responses to Privatisation and Outsourcing, in *The Province of Administrative Law* 40 (Michael Taggart ed., Oxford: Hart Publishing, 1997).

Bamforth, Nicholas & Peter Leyland, Public Law in a Multi-Layered Constitution, in *Public Law in a Multi-Layered Constitution* 247 (Nicholas, Bamforth & Peter Leyland eds., Oxford & Portland, Oregon: Hart, 2003).

Brooks, Richard R. W., Knowledge in Fiduciary Relations, in *Philosophical Foundations of Fiduciary Law* 225 (Andrew S. Gold & Paul B. Miller eds., Oxford: Oxford University Press, 2014).

Brown, Chester, William Burke-White & Andreas von Staden; Alessandra Asteriti & Christian J. Tams; and Irmgard Marboe, all in *The Multilateralization of International Investment Law* (Stephan W. Schill, ed., Cambridge & New York: Cambridge University Press, 2009).

della Cananea, Giacinto, Procedural Due Process of Law Beyond the State, in *The Exercise of Public Authority by International Institutions* 965 (Armin von Bogdandy, Rüdiger Wolfrum, Jochen von Bernstorff, Philipp Dann & Matthias Goldmann eds., Berlin, Heidelberg: Springer Berlin Heidelberg, 2010).

Cane, Peter, Accountability and the Public/Private Distinction, in *Public Law in a Multi-Layered Constitution* 247 (Nicholas Bamforth & Peter Leyland eds., Oxford & Portland, Oregon: Hart, 2003).

Theory and Values in Public Law, in *Law and Administration in Europe: Essays in Honour of Carol Harlow* 15 (Paul Craig & Richard Rawlings eds., Oxford & New York: Oxford University Press, 2003).

Cherednychenko, Olha O., Subordinating Contract Law to Fundamental Rights: Towards a Major Breakthrough or Towards Walking in Circles?, in *Constitutional Values and European Contract Law* 35 (Stefan Grundmann ed., Alphen aan den Rijn, The Netherlands: Kluwer Law International, 2008).

Dagan, Hanoch & Sharon Hannes, Managing Our Money: The Law of Financial Fiduciaries as a Private Law Institution, in *Philosophical Foundations of Fiduciary Law* 91 (Andrew S. Gold & Paul B. Miller eds., Oxford: Oxford University Press, 2014).

Davis, Dennis M., Socio-Economic Rights, in *The Oxford Handbook of Comparative Constitutional Law* 1020 (Michel Rosenfeld & András Sajó eds., Oxford: Oxford University Press, 2012).

Dupuy, Pierre-Marie, Unification Rather than Fragmentation of International Law? The Case of International Investment Law and Human Rights Law, in *Human Rights in International Investment Law and Arbitration* 45 (Pierre-Marie Dupuy, Francesco Francioni & Ernst-Ulrich Petersmann eds., Oxford & New York: Oxford University Press, 2009).

Dürig, Günter, Grundrechte und Zivilrechtsprechung, in *Vom Bonner Grundgesetz zur gesamtdeutschen Verfassung. Festschrift zum 75. Geburtstag von Hans Nawiasky* 177–82 (Theodor Maunz ed., Munich: Isar Verlag, 1956) (Ger.).

Dworkin, Ronald, Political Judges and the Rule of Law, in *A Matter of Principle*, ch. I (Cambridge, Mass & London, England: Harvard University Press, 1985).

Ewing, Keith D., Economic Rights, in *Oxford Handbook of Comparative Constitutional Law* 1036 (Michel Rosenfeld & András Sajó eds., Oxford: Oxford University Press, 2012).

Feinäugle, Clemens A., The UN Security Council Al-Qaida and Taliban Sanctions Committee, in *The Exercise of Public Authority by International Institutions* 101 (Armin von Bogdandy, Rüdiger Wolfrum, Jochen von Bernstorff, Philipp Dann & Matthias Goldmann eds., Berlin, Heidelberg: Springer Berlin Heidelberg, 2010).

Ferrari, Franco, Forum Shopping in the International Arbitration Context: Setting the Stage, in *Franco Ferrari, Forum Shopping in the International Commercial Arbitration Context* 1 (Munich: Sellier European Law Publishers, 2013).

Finn, Paul, The Forgotten 'Trust': The People and the State, in *Equity: Issues and Trends* 131 (Malcolm Cope ed., Leichhardt, NSW: Federation Press, 1995).

Fox-Decent, Evan, Fiduciary Authority and the Service Conception, in *Philosophical Foundations of Fiduciary Law* 363 (Andrew S. Gold & Paul B. Miller eds., Oxford: Oxford University Press, 2014).

From Fiduciary States to Joint Trusteeship of the Atmosphere: The Right to a Healthy Environment through a Fiduciary Prism, in *Fiduciary Duty and the Atmospheric Trust* 253 (Ken Coghill, Charles Sampford & Tim Smith eds., Surrey & Burlington, VT: Ashgate, 2012).

Freedland, Mark, Law, Public Services, and Citizenship—New Domains, New Regimes?, in *Public Service and Citizenship in European Law—Public and Labour Law Perspectives* E11 (Mark Freedland & Silvana Sciarra eds., Oxford: Clarendon Press, 1998).

Gold, Andrew S., The Loyalties of Fiduciary Law, in *Philosophical Foundations of Fiduciary Law* 176 (Andrew S. Gold & Paul B. Miller eds., Oxford: Oxford University Press, 2014).

Goldmann, Matthias, Inside Relative Normativity: From Sources to Standard Instruments for the Exercise of International Public Authority, in *The Exercise of Public Authority by International Institutions* 661 (Armin von Bogdandy, Rüdiger Wolfrum, Jochen von Bernstorff, Philipp Dann & Matthias Goldmann eds., Berlin, Heidelberg: Springer Berlin Heidelberg, 2010).

Gutmann, Amy, Freedom of Association, in *Freedom of Association* 3 (Amy Gutmann ed., Princeton: Princeton University Press, 1998).

Hershkoff, Helen, in this volume.

State Common Law and the Dual Enforcement of Constitutional Norms, in *New Frontiers of State Constitutional Law: Dual Enforcement of Norms* 151 (James A. Gardner and Jim Rossi eds., New York: Oxford University Press, 2011).

Transforming Legal Theory in the Light of Practice: The Judicial Application of Social and Economic Rights to Private Orderings, in *Courting Social Justice: Judicial Enforcement of Social and Economic Rights in the Developing World* 268 (Varun Gauri & Daniel M. Brinks eds., New York: Cambridge University Press, 2008).

Hirsch, Moshe, Investment Tribunals and Human Rights Treaties: A Sociological Perspective, in *Investment Law within International Law: Integrationist Perspectives* 85 (Freya Baetens ed., Cambridge: Cambridge University Press, 2013).

Investment Tribunals and Human Rights: Divergent Paths, in *Human Rights in International Investment Law and Arbitration* 97 (Pierre-Marie Dupuy, Francesco Francioni & Ernst-Ulrich Petersmann eds., 2009).

Interactions between Investment and Non-Investment Obligations, in *The Oxford Handbook of International Investment Law* 154 (Peter Muchlinski, Federico Ortino & Christoph Schreuer eds., Oxford & New York: Oxford University Press, 2008).

Holmes, Stephen & Cass R. Sunstein, The Politics of Constitutional Revision in Eastern Europe, in *Responding to Imperfection: The Theory and Practice of Constitutional Amendment* 275 (Sanford Levinson, ed., Princeton: Princeton University Press, 1995).

Howard, Rhoda, Dignity, Community and Human Rights, in *Human Rights in Cross-Cultural Perspectives: A Quest for Consensus* 81 (Abdullahi Ahmed An-Na'im ed., Philadelphia: University of Pennsylvania Press, 1992).

Hunt, Murray., Constitutionalism and Contractualisation of Government in the United Kingdom, in *The Province of Administrative Law* (Michael Taggart ed., Oxford, UK: Hart Publishing, 1997).

Jackson, Vicki C. Unconstitutional Constitutional Amendments: A Window into Constitutional Theory and Transnational Constitutionalism, in *Democracy perspectives: Festschrift for Brun-Otto Bryde's 70th Birthday* (Michael Bäuerle, Philipp Dann & Astrid Wall Rabenstein eds., Tübingen: Mohr Siebeck, 2013).

Jenson, Jane & Ron Levi, Narratives and Regimes of Social and Human Rights: The Jack Pines of the Neoliberal Era, in *Social Resilience in the Neoliberal Era* 69 (Peter A. Hall & Michèle Lamont eds., New York: Cambridge University Press, 2013).

Kateb, George, The Value of Associations, in *Freedom of Association* 35 (Amy Gutmann ed., Princeton: Princeton University Press, 1998).

Kingsbury, Benedict, International Law as Inter-Public Law, in *Nomos XLIX: Moral Universalism and Pluralism* 167 (Henry R. Richardson & Melissa S. Williams eds., New York: New York University Press, 2009).

Kingsbury, Benedict & Megan Donaldson, From Bilateralism to Publicness in International Law, in *From Bilateralism to Community Interest: Essays in Honour of Bruno Simma* 79 (Ulrich Fastenrath, Rudolf Geiger, Daniel-Erasmus Khan, Andreas Paulus, Sabine von Schorlemer & Christoph Vedder eds., Oxford: Oxford University Press, 2011).

Kingsbury, Benedict & Stephan Schill, Investor-State Arbitration as Governance: Fair and Equitable Treatment, Proportionality, and the Emerging Global Administrative Law, in *El Nuevo Derecho Administrative Global En América Latina: Desafíos Par Alas Inversions Extrajeras, La Regulación Nacional Y El Financiamiento Para El Desarrollo* 221 (Buenos Aires: RPA, 2009).

Klabbers, Jan, Beyond the Vienna Convention: Conflicting Treaty Provisions, in *The Law of Treaties beyond the Vienna Convention* (Enzo Cannizazaro ed., Oxford: Oxford University Press, 2011).

Reluctant Grundnormen: Articles 31(3)(C) and 42 of the Vienna Convention on the Laws of Treaties and the Fragmentation of International Law, in *Time, History and International Law* 141 (Matthew Craven, Malgosia Fitzmaurice & Maria Vogiatzi eds., Leiden & Boston: Martinus Nijhoff Publishers, 2007).

Koremenos, Barbara & Timm Betz, The Design of Dispute Settlement Procedures in International Agreements, in *Interdisciplinary Perspectives on International Law and International Relations* 371 (Jeffrey L. Dunoff & Mark A. Pollack eds., New York: Cambridge University Press, 2013).

Kriebaum, Ursula, Privatizing Human Rights: The Interface between International Investment Protection and Human Rights, in *The Law of International Relations—Liber Amicorum Hanspeter Neuhold* 165 (August Reinsch & Ursula Kriebaum eds., Ultrecht, Netherlands: Eleven International Pub, 2007).

Kumm, Mattias, Political Liberalism and the Structures of Rights: On the Place and Limits of the Proportionality Requirement, in *Law, Rights and Discourse: Themes from the Legal Philosophy of Robert Alexy* 7 (George Pavlakos ed., Portland, Oregon: Hart Publishing, 2006).

Kurtz, Jürgen, The Merits and Limits of Comparativism: National Treatment in International Investment Law and the WTO, in *The Multilateralization of International Investment Law* 243 (Stephan W. Schill, ed., Cambridge & New York: Cambridge University Press, 2009).

Langford, Malcolm, The Justiciability of Social Rights: From Practice to Theory, in *Social Rights Jurisprudence: Emerging Trends in International and Comparative Law* 3 (Malcolm Langford ed., Cambridge & New York: Cambridge University Press, 2009).

Locke, John, Second Treatise, in *Two Treatises of Government*, 265 (Peter Laslett ed., Cambridge & New York: Cambridge University Press, 1988).

Lucy, William, Private and Public: Some Banalities about a Platitude, in *After Public Law* 56 (Cormac Mac Amhlaigh, Claudio Michelon & Neil Walker eds., Oxford: Oxford University Press, 2013).

Lutz, Donald S., Toward a Theory of Constitutional Amendment, in *Responding to Imperfection: The Theory and Practice of Constitutional Amendment* 237 (Sanford Levinson, ed., Princeton: Princeton University Press, 1995).

Metzger, Gillian E., Private Delegations, Due Process, and the Duty to Supervise, in *Government by Contract: Outsourcing and American Democracy* 291 (Jody Freeman & Martha Minow eds., Cambridge, Mass. & London, England: Harvard University Press, 2009).

Michelman, Frank I., The Interplay of Constitutional and Ordinary Jurisdiction, in *Comparative Constitutional Law* 278 (Tom Ginsburg & Rosalind Dixon eds., Cheltenham, UK & Northampton, MA: Edward Elgar, 2011).

Miller, Paul B., The Fiduciary Relationship, in *Philosophical Foundations of Fiduciary Law* 63 (Andrew S. Gold & Paul B. Miller eds., Oxford: Oxford University Press, 2014).

Moravcsik, Andrew, Liberal Theories of International Law, in *Interdisciplinary Perspectives on International Law and International Relations* 83 (Jeffrey L. Dunoff & Mark A. Pollack eds., New York: Cambridge University Press, 2013).

Morijn, John & Jasper Krommendijk, "Proportional" by What Measure(s)? Balancing Investor Interests and Human Rights by Way of Applying the Proportionality Principle in Investor-State Arbitration, in *Human Rights in International Investment Law and Arbitration* 422 (Pierre-Marie Dupuy, Francesco Francioni & Ernst-Ulrich Petersmann eds., Oxford & New York: Oxford University Press, 2009).

Oliver, Dawn, The Underlying Values of Public and Private Law, in *The Province of Administrative Law* 217 (Michael Taggart ed., Oxford: Hart Publishing, 1997).

Osiatynski, Wictor, Social and Economic Rights in a New Constitution for Poland, in *Western Rights? Post-Communist Application* 233 (András Sajó ed., The Hague, The Netherlands & Cambridge, MA: Kluwer Law International, 1996)

Petersmann, Ernst-Ulrich, Multilevel Trade Governance in the WTO Requires Multilevel Constitutionalism, in *Constitutionalism, Multilevel Trade Governance and Social Regulation* 5 (Christian Joerges & Ernst-Ultrich Petersmann eds., Oxford & Portland, Oregon: Hart Publishing, 2006).

Raustiala, Kal, International Proliferation and the International Legal Order, in *Interdisciplinary Perspectives on International Law and International Relations* 293 (Jeffrey L. Dunoff & Mark A. Pollack eds., New York: Cambridge University Press, 2013).

Raz, Joseph, Human Rights without Foundations, in *The Philosophy of International Law* 321 (Samantha Besson & John Tasioulas eds., Oxford: Oxford University Press, 2010).

On the Authority and Interpretation of Constitutions: Some Preliminaries, in *Constitutionalism: Philosophical Foundations* 152 (Larry Alexander ed., Cambridge, UK: Cambridge University Press, 1998).

Reiner, Clara & Christoph Schreuer, Human Rights and International Investment Arbitration, in *Human Rights in International Investment Law and Arbitration* 82 (Pierre-Marie Dupuy, Francesco Francioni & Ernst-Ulrich Petersmann eds., Oxford & New York: Oxford University Press, 2009).

Schill, Stephan, International Investment Law and Comparative Public Law—An Introduction, in *The Multilateralization of International Investment Law* 3 (Stephan W. Schill, ed., Cambridge & New York: Cambridge University Press, 2009).

Schneiderman, David, in this volume.

Scheinin, Martin, Impact on the Law of Treaties, in *The Impact of Human Rights Law on General International Law* 23 (Martin Scheinin & Menno T. Kamminga eds., Oxford: Oxford University Press, 2009).

Smith, Lionel D., Can We Be Obliged to Be Selfless?, in *Philosophical Foundations of Fiduciary Law* 141 (Andrew S. Gold & Paul B. Miller eds., Oxford: Oxford University Press, 2014).

Steiner, Hillel, Working Rights, in *A Debate over Rights: Philosophical Enquiries*, Mathew H. Kramer, Nigel E. Simmonds & Hillel Steiner eds. (Oxford: Clarendon Press, 1998).

Sunstein, Cass, Against Positive Rights, in *Western Rights? Post-Communist Application* 225 (András Sajó ed., The Hague, The Netherlands & Cambridge, MA: Kluwer Law International,1996).

Teubner, Gunther, A Constitutional Moment? The Logics of "Hit the Bottom," in *The Financial Crisis in Constitutional Perspective: The Dark Side of Functional Differentiation* 3 (Poul Kjaer & Gunther Teubner eds., Oxford & Portland, Oregon: Hart Publishing, 2011).

"Global Bukowina": Legal Pluralism in the World Society, in *Global Law without a State* (Gunther Teubner ed., Aldershot, Dartmouth: Ashgate Publishing Company, 1996).

Societal Constitutionalism: Alternatives to State-Centered Constitutional Theory?, in *Transnational Governance and Constitutionalism* 3 (Christian Joerges, Inger-Johanne Sand & Gunther Teuber eds., Portland, Oregon: Hart Publishing, 2004).

von Bogdandy, Armin, Philipp Dann & Matthias Goldmann, Developing the Publicness of Public International Law: Towards a Legal Framework for Global Governance Activities, in *The Exercise of Public Authority by International Institutions* 4 (Armin von Bogdandy, Rüdiger Wolfrum, Jochen von Bernstorff, Philipp Dann & Matthias Goldmann eds., Berlin, Heidelberg: Springer Berlin Heidelberg, 2010).

Waibel, Michael Asha Kaushal, Kyo-Hwa Liz Chung & Claire Balchin, The Backlash against Investment Arbitration: Perceptions and Reality, in *The Backlash against Investment Arbitration: Perceptions and Reality* xxxvii (Michael Weibel, Asha Kaushal, Kyo-Hwa Liz Chung & Claire Balchin eds., Alphen aan den Rijn, The Netherlands: Kluwer Law International, 2010).

Waldron, Jeremy, Property and Ownership, in *The Stanford Encyclopedia of Philosophy* (Edward N Zalta ed., Standford, CA: Standford University 2012).

Rights in Conflict, in *Liberal Rights: Collected Papers 1981–1991* 203 (Cambridge & New York & Victoria: Cambridge University Press, 1993).

Weinrib, Lorraine, Constitutional Conceptions and Constitutional Comparativism, in *Defining the Field of Comparative Constitutional Law* 3 (Vicki Jackson & Mark Tushnet eds., Westport, Connecticut: Praeger Publishers, 2002).

Williams, Alexander, Public Authorities, in *The Impact of the UK Human Rights Act on Private Law* 48 (David Hoffman ed., New York: Cambridge University Press, 2011).

Williamson, John, What Washington Means by Policy Reform, in *Latin American Adjustment: How Much Has Happened* (John Williamson ed., Washington, DC: Institute for International Economics, 1990).

Young, Alison L., Mapping Horizontal Effect, in *The Impact of the UK Human Rights Act on Private Law* 16 (David Hoffman ed., New York: Cambridge University Press, 2011).

## Journals/Working Papers/Newspaper Articles

Adler, Matthew D., Rights against Rules; The Moral Structure of American Constitutional Law, 97 *Mich. L. Rev.* 1 (1998).

Akehurst, Michael, Equity and General Principles of Law, 25 *Int'l & Comp. L. Q.* 801 (1976).

Aleinikoff, Thomas Alexander, Constitutional Law in the Age of Balancing, 96 *Yale L.J.* 943 (1987).

Alexander, Larry, The Public/Private Distinction and Constitutional Limits on Private Power, 10 *Const. Comment.* 361 (1993).

Alexy, Robert, The Construction of Constitutional Rights, 4 *Law & Ethics Hum. Rts.* 20 (2010).

Allen, Tom, Compensation for Property under the European Convention on Human Rights, 28 *Mich. J. Int'l Law* 287 (2007).

Liberalism, Social Democracy and the Value of Property under the European Convention on Human Rights, 59 *Int'l & Comp. L.Q.* 1055 (2010).

Alvarez, José E., Are Corporations "Subjects" of International Law?, 9 *Santa Clara J. Int'l L.* 1 (2011).

How Not to Link: Institutional Conundrums of an Expanded Trade Regime, 7 *Widener L. Symp. J.* 1 (2001).

International Organizations: Accountability or Responsibility, in Responsibility of Individuals, States and Organizations: Proceedings of the 35th Annual Conference of the Canadian Council on International Law, Ottawa, October 26–28, 2006,121 (Canadian Council on International Law, 2007).

The Paradoxical Argentina Crisis Cases, 6 *World Arb. & Mediation Rev.* 143 (2010).

The Return of the State, 20 *Minn. J. Int'l L.* 223 (2011).

Alvarez, José E. & Tegan Brink, Revisiting the Necessity Defense: Continental Casualty v. Argentina, 2010–11 Y.B. on Int'l Investment L. & Pol'y 319 (2011).

Alvarez, José E. & Kathryn Khamsi, The Argentine Crisis and Foreign Investors: A Glimpse into the Heart of the Investment Regime, 2008–09 Y.B. on Int'l Investment L. & Pol'y 379 (2009).

Alvarez-Jiménez & Alberto, The Interpretation of Necessity Clauses in Bilateral Investment Treaties after the Recent ICSDI Annulment Decisions, 2010–11 Y.B. on Int'l Investment L. & Pol'y 419 (2011).

Ancelovici, Marcos & Jane Jenson, La standardisation et les mécanismes du transfert transnational, 1 *Rev. Gouv't Action Pub.* 37 (2012) (Fr.).

Atkinson, Rob, Obedience as the Foundation of Fiduciary Duty, 34 *J. Corp. L.* 45 (2008).

Bandes, Susan A., The Negative Constitution: A Critique, 88 *Mich. L. Rev.* 8 (1990).

Bandura, Romina, A Survey of Composite Indices Measuring Country Performance: 2006 Update, (U.N.D.P/O.D.S. Working Background Paper, 2006).

Barak-Erez, Daphne, The Private Prison Controversy and the Privatisation Continuum, 5 *L. & Ethics of Hum. Rts.* 138 (2011).

A State Action Doctrine for an Age of Privatization, 45 *Syracuse L. Rev.* 1169 (1995).

Barsh, Russel Lawrence, Measuring Human Rights: Problems of Methodology and Purpose, 15 *Hum. Rts. Q.* 87 (1993).

Bartholomew, Amy & Jennifer Breakspear, Human Rights as Swords of Empire?, 40 *Socialist Reg.* 125 (2009).

Baxi, Upendra, Voices of Suffering and the Future of Human Rights (1998) 8 *Transnat'l L. & Contemp. Probs.* 125.

Beale, L.K., Charter Schools, Common Schools and the Washington State Constitution, 72 *Wash. L. Rev.* 535 (1997).

Beermann, Jack M., Administrative-Law-Like Obligations on Private[ized] Entities, 49 *UCLA L. Rev.* 1717 (2002).

Privatization and Political Accountability, 28 *Fordham Urb. L.J.* 1507 (2001).

Benvenisti, Eyal & George W. Downs, The Empire's New Clothes: Political Economy and the Fragmentation of International Law, 60 *Stanford L. Rev.* 595 (2007).
Berle, Adolf A. Jr., Constitutional Limitations on Corporate Activity—Protection of Personal Rights from Invasion through Economic Power, 100 *U. Pa. L. Rev.* 933 (1952).
Bermann, George, Taking Subsidiarity Seriously: Federalism in the European Community and the United States, 94 *Colum. L. Rev.* 331 (1994).
Bernal, Carlos, Unconstitutional Constitutional Amendments in the Case Study of Colombia: An Analysis of the Justification and Meaning of the Constitutional Replacement Doctrine, 11 *I.CON* 339 (2013).
BeVier, Lillian & John Harrison, The State Action Principle and Its Critics, 96 *Va. L. Rev.* 1767 (2010).
Blank, Yishai, Federalism, Subsidiarity, and the Role of Local Governments in an Age of Global Multilevel Governance, 37 *Fordham Urb. L.J.* 509 (2010).
Branch, H. N. & Leo Stanton Rowe, The Mexican Constitution of 1917 compared with the Constitution of 1857, 71 *Annals Am. Pol. Sci. Ass'n* 1, 2 (Supp. May 1917) (translating both constitutions).
Brower II, Charles H., NAFTA's Investment Chapter: Initial Thoughts about Second-Generation Rights 36 *Vand. J. Transnat'l L.* 1533 (2003).
Buchanan, G. Sidney, A Conceptual History of the State Action Doctrine: The Search for Governmental Responsibility, 34 *Hous. L. Rev.* 333 (1997).
Carozza, Paolo G., Subsidiarity as a Structural Principle of International Human Rights Law, 97 *Am. J. Int'l L.* 38 (2003).
Chemerinsky, Erwin, The Assumptions of Federalism, 58 *Stan. L. Rev.* 1763 (2006).
  Reconceptualizing Federalism, 50 *N.Y.L. Sch. L. Rev.* 729 (2006).
  Rethinking State Action, 80 *Nw. U. L. Rev.* 503 (1985).
  Empowering States When It Matters, 69 *Brook. L. Rev.* 1313 (2004).
  The Values of Federalism, 47 *Fla. L. Rev.* 499 (1995).
Cherednychenko, Olha O., Fundamental Rights and Private Law: A Relationship of Subordination or Complementarity?, 3 *Utrecht L. Rev.* 1 (2007).
Chmielewski, Philip J., Workers' Participation in the United States: Catholic Social Teaching and Democratic Theory, 55 *Rev. Soc. Econ.* 487 (1997).
Cohen-Eliya, Moshe & Iddo Porat, The Hidden Foreign Law Debate in Heller: The Proportionality Approach in American Constitutional Law, 16 *San Diego L. Rev.* 367 (2009).
Collins, Hugh, Ascription of Legal Responsibility to Groups in Complex Patterns of Economic Integration, 53 *Mod. L. Rev.* 731 (1990).
Craig, Paul, Contracting Out, the Human Rights Act and the Scope of Judicial Review, 118 *L. Q. Rev.* 551 (2002).

Criddle, Evan J., Fiduciary Administration: Rethinking Popular Representation in Agency Rulemaking, 88 *Tex. L. Rev.* 441 (2010).

Fiduciary Foundations of Administrative Law, 54 *UCLA L. Rev.* 117 (2006).

Criddle, Evan J. & Evan Fox-Decent, Human Rights, Emergencies, and the Rule of Law, 34 *Hum. Rts. Q.* 39 (2012).

Darwall, Stephen & Julian Darwall, Civil Recourse as Mutual Accountability, 39 *Fla. St. U. L. R.* 17 (2011).

Davies, Anne C.L., This Time It's for Real: The Health and Social Care Act 2012, 76 *Mod. L. Rev.* 564 (2013).

Ultra Vires problems in Government Contracts, 122 *L.Q. Rev.* 98 (2006).

Davis, Kevin, Benedict Kingsbury & Sally Engle Merry, Indicators as a Technology of Global Governance (Global Admin. L. Series, Inst. for Int'l L. & Just., Working Paper 2010/2, 2010).

DeMott, Deborah A., Beyond Metaphor: An Analysis of Fiduciary Obligation, 1988 *Duke L.J* 879 (1988).

Dersnah, Megan, Background Paper, A Review of National MDG Reports from a Gender Perspective, U.N. Women, Expert Grp. Meeting, Oct. 21–24, 2013.

Dezalay, Yves & Bryant Garth, From the Cold War to Kosovo: The Rise and Renewal of the Field of International Human Rights, 2 *Ann. Rev. L. Soc. Sci.* 231 (2006).

Dickinson, Laura A., Public Law Values in a Privatized World, 31 *Yale J. Int'l L.* 383 (2006).

Donnelly, Catherine, Positive Obligations and Privatisation, 61 *N. Ir. Legal Q.* 209 (2010).

Donnelly, Catherine M. & Leonard Cheshire, Again and Beyond: Private Contractors, Contract and s 6(3)(b) of the Human Rights Act, 2005 *Pub. L.* 785.

Dumberry, Patrick & Gabrielle Dumas-Aubin, How to Impose Human Rights Obligations on Corporations, 4 *Y.B. on Int'l Investment L. & Pol'y* 569 (2011–12).

Eberle, Edward J., The Architecture of First Amendment Free Speech, Mich. St. L. Rev. 1191 (2011).

Edwards, Denis J., Fearing Federalism's Failure: Subsidiarity in the European Union, 44 *Am. J. Comp. L.* 537 (1996).

El-Hage, Javier, How May Tribunals Apply the Customary Necessity Rule to the Argentine Cases?, 2011–12 *Y.B. on Int'l Investment L. & Pol'y* 445 (2012).

Emberland, Marius, The Corporate Veil in the Case Law of the European Court of Human Rights, 63 *ZaöRV* 945 (2003).

Fallon, Richard, Legitimacy and the Constitution, 118 *Harv. L. Rev.* 1787 (2005).

Ferraz, Octavio Luiz Motta, Harming the Poor through Social Rights Litigation: Lessons From Brazil, 89 *Tex. L. Rev.* 1643 (2011).

Social and Economic Rights: Harming the Poor through Social Rights Litigation: Lessons from Brazil, 59 *Tex. L. Rev.* 1643 (2011).

Finn, Paul, Fiduciary Reflections, 88 *Austl. L.J.* 127 (2014).
Fischer, Thomas C., "Federalism" in the European Community and the United States: A Rose by Any Other Name ... , 17 *Fordham Int'l L.J.* 389 (1994).
Fisher-Lescano, Andrea & Gunther Teubner, Regime Collisions: The Vain Search for Legal Unity in the Fragmentation of Global Law, 25 *Mich. J. Int'l. Law* 999, 1004 (2004).
Fleming, James E., The Missing Selves in Constitutional Self-Government, 71 *Fordham L. Rev.* 1789 (2003).
Fombad, Charles Manga, Some Perspectives on Durability and Change under Modern African Constitutions, 11 *Int'l J. Const. L. (I•CON)* 382 (2013).
Frankel, Richard, Regulating Privatized Government Through § 1983, 76 *U. Chi. L. Rev.* 1449 (2009).
Frankel, Tamar, Fiduciary Law, 71 *Calif. L. Rev.* 795 (1983).
Freedland, Mark, Privatising Carltona: Part II of the Deregulation and Contracting Out Act 1994, *Pub. L.* 21 (1995).
  Public Law and Private Finance: Placing the Private Finance Initiative in a Public Law Frame, *Pub. L.* 288 (1998).
Freeman, Jody, Extending Public Law Norms through Privatization, 116 *Harv. L. Rev.* 1285 (2003).
  The Private Role in Public Governance, 75 *N.Y.U. L. Rev.* 543 (2000).
Friedman, Barry, Dialogue and Judicial Review, 91 *Mich. L. Rev.* 577 (1993).
Friedmann, W.G., Public and Private Law Thinking: The Need for Synthesis, 5 *Wayne L. Rev.* 291 (1958–59).
Friendly, Henry J., The Public-Private Penumbra—Fourteen Years Later, 130 *U. Pa. L. Rev.* 1289 (1982).
Fox-Decent, Evan & Evan J. Criddle, The Fiduciary Constitution of Human Rights, 15 *Legal Theory* 301 (2009).
Gallagher, Paul, The Irish Constitution—Its Unique Nature and the Relevance of International Jurisprudence, 45 *Irish Jurist* 22 (2010).
Gardbaum, Stephen, The Horizontal Effect of Constitutional Rights, 102 *Mich. L. Rev.* 387 (2003).
Geistfeld, Mark A., The Doctrinal Unity of Alternative Liability and Market-Share Liability, 155 *U. Pa. L. Rev.* 447 (2006).
Giegerich, Thomas, The Is and the Ought of International Constitutionalism: How Far Have We Come on Habermans's Road to a "Well-Considered Constitutionalization of International Law"?, 10 *German L. J.* 31 (2009).
Gilman, Michele Estrin, Legal Accountability in an Era of Privatized Welfare, 89 *Cal. L. Rev.* 569 (2001).
Ginsburg, Tom & James Melton, Does the Constitutional Amendment Rule Matter at All? Amendment Cultures and the Challenges of Measuring Amendment Difficulty (May 3, 2014), University of Chicago Coase-

Sandor Institute for Law & Economics Research Paper No. 682, University of Chicago, Public Law Working Paper No. 472, available at SSRN: ssrn.com/abstract=2432520.

Glennon, Robert J. Jr. & John E. Nowak, A Functional Analysis of the Fourteenth Amendment "State Action" Requirement, 1976 *Sup. Ct. Rev.* 221 (1976).

Gold, Andrew S., Reflections on the State as Fiduciary, 63 *U. of Toronto L.J.* 655 (2013).

Gore, Charles, The Rise and Fall of the Washington Consensus as a Paradigm for Developing Countries, 28 *World Dev.* 789 (2000).

Gosling, Martin, The Global Trend towards Private Prisons, 170 *Just. of the Peace & Loc. Gov't L.* 892 (2006).

Grant, Ruth W. & Robert O. Keohane, Accountability and Abuses of Power in World Politics, 99 *Am. Pol. Sci. Rev.* 29 (Feb. 2005).

Green, Leslie, Two Views of Collective Rights, 4 *Can. J. Law Jurisprudence* 315 (1991).

Greene, Abner S., The Irreducible Constitution, 7 *J. Contemp. Legal Issues* 293 (1996).

Grey, Thomas C., Molecular Motions: The Holmesian Judge in Theory and Practice, 37 *Wm. & Mary L. Rev.* 19 (1995).

Habermas, Jürgen, The Constitutionalization of International Law and the Legitimation Problems of a Constitution for a World Society, 15 *Constellations* 445 (2008).

Hamilton, Alexander, The Federalist No. 70, No. 72 (J. Cooke ed., 1961).

Harlow, Carol, 'Public' and 'Private' Law: Definition without Distinction, 43 *Mod. L. Rev.* 241 (1980).

Hershkoff, Helen, Foreword: Positive Rights and State Constitutions, 33 *Rutgers L.J.* 799 (2002).

  Horizontality and the "Spooky" Doctrines of American Law, 59 *Buff. L. Rev.* 455 (2011).

  "Just Words": Common Law and the Enforcement of State Constitutional Social and Economic Rights, 62 *Stan. L. Rev.* 1521 (2010).

  Lecture, The Private Life of Public Rights: State Constitutions and the Common Law, 88 *N.Y.U. L. Rev.* Online 1 (2013).

  The New Jersey Constitution: Positive Rights, Common Law Entitlements, and State Action, 69 *Alb. L. Rev.* 553 (2006).

  Positive Rights and State Constitutions: The Limits of Federal Rationality Review, 112 *Harv. L. Rev.* 1131 (1999).

  Welfare Devolution and State Constitutions, 67 *Fordham L. Rev.* 1403 (1999).

Hershkoff, Helen & Stephen Loffredo, State Courts and Constitutional Socio-Economic Rights: Exploring the Underutilization Thesis, 115 *Penn St. L. Rev.* 923 (2011).

Higgins, Tracy E., Anti-Essentialism, Relativism, and Human Rights, 19 *Harv. Women's L.J.* 89 (1996).

Hogan, Gerard, Directive Principles, Socio-Economic Rights and the Constitution, 36 *Irish Jurist* 174 (2001).

Hogg, Peter W. & Allison A. Bushell, The Charter Dialogue between Courts and Legislatures (Or Perhaps the Charter of Rights Isn't Such a Bad Thing after All), 35 *Osgoode Hall L.J.* 75 (1997).

Hohfeld, Wesley Newcomb, Some Fundamental Legal Conceptions as Applied to Legal Reasoning, 23 *Yale L.J.* 16 (1913).

Horowitz, Harold W., The Misleading Search for "State Action" under the Fourteenth Amendment, 30 *S. Cal. L. Rev.* 208 (1956–57).

Iacobucci, Frank, The Charter: 20 Years Later, 21 *Windsor Y.B. Access to Just.* 3 (2002).

Jackson, Vicki C., Being Proportional about Proportionality, 21 *Const. Comment.* 803 (2004).

Jacoby, Tamar, The Reagan Turnaround on Human Rights, 64 *Foreign Aff.* 1066 (1986).

Jain, Neha, General Principles of Law as Gap-Fillers (forthcoming).

Jensen, Darryn, Prescription and Proscription in Fiduciary Obligations, 21 *King's L.J.* 333 (2010).

Johnson, Bruce & Kyu Ho Youm, Commercial Speech and Free Expression: The United States and Europe Compared, 2 *J. Int'l Media & Ent. L.* 159 (2008).

Kabeer, Naila, Gender Equality and Women's Empowerment: A Critical Analysis of the Third Millennium Development Goal, 13 *Gender & Dev.* 13 (2005).

Kadens, Emily, The Myth of Customary Law Merchant, 90 *Tex. L. Rev.* 1153 (2012).

Katz, Al, Studies in Boundary Theory: Three Essays in Adjudication and Politics, 28 *Buff. L. Rev.* 383 (1978).

Kaye, Judith S., Foreword: The Common Law and State Constitutional Law as Full Partners in the Protection of Individual Rights, 23 *Rutgers L.J.* 727 (1992).

Keohane, Robert O., Andrew Moravcsik & Anne-Marie Slaughter, Legalized Dispute Resolution: Interstate and Transnational, 54 *Int'l Org.* 457 (2000).

Kim, Sung Hui, The Last Temptation of Congress: Legislator Insider Trading and the Fiduciary Norm against Corruption, 98 *Cornell L. Rev.* 845 (2013).

Kincaid, John, From Cooperative to Coercive Federalism, 509 *Annals Am. Acad. Pol. & Soc. Sci.* 139 (1990).

Kingsbury, Benedict & Richard Stewart, The Emergence of Global Administrative Law, 68 *Law & Contemp. Probs.* 15 (2005).

Knop, Karen, Here and There: International Law in Domestic Courts, 32 *NYU J. Int'l L. & Politics* 501 (2000).

Koskenniemi, Martti, Constitutionalism as Mindset: Reflections on Kantian Themes about International Law and Globalization, 8 *Theoretical Inquiries in L.* 9, 17 (2006).

Fragmentation of International Law—The Function and Scope of the Lex Specialis Rule and the Question of "Self-Contained Regimes": An Outline, 6(1) *Transnat'l Disp. Mgmt* (2009).

The Fate of Public International Law: Between Technique and Politics, 70 *Mod. L. Rev.* 1 (2007).

Koskenniemi, Martti & Päivi Leino, Fragmentation of International Law? Postmodern Anxieties, 15 *Leiden J. Int' l L.* 553 (2002).

Kramer, Larry & Alan O. Sykes, Municipal Liability Under § 1983: A Legal and Economic Analysis, 1987 *Sup. Ct. Rev.* 249 (1987).

Krent, Harold J., Federal Power, Non-Federal Actors: The Ramifications of Free Enterprise Fund, 79 *Fordham L. Rev.* 2425 (2011).

Reconceptualizing Sovereign Immunity, 45 *Vand. L. Rev.* 1529, 1529 (1992).

Kritchevsky, Barbara, Civil Rights Liability of Private Entities, 26 *Cardozo L. Rev.* 35 (2004).

Landau, David, The Reality of Social Rights Enforcement, 53 *Harv. Int'l L.J.* 402 (2012).

Law, David S., The Anatomy of a Conservative Court, 87 *Tex L Rev.* 1545 (2009).

Why Has Judicial Review Failed in Japan?, 88 *Wash. U. L. Rev.* 1425 (2011).

Law, David S. & Mila Versteeg, The Evolution and Ideology of Global Constitutionalism, 99 *Cal. L. Rev.* 1163, 1170 (2011).

Leib, Ethan J. & David L. Ponet, Fiduciary Representation and Deliberative Engagement with Children, 20 *J. Pol. Phil.* 178 (2012).

Lerner, Ralph, The Supreme Court as Republican Schoolmaster, 1967 *Sup. Ct. Rev.* 127.

Levinson, Daryl J., Making Government Pay: Markets, Politics, and the Allocation of Constitutional Costs, 67 *U. Chi. L. Rev.* 345 (2000).

Loffredo, Stephen, Poverty, Inequality, and Class in the Structural Constitutional Law Course, 34 *Fordham Urb. L.J.* 1239 (2007).

Löwenheim, Oded, Examining the State: A Foucauldian Perspective on International 'Governance Indicators', 29 *Third World Q.* 255 (2008).

Lutz, Donald S., The United States Constitution as an Incomplete Text, 496 *Annals Am. Acad. Pol. & Soc. Sci.* 23 (1988).

Manning, Bayless, Corporate Power and Individual Freedom: Some General Analysis and Particular Reservations, 55 *Nw. U. L. Rev.* 38 (1960).

Mashaw, Jerry L., Civil Liability of Government Officers: Property Rights and Official Accountability, 42 *Law & Contemp. Probs.* 8 (1978).

McGovern, Shannon K., Note, A New Model for States as Laboratories for Reform: How Federalism Informs Education Policy, 86 *N.Y.U. L. Rev.* 1519 (2011).

McLachlin, Campbell, Investment Treaties and General International Law, 57 *Int'l & Comp. L.Q.* 361, 369 (2008).
McLachlan, Campbell, The Principle of Systemic Integration and Article 31(3)(c) of the Vienna Convention, 54 *Int'l & Comp. L.Q.* 279 (2005).
Medina, Barak, Constitutional Limits to Privatization: The Israeli Supreme Court Decision to Invalidate Prison Privatization, 8 *Int'l J. Const. L.* 690 (2010).
Merry, Sally Engle, Measuring the World: Indicators, Human Rights, and Global Governance, 103 *Am. Soc'y of Int'l L. Proc. Ann. Meeting* 239 (2009).
 Measuring the World: Indicators, Human Rights, and Global Governance, 52 *Current Anthropology* S83 (2011).
Michelman, Frank I., On the Uses of Interpretive 'Charity': Some Notes on Application, Avoidance, Equality, and Objective Unconstitutionality from the 2007 Term of the Constitutional Court of South Africa, 1 *Const. Ct. Rev.* 1 (2008).
 The Bill of Rights, The Common Law, and the Freedom-Friendly State, 58 *U. Miami L. Rev.* 401 (2003).
 The Supreme Court and Litigation Access Fees: The Right to Protect One's Rights—Part I 1973, *Duke L.J.* 1153 (1973).
 W(H)ither the Constitution?, 21 *Cardozo L. Rev.* 1063 (2000).
Miller, Paul B., Justifying Fiduciary Remedies, 63 *U. Toronto L.J.* 570 (2013).
 Multiple Loyalties and the Conflicted Fiduciary, 40 *Queen's L.J.* 301 (2014).
Minow, Martha, Public and Private Partnerships: Accounting for the New Religion, 116 *Harv. L. Rev.* 1229 (2002–03).
Mokhiber, Craig G., Toward a Measure of Dignity: Indicators for Rights-Based Development, 18 *Stat. J. United Nations Econ. Commission Eur.* 155 (2001).
Mortenson, Julian Davis, The Travaux of Travaux: Is the Vienna Convention Hostile to Drafting History, 107 *Am. J. Int'l L.* 780 (2013).
Moyn, Samuel, A Powerless Companion: Human Rights in the Age of Neoliberalism, 77 *Law & Contemp. Probs.* 147(2015).
Mullan, David, Underlying Constitutional Principles: The Legacy of Justice Rand, 34 *Manitoba L.J.* 1 (2010).
Mureinik, Etienne, A Bridge to Where? Introducing the Interim Bill of Rights, (1994) 10 *S. Afr. J. on Hum. Rts.* 31.
Nelson, Caleb, Sovereign Immunity as a Doctrine of Personal Jurisdiction, 115 *Harv. L. Rev.* 1559 (2002).
de Neufville, Judith Innes, Social Indicators of Basic Needs: Quantitative Data for Human Rights Policy, 11 *Soc. Indicators Res.* 383 (1982).
O'Neill, Onora, The Dark Side of Human Rights, 81 *Int'l Aff.* 427 (2005).
Odomusu, Ibironke T., The Law and Politics of Engaging Resistance in Investment Dispute Settlement, 26 *Penn St. Int'l L. Rev.* 251 (2007).
Oliver, Dawn, Common Values in Public and Private Law and the Public/Private Divide, *Pub. L.* 630 (1997).

Palmer, Stephanie, Public Functions and Private Services: A Gap in Human Rights Protection, 6 *Int'l J. Const. L.* 585 (2008).

Paparinskis, Martins, Investment Treaty Arbitration and the (New) Law of State Responsibility, 24 *Eur. J. Int'l.* 617 (2013).

Perry, Michael J., The Morality of Human Rights, 50 *San Diego L. Rev* 775 (2013).

Perry, Stephen R., Protected Interests and Undertakings in the Law of Negligence, 42 *U. Toronto L.J.* 247 (1992).

Peters, Anne, Compensatory Constitutionalism: The Function and Potential of Fundamental International Norms and Structures, 19 *Leiden J. Int'l. L.* 570 (2006).

Pildes, Richard H., Avoiding Balancing: The Role of Exclusionary Reasons in Constitutional Law, 45 *Hastings L J.* 711 (1994).

Ponet, David L. & Ethan J. Leib, Fiduciary Law's Lessons for Deliberative Democracy, 91 *B.U. L. Rev.* 1207 (2011).

Posit, Dorrit & Daniela Casale, Expert Paper, Gender, Education and Labour Market Outcomes, U.N. Women, Expert Grp. Meeting, Nov. 3–5, 2014.

Poto, Margherita, The Principle of Proportionality in Comparative Perspective, 8 *German L.J.* 835 (2007).

Quinn, Thomas G., State Action: A Pathology and a Proposed Cure, 64 *Cal. L. Rev.* 146 (1976).

Ratliff, Warren L., The Due Process Failure of America's Prison Privatization Statutes, 21 *Seton Hall Legis. J.* 371 (1997).

Randall, Maya Hertig, Commercial Speech under the European Convention on Human Rights: Subordinate or Equal?, 6 *Hum. Rts. L. Rev.* 53 (2006).

Rave, D. Theodore, Politicians as Fiduciaries, 126 *Harv. L. Rev.* 671 (2013).

Redish, Martin H. & Lawrence C. Marshall, Adjudicatory Independence and the Values of Procedural Due Process, 95 *Yale L. J.* 455 (1986).

Roberts, Anthea, Clash of Paradigms: Actors and Analogies Shaping the Investment Treaty System, 107 *Am. J. Int'l L.* 45 (2013).

Rodriguez, Daniel B., State Constitutional Failure, 2011 *U. Ill. L. Rev.* 1243 (2011).

Rodríguez-Garavito, César, Beyond the Courtroom: The Impact of Judicial Activism on Socioeconomic Rights in Latin America, 89 *Tex. L. Rev.* 1669 (2011)

Rodrik, Dani, Goodbye Washington Consensus, Hello Washington Confusion?, XLIV *J Econ. Literature* 973 (2006).

Roosevelt, Franklin D., "Unless There is Security Here at Home, There Cannot Be Lasting Peace in the World"—Message to the Congress on the State of the Union, 13 *Pub. Papers* 32, 41 (Jan. 11, 1944).

Rosatti, Horacio Daniel, Los tratados bilaterales de inversión, el arbitraje internacional obligatorio y el sistema constitucional argentine, No. 198 *La Ley* 198 (Oct. 15, 2003).

Rosenthal, Lawrence, A Theory of Governmental Damages Liability: Torts, Constitutional Torts, and Takings, 9 *U. Pa. J. Const. L.* 797 (2007).

Rosga, AnnJannette & Margaret L. Satterthwaite, The Trust in Indicators: Measuring Human Rights 2 (Ctr. for Hum. Rts. & Global Just. Working paper, Number 20).

Ross, Howard, UN Body Criticizes Development Aid: Report Urges Wealthy Countries to Divert Spending to Basic Needs, The Globe and Mail, May 21, 1991.

Rostow, Eugene V., The Democratic Character of Judicial Review, 66 *Harv. L. Rev.* 193 (1952).

Rostron, Allen, Beyond Market Share Liability: A Theory of Proportional Share Liability for Non-Fungible Products, 52 *UCLA L. Rev.* 151 (2004).

Rozakis, C., The Right to a Fair Trial in Civil Cases, 4 *Jud. Stud. Inst. J.* 96 (2004).

Rubenstein, W.B., The Concept of Equality in Civil Procedure (UCLA Research Paper Series, Research Paper No. 01–18).

Salmon, J., A Perspective on the Corporate Transformation of Healthcare, 25 *Int'l J. Health Services* 11 (1995).

Sarfaty, Galit A., Why Culture Matters in International Institutions: The Marginality of Human Rights at the World Bank, 103 *Am. J. Int'l L.* 647 (2009).

Schauer, Frederick, Ashwander Revisited, 1995 *Sup. Ct. Rev.* 71 (1995).

Schneiderman, David, The Global Regime of Investor Rights: Return to the Standards of Civilised Justice? 5 *Transnat'l Legal Theory* 60 (2014).

   Legitimacy and Reflexivity in International Investment Arbitration: A New Self-Restraint?, 2 *Int'l J. Disp. Mgmt.* 47 (2011).

   Revisiting the Depoliticization of Investment Disputes, 2010–11 *Y.B. on Int'l Investment L. & Pol'y* 693 (2012).

Schreuer, Christoph, From ICSID Annulment to Appeal Half Way Down the Slippery Slope, 10 *L. & Prac. of Int'l Cts. & Tribunals* 211 (2011).

Scolnicov, Anat., Lifeless and Lifelike in Law: Do Corporations Have Human Rights?, available at dx.doi.org/10.2139/ssrn.2268537.

Seidman, Louis Michael, The State Action Paradox, 10 *Const. Comment.* 379 (1993).

Simma, Bruno, From Bilateralism to Community Interest in International Law, 250 *Recueil des Cours, Acad. de Droit Int'l de la Haye* 217 (1997).

   Foreign Investment Arbitration: A Place for Human Rights, 60 *Int'l & Comp. L.Q.* 573 (2011).

   Self-Contained Regimes, 15 *Neth. Y.B. Int'l Law* 111 (1985).

Singer, Joseph W., The Legal Rights Debate in Analytical Jurisprudence from Bentham to Hohfeld, 1982 *Wis. L. Rev.* 975(1982).

Sklansky, David A., Private Policing and Human Rights, 5 *L. & Ethics of Hum. Rts.* (2011).

Sloane, Robert D., On the Use and Abuse of Necessity in the Law of State Responsibility, 106 *Am. J. Int'l L.* 447 (2012).

Snyder, Barbara Rook, Private Motivation, State Action and the Allocation of Responsibility for Fourteenth Amendment Violations, 75 *Cornell L. Rev.* 1052 (1990).

Spector, Horacio, Constitutional Transplants and the Mutation Effect, 83 *Chi.-Kent L. Rev.* 129 (2008).

Sripati, Vijayashri & Arun K. Thiruvengedam, India: Constitutional Amendment Making the Right to Education a Fundamental Right, 2 *Int'l. J of Const. L.* 148 (2004).

Stewart, Richard B., Remedying Disregard in Global Regulatory Governance: Participation and Responsiveness, 108 *Am. J. Int'l L.* 211 (2014).

Strine, Leo, Lawrence Hamermesh, R. Franklin Balotti & Jeffrey M. Gorris, Loyalty's Core Demand: The Defining Role of Good Faith in Corporation Law, 93 *Geo. L.J.* 629 (2010).

Supiot, Alain, État social et mondialisation: analyse juridique des solidarités, 2012–2013 Year 113 (113e année) *Annuarie C. France* 717 (2014).

Le rêve de l'harmonie par le calcul, Le Monde Diplomatique, Feb. 2015 (Fr.).

Sweet, Alex Stone, Investor-State Arbitration: Proportionality's New Frontier, 4 *L. & Ethics of Hum. Rts.* 47 (2010).

Sweet, Alec Stone & Giacinto della Cananea, Proportionality, General Principles of Law, and Investor-State Arbitration: A Response to Jose Alvarez, 46 (3) *N.Y.U. J. Int'l L. & Pol.* 911, 940 (2014)

Sweet, Alec Stone & Jud Mathews, Proportionality Balancing and Global Constitutionalism, 47 *Colum. J. Transnat'l L.* 72 (2008).

Sykes, Alan O., The Economics of Vicarious Liability, 93 *Yale L.J.* 1231 (1984).

Symposium, Charter Dialogue: Ten Years Later, 45 *Osgoode Hall L.J.* 1 (2007).

The Proliferation of International Tribunals: Piercing together the Puzzle, 31 *N.Y.U. J. Int'l L. & Pol.* 679 (1999).

Tasioulas, John, Taking Rights out of Human Rights, 120 *Ethics* 647 (2010).

Teubner, Gunther, The Anonymous Matrix: Human Rights Violations by 'Private' Transnational Actors, 69 *Mod. L. Rev.* 327 (2006).

Constitutionalizing Polycontexturality, 20 *Soc. & Legal Stud.* 210 (2011).

Legal Irritants: Good Faith in British Law or How Unifying Law Ends Up in New Divergences, 61 *Mod. L. Rev.* 11 (1998).

Substantive and Reflexive Elements in Modern Law, 17 *Law & Soc'y Rev* 239 (1982–83).

Thirlway, Hugh, The Law and Procedure of the International Court of Justice, 61 (1) *Y.B. Int'l L.* 1, 113 (1990).

Tribe, Laurence H., A Constitution We are Amending: In Defense of a Restrained Judicial Role, 97 *Harv. L. Rev.* 433 (1983).

Unraveling National League of Cities: The New Federalism and Affirmative Rights to Essential Government Services, 90 *Harv. L. Rev.* 1065 (1977).

Turano, Leslie., Charitable Trusts and the Public Service: The Public Accountability of Private Care Providers, 18 *King's L.J.* 427 (2007).
Tushnet, Mark, An Essay on Right, 62 *Tex. L. Rev.* 1363 (1984).
 Civil Rights and Social Rights: The Future of the Reconstruction Amendments, 25 *Loyola L.A. L. Rev.* 1207 (1992).
 A Response to David Landau, 53 *Harv. Int'l L.J. Online* 155 (2012).
 Shelley v. Kraemer and Theories of Equality, 33 *N.Y.L. Sch. L. Rev.* 383 (1988).
Unterhalter, Elaine, Expert Paper, The MDGs, Girls' Education and Gender Equality, U.N. Women, Expert Grp. Meeting, Oct. 21–24, 2013.
Van Aaken, Anne, Fragmentation of International Law: The Case of International Investment Law, 17 *Fin. Y.B. Int'l Inv. L.* 91 (2006).
van der Walt, Johan, Horizontal Effect of Fundamental Rights and the Threshold of the Law in View of the Carmichele Saga, 19 *S. Afr. J. Hum. Rts.* 517 (2003).
 Progressive Indirect Horizontal Effect of the Bill of Rights: Towards a Co-Operative Relation Between Common-Law and Constitutional Jurisprudence, 17 *S. Afr. J. Hum. Rts.* 341 (2001).
Velasco, Julian, How Many Fiduciary Duties Are There in Corporate Law, 83 *S. Cal. L. Rev.* 1231 (2010).
Verkuil, Paul R., Privatizing Due Process, 57 *Admin. L. Rev.* 963 (2005).
Verschraegen, Gert, Human Rights and Modern Society: A Sociological Analysis from the Perspective of Systems Theory, 29 *J.L. & Soc'y* 258 (2002).
Vischer, Robert K., Subsidiarity as a Principle of Governance: Beyond Devolution, 35 *Ind. L. Rev.* 103 (2001).
Voeten, Erik, International Judicial Independence, (Sept. 2011) (unpublished manuscript).
von Borries, Reimer & Malte Hauschild, Implementing the Subsidiarity Principle, 5 *Colum. J. Eur. L.* 369 (1999).
Waldron, Jeremy, Are Sovereigns Entitled to the Benefit of the International Rule of Law?, 22 *Eur. J. Int'l.* 315 (2011).
 The Concept and the Rule of Law, 43 *Ga. L. Rev.* 1 (2008).
 Property, Justification and Need, 6 *Can. J. L. and Jurisprudence* 185 (1993).
Weil, Prosper, The Court Cannot Conclude Definitely . . . Non Liquet Revisited, 36 *Colum. J. Transnat'l L.* 109 (1997).
Wells, Michael L., Identifying State Actors in Constitutional Litigation: Reviving the Role of Substantive Context, 26 *Cardozo L. Rev.* 99 (2004).
Zipursky, Benjamin C., Snyder v. Phelps, Outrageousness, and the Open Texture of Tort Law, 60 *DePaul L. Rev.* 473 (2011).
Zumbansen, Peer, Transnational Private Regulatory Governance: Ambiguities of Public Authority and Private Power, 76 *Law & Contemp. Probs.* 117 (2013).

## Cases

Bundesverfassungsgericht [Federal Constitutional Court] Feb. 9, 2010, 1 BvL 1/09, Absatz-Nr., www.bverfg.de/entscheidungen/ls20100209_1bvl000109en.html (official translation by the Court) (Ger.).
1 BverfGE 14 Walter F. Murphy & Joseph T. Tanenhaus, Comparative Constitutional Law: Cases and Commentaries 209 (1977)) [Southwest Case].
24 BVerfG 278 (Ger.).
25 BVerfG 256 (Ger.).
30 BVerfG 173 (Ger.).
34 BVerfG ### (Ger.).
35 BVerfG 202 (Ger.).
42 BVerfG 142 (Ger.).
46 BVerfG 325 (Ger.).
54 BVerfG 129 (Ger.).
54 BVerfG 148 (Ger.).
60 BVerfG 234 (Ger.).
61 BVerfG 1 (Ger.).
62 BVerfG 230 (Ger.).
66 BVerfG 116 (Ger.).
73 BVerfG 261 (Ger.).
92.9 Hit FM Radio v. Austria, App. No. 6754/05.
A and H v. Austria, App. No. 9905/82, (1984) D.R. 18.
AB Kurt Kellermann v. Sweden, App. No. 41579/98.
Airey v. Ireland, 2 Eur. H.R. Rep. 305 (1979).
Agrotexim v. Greece, 21 Eur. H.R. Rep. 250 (1996).
Agrotexim v. Greece, App. No. 14807/89.
American Mfrs. Mut. Ins. Co. v. Sullivan, 526 U.S. 40 (1999).
Amoco Int'l Fin. Corp. v. Iran, 15 Iran-U.S. Cl. Trib. Rep. 189 (1987).
Andrews v. Law Soc'y of B.C., [1989] 1 S.C.R. 143, 56 D.L.R. (4th) 1 (Can.).
Asahi v. Japan [Sup. Ct.] 1967, 21 Saikō Saibansho Minji Hanreishū [Minshū] 5, 1043. English transl. available at www.courts.go.jp/english/judgments/text/1967.05.24-1964-Gyo-Tsu-No.14.html).
Aston Cantlow v. Wallbank, [2003] UKHL 37, [2004] 1 A.C. 546.
Autronic v. Switzerland, App. No. 12726/87, Eur. Comm'n H.R. 22 May 1990.
Baier v. Alta, 2007 SCC 31, [2007] 2 S.C.R. 673 (Can.).
Baker v. Carr, 369 U.S. 186, 209 (1962).
Barsky v. Bd. of Regents, 347 U.S. 422 (1954).
Barrows v. Jackson, 346 U.S. 249 (1953).
Bellis v. U.S., 417 U.S. 85 (1974).
Biloune and Marine Drive Complex Ltd. v. Ghana Investments Centre and the Government of Ghana 95 I.L.R. 184 (1989) (award on jurisdiction and liability).

Black v. Cutter Laboratories, 351 U.S. 292 (1956).
Blum v. Yaretsky, 457 U.S. 991 (1982).
Botta v. Italy 1998-I Eur. Ct. H.R.
Brown v. Entertainment Merchants Ass'n, 131 S.Ct. 2729 (2011).
Bundesverfassungsgericht [BVerfG] [Federal Constitutional Court] Jan. 15, 1958, 7 entscheidungen des Bundesverwaltungsgerichts [BVerfGE] 198 (Ger.) [Lüth].
Burwell v. Hobby Lobby Stores, Inc., 573 U.S. ___ (2014), Docket No. 13-354, 20.
Cameron v. Network Rail Infrastructure Ltd., [2006] EWHC 1133 (Q.B.).
Campbell v. MGN Ltd., [2004] UKHL 22.
Carltona Ltd v. Comm'rs of Works, [1943] 2 All E.R. 560 (CA).
Carmichele v. Minister of Safety and Security and Another 2001 (4) SA 938 (CC) (S. Afr.).
Casado Coca v. Spain App. No. 15450/89.
Church of Scientology v. France, App. No. 1950/.
Church of Scientology Moscow v. Russia, App. No. 18147/02.
Citizens United v. Fed. Election Comm'n, 558 U.S. 310, 466 (2010).
City of Johannesburg v. Blue Moonlight Properties [2011] ZACC 33 (S. Afr.).
CMS Gas Transmission Co. v. The Argentine Republic, ICSID Case No. ARB/01/8, Award, May 12 2005.
Coleman v. Miller, 307 U.S. 433 (1939).
Collins V. Eli Lilly & Co., 116 Wis.2d 166, 342 N.W.2d 37 (1984), cert. denied, 469 U.S. 826 (1984).
Compare West v. Atkins, 487 U.S. 42 (1988).
Continental Casualty v. Argentine Republic, ICSID Case No. ARB/03/9.
Correctional Services Corp. v. Malesko, 534 U.S. 61 (2001).
Costello-Roberts v. United Kingdom, 247-C Eur. Ct. H.R. (ser. A) (1993).
Credit and Industrial Bank v. Czech Republic, 26 Eur. H.R. Rep. 88 (1998).
Delisle v. Can. (Att'y Gen.), [1999] 2 S.C.R. 989, 176 D.L.R. (4th) 513 (Can.).
Demuth v. Switzerland, 31 Eur. H.R. Rep. 772.
DeShaney v. Winnebago County Department of Social Services, 489 U.S. 189 (1989).
Donoghue v. Poplar Housing, [2001] EWCA (Civ) 595, [2002] Q.B. 48.
Du Plessis v. De Klerk 1996 (5) BCLR 658 (CC) (S. Afr.).
Dunmore v. Ont., 2001 SCC 94, [2001] 3 S.C.R. 1016 (Can.).
Dunsmuir v. N.B., 2009 SCC 9, [2008] 1 S.C.R. 190 (Can.).
Eldridge v. B.C. (Att'y Gen.), [1997] 3 S.C.R. 624, 151 D.L.R. (4th) 577 (Can.).
Elettronica Sicula S.p.A. (ELSI) (U.S. v. Italy), 1989 I.C.J. 15 (July 20).
Enron Creditors Recovery Corp. Ponderosa Assets, L.P. v. The Argentine Republic, ICSID Case No. ARB/01/3, Decision on the Application for Annulment of the Argentine Republic (July 30, 2010).
Eugenia Michaelidou Developments Ltd v. Turkey, App. No. 16163/90.

Ex Parte Virginia, 100 U.S. 339 (1880).
Farraj v. King's Healthcare NHS Trust, [2009] EWCA (Civ) 1203, [2010] 1 W.L.R. 2139.
Fayed v. United Kingdom, 18 Eur. H.R. Rep. 393 (1994).
Finska församlingen and Hautaniemi v. Sweden, App. No. 24019/94, (1996) D.R. 85.
Flagg Brothers, Inc. v. Brooks, 436 U.S. 149 (1978).
Free Enter. Fund v. Public Co. Accounting Oversight Bd., 561 U.S. 477 (2010).
G.J. v. Luxemburg, 36 Eur. H.R. Rep. 40 (2003).
Gosselin v. Que. (Att'y Gen.), 2002 S.C.C. 84, [2002] 4 S.C.R. 429 (Can.).
Gov't of the Republic of S. Afr. v. Grootboom, (CCT11/00), (11) B.C.L.R. 1169 (S. Afr.).
Groppera Radio v. Switzerland, App. No. 10890/84.
Groppera Radio v. Switzerland, (1990) 12 Eur. H.R. Rep. 321.
Haig v. Can. (Chief Electoral Officer), [1993] 2 S.C.R. 995, [1993] S.C.J. No. 84 (Can.).
Hague v. C.I.O., 307 U.S. 496 (1939).
Hall v. E.I Du Pont De Nemours & Co., 345 F. Supp. 353 (E.D.N.Y. 1972).
Harper v. Can. (Att'y. Gen.), 2004 SCC 33, [2004] 1 S.C.R. 827 (Can.).
HCJ 366/03 Commitment to Peace & Social Justice Soc'y v. Minister of Fin. [2005] (Isr.).
HCJ 888/03 Rubinova v. Minister of Fin. [2005] (Isr.).
HCJ 2605/05 The Academic Ctr. of Law and Bus. v. The Minister of Fin. [2009] (Isr.).
Holy Monasteries v. Greece, App. No. 13092/87; 13984/88.
Hosanna-Tabor Evangelical Lutheran Church and School v. EEOC, 565 U.S. ___ (2012), Docket No. 10-553.
Immobiliare Saffi v. Italy, 30 Eur. H.R. Rep. 756.
Jackson v. Metro. Edison Co., 419 U.S. 345 (1974).
James v. London Elec. Plc., [2004] EWHC 3226 (Q.B.).
James v. United Kingdom, 8 Eur. H.R. Rep. 123 (1986).
Kesavananda Bharati v. State of Kerala, A.I.R. (1973) S.C. 1461 (India).
Kiobel v. Royal Dutch Petroleum Co., 133 S. Ct. 1659 (2013).
Khumalo v. Holomisa 2002 (5) SA 401 (CC) (S. Afr.).
Krone Verlag v. Austria (No 3), App. No. 39069/97.
Labor v. Swing, 312 U.S. 321 (1941).
Law v. Can. (Minister of Emp't and Immigration), [1989] 1 S.C.R. 143, 56 D.L.R. (4th) 1 (Can.).
Leser v. Garnett, 258 U.S. 130, 136 (1922).
Lloyd Corp. v. Whiffen, 773 P.2d 1294 (Or. 1989).
Lochner v. New York, 198 U.S. 45 (1905).

Loewen Group, Inc. v. United States, ICSID Case No. ARB (AF)/98/3, 42 I.L.M. 811 (2003), 7 ICSID Rep. 442 (2005).
Lugar v. Edmondson Oil Co., 457 U.S. 922 (1982).
Malcolm v. Mackenzie, [2004] EWCA (Civ) 1748.
Marbury v. Madison, 5 U.S. 137 (1803).
Maric v. Thames Water Ltd., [2003] UKHL 66.
Markt Intern and Beerman v. Germany, (1990) 12 Eur. H.R. Rep. 161.
Marzari v. Italy, App. No. 36448/97, 28 Eur. H.R. Rep. Comm'n Dec. 175 (1999).
Matos e Silva Lda v. Portugal, 24 Eur. H.R. Rep. 573.
Mazibuko v. City of Johannesburg 2010 (4) SA 1 (S. Afr.).
Metalclad Corp. v. United Mexican States, ICSID Case No. ARB(AF)/97/1, Award (Aug. 30, 2010).
Minister of Health v. Treatment Action Campaign (2002) 5 SA 721, (CCT8/02) [2002] ZACC 15 (S. Afr.).
Minneapolis & St. Louis Railway v. Beckwith, 129 U.S. 26 (1889).
Minneci v. Pollard, 132 S. Ct. 617 (2012).
Montréal (City) v. 2952-1366 Que. Inc., 2005 SCC 62, [2005] 3 S.C.R. 141 (Can.).
Moscow Branch of the Salvation Army v. Russia, App. No. 72881/01.
Nandini Sundar v. Chattisgarh, (2011) 7 S.C.C. 547 (India).
National Media v. Bogoshi 1998 (4) SA 1196 (SCA) (S. Afr.).
New State Ice Co. v. Liebmann, 285 U.S. 262 (1932).
New York Times v. Sullivan, 376 U.S. 254 (1964).
News Verlag v. Austria , 31 Eur. H.R. Rep. 246.
Nike, Inc. v. Kasky, 539 U.S. 65.
Occupiers of 51 Olivia Road v. City of Johannesburg, (CCT 24/07), [2008] ZACC 1 (S. Afr.).
Oil Platforms (Iran v. U.S.), 2003 I.C.J. REP. 161 (Nov. 6), 42 I.L.M. 1334 (2003).
Ont. v. Criminal Lawyers' Ass'n of Ont., 2010 SCC 23, [2010] 1 S.C.R. 815 (Can.).
Ont. (Att'y Gen.) v. Fraser, 2011 SCC 20, [2011] 2 S.C.R. 3 (Can.).
Osman v. United Kingdom, 29 Eur. H.R. Rep. 245 (1998).
Pincová and Pinc v. Czech Republic, App. No. 36548/97.
Potvin v. Metro. Life. Ins. Co., 997 P.2d 1153 (Cal. 2000).
Prosecutor v. Erdemovic, IT-96-22-A.
R v. Bembridge, (1783) 22 State Tr. 1 [155-56] (H.L.) (appeal taken from Eng.) (Gr. Brit.).
R v. Chief Rabbi of the United Hebrew Congregations of Great Britain and the Commonwealth, ex parte Wachmann, [1992] 1 W.L.R. 1036.
R v. Disciplinary Comm. of the Jockey Club, ex parte Aga Khan, [1993] 1 W.L.R. 909 (CA).

R v. Inland Revenue Comm'rs, exp. National Federation of Self-Employed and Small Businesses Ltd., [1982] A.C. 617 (H.L.) (appeal taken from Eng.) (U.K.).
R v. N. & E. Devon Health Authority, ex parte Coughlan, [1999] EWCA (Civ) 1871, [2001] Q.B. 213 (CA).
R. v. Oakes, [1986] 1 S.C.R. 103, 26 D.L.R. (4th) 200 (Can.).
R v. Panel on Takeovers & Mergers, ex parte Datafin, [1987] Q.B. 815 (CA) 824.
R v. Servite Houses, ex parte Goldsmith, [2000] EWHC (Admin) 338, (2001), 33 H.L.R. 35 (Q.B.).
R. v. Sharpe, 2001 SCC 2, [2001] 1 S.C.R. 45 (Can.).
R (A) v. Partnerships in Care Ltd., [2002] EWHC (Admin) 529, [2002] 1 W.L.R. 2610.
R (Heather) v. Leonard Cheshire Found., [2002] EWCA (Civ) 366, [33], [2002] 2 All E.R. 936.
R (Johnson) v. Havering LBC, [2007] EWCA (Civ) 26, [2008] Q.B. 1.
R (Mullins) v. Jockey Club App. Bd. (No.1), [2005] EWHC (Admin) 2197, [2006] A.C.D. 2.
R (Weaver) v. London & Quadrant Housing Trust, [2009] EWCA (Civ) 587, [2010] 1 W.L.R. 363.
R (Wilkinson) v. Broadmoor Special Hosp. Auth., [2001] EWCA (Civ) 1545.
R.T.B.F. v Belgium, App. No. 50084/06.
R.W.D.S.U., Local 558 v. Pepsi-Cola Canada Beverages (West) Ltd., 2002 SCC 8, [2002] 1 S.C.R. 156 (Can.).
R.W.D.S.U., Local 580 v. Dolphin Delivery Ltd., [1986] 2 S.C.R. 573, 33 D.L.R. (4th) 174.
Radio France v. France, App. No. 53984/00.
Reference re Remuneration of Judges of the Provincial Ct. of P.E.I., [1997] 3 S.C.R. 3, 150 D.L.R. (4th) 577 (Can.).
Reference re Secession of Quebec, [1998] 2 S.C.R. 217, 161 D.L.R. (4th) 385 (Can.).
Reparation for Injuries Suffered in the Service of the United Nations, Advisory Opinion, 1949 I.C.J. 174 (Apr. 11).
S.D. Myers Inc. v. Government of Canada, UNCITRAL, Partial Award, Nov. 13 2000.
Saunders v. United Kingdom, 23 Eur. H.R. Rep. 313 (1996).
Sempra Energy Int'l v. Argentine Republic, ICSID No. ARB/02/16, Award (Sept. 28, 2007).
Shelley v. Kraemer, 334 U.S. 1 (1948).
Siemens A.G. v. Argentina, Award, Feb. 6, 2007, ICSID Case No. ARB/02/8.
Sindell v. Abbott Laboratories, 607 P.2d 924 (Cal. 1980).
Société Colas Est. v. France, 39 Eur. H.R. Rep. 17 (2004).
Soobramoney v. Minister of Health Kwazulu-Natal (12) B.C.L.R. 1696 (S. Afr.).
South West Africa Case (Ethiopia v. S. Air.; Liberia v. S. Mr.), 1966 I.C.J. 4, 298 (July 18).

Sporrong and Lönnroth v. Sweden, App. No. 7151/75.
Stavebná v. Slovakia, App. No.7261/06.
Storck v. Germany, 2005-V Eur. Ct. H.R.
Suez, Societad General de Aguas de Barcelona S.A., and Inter Agua Servicios Integrales del Agua S.A. v. The Argentine Republic, ICSID Case No. ARB/ 03/17, Decision on Liability (Jul. 30, 2010) [Suez v. Argentina].
Summers v. Tice, 33 Cal.2d 80 (1948).
Sychev v. Ukraine, App. No. 4773/02 (2005).
Snyder v. Phelps, 131 S.Ct. 1207 (2011).
Thomson Newspapers Co. v. Can, (Att'y Gen.), [1998] 1 S.C.R. 877, 159 D.L.R. (4th) 385 (Can.).
Southern Pacific Co. v. Jensen, 244 U.S. 205 (1917).
Submission on Behalf of the Amicus Curiae Inner City Resources Centre, Maphango v. Aengus Lifestyle Property, CCT Case No. 57/2011.
Sunday Times v. United Kingdom, 2 Eur. H.R. Rep. 245.
Swiss Radio and Television v. Switzerland, App. No. 34124/06.
Texaco Overseas Petroleum v. Libya, 104 J. Droit Int'l 350 (1977), 17 I.L.M. 1 (1978).
The Civil Rights Cases, 109 U.S. 3 (1883).
Tifoyo v. United Kingdom, 48 Eur. H.R. Rep. 18, 39 (2009).
Unni Krishnan v. State of Andhra Pradesh, 1993 S.C.R. (1) 594 (India).
United States v. Alvarez, 132 S.Ct. 2537 (2012).
United States v. Ewell, 383 U.S. 116, 120 (1966).
United States v. Lopez, 514 U.S. 549 (1995).
United States v. Stevens, 559 U.S. 460 (2010).
United States v. White, 322 U.S. 694 (1944).
Van der Mussele v. Belgium, 70 Eur. Ct. H.R. (ser. A) (1983).
Various Claimants v. Inst. of the Bros. of the Christian Sch., [2012] UKSC 56, [2013] 2 A.C. 1.
Velantzas v. Colgate-Palmolive Co., Inc., 109 N.J. 189, 536 A.2d 237 (1988).
Vereinigung Soldaten Österreichs and Gubi v. Austria, App. No. 15153/89.
Virginia v. Rives, 100 U.S. 313 (1880).
von Hannover v. Germany, 40 Eur. H.R. Rep. 1, 57 (2004).
Walz v. Tax Comm'n of the City of New York, 397 U.S. 664 (1970).
Woodland v Swimming Teachers Association, [2013] UKSC 66, [2014] A.C. 537.
Wos v. Poland, 2005-IV Eur. Ct. H.R.
X and Church of Scientology v. Sweden, App. No. 7805/77, (1979) 16 D.R. 68.
X & Y v. The Netherlands, 91 Eur. Ct. H.R. (ser. A) (1985).
YL v. Birmingham City Council, [2007] UKHL 27, [2007] 3 W.L.R. 112.
Younger v. Harris, 401 U.S. 37 (1971).
Yukos v. Russia, App. No. 14902/04.
Z v. United Kingdom, 34 Eur. H.R. Rep. 97 (2001).

## Legislation/Constitutions/Treaties/International & Government Documents (including statistics and proceedings)

314 Parl. Deb., H.C. (6th ser.) (1998).
1789 Const. Déclaration des Droits de l'Homme et du Citoyen [Declaration of the Rights of Man and the Citizen] (Fr.).
1918 Russian Constitution.
Accountability Office, U.S. Gov't, GAO-16-97, Federal Judiciary: Improved Cost Savings Estimates Could Help Better Assess Cost Containment Efforts (Nov. 2015), available at www.gao.gov/assets/680/673581.pdf.
African (Banjul) Charter on Human and Peoples' Rights, adopted June 27, 1981, 1520 U.N.T.S. 217 (entered into force Oct. 21, 1986).
Alien Tort Statute, 28 USC § 1350.
American Convention on Human Rights, Nov. 22, 1969, 1144 U.N.T.S. 123.
Canada Labour Code, R.S.C. 1985, c. L-2
Canadian Charter of Rights and Freedoms, Part I of the Constitution Act, 1982, being Schedule B to the Canada Act, 1982 c. 11 (U.K.).
Certification of the Const. of the Republic of S. Afr. (1996) (10) BCLR 1253.
Constitution of Portugal, Translation Provided by the Portuguese Parliament, app.parlamento.pt/site_antigo/ingles/cons_leg/Constitution_VII_revisao_definitive.pdf.
Contracts (Rights of Third Parties) Act 1999, c. 31 (U.K.).
Convention for the Protection of Human Rights and Fundamental Freedoms, Nov. 4, 1950, Europ.T.S. No. 5; 213 U.N.T.S. 221.
Convention on the Settlement of Investment Disputes between States and Nationals of Other States, Mar. 18, 1965, 17 U.S.T. 1270, 575 U.N.T.S. 159.
James Crawford, The International Law Commission's Articles on State Responsibility: Introduction, Text and Commentaries (2002).
José E. Alvarez, International Organizations: Accountability or Responsibility (Oct. 27, 2006).
Deregulation and Contracting Out Act 1994, c. 40 (U.K.).
Draft Articles on Responsibility of International Organizations, Yearbook of the International Law Commission, 2011, Vol. II.
Enabling Act, An act to provide for the division of Dakota into two states and to enable the people of North Dakota, South Dakota, Montana, and Washington to form constitutions and state governments and to be admitted into the union on an equal footing with the original states, and to make donations of public lands to such states, 25 U.S. Statutes at Large, c 180 (approved Feb. 22, 1889).
European Communities—Measures Concerning Meat and Meat Products (Hormones), WTO Doc. WT/DS26/AB/R, at 41–42 (adopted Feb. 13, 1998).
European Convention for the Protection of Human Rights and Fundamental Freedoms, Nov. 4, 1950, 213 U.N.T.S. 222.

Freedom of Information Act, 2000, c. 36.
General Agreement on Tariffs and Trade, Oct. 30, 1947, 61 Stat. A–11, 55 U.N.T.S. 194.
Hans Otto Sano & Lone Lindholt, Human Rights Indicators 2000: Country Data and Methodology (2000).
Health and Social Care Act 2008, c. 14 (U.K).
HM Treasury, Standardisation of PF2 Contracts, 2012, (U.K.) (draft).
Home Office, Rights Brought Home: The Human Rights Bill, 1997, Cm. 3782.
Honduras Constitution, 1982.
Human Rights Act 1998, c. 42.
India Constitution.
International Chamber of Commerce, Dispute Board Rules (2011), available at www.iccwbo.org/ICCDRSRules/.
International Covenant on Civil and Political Rights, G.A. Res. 2200A (XXI), U.N. Doc. A/6316, 999 U.N.T.S. 171 (Dec. 16,1966).
International Covenant on Economic, Social and Cultural Rights, G.A. Res. 2200A (XXI), U.N. Doc. A/6316, 993 U.N.T.S. 3 (Dec. 16, 1966).
International Financial Corporation, IFC Sustainability Framework: Policy and Performance Standards on Environmental and Social Sustainability Access to Information Policy (2012).
Int'l Law Comm'n, Report of the Study Group, Fragmentation of International Law: Difficulties Arising From the Diversification and Expansion of International Law (U.N. Doc A/CN.4/ L682, 2006).
Labour Relations Act, 1995, S.O. 1995, c. 1, Sched. A (Can.).
Legal Consequences for States of the Continued Presence of South Africa in Namibia (South West Africa) Notwithstanding Security Council Resolution 276 (1970), Advisory Opinion, 1971 I.C.J. 16, 47 (June 21).
Local Authorities Election Act, R.S.A. 2000, c. L-21 (Can.).
Magna Carta, 1215, 17 John, (Eng.), translated in English Translation of Magna Carta (British Library).
Magna Carta, 1225, 9 Hen. 3, (Eng.).
Martti Koskenniemi, Fragmentation of International Law: Difficulties Arising from the Diversification and Expansion of International Law, UN Doc. A/CN.4/ L.682 (Apr. 13, 2006).
Mexican Constitution, 1857.
Office of Management and Budget, Executive Office of the President, Budget of the United States Government: Summary Tables, Fiscal Year 2012 (2011), available at www.gpo.gov/fdsys/pkg/BUDGET-2012-BUD/pdf/BUDGET-2012-BUD-29.pdf.
Police and Justice Act 2006, c. 48 (U.K.).
Rajeev Malhotra & Nicolas Fasel, Quantitative Human Rights Indicators: A Survey of Major Initiatives, Abo Akedemi University, Expert Meeting on Human Rights Indicators, Mar. 2005 (Fin.).

Religious Freedom Restoration Act, 42 U.S.C. §§2000bb–2000bb-4.
Report of the Expert Group Meeting on Envisioning Women's Rights in the Post-2015 Context, U.N. Women, Expert Grp. Meeting, Nov. 3–5, 2014.
Rules and Procedures Governing the Settlement of Disputes, Apr. 15, 1994, Marrakesh Agreement Establishing the World Trade Organization, Annex 2, 1869 U.N.T.S. 401.
South African Constitution, 1996.
Supreme Court Act, 1981, c. 54 (U.K.).
The Baku-Tbilisi-Ceyhan Pipeline.
The Children and Families Act, 2014, c. 6.
The Civil Rights Act of 1875, 8 Stat. 335 (1875).
The Declaration of Independence (U.S. 1776).
The Human Right to Water and Sanitation, G.A. Res. 64/292, U.N. Doc. A/RES/64/292 (Aug. 3, 2010).
The Soviet Constitution of 1936.
Treaty between the United States of America and the Argentine Republic Concerning the Reciprocal Encouragement and Protection of Investment, 31 I.L.M. 124 (entered into force Oct. 20, 1994).
Treaty of Canterbury, U.K.-Fr., Feb. 12, 1986, 1985/86 Cmnd. 9745 France No. 1 (1986) (U.K.) (English Channel Tunnel Agreement).
Treaty on European Union, Feb. 7, 1992, 1992 OJ (191) 1.
U.N. Conf. on Trade & Dev., Selected Developments in IIA Arbitration and Human Rights IIA Monito No.2 (2009) UNCTAD/WB/DIAE/IA/2009/7.
U.N. Conf. on Trade & Dev., World Investment Report 2013: Global Value Chains: Investment and Trade for Development 101 (2013).
U.N. Dev. Program, Human Development Report 1991: Financing Human Development (1991).
U.N. Dev. Program, Human Development Report, 1992: Global Dimensions of Human Development (1992).
U.N. Dev. Program, Response by William H. Draper III Administrator of the United Nations Development Programme to the General Debate (June 12, 1991) (William H. Draper).
U.N. Office of the High Comm'r for Human Rights, Frequently Asked Questions about the Guiding Principles on Business and Human Rights (2014).
U.N. Office of the High Comm'r for Human Rights, Human Rights Indicators: A Guide to Measurement and Implementation (2012).
U.N. Office of the High Comm'r for Human Rights, Rep. on Indicators for Promoting and Monitoring the Implementation of Human Rights, HRI/MC/2008/3, June 6, 2008.
U.N. Special Representative of the Secretary-General, Guiding Principles on Business and Human Rights: Implementing the United Nations 'Protect,

Respect and Remedy' Framework, H.R.C. Doc. A/HRC/17/31 (Mar. 21, 2011) (John Ruggie).
U.N. Women, Promoting UN Accountability (UN-SWAP) (2014).
United States Constitution.
United Nations, Econ. & Soc. Council, Comm'n on Human Rights, Promotion and Protection of Human Rights: Interim Report of the Special Representative of the Secretary-General on the Issue of Human Rights and Transnational Corporations and Other Business Enterprises, 60, U.N. Doc. E/CN.4/2006/97 (Feb. 22, 2006).
United States-Trade Measures Affecting Nicaragua, Oct. 13, 1986 (unadopted), GATT Doc. L/6053.
United States, Treaty Concerning the Encouragement and Reciprocal Protection of Investment, (2004).
Universal Declaration of Human Rights, G.A. Res. 217 (III) A, U.N. Doc. A/RES/217(III) (Dec. 10, 1948).
Vienna Convention on the Law of Treaties, opened for signature May 23, 1969, 1155 U.N.T.S. 331, 8 I.L.M. 679 (1969).
World Bank, Economic Growth in the 1990s: Learning from a Decade of Reform (2005).
World Bank, World Development Report 1991: The Challenge of Development (1991).

## Movies

John Ford, *The Man Who Shot Liberty Valance* (Paramount Pictures 1962).

# INDEX

*AB Kurt Kellermann v. Sweden*, 212
Ackerman, Bruce, 118
*Affordable Care Act*, 206
Alexy, Robert, 131, 138–39
Alito, Justice Samuel, 206
Allen, Thomas, 200
Alvarez, José E., 2–3, 43, 199
Amendment, constitutional, 109
  and democracy, 116–17, 119, 121, 124
  and good or just norms, 117, 119
  and the rule of law, 117, 119, 123, 125
  eternity clauses, 110, 116, 120
  judicial review of, 117, 121
  procedure, 115
Amnesty International, 275–76
Annan, Kofi, 282
Arndt, Christiane, 278
*Autronic v. Switzerland*, 202–3

*Baier v. Alberta*, 174–75, 179–80
*Barrows v. Jackson*, 159
Basel Convention on the Control of Transboundary Movement of Hazardous Waste, 40
Bastarache, Justice J. E. Michel, 178–79, 184–85, 187, 189, 192
Baxi, Upendra, 25, 34
Beinisch, President Dorit, 249
*Bellis v. U.S.*, 210
Benvenisti, Eyal, 49, 92–93
Berlin, Isaiah, 8
Bilateral Investment Treaty, 26, 35, 39, 44–45, 55, 57–62

*Biloune and Marine Drive Complex Ltd. v. Ghana Investments Centre and the Government of Ghana*, 33
Bingham, Lord Thomas, 243, 245
*Black v. Cutter Laboratories*, 159
Black, Justice Hugo, 159
*Blood Meridian*, 160–61
Boundary crossing, 45, 47, 50–51, 54, 56, 58, 60–62, 71, 73, 76, 78, 80, 84, 87–89, 93, 273
  and hybridity, 192
  horizontal v vertical, 52–53, 55, 82, 92
  human rights and development, 282, 288–89
  legitimate and legitimating, 84, 92
  public to private, 134
Bradley, Justice Joseph P., 154–55
Brennan, Justice William J., 156–57
*Burwell v. Hobby Lobby Stores Inc.*, 206
Buxton, Lord Justice Richard, 229

Calvo, Carlos, 83
Canadian Charter of Rights and Freedoms, 114, 173, 190
  equality, 174, 176–77, 182, 186, 189
  freedom of association, 176, 180
  freedom of expression, 161, 179, 183–84, 189
  hybrid rights claim, 175, 188–89, 192
  limitations clause, 161, 193
  right to life, liberty and security of the person, 173–74, 181
  underlying values, 191
Cane, Peter, 234, 240–41
*Carltona* principle, 226

## INDEX

Carmichele v. Minister of Safety and Security and Another, 166, 170
Carter, President James, 275
Chilean Human Rights Commission, 274
Church of Scientology Moscow v. Russia, 205
Citizens United v. Federal Election Commission, 206
City of Johannesburg v. Blue Moonlight Properties, 101
Civil Rights Cases, 137, 146, 154, 158
CMS Gas Transmission Co. v. The Argentine Republic, 39
Cohen-Eliya, Moshe, 140
Committee on Economic, Social and Cultural Rights, 281
Committee on the Rights of the Child, 281
Comparative public law, 55–56, 58, 85–86, 91
Constitution of India, 112, 126
Constitution of Ireland, 112
Constitution of Japan, 113
Constitution of Mexico, 110
Constitution of South Africa, 114, 126, 164, 170
Constitution of the Italian Republic, 113–14
Constitutionalism, 95, 109, 124, 127
  American, 132, 134, 136–37
  as mindset, 41
  compensatory, 25, 41
  democracy and the rule of law, 119, 125, 160
  global, 28, 85
  judicial v political, 94
  societal, 27, 29
Continental Casualty v. Argentina, 60–68, 71–72, 80, 83–84, 93
Corporate human rights, 75, 195–96, 198–99, 214
  derivative rights, 196, 201, 203–5, 207
  justification, 201, 208, 211–12, 214
Court of Appeal of England and Wales, 218, 229, 242, 244
Craig, Paul, 222–23

Criddle, Evan J., 252
Customary international law, 41, 50–51, 61, 66

Daft, Douglas, 282
Davies, A.C.L., 4, 215
Declaration of the Rights of Man and of the Citizen, 9–10
Delisle v. Canada, 174, 176, 184
Demuth v. Switzerland, 203–4
Dependency, 21–24
Deregulation and Contracting Out Act, 1994, 226, 231
Dersnah, Megan, 4, 271
Deschampes, Justice Marie, 189
DeShaney v. Winnebago County Department of Social Services, 160–61
Dezalay, Yves, 276
Dialogue, constitutional, 94–97, 107–8
  common-law dialogues, 99, 101, 104
  conditions of unconstitutionality, 97–99
  judicially initiated, 102–4, 106–7
  reading up v reading down, 104
  unconstitutionality by omission, 96–97
Dicey, Albert Venn, 234
Directive principles, 112–13, 126
Donoghue v. Poplar Housing, 219, 221, 241–42
Douglas, Justice William O., 134, 159
Downs, George, 49, 92
Drittwirkung doctrine, 140, 150, 166
Du Plessis v. De Klerk, 164–65, 168–69, 171–72
Dunmore v. Ontario, 174–88, 192
Dupuy, Pierre-Marie, 37
Dürig, Günter, 168
Dworkin, Ronald, 87

Engle Merry, Sally, 273
Enron v. Argentina, 60–73, 80, 83–84, 93
Equality, 102
  formal v substantive, 13
  gender, 272, 282, 284–87

European Convention on Human
    Rights, 2, 196–97, 199, 214,
    238–39, 241, 245–47, 249
  freedom of association, 198, 205, 211
  freedom of religion, 196, 201, 204–5
  prohibition on retroactivity of
    criminal punishment, 196, 198,
    210
  right of nondiscrimination, 196, 201,
    204
  right to a fair trial, 196, 198, 208, 210
  right to free speech, 196, 201–2, 204
  Right to free speech, 202
  right to life, 248
  right to property, 196–97, 199–200,
    212–13
  right to respect for private life, family
    and home, 198, 241–42
European Court of Human Rights, 79,
    132, 196–97, 199, 202–3, 208, 210,
    212, 233, 245–47
Ex Parte Virginia, 158

Fayed v. United Kingdom, 209
Federal Constitutional Court of
    Germany, 3, 117, 120, 138, 140,
    150, 164, 166–67
Federalism, 132, 136–37
Finska församlingen and Hautaniemi v.
    Sweden, 199
Fisher-Lescano, Andrea, 27
Flagg Brothers, Inc. v. Brooks, 159
Forum-shopping, 49–50, 81–82, 84, 92
Fox-Decent, Evan, 251, 254, 263, 269
Frankfurter, Justice Felix, 157, 161
Freedland, Mark, 235
Freeman, Jody, 236
Friedmann, Wolfgang G., 146

Gardbaum, Stephen, 153
Garth, Bryant, 276
General Agreement on Tariffs and
    Trade, 48, 61–62, 64–65
  general exceptions clause, 60–66
German Basic Law, 116, 120
Ginsburg, Justice Ruth Bader, 206
Global administrative law, 51–54, 69,
    71, 73, 78, 87, 89–90, 92

Globalization, 7, 51, 234
Gosselin v. Quebec, 174
Grootboom, 127

Habermas, Jürgen, 25
Haig v. Canada, 174
Hale, Baroness Brenda, 243, 245–46
Harlow, Carol, 235
Hartz IV, 120
Health and Social Care Act, 2008, 245
Health and Social Care Act, 2012, 237
Hegel, Georg Wilhelm Friedrich, 212
Hershkoff, Helen, 3, 90, 129
Hirsch, Moshe, 38, 40
Hobbes, 7–8, 12, 255
Hogg, Peter, 163–64
Hohfeld, Wesley, 151, 153, 159
Hohfeldian point, 149–54, 159, 171
Holy Monasteries v. Greece, 199
House of Lords, 219, 243
Human Rights Act, 1998, 4, 216,
    219–25, 227, 229–32, 235, 238–39,
    241–45, 248
Human rights indicators, 271–74, 278,
    280–84, 286, 288

Individualism, 6–7
Inter-American Convention on Human
    Rights, 209
Inter-American Court of Human
    Rights, 79
International Centre for Settlement of
    Investment Disputes, 36, 69,
    71–72, 92
International Centre for Settlement of
    Investment Disputes Convention,
    69, 71–72, 87
International Chamber of Commerce,
    36
International Court of Justice, 45, 49,
    73–74, 76, 82, 199
International Covenant on Civil and
    Political Rights, 16, 44, 209,
    212–13
International Covenant on Economic,
    Social and Cultural Rights, 16
International Criminal Court, 45,
    75

INDEX 327

International investment law, 26,
    29, 31–32, 36–37, 41, 55–56, 58,
    62, 80
International Labor Organization, 111
International Law Commission, 25–26,
    47, 71, 74, 76, 78
    Articles of Responsibility for
        International Organizations,
        75–77, 84
    Articles of State Responsibility, 47,
        59–60, 69, 75, 86
    Study on Fragmentation, 50, 62, 84
International law, constitutional
    approach to, 41
International law, fragmentation of,
    25–26, 29, 31, 48–49, 56, 84
    *autopoietic* systems, 27, 32
    and forum-shopping, 92
    regime collision, 32, 37
    systems theory, 26–27, 30, 42
International legal personhood, 73, 75,
    84
International Monetary Fund, 75–78
International public authority, 52, 85
Israel, Basic Law
    Human Freedom and Dignity, 114

Jackson, Vicki C., 3, 109
Jenson, Jane, 274
Judicial activism, 87, 89
Judicial review, 52, 90, 118, 135, 190,
    216–20, 222, 224, 227, 230–32,
    234, 244, 257–58
    International, 55

Kahana, Tsvi, 3–4, 173
Kaye, Justice Judith S., 139
*Khumalo v. Holomisa*, 169–70
Kingsbury, Benedict, 55
Koskenniemmi, Martti, 38, 41, 48
Kriegler, Justice Johann, 165, 171–72
Kumm, Matthias, 171

*Labor v. Swing*, 155, 157, 161–64, 170
*Labour Relations Act, 1995*, 176
Levi, Ron, 4, 271, 274
*Lex specialis*, 30, 47–48, 50–51, 57, 72,
    75, 77

Liberal tradition, 6–7, 23
Liberal rights, 8–9, 122
Local Authorities Election Act,
    179
Locke, 7, 12, 23–24, 213
Löwenheim, Oded, 279, 287
Luhmann, Niklas, 26, 28
*Lüth*, 150, 164, 166–67

Magna Carta, 8–9
Mance, Lord Jonathan, 243–44, 247–48
Manning, Bayless, 130
*Marbury v. Madison*, 126, 159
*Markt Intern and Beerman v. Germany*,
    203
Marshall, Chief Justice John, 158
Max Planck Institute, 52
*Mazibuko v. City of Johannesburg*,
    108
McIntyre, Justice William, 162–64
McLachlan, Campbell, 31, 37
Mental Health Act, 1983, 217
*Metalclad Corporation v. United
    Mexican States*, 36
Metzger, Gillian, 145
Michelman, Frank I., 99, 149, 152, 157,
    159
Millennium Development Goals, 282,
    284, 286
Miller, Paul B., 3, 251
*Minister of Health v. Treatment Action
    Campaign*, 107
*Moscow Branch of the Salvation Army
    v. Russia*, 205
Moyn, Samuel, 33, 274

*National Assistance Act, 1948*, 217, 229,
    244
Neoliberalism, 272, 274, 276, 278–80,
    288
Neuberger, Lord David, 221–22,
    243–44, 248
New Jersey Supreme Court, 139
New York Court of Appeals, 139
*New York Times v. Sullivan*, 137, 155,
    157, 161–64, 169–70
*News Verlag v. Austria*, 202
*Nike, Inc. v Kasky*, 203

*Non liquet*, 45–46, 57
North Atlantic Free Trade Agreement, 40

O'Regan, Justice Catherine, 108, 169–70
*Oakes* test, 193
Obligations, fiduciary
  duty of loyalty, 261, 263–64, 266
  fiduciary authority, 252–55, 257–58
  fiduciary theory of state authority, 251, 259, 265
  judicial review, 258
  principle of consensualism, 265, 269
  principle of fidelity, 265–66
  principle of prudence, 265, 267
  principle of transparency, 265, 267, 269
  public v private fiduciary law, 252, 256–57, 260–66, 270
Oliver, Dawn, 235
Oman, Charles, 278
Organisation for Economic Co-operation and Development, 85–86, 271, 278
  Development Co-Operation Directorate gender marker, 287

*Pacta sunt servanda*, 72, 81
Palmer, Stephanie, 4, 233
Peterson, Luke, 38
Pillay, Navi, 282
Porat, Iddo, 140
Positive obligations, 3–4, 109–10, 112, 127, 129, 132, 137, 173–74, 178, 233, 245–49, 252, 264–65
Precautionary principle, 48
Privatization, 2, 5, 90, 130–31, 142–43, 233–34, 236–37, 240, 244–50
Proportionality, 36, 52, 61, 68, 86, 131–33, 138, 140–41, 144–47
Public-private partnership, 215, 234, 236
  contractor liability, 216, 222, 229, 231–32
  hybrid public authorities, 4, 53, 90, 219, 239, 241, 243, 250

liability of the public authority, 142–43, 224, 227, 230, 232
outsourcing v transfer of assets, 237
vicarious public law liability, 228, 231

*R (A) v. Partnerships in Care Ltd.*, 217
*R (Heather) v. Leonard Cheshire Foundation*, 225, 229, 242, 245
*R (Johnson) v. Havering LBC*, 229
*R (Weaver) v. London & Quadrant Housing Trust*, 219
*R v. Panel on Takeovers and Mergers*, ex parte *Datafin*, 218, 244
*R v. Servite Houses*, ex parte *Goldsmith*, 217
Rational design, 80–81
Reagan, President Ronald, 275
Rehnquist, Chief Justice William, 159, 161
Reiner, Clara, 33, 38
*Respondeat superior*, 143
Right
  freedom of association, 176, 180, 182, 184, 187–89, 192, 205, 211–12, *See* European Convention on Human Rights, *See* Canadian Charter of Rights and Freedoms
  to free speech, 100, 106, 155, 162, 167, 174, 179–80, 196, 201–4, *See* European Convention on Human Rights
  to housing, 101
  positive v negative, 3, 8, 17–18, 23, 122, 176, 183, 283–84
  to privacy, 18, 105–6, 140, 202, 230
  to property, 2, 39, 58, 102, 197, 199–200, 208, 212–14, *See* European Convention on Human Rights
  right to free speech, 161
  to reputation, 102
  to water, 35, 40
Roosevelt, President Franklin Delano, 134
Rosatti, Horacio, 39
Rose, Nikolas, 278, 280
Rothstein, Justice Marshall, 179

Rule-of-law, 91, 118–19, 125, 127
Russian Constitution of 1918, 111
*RWDSU v. Dolphin Delivery Ltd*, 161, 163–65

*S.D. Myers v. Government of Canada*, 40
*Saunders v. United Kingdom*, 210
Scheinin, Martin, 40–41
Schill, Steven, 54–55, 57–58, 84–85
Schneiderman, David, 25
Schneidermann, David, 2
Schreuer, Christoph, 33, 38
Scolnicov, Anat, 2, 194
Seidman, Louis, 171–72
*Shelley v. Kraemer*, 137, 155, 157, 159, 161–65, 167
Simma, Bruno, 33, 37, 45, 58
Social contract tradition, 12
 and the fiduciary theory of state authority, 251, 253, 270
 and the state of nature, 7, 11
 and violability, 23
Social welfare obligations,
 constitutional, 109, 113, 121–22
 justiciable v non-justiciable social welfare rights, 114–15
 with v without an accompanying right, 125, 127
*Société Colas Est. v. France*, 198
South African Bill of Rights, 100
South African Constitutional Assembly, 165
South African Constitutional Court, 3, 100, 107, 117, 164, 167
South Korean Constitution of 1987, 114
*Southwest Case*, 116
Spector, Horacio, 39
State sovereignty, 119, 138, 152, 154, 160, 167
State-action doctrine, 133, 138–39, 141–42, 144
 exclusion and state accountability, 178, 181–84, 186–89
 horizontal effect, 149–53, 164, 166, 168–72
Statelessness, 11
*Storck v. Germany*, 246–47

Subsidiarity, 131–32, 135–36, 140–41, 144, 147
*Suez v. Argentina*, 35, 39
Sumption, Lord Jonathon, 228
*Sunday Times v. United Kingdom*, 202
Supiot, Alain, 272, 289
Supreme Court of Canada, 4, 161–62, 173, 176, 190–91
Supreme Court of India, 113, 117
Supreme Court of Israel, 248
*Sychev v. Ukraine*, 247

Teubner, Gunther, 26–29, 42
The Deregulation and Contracting Out Act, 1994, 226
Thomas, Jean, 3, 6
Thurlow, Baron, 209
Tushnet, Mark, 94, 122, 146

United Nations, 49, 112, 199, 273
United Nations Conference on Trade and Development, 34
United Nations Development Plan, 271, 277, 282, 287
 Human Development Report, 282, 286
United Nations General Assembly Declaration on the Right to Water, 40
United Nations Global Compact, 34, 289
United Nations Human Rights Council, 289
United Nations Office of the High Commissioner for Human Rights, 281–83
 Report on Human Rights Indicators, 284
United Nations Universal Declaration of Human Rights, 10, 15–16, 44, 112
United States Constitution, 140, 153, 161
 Fifteenth Amendment, 119
 Fourteenth Amendment, 119, 137, 146, 154–57, 160, 209
 Nineteenth Amendment, 119
 Supremacy Clause, 153
 Thirteenth Amendment, 119

United States Declaration of
    Independence, 9–10
United States Supreme Court, 134, 156,
    158, 161, 203, 209–10
*US Alien Tort Act*, 4, 74–75, 77

Van der Walt, Johan, 3, 149
Vienna Convention on the Law of
    Treaties, 40–41, 77
    sources of international law, 46, 51,
    62
    treaty interpretation, 37, 41, 43, 45,
    47
Vinson, Chief Justice Fred M., 157–59
Violability, 12–15, 19, 23–24
*Virginia v. Rives*, 158

Waldron, Jeremy, 87, 91, 212
Warren, Chief Justice Earl, 159
Washington State Constitution, 111
Weberian, 22, 274, 278

Weimar Constitution of 1919, 110,
    112
*Woodland v. Swimming Teachers
    Association*, 228
Woolf, Lord Chief Justice Harry, 221,
    225, 229, 241–42
World Bank, 271, 275–76, 278
    International Finance Corporation,
    288
World Trade Organization, 43, 52, 55,
    60–67, 71, 76, 79, 82–83, 85
    Appellate Body, 45, 76
World Trade Organization Dispute
    Settlement Understanding, 43, 62
*Wos v. Poland*, 247

*X and Church of Scientology v. Sweden*,
    204

*YL v. Birmingham City Council*,
    220–22, 224, 229, 242, 244–48

Lightning Source UK Ltd.
Milton Keynes UK
UKHW02f1908031018
329919UK00017B/433/P